QUALITATIVE COMPLEXITY

Offering a critique of the humanist paradigm in contemporary social theory, *Qualitative Complexity* is the first comprehensive sociological analysis of complexity theory. Drawing from sources in sociology, philosophy, complexity theory, 'fuzzy logic', systems theory, cognitive science and evolutionary biology, John Smith and Chris Jenks present a new series of interdisciplinary perspectives on the sociology of complex, self-organising structures.

John Smith has taught at Goldsmiths College, University of London; Lancaster University; and Greenwich University. He is a sociologist and a painter trained at the Royal College of Art. He is interested in sociological theory, philosophy and visual culture, and has published in all of these areas.

Chris Jenks is Pro-Vice-Chancellor and Professor of Sociology at Brunel University. He has published extensively in the areas of sociological theory, childhood, cultural theory and visual and urban culture.

The two authors met at Goldsmiths College and have subsequently published together in *Cultural Reproduction* (edited by Jenks; Routledge 1993); *Visual Culture* (edited by Jenks; Routledge 1995); *Images of Community: Durkheim, Social Systems and the Sociology of Art* (jointly authored by Smith and Jenks; Ashgate 2000); and an article on Complexity Theory in *Theory, Culture and Society* (October 2005).

INTERNATIONAL LIBRARY
OF SOCIOLOGY
Founded by Karl Mannheim
Editor: John Urry, Lancaster University

QUALITATIVE COMPLEXITY

Ecology, cognitive processes and
the re-emergence of structures
in post-humanist social theory

John Smith and Chris Jenks

Routledge
Taylor & Francis Group

LONDON AND NEW YORK

First published 2006
by Routledge
2 Park Square, Milton Park, Abingdon, Oxon OX14 4RN

Simultaneously published in the USA and Canada
by Routledge
270 Madison Ave, New York, NY 10016

Routledge is an imprint of the Taylor & Francis Group, an informa business

Transferred to Digital Printing 2007

© 2006 John Smith and Chris Jenks

Typeset in Bembo by
RefineCatch Limited, Bungay, Suffolk

British Library Cataloguing in Publication Data
A catalogue record for this book is available from the British Library

Library of Congress Cataloging in Publication Data
A catalog record for this book has been requested

ISBN10: 0–415–33650–3 (hbk)
ISBN10: 0–415–43967–1 (pbk)

ISBN13: 978–0–415–33650–5 (hbk)
ISBN13: 978–0–415–43967–1 (pbk)

CONTENTS

CONTENTS

Part I

THE INTERDISCIPLINARY FIELD

1

COMPLEXITY THEORY

A positioning paper

Complexity theory and its precursors have been influential in science, technology and mathematics for some time. This influence is newer and less developed in social science. In the perspectives of critical phenomenology, post-modern critical theory, post-structuralism and contemporary aesthetics, it is at times completely absent, much to their cost. Some derivatives of post-structuralism seem to believe that a more materialistic outlook, sometimes ironically called the 'semiotics of materiality'[1], or more recognisably, actor-network theory (ANT), is sufficient to meet the challenge of complexity. This is, in our view, both insufficient and prone to seed the belief that the detailed arguments of complexity theory, especially the development we essay below, can be anticipated and pre-empted; they can be taken, so to speak, as already in the discipline of sociology. This is not the case, but rather a recipe, for insularity. True, the notion of 'complexity' appears in socio-logical discourse, but is so permeated by the inappropriate idioms of post-structuralism that its qualitative impact is massively diminished, if not lost altogether.

Indeed, our earlier work on such topics as childhood, visual culture and language came directly from these traditions, complete with the critique of over-emphasis on language that ANT also denounced. In our case, the emphasis was not on ANT's interests in the hybrid networks of humans and non-humans but, for example, on the differences of discipline and possibility presented by the visual and the verbal and, more generally, on similar issues of functional differentiation. Yet we found that, to the extent we were critical of post-structuralist foundations, our positions followed concerns closely parallel, though from completely different directions, to those of complexity theory. The synthesis we shall go on to describe is our version of a way forward and also an attempt to re-direct or re-focus the insights of complexity theory, in many other disciplines, for the analysis of culture interactive with a number of other systems, notably the biosphere, with its own past, its energy require-ments and the interplay of order and disorder. What is implied here is a core of shared requirements and specific new directions of emphasis. These do not constitute a meta-narrative, in Lyotard's sense; indeed, they resist it. A totalised

3

theory of complexity is a contradiction in terms: it would fragment into forms demanded by specific complex orders. It is possible, however, to represent a set of conclusions, observations, even frustrations that are perhaps not necessary in the Kantian sense but are unavoidable – and, crucially, unavoidable across a variety of disciplines. It is as though complexity has sometimes independently, and sometimes through concerted inquiry insisted that it has to be taken into very serious account because it is not a peripheral phenomenon. Strategies of simplification are likely to produce a pandemonium of unintended, unforeseen, dangerous and costly consequences.

The emergence of complexity (or chaos) theory

Hegel said that true thinking is thinking that looks death straight in the face. We could add that true thinking is thinking that looks disorder and uncertainty straight in the face.

(Morin 2002: 329)

The origins of complexity theory are themselves complex and this is not the place for a documentary history. Amongst others,[2] Gleik (1987) provides a lively description and analysis. Hayles (1990, 1991 and 1999) provides an influential and challenging analysis. There are several edited collections, such as Eve *et al.* (1997) and Schnitman and Schnitman (2002). For developed accounts of complexity and sociology, Cilliers (1998) and Byrne (1998) come from quite different though equally illuminating perspectives. From the 'older generation' of complexity theory we shall choose Lorenz, Prigogine, and Maturana and Varela; meteorologist, thermodynamicist, and cognitive biologists respectively. Lorenz will stand as the example here.

In the early 1960s Lorenz constructed a computer model of a simple weather system. Starting a continuation of a previous run he was surprised to see that instead of repetition he found widely and rapidly diverging patterns. He suspected a malfunction. In fact, the computer had rounded off the numbers he had previously used, from six decimal places to three, 'assuming the difference – one part in a thousand – to be inconsequential' (see Gleik 1987: 11–31). It was not inconsequential. The weather system was shown to be complex and, more importantly, in the sense of 'extreme sensitivity to initial conditions' and its counterpart: non-linearity. This notion of initial conditions is perhaps disconcerting for a process discipline like sociology set against the more limited practices of computer modelling. Instead, then, a small variation may generate unexpected outcomes – the so-called 'butterfly effect'. For example:

Nonlinear behaviour is often referred to as positive feedback in which internal or external changes to a system produce amplifying effects. In short, nonlinear means that small changes in system variables can have

4

disproportionate outcomes . . . [I]t is . . . *interactions* . . . that produce
the nonlinearities that make the social world a world of surprises.
(Eve *et al.* 1997: 66, our emphases)

The word 'disproportionate' is questionable in this context. Surprising outcomes happen only when the situation is prone to, or capable of, generating
that outcome. More formally, the system and its interactions with other systems
must inherently contain or seed these possibilities. There is no occult multipli-
cation of effects *ex nihilo*. Unfortunately, the more playful reporting of chaos/
complexity theory sometimes plays up weirdness. The butterfly effect is classic:
the beating of a butterfly's wings in one hemisphere can end up as a tornado in
another. Ironically what is implied in this wording is actually linear causality:
a small flap here causes an almighty force elsewhere. Misleadingly left out is the
massive non-linear instability of planetary weather systems whose interaction,
just like social interaction, produces the non-linearities and the surprises. The
butterfly's wingbeat is a minuscule variable and remains so. It may or may not
contribute to something bigger, depending entirely on whether its feedback is
added to or cancelled out by other such feedback variables. It is the number of
active variables, interactions and possibilities that cause non-predictability
except in the relatively short term, not some magical magnifier.

Another example might be a discarded match that in one place discharges
its free energy harmlessly, but in another the same energy discharge is propa-
gated to cause a minor or a catastrophic forest fire according to the *critical
state* of the environment. Crucially, this continued or chain reaction depends
on available energy, in this case stored and potentially available as wood in a
combustible state.[3] Other systems such as wind, rainfall and ambient temperature are also very likely to be co-influential. There are stranger phenomena,
such as Prigogine's 'brussellator'[4] – an oscillating chemical reaction that seems
perversely active or inactive in discrete places with no apparent cause. But
oscillation is not alchemical; it depends on structural probabilities and
possibilities.

At this stage, complexity theory could be, and was often, referred to as chaos
theory. However, phenomena known as 'strange attractors' were soon to
appear in the literature, and these showed that complex phenomena could, at
least temporarily, permit themselves to be contained within certain loose
parameters, patterned limits, pathways and recurrences. Note that linear systems, those whose future state can be reliably predicted, can become non-linear
through the interaction of external factors. Similarly, non-linear systems could
become more linear, or static, through the dissipation of energy or the removal
of interaction. Clearly, here chaos is not a good description in the sense of
permanent or universal upheaval or randomness. Nor does it square with post-
structuralism's notions of randomness, conventionality or presumed infinite or
autonomous possibilities of deconstruction, interpretation or reconstruction.
On the contrary, complex systems can, and do, exhibit different degrees of

complexity, interdependence and robustness of self-organisation. They can also die. That brings us to Maturana and Varela.[5]

Autopoiesis

The concept 'autopoiesis' means, roughly, self-structuring. This crucial term, autopoiesis, so central to systems theory and Luhmann's sociology, is borrowed from cognitive biology. Scholars from more humanistic disciplines are aware that the term was coined by Maturana and Varela, but possibly less aware of their subsequent disputes or influence in cognitive theory, epistemology and cybernetics.[6] Moreover, autopoiesis is a term with an explicit relationship to evolutionary theory, a corpus that sociology, to say the least, finds difficult. There is also an implicit criticism of evolutionary theory, that it had stressed change at the expense of adequate attention to *homeostasis* or the ability of a system, in this case an organism, to maintain a coherent identity over time. This, then, is complexity from almost the opposite point of view, not chaos but evolved complexity in two senses: heterogeny of species and homeostasis in the sense of self-reproduction of an organism or system that is itself massively complex. We shall return to ramifications of this issue in detail.

Autopoiesis in its original form stressed that the living organism produced and organised the relationships between its components. Crucially, it also organised its relationship to its environment. Despite 'structural coupling' or evolved adaptation, 'the organism decides what counts as environment' and so also maintains its 'operational closure'[7]. It is, of course, central to the application of complexity theory to sociology (Luhmann 1984, 1995), but it should be noted that Varela objected to the application of autopoiesis to social systems, even the operationally closed models developed by Luhmann. The versions explored here are much more open. Indeed, it is a characteristic of complex systems that boundaries are extremely difficult to draw. For example, in sociology how do we draw the boundary between individual and member? We shall return at length to Maturana Varela and Luhmann below. For the moment, it is important to stress that autopoiesis is completely unlike the ideas of self-autonomy assumed by post-modern or post-structural notions of freedom, negation and deconstruction.

> Though self-organisation obviously signifies autonomy, a self-organising system . . . must work to construct and reconstruct its autonomy and this requires energy . . . [T]he system must draw energy from the outside; to be autonomous . . . it must be [also] dependent.
> (Morin 2002: 45, following von Foerster 1984)

The inexorable fate of any system that does not draw energy from its environment is entropic equilibrium: it will cease to be dynamic or, in the case of the living, it will die. A full discussion of entropy and negative entropy together with their implications for order and disorder will be given below in our discussion of Prigogine's thermodynamics.

Morin's comment is characteristically scientific in tone. Nevertheless, it is derived from a truly interdisciplinary book, *New Paradigms, Culture and Subjectivity* (2002; edited by D.F. and J. Schnitman) whose contributions range from physics to psychotherapy. Morin's paradox can be resolved by an ecological perspective: a self-organising system in an environment (of self-organising systems) is reciprocal in terms of cause and effect. It has to be *viable* and at other times it may not be viable. Morin (2002) offers the concept *auto-eco-organisation*. Autopoiesis and especially the adjectival form *autopoietic* are, usefully, less cumbersome. We stress interdependence, and indeed the co-postulation of both 'ecology' and 'operational closure'. Or: an animal or a phenomenon, like a social fact, is only recognisable on account of its closure or identity *vis-à-vis* an environment. That is also the basis of its extinction, as individual or species, at the hands of that environment. This kind of critically balanced, potentially fallible interdependence is characteristic in complexity theory. How does this differ from post-modern or late humanist, critical theory?

The central analytic tool of post-modern criticism is negation or *deconstruction*. It has many antecedents in the phenomenological tradition, broadly collectable[8] as 'suspension', 'bracketing', or putting in radical doubt. It is always possible to deconstruct in imagination, that is, through environmental disconnection. From an eco-auto-organisational point of view, the idea that such negations are *always* possible in systems environment relations is questionable. Further, the idea that to negate is to open the possibility of renewal becomes untenably optimistic, or indeed simplistic. Every such action will have an effect: no negation is costless or innocent; the substitute form will have to draw its energy and resources from what it supplanted and is likely to be confronted with the debris of what went before. Consequently, as we see in practice, negation is both adversarial and limited to contexts in which it has a reasonable chance of confiscating resources for itself. It will not be free but patterned, and linked to the maintenance of discipline boundaries. The shift from linguistic construction and its connotations of relative autonomy and conventionality to the notion of autopoiesis implies a shift from post-modernity's innocence to a reflexive assessment of its own structural or political implications and its economic (ecological) requirements. This exactly parallels the realisation in the last few decades that human development is not simply a dream or an ideal but an ecological process with huge environmental impacts. It also parallels the gradual political realisation that for its cultural opponents, or even some of its adherents, post-modernism is at best over-optimistic, and at worst, not an inclusive, but a specific, even an aggressive, political doctrine.

Furthermore, it insists that so far as action, construction or destruction requires the real-time import of energy, self-reference loses something of its closure or autonomy. Just as auto-organisation becomes eco-auto-organisation, so self-reference becomes auto-exo-reference. The term is again derived from Morin (2002: 49). The implications of this change and its impact on informatics will occupy us throughout the work. That brings us to preliminary remarks on Prigogine and his approach to the significance of far-from-equilibrium systems.

Systems and dissipative structures

To many sociologists systems theory will have a conservative, Parsonian ring, obsessed with stasis. But Prigogine and his followers stress thermodynamics, such that systems theory and systems theory *in sociology* are not the same thing. Luhmann has built many theoretically productive bridges between systems, complexity and social theories, but we shall also differ from him in many respects. Then there is the body of sociology-led but interdisciplinary inquiry broadly called 'world-systems analysis' which also cites Prigogine.

When societies are viewed as systems that, like organisms, survive only by virtue of:

- acquiring energy from the environment; and then
- channelling that energy in a controlled way so as to maintain their structure against their entropic tendency to fall apart; and, finally
- expelling the energy as pollution, garbage and heat,

then they fit into the definition created by Prigogine (1984, 1996) of a dissipative structure (Grimes 2000: 33).

Grimes' third point can be misleading. If energy is acquired only to be expelled, the relationship to an environment would be a sort of non-functional accident, as insignificant as wind happening to blow through a tunnel. True, it is the by-products of the conversion of environmental energy into system specific energy that are expelled. The system avoids entropy by capturing energy from outside. The system may become 'prey' in due course, either in the organic or socio-economic sense. But this relationship is also necessarily structural. Pollution or waste is itself potentially dissipative at the level of *ecosystem*. If by-products remain as garbage and are not recycled into the active energy system, any finite source of energy will eventually run out. This could be understood at the level of prey/predator: so long as there are waste products in predation, the numbers of active predators relative to prey must decrease as you move 'up' the food chain; few lions, lots of antelopes. And unless these wastes are scavenged, that is, recycled, the food chain will inevitably collapse as a whole. If for food chain we substitute social hierarchy, the result is the same. Increased satiation at the top requires the increased work or increased number of workers below. Waste products left un-recycled (surplus value, unsold stocks, worked-out land, failures to reinvest) will tend toward depression or collapse. At the level of economic production, energy wasteful practices are more likely

8

to die out sooner than energy efficient ones. The relentless accumulation of un-recycled, or worse, un-recyclable, waste products is a direct indicator that the system as a whole is indicating the potential for collapse. It is important to note that the disorder referred to here is a consequence of other orderings; it is not a sort of background against which ordering processes take place.

There is another structural implication:

> . . . when a variable affecting a dissipative structure changes enough, the structure either reorganises itself or collapses. This crisis point is called a 'bifurcation'. When collapse is avoided, the reorganisation process takes pieces of the earlier structure and changes their functions and relative importance so as to allow the system to continue, although now in a new form. An example is the stress caused by rising populations, which ultimately compels a society to become more hierarchical or collapse into fragments.
>
> (Grimes 2000: 33)

We emphasise the relative limitations of this systems ecology even in the most formal expression. The collapse of a series of system/environment relationships leaves the landscape littered with the debris of the previous relationships in various states of functional viability. Contrasted with the more open landscapes of post-structuralism, this is a much more mortal, burdened and history saturated panorama. Finite possibility and a huge dose of *impossibility* is its keynote.

The distinction between a system and an environment of systems is itself structural. For those critics who see a propensity towards stasis in social systems theory we can only reply that systems theory in general is far more inclined toward the dynamic, the chaotic, and the non-linear. In truth, the static *versus* the dynamic is a ridiculous polarity; they presuppose each other. It is only on the back of the dynamics of differentiation that any systems/environment relationship is conceivable and only on the back of that finite homeostasis, or relative ecological robustness, that complexity can co-evolve. Similarly, it is only on the basis of extant homeostasis that change in the sense of bifurcation or collapse or extinction can occur. And it is only on the basis of the homeostatic identity of variables that near-chaotic phenomena can emerge out of their interaction.

Prigogine also insists on the irreversibility of time. This may seem odd to readers from disciplines other than physics. His argument, which will have important implications later in the text, is as follows:

> Newton's law of motion, $ma = f$ [states] that mass multiplied by acceleration is equal to force. The basic characteristic of this law is its deterministic character. Once we know the initial conditions, we can predict any future or past position of the trajectory. Moreover,

9

Newton's law is irreversible. If we replace time by minus time, Newton's law remains invariant.

(Prigogine 2002: 22)

Or:

Einstein has often repeated that time, as associated to irreversibility, is an 'illusion' . . . This radical denial of time . . . is being reiterated today by such distinguished physicists as Feynman and Hawking. It is suggested that irreversibility may be the result of our approximations, our 'coarse graining', which *we* introduce into a time reversible universe described by the classic laws of nature.

(ibid. p. 26)

By contrast, complex systems, which operate in non-equilibrium conditions, require energy inputs to maintain their self-organisation, but moreover, every future state of the system is extremely sensitive to its current, or initial, state. Such systems are necessarily historical or irreversible. That is implied in the very notion of non-linearity. 'Irreversibilty [for Prigogine] leads to both disorder and order. [It] plays a constructive role' (ibid. p. 27). This underlines the point we made above.

The fingerprints of complexity for sociology

Here we propose a transition. From the various ways in which complexity theory has emerged, we now want to look at what we described above as core beliefs, observations or even frustrations.

Cilliers (1998) cites 'two indispensable characteristics of *capabilities* of complex systems' (p. 10, our emphasis): 'The first of these will be discussed as the process of *representation*; the second, which concerns the development and change of internal structure without the a priori necessity of an external designer, as the process of *self-organisation*.'

Before mentioning any more characteristics, this brings us to the controversial core of complex systems. Cilliers uses the word 'capabilties'; others use 'knowledge' and 'information' (in scare quotes). One can see why. Accepting that complex systems include things like thermodynamic change, human representation and simple multicellular organisms, it is difficult to assert without qualification that: 'In order to respond adequately to its environment, a complex system must be able to *gather* information about that environment and *store* it for future *use*' (ibid. p. 11, our emphases; perhaps 'future' should be questioned too).

Cilliers does provide such qualifications and they constitute a powerful case, part of which we shall strongly affirm and part of which we shall challenge. Solutions to the problematic relation of inside/outside (environment and

10

information) 'usually postulate a one to one correspondence between elements of the system and specific external causes' (ibid.). Cillier proposes instead the notion of *distributed representation*, which we shall consider in due course. Let us rework the ground of the inside/outside relationship as follows:

1. There cannot possibly be any direct one-to-one correspondence between the environment and the system as a whole. Both difference and complexity preclude it. It is not practically possible.
2. At best, correspondence occurs across an interface of difference where the elements that characterise the system and the elements that constitute the environment are by definition of different orders. Furthermore, only *elements* can relate to other elements. There is still the problem of distribution within the system.
3. It is possible to imagine a scenario in which a single element, or small group of elements, contains the complexity of the system in whole or in part – something like a seed or code *for*. (Cilliers rules out such a possibility. See below.) But this still leaves us with a double distribution problem: how does the totality get compressed/coded/represented in the part? If that *is* possible, how does the part control, organise, 'exert its will' on the whole? That would seem to throw enormous problems on the basic premise that simple elements interact to form complex systems. Or, it assumes evolution whilst throwing enormous obstacles in its path.

We can now rework each point, almost with its counterpoint:

1. There must be a direct exchange of energy between the system and environment.
2. This exchange is *mediated*. This point is crucial and we cannot emphasise it enough. We suggest that the mediation of material into another material and the mediation of material into information belong to a continuum of which the latter is a special case. The human versions of this are even more 'special' and latecomers on the scene. This is where post-humanism begins to assert its special relation to complexity theory.
3. Cilliers' objections to one super-component turn on the idea that it is not the individual that is crucial but the complex structure of the system. But not all elements are simple in the sense he implies here. To cast them all as individuals is an understandable formalisation, but it violates complexity. Complex systems are not formal systems; they consist of (sometimes living) discrete elements of differing complexity, importance and redundancy. Cilliers does not deny this – the rest of his excellent book is dedicated to precisely this problem. But the ghost of formalism continues to haunt all of us. We want to emphasise that the landscape of complexity may be littered with simple components, but some of these may have reorganised

11

themselves as super-components, especially *self-replicators*, which for many reasons persist *vis-à-vis* an environment of other systems, or fragments, or residues, or obstacles, or redundancies, or routes through which complexity must flow. Collectively taken, this is our sense of what are called in the literature strange attractors. Their location may be inside, outside or, so to speak, between organisms, systems, individuals and their social and physical environment.

It is essential *not* to try to define strange attractors. Byrne (1998) provides an informative tour ranging from the graphical patterns that emerge from mapping the complex positions of a pendulum to 'fitness landscapes' in evolutionary biology:

> . . . the fitness landscape peak is in a sense the bottom of the attractor basin turned upside down. It represents a *for the moment* optimal form . . . The marsupial wolf looked very much like a wolf, although the evolutionary gap between the two was far greater than that between a wolf and a human being. There is a strange attractor for that body form . . .

> (p. 29)

Later we shall draw on sources of attractors as diverse as 'evolutionarily stable strategies' (see, for example, Dennet 2003; Maynard Smith 1982, 1988; Skyrms 1996), reproductive need, or the fashioning of semi-permanent images (see Dissanayake 1993; Smith and Jenks 2000). What we are at pains to *deny* is:

1. The supposition that all manner of heterogeny is possible and indeed can co-habit.
2. That for humans the only, or primary, means of access to other attractors is language.
3. That frequent or habitual structures are contingent, i.e. random, but instead are contingent *upon*, i.e. depend on, ecological relationships.
4. Possibility is open and infinite. On the contrary, impossibility is at least as important.
5. History, especially human prehistory, is not crucial to contemporary possibilities. Instead, both the limits and the plasticity of culture are organically related not simply to the human past but to the planet and its biosphere.

We might put the last point differently by saying that we inherit a significant degree of freedom won for us by the totality of the evolutionary process. Opportunities and responsibilities are therefore at stake. There is such a thing as misuse or abuse which will bear costs in relation to our powers. Attractors, then, are not particularly strange. They are a diverse group of topographies, mappings, routes, regularities, successful outcomes, capabilities, knowledge, forces and powers that pattern complexity. Conversely, they are negatively defined by no-go areas, obstacles, deserts, extravagant use of energy, propensity to catastrophic predation, poverty, ignorance, powerlessness, lack of freedom and opportunity.

Cilliers (1998: 3–5) further offers a ten-point sketch of complex systems adapted, according to the endnote, 'from Nicolis and Prigogine (1989), Serra and Zanarini (1990) and Jen (1990)' which we have further abbreviated. Number 8 is stated in full. Number 10 is explicitly discussed above in connection with the formalisation of complexity. This material inevitably restates some of the issues above. We include it to show something of the flavour of Cilliers' categorisation, compared to our own, and as a parallel specification other readers may prefer:

1. Complex systems consist of a large number of elements.
2. [Complexity arises from their dynamic interaction.] A complex system changes with time. The interactions do not have to be physical; they can also be thought of as the transference of information.
3. The interaction is fairly rich, i.e. any element in the system influences, and is influenced by, quite a few others.
4. [I]nteraction is *non-linear* ... Non-linearity also guarantees that small causes can have large results and vice versa. It is a precondition for complexity.
5. Interactions normally have a fairly short range ... this does not preclude wide-ranging influence.
6. There are [feed]back loops in the interactions ... positive (enhancing, stimulating) or negative (detracting, inhibiting).
7. Complex systems are usually open systems, i.e. they usually interact with their environment.
8. Complex systems operate under conditions far from equilibrium. There has to be a constant flow of energy to maintain the organisation of the system and ensure its survival. Equilibrium is another word for death.
9. Complex systems have a history. Not only do they evolve through time but their past is co-responsible for their present behaviour.
10. Each element of the system is ignorant of the behaviour of the system as a whole; it responds only to information that is available locally. This point is vitally important. If each element 'knew' what was happening to the system as a whole, all of the complexity would have to be present *in that element*. This would either entail a physical impossibility ... or constitute a metaphysical move in the sense that the 'consciousness' of the whole is contained in one particular unit. Complexity is the result of a rich interaction of simple elements that only respond to the limited information each of them are presented with ... (original emphases).

Responding again to number 10, reference to metaphysics and consciousness, for us, introduces an unnecessary polarity between the physical and, if the polarity is granted, what can only be called the weird. But there is nothing strange, conscious or metaphysical about components (e.g. the seed) that in some sense store the possibility of subsequent, different components. True, the seed does not store all the interactive possibilities of the subsequent components with the environment, though it might code for, say, leaf fall. The crucial point is that the degree of complexity of the component (the seed) is itself a product of environmental interactions, that is, exactly the same process. If, then, we do not allow, either implicitly or explicitly, heterogeneous degrees of complexity in the components themselves (in Cilliers' case through misplaced formalism), the issue eventually returns in the forced and false polarity of physics and metaphysics. We have only to look around us to see that the rest of Nature has no trace of this peculiar human(ist) preoccupation. At the same time, it makes massive use of the informational substrate DNA. In this sense 'degrees of complexity' is itself too formalistic, too aggregative, modelled too much on units and numbers. This is why our title, *Qualitative* Complexity, is necessary.

Byrne (1998) has a somewhat different approach. He begins, as we do, with the point about the newness of complexity theory, and so:

> It is necessary to begin the book with this chapter [i.e. the first] to which I had considered giving the title 'naming of parts'. However one of the most important things about this approach is precisely its rejection of the validity of analytical strategies in which things are reducible to the sum of their parts. We are dealing with emergent properties and therefore must begin with a holistic statement.
>
> (p. 14)

Contrasted with, but not excluding, Cilliers' two priorities of representation and self-organisation, Byrne opens his account with 'two themes of evolutionary development and holism which have to be taken together' (ibid. p. 15) and partly concludes this reflection with this interesting statement:

> Not only can the complex not always be derived, even in principle from the less complex, but, . . . we can often only understand the simpler in terms of its origins in the more complex.
>
> (ibid. p. 16)[9]

This is a rather important point that is also a source of confusion. In this context it means that a system, especially a complex system, is not defined as or by the aggregate of its component parts. This is an axiom of general systems theory. It should not be confused with the fallacy shorthanded as 'the conservation of complexity' – or the proposition that what is complex must be descended from complex beginnings. In fact, in order for auto-eco-organisation to be autonomous, not needing either 'designers' or some principle of 'vitalism', its originating processes must be in some sense simple, precisely in order to build complexity. This can be seen in the history of evolution. The systems axiom thus relates to the impossibility of reductionism; the further considerations refer, quite differently, to a history of nested development. It is crucial that they are not confused.

Citing Hayles, Byrne continues by distinguishing between:

> The contrast between order and disorder is a continuing dichotomy in the Western mind-set. [Hayles] contrasts this binary logic with the four-valued logic of Taoism in which not-order is not equivalent to anti-order. This is persuasive and the point being made is that whilst 'chaos' in its popular usage is to be understood as a description of anti-order, to all intents and purposes a synonym for randomness, the scientific usage is far more equivalent to not-order, and indeed sees chaos as containing/preceding order. The and/or is necessary because there are at least two approaches, which as Hayles indicates seem determined to ignore each other.
>
> (1998: 12)
>
> One is essentially concerned with the order that lies hidden within chaos and is essentially US-based. The other, European and represented particularly by Prigogine focuses on the order that emerges from chaos.
>
> (p. 16)

At least the citations are common, the core is emerging, and perhaps the divide has improved somewhat. We hesitate on the 'four-valued logic of Taoism' and normally we would do the same on 'the continuing dichotomy in the Western mind-set', but in this latter respect Byrne/Hayles are spot-on. We would take it further: not only is chaos a synonym for randomness in popular usage, it is a crucial linguistic habit in philosophical usage that serves only to mask, frustrate and confuse any significant analysis of complexity. Suffice to say that humanism, in the form of the posited centrality of the human subject, is the diametric opposite of holism and evolutionary development. This is tantamount to the assertion that popular and philosophical usage, in which we include the majority of study of culture, is trapped in a 'mind-set' that has not yet taken proper account of Darwin, let alone the subsequent shapes of post-Darwinian analyses.

Byrne announces 'A naming of parts' (p. 18). His first part is the distinction between linear and non-linear relationships. Linearity implies a relationship that is predictable over time. Some writers, in the tradition of post-modernism, are apt to find the uncertainties of non-linearity more glamorous. This is

15

sentimental. We therefore applaud Byrne's concluding, cautionary remark on linearity:

> Once we can predict, we can engineer the world and make it work in the ways we want it to. We can turn from reflection to engagement. This is a wholly honourable project so far as I am concerned. It is the technological foundation of modernity itself.
>
> The trouble is that much, and probably most, of the world doesn't work in this way.
>
> (ibid. p. 19)

This remark offers the first trace of a deep schism in the face of complexity. There are the sentimentalists and they are simply foolish or naïve. Many celebrants of benign heterogeny will have had their beliefs shaken after 9/11 and Beslan. Yet the cut is deeper. The clear support of the 'technological foundations of modernity' is anathema to those who have reached complexity by way of Heidegger (such as Dillon 1993) or by way of Derrida (such as Cilliers). Cilliers goes on to cite Derrida positively, whilst Byrne explicitly titles one section of his work, *Complexity against Postmodernism*. Both are drawn together by the force of complexity itself; indeed they endorse each other's work on the covers. But the argument does not and cannot go away. Moreover, it finds precisely analogous forms in the various disciplines that have brought complexity to the fore. It is the basis of the well-reported spat between Dennett, Pinker, Dawkins *et al.* on the one hand and Gould, Rose, or Lewontin on the other. These are just some of the more recent (or most publicised) incidents in a dispute running throughout the history of ideas, superheated perhaps, since *The Origin of Species*. Such disputes concern what we shall call *degrees* of determinism and of freedom. Crucially, without a level of determinism (impossibility, attractors, holism, evolutionary development) and a large dose of freedom (non-linearity, several possibilities at once, rich interaction) we should not be talking about complexity but the old polarisation: order and chaos-as-randomness. The point is *not* to join one of the camps, rather than both, and certainly not a priori. Degrees of complexity, stability and so on must be decided on their merits, and disorder will often follow from order. Only the older forms of humanism can propose positions in advance, as though 'we' (or the Deity) called the shots.

Most of the remaining content in Byrne's 'naming of parts' has been introduced above, apart from one emphasis. He spends much time on the issue of bifurcation. He cites Harvey and Reed (1994: 385) – which we shall also use for its succinctness:

> In the absence of significant perturbations a dissipative system will usually follow a 'normal' linear trajectory. Of course there will be the

usual boundary testing, but in the absence of any sustained increase in environmental energy the system will return to its original point of reference. At some point, however, this stable regimen is disrupted, and, if the internal movement of the system is propitious, the system's stable behaviour gives way to random fluctuations.

Abandoning its original trajectory, the system destabilises and exhibits a so-called 'pitchfork bifurcation' pattern. That is, once destabilised, the system begins to fluctuate between two or more points [or paths, or alternatives, or alliances . . .] The oscillation continues until it abandons its original path and takes one or more of the alternative points [or directions etc.] as its path of development.

(Byrne 1998: 23)

Much of this terminology is embedded in extremely difficult mathematics, such as Feigenbaum sequences, whilst the influence of Prigogine is more ordinarily obvious. Let us unpack the passage further. Points and pitchfork patterns may well refer to plotted data, but they may equally well refer to behaviours, events and places; indeed the data represents them. Our point is that the process does not belong to mathematicians, to any other discipline, or even to humans. British education, for example, has been 'bifurcating' for the last decade to the point of exasperation in the view of many of its practitioners, with or without data in the narrow sense. Convection patterns in heated liquids exhibit similar changes from micro to macro movements: the simmer as opposed to the rolling boil. Bifurcation is visible and intelligible in the world.

Byrne concludes this section by allying himself to the 'both camps' position:

In 'absolute chaos' (popular chaos, postmodernism's vision of chaos) small changes through time produce indeterminate results: anything could happen. The interesting thing about complex solutions is that we can't predict what will happen but we know that what will happen will be drawn from a set of alternatives greater than one but less than too many to cope with – the realm of *determined* chaos.

(ibid. p. 26, our emphasis)

'Less than too many to cope with' puts Byrne alongside the optimists, as opposed to Gray's (2003) bleak vision. Ironically, as a post-Marxist, it also puts him closer to the 'right-wing', especially Dennett, from the post-modern or anti-determinist viewpoint. From our standpoint, the description 'deterministic chaos' is correct, though counter-intuitive, and we have to be strategically optimistic even though in the long term, and in the face of near-term catastrophe or local impossibility, that may be absurd.

17

Fuzzy logic

Fuzzy logic is a mathematically sophisticated and philosophically persuasive stance. It is also of immense practical utility in electronic technology. The best and very accessible account is given by its founder, Kosko (1994). A short account occurs in Eve *et al.* (1994). Fuzzy logic may be briefly illustrated as follows. Imagine two sets of apples: one green, one red. Easy – but in a complex world, even in a world complicated only by apples, you can get red-green apples. All right, let the two sets overlap: reds on one side, greens on the other, red-greens in the intersection. But how do you set the boundaries? Where does red stop and red-green begin? Where does red-green stop and green begin? In other words, the recognition of an overlapping subset, or red-green, implies an infinite possibility of further subsets according to the degree of 'pure' redness or greenness. This will prove crucial in the discussion of conceptualisation or categorisation. To say that 'X is true' may be misleading in a complex environment. To say 'X is true sometimes or to a degree', may be more accurate. In a complex world fuzziness may increase accuracy whilst assertive certainty may decrease it. Try that on the well-aired notion of the post-modern disbelief in meta-narratives. Do you disbelieve in traditional cultural hierarchies, the fine arts and such like? What about the desirability of democracy, human rights, policies against discrimination, meritocracy? Not quite so clear cut? And how do you like your dentist? Do you want competence, qualifications, authority, correct diagnosis, bags of relevant experience, and enough technological saturation to minimise your pain and perhaps cosmetically maximise your looks? Or an alternative practitioner who deconstructs the claim to expertise? Will you concede that 'post-modern' dentistry (the cosmetics and so on) is only possible once the nuts and bolts of ordinary belief-in-metanarratives-competence have been done up? Are we post-modern to a degree? Are we modern where necessary? Is the situation clear cut, or complex, or fuzzy? Which is the more truthful description?

If you have an ambivalent opinion on that, you cannot belong to either the positivist camp or the post-modern–post-structural persuasion. You might belong to both, but we suspect (if you are a professional social theorist, philosopher, or scientist, amongst many other such trades) that you have earned your living in the business of denying that fact. Welcome to the ice-cold clarity of fuzzy complexity!

Under the counter-intuitive heading, *The Whole in the Part*, Kosko exploits 'subsethood' to reframe the discussion of possibility. He imagines a set of 100 throws of a coin, divided into two component subsets of heads/tails or successes/failures. The two subsets precisely add up to the total set; both subsets precisely exclude each other (Kosko 1994: 56–7). Traditional, Aristotelian logic treats this, and like arrangements, according to Kosko as the central or normal position. Kosko insists this is only the extreme position, the black and white case; no 'grey':

Traditional fuzzy [probability] theory was bivalent, all or none, 100% or 0%. That seemed as extreme as any other black and white claim. Very tall men made up a 100% subset of tall men. That I could buy. Every tall man is tall. But the old view that said tall men made up a 0% subset of *very* tall men. That I could not buy. It was a matter of degree. Every tall man is very tall to some degree, often to a very slight degree.

(ibid. p. 55, our emphasis).

Kosko then offers a brilliantly simple set diagram:

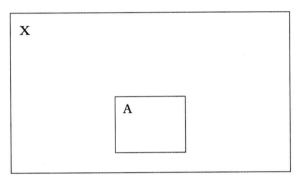

Supposing the set A shrinks to a point. In that extreme case, the part . . . does not contain the whole at all . . . Nothing cannot contain something, let alone everything . . . [C]ontainment or subsethood is 0%. Now suppose A comes back into existence and grows . . . and [e]ventually fills up the whole rectangle. Then part A equals the whole X. In that extreme case the part contains the whole 100% because the part *is* the whole. What happens between the extremes? Containment takes on degrees. It varies smoothly from 0 to 1 [0% to 100%] as A grows in area. The bigger the subset A, the more it contains the whole.

So there it was. The part cannot contain the whole unless the part equals the whole. That much and only that much scientists had gotten right. Otherwise the part partially contains the whole. The part contains the whole in direct proportion to its size . . . in relation to the whole. For centuries scientists and mathematicians had missed this simple idea . . . for the same reason I had missed it: Aristotle had outlawed the very idea of it.

[Now comes the punch line.] What is the whole in the part? . . . *The whole in the part is probability.*

(ibid. p. 59, original emphases)

For the moment, think of fuzzy theory's influence on the inter-permeation of modernism and post-modernism, or our tendency to categorise phenomena, our attitude to whether the clear cut is less true than the fuzzy. That implies a radical reflection on what we shall call our *strategies* rather than our concept of reason. For sociology in particular its impact is devastating. The whole discipline is founded on the study of distinctly and explicitly social phenomena. If we instead suggest that social phenomena are only social to a degree, then sociology loses credibility as uni-disciplinary. It is pitched immediately into the 'chaos', in the sense of complexity, of interdisciplinary imperatives.

World-systems theory

We continue to stress eco-auto-organisation. That too is characteristic of world-systems theory. Following Wallerstein, 'my "world-system" is not a system "of the world" nor "in the world". It is a system that "is the world".' (Wallerstein 1993: 294, in Hall 2000: 4). Hall asserts, 'the world-system must be studied as a whole. Therefore the study of social, political, economic or cultural change in any component of the system must begin by understanding that component's role within the system' (ibid. p. 6).

There are a series of compelling and conflicting positions. The proposition that 'my world-system is *the* world-system' indicates a questionable confusion. But what is interesting about world-systems theory is the claim that structures, cycles of relationship, announce themselves to attentive thinkers. This is a direct counter-claim to post-modernism in the form of a 'science' of history, related to the aspirations of neo-Marxism; a project not dissimilar to Byrne's hope that it is possible to meet complexity with a kind of practical optimism.

Here a difference must be asserted. Both Byrne and Hall are concerned with substantive matters of relationship. Here we are concerned with re-opening the philosophy of social inquiry. The substantive research is not yet possible; it would still be too influenced by the humanist paradigm. World-systems will be taken instead, then, as a proposal of structures that sit across system/environment distinctions, as a proposal of a class of large-scale attractors.

The contribution of biology and cognitive science

Here we stress that viable cognitive processes are the result of adaptation and evolution, and that consequently (a) what we call 'the mind' has an adaptive architecture, and (b) the evolution of that architecture implies a history shared between humankind and other sentient species on the planet. Creation *ex nihilo* has no place in this paradigm, even when it is disguised under the rubrics of linguistic construction.

Again, this is a fundamentally ecological proposition. It may be contrasted with the traditions of humanism by considering the question of human sovereignty. For such writers as Nietzsche, the idea of limit is anti-human. Even for Kant, the subject constitutes itself. In Derrida, the absence of limit or undecidability is tragically congruent with the horizon of text that can recognise no 'outside-text' to warrant its truth, discipline or authenticity. For modernism and for some of the more IT-saturated tendencies of post-modernism–post-humanism, the new or post-human is (de)limited by technology amid metaphors of transformation from maggot to winged insect. The irony of that reduction from human 'autonomy' to insect automatism is of course always missed. Nothing that is going to die or has a definite gender or is a member of a specific culture is autonomous. That would be a humanistic over-exaggeration. Cognitive biology has the cooler, more realistic term 'post-natal plasticity'. Humans exhibit relatively high levels of post-natal plasticity compared with, say, antelopes. Dogs come somewhere in between. Post-natal plasticity implies the ability to reconfigure, learn, reprogramme mental processes and behaviours, and, to borrow from fuzziness, this is clearly available to many species to a degree. But post-natal is also post-architecture and, as such, plasticity is limited by evolutionary adaptation in all species, including humans. This functions to our advantage: it would be impossible to acquire language if the architecture was not already there. It also means that Nietzsche and Kant have to be discarded from epistemology.

The ground of complexity cannot be chaos in the sense of total randomness. Equally, neither can complexity arise from total freedom. Complexity can only arise from relative plasticity that is, therefore, subsequently drawn into interaction. Given that limit and the interdisciplinary 'shove' generated by fuzzy logic, the traditional distinction between ethology and ethnology, if not erased, has become (to use Dillon's term *not* in the sense intended) 'radically relational'. Returning to the themes of time and holism, these frames are now placed in question. Time becomes, in Prigogine's sense, neither background, nor theatre, but agent.

Our interest can be heuristically divided in two, actually overlapping, parts. The first considers the objections to the centralisation of consciousness, sometimes called the 'Cartesian Theatre'. Drawn from sources such as Dennett (1991) and Damasio (1995), it stresses the *parallel* contributions of the totality of human faculties in the generation of both consciousness and reason, or reasonableness. This is set radically against the *serial* view of the *cogito* or the subject, or indeed language, as the constrained access to human self-reflexive understanding. The second concerns the relationship of evolutionary biology and psychology to the generation of culture. This is politically controversial. We cite Barkow *et al.* (1992) and Pinker's (1993) insistence that their proposals are not right-wing, and Dennett's (2003) insistence that to discuss the very idea of human nature's relation to culture is not taboo. Human nature as opposed to the blank slate is no more taboo than the discussion of human culture's impact on Nature. Humans are an identifiable species with a number of characteristics in common. Language is not the least of these. It is absurd to think of language, as one example, as random in either origin or structure. This is the opening position of Barkow *et al.* (1992):

Culture is not causeless and disembodied. It is generated in rich and intricate ways by information-processing mechanisms situated in human minds. These mechanisms are, in turn, the elaborately sculpted product of the evolutionary process. Therefore to understand the relationship between biology and culture one must first [we prefer 'also'] understand the architecture of our evolved psychology.

(p. 3)

Further:

The information-processing mechanisms that collectively comprise the human mind differ in many ways from those that comprise the mind of an alligator or a bee or a sparrow or a wolf . . . [D]ifferent design features: different perceptual processes, different ways of categorizing the world, different preferences, different rules of inference, different memory systems, different learning mechanisms . . . [P]erceiving a rattlesnake, a coyote might run from it, but another rattlesnake may try to mate with it.

(ibid. p. 8)

This example is interesting. It has a common core, a common reality, that is nevertheless highly differentiated for the various parties. Nor is the common core simply a product of 'our' understanding; it is complexly shared in and with the world. If that looks like positivism, then let us turn the point into its counter-point.

If you accept that the mind's architecture is adapted to the possibility of language, then it follows that culture, to the extent it is rooted in language, is also rooted in evolutionary adaptation. That relationship is only insignificant to the extent that languages are themselves neutral. This is not what post-modernism teaches; rather, it teaches that concrete, culturally embedded languages are agents of reality-construction. We want to argue that language as a whole is similarly an agent, prone to construct according to its own rules and tendencies. Particularly important here is the universal tendency to categorial formalism. Fuzzy theory cuts right across this. It is a challenge to language in general, not just in particular. Our earlier book *Images of Community* (2000) was concerned with precisely this problem in terms of the distinction between verbal and visual culture.

Barkow *et al.* also provide a devastatingly sharp and detailed critique of what they call the 'standard social science model' (SSSM). Of course they include the researchers, the philosophers, especially Foucault and Derrida, and the social theorists, especially Durkheim and Geertz. One may disagree in whole or in part with their positions, but it is an unmistakable requirement that sociology's relationship to science must be re-examined. Both terms are at present mutual caricatures. Barkow *et al.* aim at congruence between the fields. We go further:

22

as we argued in *Images of Community* (especially chapter 11) what is at stake is the possibility of a unified ontology. By implication the present position is not unified. It seems to us absurd that a special ontology has to be invoked for humans and their culture. That schism is humanism.

Our title is: *Qualitative Complexity: Ecology, Cognitive Processes and the Re-emergence of Structures in Post-humanist Social Theory.* What does this imply?

Why *qualitative* complexity? All complexity is qualitative, because it is self-organising in the ecological sense. The complex relationships between phenomena generate landscapes of possibility and impossibility, which inform their actual qualitative organisation(s). There is, then, no independent organisation, and moreover, no independent disorder either: they are co-determining. Let us draw the converse implication: to treat complexity in a quantitative or formal sense becomes increasingly untenable: complex systems have histories and futures, paths by which they come into being and possible directions dependent on many factors (such as energy, habitat, habit). They are not 'things' in the noun like sense but processes; nor are they 'things' in the categorical sense because nothing underwrites the linguistic academic habit of collecting them together. For example, to speak of a democratic society and a theocratic society, to take a topical case, assumes a continuity in the word 'society' that complexity theory, fuzzy logic, and international relations now tell us is, to say the least, problematic and deeply risk-laden.

The next key word we emphasise is structure. Structure has become a neglected subject in social theory, apart perhaps from the recent renewal of interest in social systems led by Niklas Luhmann. But complexity theory is beginning to formulate accounts of structural phenomena that the limited means of older paradigms could not focus or even acknowledge. The former rigidities connoted by structure, now reconceptualised as the self-structuring of complex systems, is one such field. Whether understood through the disciplines of sociology, philosophy, critical theory, critical aesthetics, ethics, cultural study and many more cross-fertilisations, much social theory has recently been at pains to deny structures, or at least external structures. Indeed, a catch-all term for a huge body of contemporary critical theory across these disciplines is 'post-structuralism'. More specifically, for post-structuralism, the primary set of limits to human society is provided by language, custom, convention or, more rarely, position. On the nature *versus* nurture spectrum, post-structuralism is firmly at the nurture side and undoubtedly carries with it connotations of political progress, opportunity and pluralist commitments, perhaps not entirely deserved. On the other hand, what could be called structuralism carries with it notions of established limit, constraint and rank. There is some justice in both sides of this mutually induced caricature. Older notions of social structure do indeed stress homeostasis, in the face of dynamic diversity, or complexity, in the loaded sense of a contrast with the primitive. Structuralism has therefore become associated with notions of conservatism, imperialism and the cultural hegemony of the developed West, parading under an assumed naturalism or progressivism. But the limits, even the guilt, of older notions of social structure do not mean that structures, or constraints, cease to exist. *Post*-structuralism is, then, untenable. So also is the opposition of nature/ nurture, a position shared by contemporary genetics, evolutionary biology and psychology, and cognitive science. Just as nature and nurture are systematically expressed through each other, we stress instead the ecology of social and non-social phenomena, another mark of a necessary interdisciplinarity.

Other forms of sociological inquiry, notably ANT and the work of Bruno Latour, also stress the interaction, or as they call it 'hybrid networks', of human and non-human. Where ANT draws a great deal of its analytic resources from post-structuralism, notably Foucault, our position is informed by complex *systems*. We may preface the matter in these terms:

Recall the confusion expressed earlier between (a) the requirement that eco–auto–organisation must evolve from simpler beginnings, and (b) that complex systems cannot be reduced to their component parts. The first relates to their ontological history, the second to their current, qualitative state. Network theorists stress what Dillon (1993) calls 'radical relationality' or what Law (1999) calls the 'semiotics of materials'. In systems terms, their hybrid networks are complex *open* systems. On the other hand, there is an influential and persuasive corpus of work descended from Varela called 'embodied philosophy', a rich amalgam of cognitive theory and phenomenology, which stresses operational *closure*, adaptive, richly content specific mechanisms, especially in the mind. Luhmann's social systems and recent developments in socio-biology and evolutionary psychology are different from but related to these structural emphases on closure. Here the argument turns not on relationality, where the components are non-existent or trivial outside the relation, but on functional differentiation and on the decisively important and irreducible characteristics of components or subsystems. This polarity must be avoided; it is both possible and evident that levels of both openness and closure, non-trivial and contingent components, both exist. To opt one way or another a priori is to close off the fuzziness of complexity and to tacitly re-admit the premise that human(ism)s 'decide'.

This distinction between openness and closure has many important implications. Here we shall point to one issue: the relationships between order and disorder. Common usage, which seeps into every discipline, evokes a figure/ ground distinction in which order functions as the figure and disorder as the ground. This is an entrenched metaphor, reflecting the acute, existential need for human beings and human societies to maintain themselves in the face of an environmental other which, designated merely as *environment*, appears less ordered or 'dis'-ordered. It is deeply homocentric; a clear example is diet. In order to maintain the order of human beings and their societies it is necessary to *undo* the order of other plants and animals that feature in the diet. The same applies to any other food chain. We emphasise that the demands of the human order (or of any animal high in the food chain) necessarily *produce* disorder elsewhere. This is not a figure/ground distinction but an ecological process.

A second example is an ordered pack of cards. If these are shuffled, an immense number of random arrangements are possible. It is easy to see that if we introduce a second pack that number will rise massively. It is equally clear, though routinely overlooked, that if all the cards were identical, the number of random arrangements declines to zero. Interim arrangements can be visualised. The point is that the possibility of disorder is directly related to the existence of order. Again, this is not a figure/ground distinction but a distribution of related variables. The homology with the previous example is instructive: the *qualitative* characteristics of the order in question are active in the determination of *consequent* disorders.

Such observations require an explicit re-examination of what is meant by contingency, randomness and disorder as it appears in socio-philosophical usage; the notions of randomness, entropic equilibrium in linear dynamics; and order and disorder relationships in complex dynamics. These are *not* matters confined to 'naïve post-structuralism'. On the contrary, despite the irreducibility of the system to its components, it does not follow that the components are themselves reducible, or trivial, or contingent. They do not necessarily owe their very existence to the system, despite the transformations it makes possible. Radical relationality becomes provisional. Only in this way do we move from the modelled *formalism* of systems/component distinctions to the sphere of the qualitative relationships of complex systems. Only the latter is appropriate to the complexity of social phenomena and their ecological embeddedness. Of course this does not rule out contingencies or trivial interactions – but they cannot be presumed. Neither can we assume, correspondingly, that networks come into or fade from being against a backdrop of randomness: relationality may not be quite so radical as we think; true, perhaps, to a degree.

It was routinely thought that sociology and human nature were incompatible. Now it is possible to argue that without a qualitatively human nature, human society and sociology cannot be grounded at all. What follows from this, at least in the complexity theory proposed here, is neither rigidity finalised by nature, nor is it arbitrary, conventional patternings, achieved in networks of contingent association, but is a grounded outcome of ecological plasticity.

Despite the opinion that naïve post-modernism has been surpassed, according to some sociologists, it is ferociously active and damaging in our politico-cultural centres of power. Nowhere more so than in the art of the spin-doctor and the current state of British education. The moral is this: analytic satisfaction is not enough; political responsibility follows, especially when sociology has been so culpable in the promoting what it *now* calls *naïve* post-modernism. A more realistic name would be *cynical* post-modernism.

The key word 'post-humanism' stems from these considerations. 'Humanism' comprises a truly complex and immense set of ideas; indeed, it may be said to represent much of Europe's intellectual history. Post-humanism therefore represents only the proposals for the beginnings of an altered theoretic strategy. What we understand as 'humanism' privileges, isolates, makes central and unique *human* being. This of course is a prime characteristic of philosophy, sociology and their associated disciplines: the 'humanities'. We do not say that humans are not 'special' or lack autonomy but that these qualities rest not on the assertions of the will (Nietzsche and his descendants) or on unlimited technological control (Modernism and Marxism), but are instead deeply rooted in the systems of terrestrial ecology. And in this respect we concur with Lovelock (1988): the Earth is not simply the surface on which life takes place but is instead a series of interactive dynamic systems that serve to permit the further development of self-organising living systems.

This proposition is disquieting because to suggest that human culture has *evolved* also suggests constraint. Ethics, and especially pluralism, are threatened; stratification is implied. This isn't the place to develop the argument in full, except to say that the right/left divide is an irrelevance. Human construction is subject to *ecological* constraint: it does not and cannot take place in the special world of 'humanism' but entirely on account of the mental and physical *adaptations* of humankind, its technology included, and its costs. This is a position shared with the Green movement, post-Marxism, 'world-systems theory' and complexity oriented studies of globalisation. And if human constructions take place in real time and space, i.e. in terrestrial ecology, two things follow: they are likely to be co-influential; they cannot be said to take place *within* human minds, cultures, custom, language or whatever else is proposed to stand as boundaries. This 'within' and the dichotomy of internal/external are a particularly entrenched topology amongst ancient and modern thought which must be resisted. Even the most abstract human idea occurs in relation to terrestrial ecology: *imagination*, defined even in the most classical sense as the faculty of representing that which it is not itself present, is *made necessary* by time.

Reform, then, is not the same as replacement and we are acutely aware that many within our discipline are engaged in similar analytic enterprises. Some will say that reform has gone further than we concede. We reject this. Whilst we agree that extremely sophisticated complexity influenced analysis is taking place in a variety of fields, we argue that the foundations of theoretical sociology remain *in transition*. In other words, whilst specific or specialised accounts of complex relationships are highly sophisticated, the *general ontology* remains confused in a number of crucial respects. This is anything other than a background issue, but on the contrary, shapes thought, language and logic across the disciplines interested in complexity, including everyday usage. Our focus, then, that which '(re)solves' how we address an immense, unknowable and untotalisable field, is *the ontology of self-organisation*, its conditions, effects, permissions and exclusions. Whilst such an ontology is, in principle, not completable and so differs in several respects from ontology's traditional meanings and aspirations, it certainly cannot resemble what Heidegger calls onto-theo-logic. Even a fragmented ontology produces strong analytic outcomes.

How does all of this square with the key words 'cognitive processes'? Let's consider Heidegger again:

> The modern form of ontology is transcendental philosophy which becomes epistemology.
>
> (Heidegger 1973: 88)

Ontology has become epistemology. The modern ontology to which Heidegger refers is that instituted by Descartes and Kant, the subjects of our next chapter. In other words, their work, ontology, broadly the theory of origins or 'being', has become the study of how 'we' recognise, respond to and interact with beings, that is things, objects, each other, the environment. We may preface the following chapter by focusing on that 'we': What does it mean here? First, it means 'we *humans*' and the authors feel this to be a major limitation and distortion. Human cognition is, from our point of view, better understood as a particular form in the evolution of cognition and not as a simply unique phenomenon, however 'special' humans feel it to be. Second, as 'we humans' it tends to connote *conscious* cognitive processes. This is a similar distorting limitation: a great deal of the 'processes of cognition' occur without or below the level of consciousness. Two respective examples are: the immune system (which 'cognises' foreign matter); expert routines such as walking, driving or playing a musical instrument (in which consciousness is divided or partly suspended once the operation has been practised sufficiently).

Central here is the series of complex relations, on the one hand, with other species and environments; and on the other, the complex 'parallelism' of part-networked, part-insulated conscious and subconscious cognitive processes. This is not a fetishism for the complex. On the contrary, over-simplification is grossly misleading, especially where conscious processes 'stand for' everything else, where that includes non-conscious processes or even objects. This again reflects the themes of fuzzy logic: our consciousness of, for example, our own immune systems or 'that tree' *both is and is not* the immune system or the tree. The identity is also a difference; it is necessarily a provisional identity – what Dennett (2003) would call 'provisional drafts' without finality. Crucially, that provisionality also applies to the self and self-consciousness. In contrast to the clear distinction of older epistemology between the subject and the object, or between consciousness and the phenomena *of* consciousness, both become 'looped' or 'smeared'. These are Dennett's terms again. There are some resemblances here with 'embodied philosophy'. We also have our differences and criticisms such that our positions more closely resemble those of Dennett's, Plotkin's or Cohen and Stewart's 'take' on the relationships between cognitive processes, complexity and the philosophical tradition. That brings us to the details of the book's structure.

Part I is intended as an extensive introduction. Its first theme will be a critical view of the founding texts of humanist philosophy, in particular the work of Descartes and Kant. We shall then contrast what we shall present as the 'classical texts' that prefigure complexity theory. This is not intended as a catalogue or a history (though the places to pursue such a study will be referenced) but as a presentation of key analytic requirements. Others present them differently. We shall attempt to present rather than criticise, where appropriate and return to more critical examinations in Parts II and III.

Part II will begin the task of distinguishing and disentangling complexity theory as it applies to social theory from the dominant schools of twentieth-century social theory – the modern versus post-modern divide. Again, we shall be exploring the founding texts or concepts, especially of Foucault, rather than derivatives and applications that obscure or lose crucial issues; especially those which, impossibly, propose to assimilate complexity theory to the quite different positions of post-structuralism. We then develop a series of counter-positions. Our first concern is a reappraisal of the relations between systems theory and cognitive processes. This involves a detailed critique of the varieties of constructivism, including Maturana and Varela and their epistemological similarities to phenomenology. We argue that the systemic and the phenomenological are eventually forced to confound each other. We then consider the evolution of intelligence, its costs, benefits and functions, and raise the crucial matter of the mind's *parallel* structure and parallel processing. We then apply these arguments to concepts of language, culture and social systems, demonstrating the limits of formal theorisation and the requirements of qualitative social theory.

Part III will propose that complexity in contemporary social theory is both fragmented and in transition, or in process of differentiation from the schools of twentieth-century social theory, its idioms and its preoccupations. We begin with a detailed critique of the proposition that complexity theory, post-structuralism and Luhmann's systems theory are in some sense compatible. Then we move to a reconsideration of both the systemic and topological characteristics of qualitative complexity. Finally we re-examine global complexity as a 're-deployment' of existing powerful topologies, in the form of networks, their ecological robustness and their relations to persistent human needs. This describes our sense of an ontology of qualitatively complex structures in persistent interaction, far from equilibrium.

2

FROM DESCARTES' CONJECTURE TO KANT'S SUBJECT AND THE *COMPUTO*

Humans cannot operate without some level of belief in their experience; nor can they mature, progress or adapt successfully to a complex or changing social and 'physical' environment without critical reflection on what they believe to be the case. Operationally, these two factors are not separable: they are multidimensional and intertwined, fed by batteries of sense-receptors acute to some stimuli, blind to others; then 'organised' and distributed by the hyper-connected networks of the human brain. It is also characteristic of human society, or at least of European thought, that the two factors become, to some extent, separated, indeed specialised, and this has unintended, undesirable outcomes. The traditional separation has taken two forms: first, the 'disciplines' associated with belief which include religion, custom, culture, common sense; and second, those associated with the criticism of belief, which are philosophy and science (with its conceptual divisions) and mathematics.

Many objections may be made to our inclusions and omissions, but they are unimportant. What *is* central is the ironic marking of disciplines, which indicates the current privileged status, or prejudice, of critical reasoning over belief. Perhaps we should say *criticism*, rather than critical reasoning, to underscore the conviction that criticism has become more idiomatic than reasonable. As a result of specialism and division, criticism has become far more what various kinds of critics *do*; an institutionalised and insular, rather than engaged, set of positions. Our objections, also grounds for our inter-disciplinary orientation, do not rest on the familiar accusations of bad faith, abuse of power and political interest – putting the objecting author in the dubious position of claiming to be a better citizen – but rather on our disbelief. The separation has run its course, it is over, or must be refashioned. The fundamentalism of certain kinds of belief has its counterpart in a fundamentalist criticism. Both are equally unfortunate. The doctrine of fundamentalist criticism is that whatever we think is the case 'could be otherwise'. This is formalised in Kant's philosophy. Of course, the beliefs of any individual could be otherwise, in the most radical form by the non-being of that individual, but that cannot mean that anything could be otherwise. Such a proposition denies ecology, indeed any kind of connectedness or networking.

If, in contrast, we admit to our environment, evolution and our social history, that a human individual living at a certain time in a certain social context, that specific member, cannot admit to the radical contingency of belief as a formal individual might; rather a certain plasticity. It is impossible to transcend fully one's own membership, in both the social and the ecological senses, and impossible to even begin to opt out of one's species. Arising from this simple observation there are a number of consequences for causality and therefore for ontology and the status of writing of this kind.

For humans and everyone else, complexity is a problem. Whether it is the manifold of sense impressions, too much traffic, too many books to catalogue or chapters to plan, an overgrown garden or an untidy house, getting lost, getting the wrong sort of bacteria in the gut, complexity costs time, money, pain, error, death. It is hardly surprising, then, that the philosophical foundations of the Enlightenment should attempt to reduce the complexity of lived experience by a sort of cataloguing, an ordering, a critical reduction, an imposition of control, where possible. That aspiration, then, should be understood as both an existential and a philosophical imperative. It is not, therefore, an error, far less a kind of theoretic perversity, but this does not mean that its formal outcomes are benign.

Those outcomes have now become subject to radical questioning. From Heidegger's critique of technology[1], to the widespread critiques of science[2], from the loss of faith in meta-narratives[3], to the dark contemplation of the frames, horizons and limits of language[4] and inscription, the criticism is relentless. But it is also strangely unreal or unproductive, or ineffective. We philosophise post-modernity but we still live an increasingly technology- and science-saturated lifestyle. In this way we have articulated an extensive philosophy of regret, but little else. This philosophy of regret is not distinct from, but part of, the old Enlightenment's paradigm, weary with itself. In this chapter we examine the establishment and limits of Descartes' and Kant's attempts to provide a secure, in the sense of less complex, basis for the critique of lived experience by establishing the centrality of the subject.

Despite good, practical reasons for its initial aspirations, the work of these philosophical giants is not primarily reasonable or logical, but in several senses negligent and contradictory. Further, if enlightenment, or reason, or criticism, is to escape regret and renew itself, it is complexity itself that must be re-addressed, confronted and brought back into the vocabulary of critical philosophy. The following, then, is not an esoteric review of an antique mode of explanation. On the contrary, the effects of Descartes and Kant are embedded in our contemporary usage, especially 'professional' social analysis, in much the same way that evolutionary adaptations and requirements are embedded in contemporary culture.

Descartes' conjecture

There is an extensive body of text from clinical psychology, cognitive science and the study of the phenomenon of self-consciousness that regards Descartes' position as simply wrong.[5] Here we are exclusively concerned with the grounds, 'idioms' and outcomes of his theoretic strategy.

Cogito ergo sum – I think therefore I am – is not so much the conjecture itself but a mid-point in the strategy the conjecture makes possible. The prior moves are:

> I resolved to pretend that nothing which had ever entered my mind was any more true than the illusions of my dreams.
>
> (4th Discourse: Descartes 1968 and 1975: 53)

> I shall suppose, therefore, that there is, not a true God, who is the sovereign source of truth but some evil demon, no less powerful who has used all his artifice to deceive me. I shall suppose that . . . all the external things that we see are only illusions and deceptions.
>
> (1st Meditation ibid. p. 100)

We should note the phrase: 'I resolved to *pretend*'; and 'I shall *suppose* . . . that there is . . . some evil demon.' This is the historic origin of humanistic rationalism. Is it a perverse or a strategic conjecture – or a little of both? In the circumstances, Descartes was prudent merely to suppose a demon and the *Meditations* and *Discourses* are full of apologies and eulogies to the perfection of God. But of course this is so much nonsense. It is essential to dispose of God in order for the human subject – the *cogito* – to become the phenomenon that underlies this new kind of truth. It is equally essential that a significant measure of perversity, the demon, be introduced into appearances-in-general. Otherwise the postulate of radical doubt (I resolved to pretend . . . that we see *only* illusions and deceptions) is exactly what it appears to be at face value: unreasonable and incredible; frankly, a silly posture. If the demon is a metaphor for the uncertainties of lived experience, it's a singularly bad one. Experience is not chaotic in the ordinary sense, but rather complex: certainty and uncertainty co-exist. The image is also characteristically insular because the lives of other sentient animals are far from chaotic. But then there is the matter of human-ism's successes! How can we deny the enormous achievements of the post-Cartesian Enlightenment? The short answer is that we do not make such a denial. But we do want to distinguish between its strengths and its weaknesses. Perhaps we should ask the following – what does the conjecture cost? What does it leave out, minimise or ignore? What is the cost/benefit, limitation, risk and destiny of the formal philosophical discipline that the conjecture makes possible?

For the contemporary reader, gods and demons are idiomatic – rather like sea serpents in early maps – scattered around more factual substance. In one sense that is also true for Descartes: despite his expressions of reverence, he is going to doubt and the only certitude in that doubt, he insists, is *cogito ergo sum*. But to see this as the factual substance is the error in both Descartes and modern readers. Any number of such residuals might have been chosen: I breathe, eat, feel pain, fear death, feel the effects of illness, experience sexual desire . . . therefore I am. The choice of 'I think' may be presented as the generalisation of all of these, but the argument is unconvincing because feeling pain or eating, for example, carry with them an ordinary kind of certitude completely incompatible with the general radicalisation of doubt. The 'I think', then, is strategic rather than logical or factual. What Descartes then proposes, and science has followed for most of the time ever since, in theory if not in practice, is a series of methodical procedures. Science works with the gradual accumulation of small certainties that can resist the general radicalisation of doubt. These may be facts, indeed crucial facts for human survival. Nevertheless, the 'I think' is still itself strategic.

It is also organisational in the sense that it grounds and controls the access to information. Where the 'I think' and its ability to doubt are privileged, they control access to and cast their shadow over everything else. Think of the model as a Venn diagram: 'I think' is the universal set; contained within it are the concrete subsets that I think about. This leads to two major consequences. First, to insist on 'I think about . . .' as the access to everything is to imply falsely that anything, however previously certain, is open to generalised radical doubt. As Descartes puts it: 'I *pretend* . . . I *suppose* demons . . .'. Second, the differentiated complexity of consciousness, for example of hunger or sexual desire, is reduced to the false simplicity of everything being thought about. In a sense, these are two sides of the same coin. The point is still twofold: first, the model is too simple, too uniform; second, the parallel autonomy of heterogeneous consciousness and less or un-conscious 'cognition'[6] has been constricted to the serial bottleneck of the 'I think'. This is humanism's cost. It is precisely this loss of complexity. It is also an ironic loss: it is only on the basis of manifest separation of the 'I think' from other aspects of consciousness that Descartes can commandeer it as the ostensible link that binds them. The common attribution of Cartesian 'dualism' is therefore radically questionable. There is the distinction between mind and 'everything else', but the mode of access is mono-polar. Yet the loss of other parallel modes of access, for example via compulsion or other such mundane certainties, passes almost unnoticed.

This 'not noticing' is a posture that founds a whole idiom of ostensibly critical philosophy. There are sound and extensive neuro-scientific arguments for a radically more 'distributed' model of the components of consciousness. Indeed, Damasio (1995) goes so far as to title his study *Descartes' Error* - quite a punchline in a liberal tradition. Similarly, Dennett (1991) criticises 'the Cartesian theatre', a kind of collecting point and control-room of consciousness, as an illusion that constantly frustrates a coherent theory of consciousness.

From *cogito* to a priori

Descartes' cumulative methodology is, in analytic terms, not radical enough for Kant in two senses: 'Experience teaches us that a thing is so and so but not that it cannot be otherwise' . . . and 'if we have a proposition which is thought as necessary . . . it is an a priori judgement' (Kant 1929-1973: 43, section B3).

These, taken together, form Kant's 'criterion' for the identification or proof of a priori 'knowledge'; that is, a cognitive domain that precedes experience. This is the formalisation of critical procedure that we spoke about in the first paragraphs of this chapter, whilst the a priori indicates the direction of its philosophical development.

It is worth unpacking these two points since they are the foundation of Kant's enterprise and central to the idiomatic structure of epistemology and critical philosophy ever since. The first proposition (the critical limitation of experience) may be taken as an implicit critique of Descartes, following Kant's interest in Hume. Both thinkers reason that experience cannot ground any certainty and so the Cartesian project is not finally worth a great deal. Similarly, the *cogito* may be certain but cannot on those grounds alone apply to any of its substantive contents.

This radicalised position remains central to both modern scientific aspiration[7] and to post-modern criticism in the positive sense as the theoretical underpinning of pluralism, and negatively as the loss of certainty, or stability, or faith, secular or otherwise. Lyotard's generalised disbelief in meta-narratives, as opposed to one by one examination, rests on precisely this ground. Derrida's metaphors of ruin, inter-permeation, and instability stand in exactly the same place, with experience modified as 'interpretation', 'inscription', 'framing' and so on. Behind them lies the enormous influence of Heidegger's insistence on, and contempt for, the importance of Kant: 'The modern form of ontology is [Kant's] transcendental philosophy which becomes epistemology' (Heidegger 1973: 88) and 'In Kant's definition . . . Being is merely the positing of the copula between the subject and the predicate' (ibid. p. 65).

Kant's second proposition ostensibly follows from the first: we find, we experience, certain phenomena as though they were necessary. There is a contradiction here. Experience apparently divides itself, insisting it is both the ground of uncertainty but also of a somewhat occult class of certainty. Kant's answer, modelling itself on the Cartesian split between the *cogito* and its substantive contents, is to distinguish between uncertain appearances for experience and the form of experience, which is 'certain' in the sense of 'inescapable'. This again is strategic rather than reasonable. All other residual types of certainty have simply been ignored.

The form of experience is inescapably necessary, or in Kant's usage, a priori. It is 'prior to' experience. It is the condition of the possibility of all subsequent experience. We must be in no doubt about the radicalism of this proposal:

time, space, cause and effect are 'certain' and therefore a priori; these and the 'certainties' of mathematics are merely the form of experience or 'appearances'.

Despite several concessions, for example the necessity of time/space is shared with all other human beings and possibly with all sentient beings, Kant's clear preference is what he calls the 'ideality' of time and space. Ideality is not quite illusion, but not too different either. Skimming through the *Transcendental Aesthetic* constantly suggests this, its title asserts it; it is clearly Kant's preference. The trouble is, he cannot get 'outside' to see. Yet there are two indicators of exteriority. The first is the necessary, or routine, or automatic suspension of time/space in the concept of God. Interestingly modern physics does exactly the same thing, except that God is replaced by 'origin' or 'singularity'. Either way space/time follows. The second we have met already, it is Kant's criterion. If space and time are 'necessary' they can only be compromised in Kant's eyes by the suggestion that they are derived from experience, however 'universal'. That universality is not open for experience or analysis. Curiously, this is again shared with one tendency within modern cognitive science called 'radical constructivism' which emphasises the closure or horizon of cognition *vis-à-vis* its environment.[8] It is also present, albeit in deteriorated form, in the various presentations of closure or horizon in language, culture, technology, simulacra in post-modern critical theory. Let us note that space/time as the literal, expansive and existential conditions of all knowledge, and experience as it appears for common sense or, some would say, for reason, are re-conceptualised in Kant as something akin to form, metaphor, code, representation, simulacra:

> Time and space, taken together, are the pure forms of all sensible intuition . . . But these are a priori sources of knowledge, being merely the conditions of our sensibility, just by this fact determine their own limits, namely that they apply to objects only so far as objects are viewed as appearances and do *not* present things as they are in themselves. This is the sole field of their validity . . . This ideality of space and time leaves, however, the certainty of empirical knowledge unaffected.
>
> (ibid. p. 80; section B56)

Kant and Descartes seek certainties. Their fundamental drive, and their fundamental error, is the reduction of complexity as, or despite, its being the source of error and uncertainty. Echoing our presentation of fuzzy logic, to try to simplify something which is essentially complex is to diminish accuracy and to court error. Heidegger's criticism is somewhat different: Being is reduced, constrained or, in more Heideggerian language, 'represented' for purposes of human control or certainty:

In that truth becomes certainty and thus the beingness (*ousia*) of
beings changes to the objectivity of the *perceptio* and the *cogitatio* of
consciouness . . . knowing and knowledge move to the foreground.

(Heidegger 1973: 88–9)

For Heidegger, 'Epistemology is the title for the increasing, essential powerlessness of modern metaphysics to know its own essence and the grounds of that
essence' (ibid.). The insistence that every form of necessity and certainty is
derived from the subject and not from experience, in other words Kant's
criterion itself, isolates both the modern subject and thought about that subject
from every other viable, terrestrial manifestation of consciousness. Heidegger's
objections are as always voiced in the need for disclosure, unconcealedness,
even the yearning for closeness to a more authentic divinity. However, the
problem is the criterion itself. It is wrong in the sense of over-simplification or
it is true to a much smaller degree than Kant's drive to ground certainty led
him to believe.

Kant chose to ignore certain types of mundane certainty, much like those
Descartes chose to ignore. Our examples in Descartes' case included such
things as hunger, respiration, sexual desire and the awareness of pain. These are
arguably 'hard-wired' responses, or not at the fullest level of consciousness.
That does not diminish their significance, but it is to our analytic advantage
to include examples specifically from conscious and calculative practices. They
are less easily ignored as special cases or as 'lower-level' phenomena.

We invite the reader, then, into a game of mundane complexity which is
nevertheless certain. What is your name? Are you certain of that? And the
date? Your sex, your childhood memories? What is your job and your medical
history? Are you married, single, divorced, gay? What is your life expectation
given that you are now well, or not well, or seriously ill? According to Kant, if
the answer to any of these questions is truly certain, then it must be an a priori
proposition. Let's tease that over the edge of absurdity: your name is certain
so it must be a priori like space and time, a law of consciousness; you cannot
have learned it from experience. Similarly, the state of your life, employment,
relationships, etc. A common response to examples such as these is that they are
trivial. But where does triviality end and complexity begin? Would it not be
more reasonable to ask that the criterion itself admits to special cases if they are
special, trivialities if they are trivial, and serious exceptions if they are serious?
Are the examples too trivial or is the criterion too simple? There is no need to
labour this point it is easy for the writers or readers to construct everyday
scenarios of mixed complexity and simplicity with intertwined levels of
certainty or uncertainty that do not necessarily correspond in any way to each
other. Thus we might conclude that Kant's axiom has nothing to do with logic.
Like Descartes it is strategic and on inspection readily dismissed; even though it
may be true in certain cases, the untruth, the illogic is the claim of universality
itself. This gives some flavour of the difference between complexity theory, or

thinking in the face of complexity, and the simple but false universals of humanism. But there is a more radical twist.

Kant's logical ploy in framing the criterion is to contrast the finite limits of actual experience with the infinity of possible experience: 'experience teaches us that a thing is so and so but not that it cannot be otherwise'. The first level of il-logic, discussed above, can be framed more formally – in establishing the certainty or truth of any specific item of experience, the totality of possible experience is not necessarily relevant but rather a certain horizon (mathematicians would say a certain 'set'). So, to know with reasonable certainty the complexities of our present employment (such as writing this book), it is neither relevant nor necessary that one should know one's co-author's date of birth, relations with his family, to say nothing of future fortune or calamity set to bless or curse one or both of us. Therefore the contrast between finite and infinite possibility, here placed in relation to experience, is impossibly unstable and will not yield any substantive result without tacit concretisation of 'infinity'.

Despite the counter-intuitive feel, it is perfectly true that the universality of space and time cannot be grounded in any finite number of human individuals' experiences. But how big is 'any finite number'? Kant is actually rather consistent here. He does not say that because all humans hitherto have regarded time/space as necessary it has somehow become necessary. That would be a degraded or derivative version and that is why the a priori version is, for him, preferable, despite its 'ideality'. Given the benefit of Darwin, however, might we not cite the evolution of consciousness, and indeed Kant's own admission, to grant that the necessity of space/time may be characteristic of all sentient beings 'to some degree'? How big is the finite number of experiences now? Is it big enough for us to say that space/time's necessity can be indeed derived? Is evolutionary time extensive enough to diminish the error term implicit in the distinction between finite experience and 'all' experience, so that it is no longer significant for all practical purposes? Certainly, this is 'only' a practical matter but with massive consequences for Kant's formalism and for philosophy generally. If we agree that evolutionary time is sufficient to ground the *derived* necessity of space and time, we have also agreed that 'infinite' has refused the definition 'not finite', a definition Hegel also detested, and become something like 'infinite enough', immense, operationally viable, or in this case 'ecologically widespread'. It is the deconcretisation and non-definition of infinity that matters. For our notion of complexity theory, 'infinity' may equally well refer to the impossibly extended, the practically widespread, the infinitely divided or divisible, like a recurring decimal, and has no fixed size, scale or number. It is a 'complex' in the sense of a contextually determined phenomenon. If, then, the contrast finite/infinite has self-similarity or relative conceptual consistency across scales, to cite mathematicians' preoccupations, it has no fixed or expected scale. This is what is intended by *qualitative* complexity. To the mathematicians' self-similarity across scales, we add a whole series of qualitative contexts ranging from 'operationally large enough' to 'practically irrelevant' to 'always reproducible for all practical purposes' to 'inexhaustible variety but gathered around certain pathways or attractors' and so on. All of these and many similar contexts are implicit in the key notions of autopoiesis, homeostasis and homeodynamics; each emphasise operational practicality in an environment with which they interact.

It is possible to generalise these two apparent sets of objections to one continuous complex, and it's because of the continuity that a new 'constant' and a new complexity can be identified, which in turn displaces Kant's apparently stable criterion with a conceptual homeodynamic. There were two related sets of objections to Kant's criterion. First, that for many, perhaps the majority, of ordinary, finite propositions the comparison with the infinite possibility of experience is simply irrelevant. Second, that such infinities are so unstable and contextual that some credence can be given to the 'sufficiently extensive'. These can now be generalised as simply as the operational contrast between the larger and the smaller; or, better for our purposes, between set and subset.

Let us take an example: Does this sample (of whatever) give me sufficient grounds to generalise? Does the experience of a subset allow me to predict the character of the set? What defines the set and the subset? These questions and distinctions are crucially important for human understanding, but where that understanding is operationally effective, illuminating and opportunistic, Kant's legislation is rigid, authoritarian and misleading; the fixed, formal criterion is not useless but certainly much less useful and much less intelligent than its contextual uses. In other words, humanity is limited, imperilled, robbed of its native intelligence by humanism's misplaced or mistaken conflation of universality and certainty. In a sense, then, Kant is far too quick to judge. For qualitative complexity theory the distinction set/subset is provisional, fuzzy, potentially effective: a strategy of maximum opportunistic plasticity, not a strategy masquerading as logical principle.

Kant's criterion is credible; it is true that experience teaches us that a thing is so and so but not that it cannot be otherwise. So now let us switch our attention from the contrast between this set of experience and all possible experiences. Let us now just concentrate on the first term: any finite set of experience. What is it that links the set? Is it being 'mine' or 'our', or just plain 'some' experience? The answer has to be: any of these so long as it is finite.

Take a statement to which Kant's criterion applies, a rather simple one: 'I like wine'. Neo-Kantians can immediately pounce: You like all wine *hitherto*. There is nothing stopping the next bottle disagreeing with you violently; being not to your taste, too sweet or too dry, or being not worth the money and so on. It is possible, even likely, you may 'change your mind' and so the criterion is proved even on such a simple proposition. Now take a more awkward case: it is certain but certainly not a priori that the Second World War happened. It might not have happened is the only neo-Kantian response. 'But it did!' is an equally valid response. Reason's task is to incorporate them both, hence 'complexity theory'. Remember that both of these propositions follow from finite, even possibly scant, experience. The analysis is as follows.

The proposition, 'I like wine' is an open set. Hence the rejoinder, 'All wine *hitherto*', is no more than a reminder that the grammar is not quite accurate – whoever said it missed out either 'all' or 'some' wine. In the first (uncorrected) case, the proposition 'all wine' is nonsense because the set is infinitely open and whoever said it or liked it, is not. In the second case, 'some' wine is the generic closure for which any specific can be substituted: this, today's, red, French, mine but not yours, etc. There are many such elastic possibilities: 'I prefer Rhones to Burgundies' is a sort of half-open set which neo-Kantians might just try to prise open. The wine drinker would be unlikely to benefit greatly from such considerations, though he might pay more attention to the rather more limited, contextual and operationally valuable statement, 'I had a wonderful Burgundy last week.'

On the other hand, despite the 'might not' reservation, the Second World War did happen. The set implied by the statement is certain, well and truly closed, and no amount of Kantian posturing can prise it open. The same is analytically true of this statement: 'I suffer from a respiratory condition which is easily enough managed but which if neglected could prove serious or fatal.' Notice again that all of these statements are based on finite experience. Perhaps we might persist with the term 'infinite enough'? That would be stretching a point as far as World War II is concerned for readers under the age of 60. But would the recollections of their parents count? After all, the essence of social understanding is that not all experience is first hand. Perhaps we might rephrase, indeed invert, the cumbersome 'infinite enough' and say that actual experience is 'too heterogeneous' for experience, in Kant's sense, to be described in the simple categorical form Kant would wish.

Kant's criterion can only apply to open sets in the sense described above and even then with some reservations. Given the complexity of the remainder of the *Critique* he should have realised this for himself, so with tongue in cheek we try a mischievous rephrasing: Experience teaches us that burning your fingers hurts but not that it cannot be otherwise.

What does this tell us? That Kant had only half the essential insight. He saw that 'experience' is too heterogeneous for us to draw conclusions about its contents with certainty. Nevertheless he treated 'experience' as a category homogeneous enough for us to draw necessary conclusions about its form, though, wisely, he restricted this necessity to 'appearances'. This is a mistake, not an interpretation, in several senses:

1. Kant concedes that the form of experience is only available from its contents but does not proceed to the conclusion that experience is therefore too heterogeneous for us to draw conclusions about itself with certainty.

2. Experience resists categorisation. Perhaps it would be better to assert the counter-intuitive rejoinder 'experience is not a category'. At best, it is a collection of categories; at worst, the term 'experience' is so varied or contradictory as to mean very little; worst, that is, for the idioms of philosophy - which likes such generalities to be stable.

3. Non-philosophers, and we can include humans and animals here, can function entirely without the category 'experience', defined or not. On the other hand, the actual experience — heterogenous, fuzzy, messy, half-conscious, operating on all sides at once, without totalisation or conscious co-ordination — is indispensable to the living. This is the sort of experience complexity theory is interested in.

4. Kant's attempt to write a proposition about experience in general succeeded in blinding him precisely to the major, and highly differentiated, dimensions of its manifestation. This is precisely the error his criterion was supposed to highlight, namely that experience is so vastly complex that necessity is massively difficult to ground. Complexity theory is also an abstraction or formalisation; a propositional or categorising ambition. That is how language works and why Heidegger is justified in his critique of language itself. Language is not 'neutral'; it is species-specific. With sufficient intellectual agility we may be able to treat that reflexively.

5. We shall also note that our mischievous example — burning one's fingers — indicates again that perceptions are not confined to a phenomenological or 'mental' realm but, on the contrary, are intensely networked in their actions with real environments. True, pain does not exist 'out there', but neither does it exist by itself 'in here'. It exists and functions solely in and for the relationship.

Along with 'experience teaches us that a thing is so and so but not that it cannot be otherwise' is another Kantian distinction. Humanism on the whole, and certainly within contemporary usage, agrees with it: whatever we understand 'to be the case' can be contrasted with 'the thing in itself'. As Kant has it: 'a pure beyond of thought'. This is conceptually identical with the strategy we described above, namely the comparison of a limited set of experiences, conclusions, cultural practices, etc. with the universal set of such practices. It is the ideological core of pluralist humanism: we/I (as limited) cannot legislate for the validity or invalidity of you/they as the possible alternatives, as 'reasonable' responses to different milieux. The 'thing in itself' is simply not 'a beyond of thought'. It is a clear postulate, moreover, of a very specific way of thinking. It is the counter-axiom to Kant's reductive definition of experience.

What, then, might it mean? Perhaps something like: all the predicates that can be asserted about this 'thing', infinitely extended. This 'thing' then begins to look decidedly strange, we can partially identify 'it', but on the other hand it is open to infinite identifications. Even after that aggregation, we could not identify 'it', though 'practically' we can. Things, never mind 'in themselves', are radically open to identifications, including predications, predation, removal, representation, use as building material and so forth. 'Things', so to speak, are in the world, open for action and re-action whilst 'in themselves'; this is a humanistic philosopher's diversion, an interesting diversion but one incredibly badly analysed, a diversion likely to lead humanistic political philosophy into the mistaken belief that political possibility is endless, costless, infinitely reasonable. In the real world, possibilities are numerous but limited, feasible but costly, interactive and so not without impact: instances of eco–auto-organisation.

It is crucial to see that this is not simply an attack on an antique form of discourse. Later we shall consider how far the idioms of post-structuralism and certain 'constructivist' positions in cognitive science rest on neo-Kantian foundations. For the moment let us remain concerned with strategy. We now turn to Morin's (2002) reappraisal of the *cogito*.

Echoing and developing our opening point, he argues:

> There are a thousand ways to prove that one exists. What is interesting here is this *ergo*: 'I cannot doubt that I am a subject.' But what Descartes did implies the *computo*. His *cogito* implies the *computo*.
>
> [O]ur *cogitos*, that is, our consciousness as subjects, depend on the fundamental *computo*, which the billions of our brain cells, in their organisational and creative interactions, incessantly cause to emerge.
>
> (p. 55)
>
> The *computo* also might be understood as the ancestral form of consciousness.
>
> With the bacterium we have neither a computer nor a machine by itself but both at once in the same thing. We have a being, a machine being that is also a computing being . . . [that] processes signs and data about its internal and external environments . . . [I]t is not simply . . . a question of binary processing, but of a more complex and more analogical mode of representing that remains a mystery . . . [T]he bacterium computes from itself, by itself and for itself, which is to say that it is animated by a kind of autofinality. It constitutes itself by itself and for itself, in a manner reminiscent of Hegel's use of the term *fur sich*.
>
> . . . The cartesian *cogito* appears much later, as it requires a well-developed brain as well as language and culture.
>
> (p. 48)

Morin's *computo* and revised *cogito* are autopoietic, or rather they are auto-eco-organisational. The tension between the more closed autopoietic and the more open auto-eco-organisational is palpable and remains so across the literature on the relationship between organism, 'information' and environment. Notice how it resonates against Kant. His subject is entirely *sui-generic*, the relationship between this 'metaphysic' and the rest of the physical environment cannot be addressed in principle. The same is true for Durkheim: his social reality is *sui-generic*, metaphysical, unable to address its *alter* except as an act of self-reference. It is true also for Luhmann, Derrida, Lyotard, Baudrillard, Foucault, radical relationality in some of its manifestations and radical constructivism, the phenomenological arm of cognitive biology.

In fact the *computo* no less than the 'body' of the bacterium arises out of the environment. Indeed, they constitute the ongoing organisational possibility of each other *vis-à-vis* the environment. The hardware/software distinction here is observable but in a sense is also absurd. It is to isolate one slice of an event within a temporal process of '*difference*'. That '*difference*' is at least tripartite, the third 'fuzzy' *agent* being the environment of systems differentiating the possibility of a specific being within and from itself. The allusion to a notion of emergence Hegel would recognise is not idle: hardware, software, environment constitute and negate their identity and difference.

Returning to the identity of the 'subject', Morin writes:

> We must now consider the basis of this principle of identity which, from the start, already appears complex because it is not readily assimilable to the Aristotelian principle of identity. This principle, which is presupposed by the act of computation and without which there would be no *computo*, is a principle of *difference and equivalence* [our emphasis] which I formulate as: 'I am me!' But just what is this 'I'? It is the occupying of an egocentric site. 'I' really means: 'I occupy an egocentric site. I speak.' 'Me,' for its part, is precisely the objectification of the I. Thus, 'I am me' means that the 'me' is not exactly the same as the I, because in the act wherein the me is formed, the me appears different – it is objectified – whereas the I is the pure uprising of the subject. The act that simultaneously posits the difference between the I and the me along with their identity allows for the *computo* to process the being as subject. Thus the bacterium can process its molecules in an objective manner while remaining a being that is animated by its auto-organisational subjectivity.
>
> (ibid. pp. 48–9)

The sudden switch from human to bacterium, which also posits a continuum, is characteristic of both the materialist and informational paradigms of complexity-influenced analysis. As Morin puts it: 'the *computo* did not descend from on high . . . neither was it installed by an engineer . . . All dimensions of life are inseparable . . . [T]he *computo* emerges from something that does not compute just as life emerges from something that is not living . . . (ibid. p. 55). It is also holistic or 'emergentist' in the sense demanded by Byrne and arguably somewhat at odds with Cilliers, though he has other challenging approaches to the emergence of order from 'distributed' components.

It is possible to see this loosening of the distinction between 'hardware', 'software' and environment, the body, the mind and nervous system, the relatively localised surroundings, as a kind of mystification. Despite the profundity of the issues, and Morin's formulations, it is quite the opposite, though not without wonder. If we accept that humans have evolved, then so, finally, has the 'subject', no matter what the character of the formulation. Evolution cannot be called mysticism by a paradigm resting on *sui-generic* creation. *Sui-generic* creation means creation *ex nihilo* unless it admits to a more than trivial ecological foundation, turning self-reference into a question of relationships. Nor is the clarity of the traditional hardware/software distinction reasonable where difference 'to a degree' or 'gradually established' is more appropriate. Most important is the refusal to make either the emergence of life or the simultaneous emergence of 'information' a matter of metaphysics. As Morin puts it:

> [just] as auto-organisaton is in fact auto-eco-organisation, self or auto reference is really auto-exo-reference, which is to say that to refer to oneself one must refer to the outside world.
>
> (ibid. p. 49)

Humanism has both failed to see this complexity and blocked the pragmatics of auto-exo-reference on spurious grounds of principle. They are spurious on the simplest possible grounds: exo-reference does not have to be 'correct', broadly or absolutely, but narrowly and practically; it only has to work ecologically. Birds know nothing about trees in the human sense. That does not stop them making use of their accessible-to-birds properties. Apparently, our philosophers have not been quite so intelligent: because we cannot know the thing-in-itself (the tree), an intellectual barrier has been erected, exo-reference is wholly and absolutely in doubt. There is no way 'out'. The evidence of life suggests there are thousands of ways out. But none of these are 'certain'. Perhaps we could do without certainty? Or, as above, re-think the certain and the necessary as the vital?

In this context it is appropriate to point out an omission. It is not so much a criticism of Morin as an addition. The identity-and-difference thought in the relation 'I' to 'me' finds parallels in what we shall call the 'spectrum' of conscious/voluntary and of the unconscious/involuntary. Between these extremes lie clusters of interwoven phenomena, from pain, to the suppression of expert operations from the attention of consciousness: one could not walk, drive, or swim, to say nothing of reading or of playing a musical instrument, if every point or movement were subject to conscious inventory, though that may have been necessary in pre-practice. Suffice to say that the *cogito* and the subject, in Kant's sense, and even the subject in Morin's sense if we concentrate on that exclusively, tend to erect the same kind of intellectual barriers that humanism builds around auto-exo-reference. We professional theorists are far too prone to posit humans as thinkers and not see our amateurish negligence. We are at least as much constituted by 'sub-' or unconscious processes ranging from those that interested Freud to digestion, the immune system and so on. This again echoes our opening themes: specialisation can produce its own insularity. However 'virtual' the contents of conscious representation, they relate to a being living in real time and space.

This chapter concludes with a final reference to the so-called 'thing-in-itself'. Hayles makes these interesting comments in relation to the work of Norbert Wiener on cybernetics. Under the heading *Crossing Boundaries: Everything is an Analogy including this Statement*, she writes:

> . . . Wiener cybernetics sees communication as a probabilistic act in a probabilistic universe, where initial conditions are never known exactly and where messages signify only through their relation to other messages . . . For Wiener no less than Saussure signification is about relation, not about the world as a thing-in-itself.
>
> It is in this context that pattern, associated with information . . . assumes paramount importance. Wiener's view of sense perception makes the point clear. Perceptions do not reflect reality directly but rather rely on transformations that preserve a pattern across multiple sensory modalities and neural interfaces. Representation arises through the analogical relation of these transformations to the original stimulus. In this respect, sense perception is like mathematics and logic, for they too deal preeminently with pattern apart from content . . . Analysis is thus constituted as a universal exchange system that allows data to move across boundaries. It is the *lingua franca* of a world (re)constructed through relation rather than grasped in essence.
>
> (Hayles 1999: 98)

Wiener's notion of analogy is less sophisticated than later formulations. There is no place in Kant's 'criterion' for probability, only the distinction between self-certainty and external chaos. Hayles employs the more developed concept of chaos outlined above, this time in the form of probability, or the probability of pattern. As opposed to the external as randomly related to the self-constituted subject, in complexity theory the 'external' is ecologically related and structured, characterised by probability and the feedback that it organises. Part of the feedback is precisely the 'self' in Morin's ambiguous sense. Hayles still talks of the world as a 'thing in itself' whilst denying the validity of doing so. She does not point out that following her argument thing in itself is entirely propositional. Moreover, thingness, as we formulate it, our very mode of access, or analogue, to the world is constantly denied, left hanging, not noticed, as a construct. Does it make sense to say that a dog distinguishes in analogic form between what it smells and the thing in itself? In seeing, do we experience a sense of loss, or discomposure, as though what we see is false? Philosophy, and what passes for ordinary 'intelligent' usage, says something like this in the routine distinction between essence and appearance. Kant uses the term 'appearances' constantly; without it his position would collapse. Nor is that an antique position; see, for example, Jay's (1993) title: *Downcast Eyes: The Denigration of Vision in French Twentieth-Century Thought*.

That does not diminish sight's authenticity; rather, it makes fools of the philosophers. A great deal of profound and scholarly nonsense has been written against 'ocularcentrism'[9] as though it indicted vision *per se*. Whereas ocularcentrism and the anti-ocularcentrism of modern French philosophy is clearly a body of writing resting on a critique of one of the worst metaphors philosophers have invented: the observer paradigm, the belief in the 'visibly' true, the idea that a mental 'picture' is correct if a counterpart in reality can be invoked. But to see is to know that appearances can be, for all practical purposes, both right and wrong, a good or bad guide to 'reality'. Limits and all, sight is still an authentic mode of engagement with the 'real' world precisely because built in to its every operation is knowledge of its limits and its strengths. It has no need at all of a clumsy arch-concept of the thing in itself or the constant distinction between essence and appearance. Sight is more complex than that. So too are 'things'.

The self-limitation of sight is not a tragedy but, as fuzzy theory teaches, an increase in accuracy. This may be tragic for those who desire absolute certainty; it is, so to speak, a 'loss of god'. The 'thing in itself' is another either/or (Aristotelian) construction. But, for the world of heterogenous conscious response, thingness is a matter of and/and. Some examples may seem contradictory (a tree is a perch, a tree is fuel) but both/many are necessary in a sense Kant cannot contain. We can resolve this by understanding the term 'necessary' to mean vital. Or better still, vital to; now the relation to another is made crucial. This should be understood in the widest possible ecological sense, not simply in relation to consciousness or purpose or life. The tree is also 'vital to' a forest fire.

The 'thing in itself as pure beyond thought' implicitly defines thingness, the being of the thing, as 'not this thought'. This is as poor a definition as saying the infinite is equal to the beyond finite. The 'thing', in relation to the thinker, is, on the contrary, part of the ground out of which a thought, or sight or hearing, that is, a complex of 'analogic' relations (in Weiner's sense) arises. It sits at one side of two grounding conditions, the world and the thinker, and evolution contains them both. This invokes fuzzy theory's 'subset theorem': the whole of the thing in itself is partly 'contained' in, established by, provokes, the thought or other analogue. That is the analogue's possibility. Further, its possibility has 'vitality' in evolutionary time; that is, opportunity, a niche; it is not ruled out by circumstance. That is not to say that its contradiction can or cannot live with or beside it in the form of and/and, not either/or. There may be ecological room. But also there may be a decisive yes/no, either/or. Eventually there was no ecological room for Nazism. The same is becoming true of post-modernism in its naïve form.

It is important to stress that this relationship of ground and analogue denies one to one correspondence, that is certainly physically impossible in relation to the whole, but rather asserts a heterogeny of analogy. Moreover, that disjuncture may occur even within the individual subject in question. Some of that complexity can be seen in this mundane example.

A family sits down to eat. Parents, grandparents and children are present. The dish is a traditional rib of beef served with vegetables. In what sense did the food ever have the status of thing in itself? Certainly not on the table. Let's start with the butcher's shop. Implied here is a vast interaction of information and 'embodiment' that, on the one hand, provides the economic systems that deliver the meat as product or commodity to this particular point in the chain of marketing. On the other are the 'embodied' skills of the butcher – embodied in him, no less than in the beef carcass, the production of his tools, the honing of his skill. The rib of beef is prepared. Is it a thing in itself? Is his expertise in cutting and preparing a kind of thing in itself? For both can be regarded as a sort of totality. Now the transaction takes place. The joint belongs to the parents of the family. Is the meat any less of a totality? Has the butcher's role become irrelevant? Yes or no? Who will decide; who can decide? The meat is cooked. Everyone agrees that a transformation has taken place – a transformation conditional on the physical properties, known or not, of the meat; a transformation conditional on the properties known or not of the cooking medium. Is the meat still a thing, a totality, in itself or not? Does it somehow lack its raw state, or any other previous state? So far we have dealt with the objects, more or less: the meat, the tools of cutting and cooking and the relatively 'simple' informational elements (such as a developed economy!). All of these questions are absurd: the thing in itself has no meaning. It is an aural illusion, a speech habit of the kind that comes from mis-hearing. The thing in itself is literally nonsense unless its specification can be decided in advance.

This could be understood in both an exalted and a mundane sense. In the exalted sense it trades off an epistemology of creationism: now the in-itself makes sense as god's 'creature'. But it has no place outside fundamental religiosity. Or, more mundanely, say I order a car and the wrong specification is delivered. Now I can say this is not the true thing I ordered. But it does not stop the dealer selling it to someone else who is happy with that specification. It would be restored; a true thing 'by itself'. The crucial thing here, like creationism, is agency: the (un)truth of the thing is decided by my agency as specifier, the failed agency of my dealer, and restored by the agency of the new customer. This is completely opposite to Kant's sense.

Now let's turn to the activity at the dining table. Amongst its many antecedents is an information saturated process that has 'established', for all practical purposes, infinitely enough, that beef is a viable part of the diet. Is eating a true thing-in-itself? Does the difference in expertise between the small child at the table and the parents make any difference? Does it matter that the guests were not party to the purchase and the cooking? Does it matter that the activity of eating is an expert physical act and that for most of the time we entirely forget its informational component – indeed have 'forgotten' so long ago that swallowing is part voluntary, part reflex? Think of the trouble Kant would have with eating: what kind of a thing is it? True, it's a process, yet its components are 'things', albeit interactive and permeated by complex information. This example is exhausted, so let us conclude.

The thing in the case of the objects car or meat, and in the case of the process, of ordering or eating, is entirely subject to agency. In one sense by specification; in another by specification in the sense of which part you mean. In neither case can 'in-itself' be attached to the thing because the scope is defined by the agent. It belongs to the agent. To say the thing in itself is to confuse and contradict the object's being with the subject's agency. The thing in itself cannot stand in opposition to the subject because it is generated by it. Thus thing denotes a formulation, a way of attending, a wording, and so is not an object. It cannot possibly be a thing-in-itself because it is a phrase. Kant cannot recognise or deal with the contradiction at the heart of his doctrine. But if we abandon his humanist paradigm it becomes clear that however manifold the ways, the world is complexly open to formulation (and other activities such as, in this case, eating). Again this is the opposite of Kant's imprisonment within mind. Unlike Kant, such 'formulations' of 'things', like eating, do not invent real objects, certainly not the space-time continuum, but demarcate and specify their interest. The paradigm here is radically materialist-informational. Our task is to maintain this complex unity that humanism has sundered. Humanism is not an external or demonic agency but a part of the history, even the destiny, of our language. We speak it as we oppose it in this sense: Kant's position might be taken as a sort of formalism that has over-simplified the issues. But what else is our project – or any academic study – than a similar 'abstraction'? What else is any everyday 'report'?

We now turn to cognitive biology's formulation of similar problems and its influence on cybernetics.

3

AUTOPOIESIS IN COGNITIVE BIOLOGY

Humanist philosophy has burdened us with the legacy of a schism between belief and criticism, which is difficult enough, but the institutional separation of disciplinary functions makes matters worse. Granted the distinction between the 'belief disciplines' and the 'critical disciplines', a difference that serves principally to reinforce mutual insularity, we find a parallel offensive front within the critical disciplines themselves. Science and reason then find themselves caught between 'realist' tendencies, to which they owe their experimental ethos and practical strength, and 'idealist' tendencies towards a general criticism of the 'constructed' status of knowledge, largely derived from post-Kantian phenomenology. The work considered below is explicitly an attempt to 'negotiate a middle course between the Scylla of cognition as the recovery of a pregiven outer world (realism) and the Charybdis of cognition of a pregiven inner world (idealism)' (Varela *et al.* 1993/2000: 172).

Maturana and Varela's *Autopoiesis and Cognition: The Realization of the Living* first appeared in 1972 in Spanish and in 1980 in English translation. Despite its origins in cognitive biology, this and their subsequent work is normally listed under philosophy, for good reasons. Like the decades, the work, its reception and subsequent development are shot through with disputed politics and aspirations. Maturana is a Chilean human rights activist, whilst Varela constantly declares his Buddhism to be central to his work as a scientist. The work is philosophically weak but nevertheless important, not least because of the first formulation of the now all-pervasive 'autopoiesis', but also for its resemblances to and differences from the philosophy of cognition in, say, Kant or Derrida. Above all, these authors' influence on 'second wave' cybernetics[1] and systems theory is decisive; they provide the grounds, despite their explicit objection, for Luhmann's renewal of systems theory in sociology. We shall strengthen, or better differentiate, the strands of its philosophical significance because it too rests on a tradition of humanistic philosophy, notably Merleau-Ponty's phenomenology, and is in danger of collapsing back into it, losing all of the real significance of its radicalism.

Given the historic interdisciplinary importance of 'autopoiesis', the amount of interpretation and explanation it has received is understandably large.

Cognitive biologists will no doubt have their own preferences, though ominously Maturana and Varela are often ignored by them. Philosophers are more attentive. The story, best told for our philosophical epistemological purposes by Hayles (1999), begins with a frog: not quite a transcendental subject, but in great danger of becoming one. Briefly, the creature was wired up by planting sensors in its visual cortex but instead of corresponding to stimuli:

> . . . fast, erratic motion elicited maximum response whereas large, slow moving objects evoked little or no response. It is easy to see how such perceptual equipment is adaptive . . . because it allows the frog to perceive flies while ignoring other phenomena irrelevant to its interests. The results implied that the frog's perceptual system does not so much register reality as *construct* it.
>
> (Hayles 1999: 135)

Frog becomes transcendental subject! The book subsequent to the study is much sounder and more complex. As was recognised at the time, a realist epistemology is presupposed for the constructivist epistemology voiced in the conclusion. This will always be the case and directly echoes Kant's presumption of a 'real' homogenous category called 'experience' in order to ostensibly deduce the impossibility of grounding certainty in experience. Kant is in this sense saying, 'I have a better concept of experience', which turns out not to be the case. Similarly, these experimenters are tacitly saying, 'Because we have a more comprehensive concept of reality, "frog-reality" is obviously constructed.' As a contribution to the understanding of reflexivity, which this whole enterprise was supposed to be, it is decidedly weak. Even weaker is the consequent supposition that human perception is also likely to be constructed, simply because both a hyper-realist epistemology and its twin, a lesser human constructivism, are asserted out of thin air. This is commonplace in what passes for contemporary critical theory.

Such examples, like Kant, trade off misplaced assertions of universality, when inexplicably concrete exceptions are both everywhere and not noticed. Let us suppose the hapless frog 'constructed' a world in which he was unaware that after the experiment it was curtains for him. If that is too ignoble, let us have a voracious and enterprising heron 'constructing' a world where laboratory frogs make good eating. Either way, he and his world get deconstructed in the literal not the more polite Derridean sense. Dead, swallowed, digested, recycled; no longer combating his own entropy but the heron's. It is truly strange that advocates of the multiple construction of realities rarely confront its savage side. Realities, constructed or not, still live in ecological competition: still 'alive', mortal, getting by, or dead. Set beside such considerations, constructivism is shot through with Cartesian and Kantian echoes: it tacitly prioritises consciousness or perception; the organism as its perceptions; the serial bottleneck, not this time of the *cogito* but of the nervous system. What is presupposed and glossed here is a relationship between 'information' systems as the key or ground of the organism's total organisation, or 'autopoiesis'. We shall return to this question in our discussion of Prigogine's thermodynamics where the relationship of material, organisation and 'information' is both central and quite different. The term 'information' is used equivocally here. In some ways it is the wrong term but to say exactly why just here would pre-empt this chapter.

Take a more human example. Speaking from the male heterosexual construction of reality, others of like orientation will notice that attractive women of childbearing age attract our attention far more than . . . practically anything else. Do we therefore 'construct' a world or, with rather less exaggeration, 'have sexual preferences'? And if after a hard day's work we want to do nothing but have a drink and go to sleep . . . have we constructed another world or have we just got tired? Supporters of constructivism in this sense are guilty on several counts: assertion without due reason, misplaced universality, dependence on anecdotes, negligence of counter-examples, massive exaggeration, but above all the failure to see that it makes no difference. Reality, constructed or not, has the same function. Nothing about construction reduces the impact of truth. Or, if your constructions do not exhibit necessity in the sense of vitality, you and your species or tribe, or culture, or orientation, are on the way to extinction. Thus the organism or culture – the short run – constructs the proposition. The world – the long run – decides the truth.

Finally we turn to the most extreme exception, which may seem absurd at first. Treat it as a preparatory to the analysis of *Autopoiesis and Cognition* and to our later return to Kant's 'thing in itself'. All of the above rest on a distinction between an organism that is both autopoietic and operates procedures, however simple or complex, that maintain its internal organisation and process 'information' about an environment. Now let us turn to a relationship between objects where no such distinctions exist. Choose, say, a hammer and nail or perhaps a car engine, or the incoming tide. Each obeys the laws of physics, which we all agree they do not construct: there is no hardware/software distinction. They are hardware all through, subject to, and part of, the laws of physics as they operate. The tide causes us fewer problems: despite variations caused by local externalities it is more or less a universal and can be treated as such. But the hammer/nail and the car are more local, more variable and not simply because they are man-made. The nail may go in straight, or bend, or break. The car may stop working (Maturana uses the same example). Neither has any preference, only you. You have the problem; they do not. The point we want to stress is that there are local variables without need for construction. Or, the outcomes are constructed out of the current, local state of physical affairs. This complex, precisely because it is local, may exclude significant aspects of the laws of physics, or better, itself regulate them in their specific interaction. No hardware, no software, remember. Water regulates gravity whether you are a swimmer or a piece of wood, but not quite so much in practical terms if you

are a stone. Cold temperatures regulate organic decay whether or not there is
human interest. Note the complexity, on the one hand of the environment
and on the other of the 'thing'. Neither are primarily linguistic categories and
this is the same problem as Kant's linguistic concretisation of 'experience'.
That proposition indicates yet again that linguistic categories (re)construct
reality. That does not make the construction binding, though it still has effects.
The assertion or observation of local variation without need for construction
indicates that the set linguistically constructed by a term such as reality is
tendentious. The set contains so many diverse elements that nothing can be
excluded, nor can it define anything. The early Wittgenstein would
call it 'literally nonsense'. This is exactly parallel to Kant's error: an infinitely
extended set is simply not a set. It follows that 'reality' in this case and
experience in Kant's are literally not defined, that is not made finite, and
therefore constitute no subject and no possible predicates either. A word
of caution: an impossible set should not be confused with a 'fuzzy' set.
This will assume greater importance in due course. 'People' is a fuzzy set.
'Everybody thinks that . . .' is an impossible set. The distinction is entirely
concrete.

Maturana and Varela developed the initial insights from the frog's visual
responses to work on colour vision in a wider range of animals, including
primates. They found:

> . . . they could not map the visible world of colour onto the the activity
> of the nervous system. There was no one to one correlation between
> perception and the world. They could, however, correlate activity in an
> animal's retina with its *experience* of colour.
>
> (Hayles 1999: 135)

Note the persistence of an entirely realist epistemology as the very ground
of the visibility of the animal's constructions. It is difficult to express the sheer
level of irony involved. Hayles argues: 'Maturana had a choice. He could continue within the prevailing assumptions of scientific objectivity, or he could
devise a new epistemology that would construct a worldview consistent with
what he thought the experimental work showed' (ibid.). This is the double-
edged error of Maturana's partly persisting in Hayles' otherwise excellent
analysis. Actually, no choice is required and the resulting epistemology is anything but new, though it has interesting variations on the truly ancient themes
of philosophical idealism. The key, positive element is autopoiesis:

> If we think of sense receptors as constituting a boundary between
> inside and outside, this implies that organizationally, the retina matches
> up with the inside, not the outside [notice again the forced (false)
> choice] . . . Maturana concluded that perception is not fundamentally
> representational . . . to speak of an objectively existing world is mis-

leading, for the very idea of a world implies a world that pre-exists its construction by an observer. Certainly there is something 'out there,' which for want of a better term we can call 'reality.' But it comes into existence for us, and for all living creatures, *only through the interaction processes determined solely by the organism's own organisation.*

(ibid.)

This is the sense in which information is a misleading term, since (for Maturana and Varela) it implies this representationalist stance. This is an over-forced, though not uncommon, choice. Everything turns on the mediate character of information as transformation. How far does the organism or the environment decide?

No general position is possible; the question of agency will vary. For Maturana and Varela (1980), a more absolutist stance appears mandatory:

No description of an absolute reality is possible [this would require] an interaction with the absolute to be described, but the representation that would arise from such an interaction would necessarily be determined by the autopoietic organisation of the observer . . .

(p. 121)

So that:

living systems operate within the boundaries of an organisation that closes in on itself and leaves the world on the outside.

(ibid. p. 136)

That proposition is to us the most interesting but, before treating this inside-outside relation in more depth, note Maturana's emphases:

. . . the activity of the nervous system is determined by the nervous system itself, and not by the external world; thus the external world would only have a triggering role in the release of the internally-determined activity of the nervous system.

(ibid. p. xv)

This self-reflexive dynamic is constantly stressed by Maturana, Varela and their interpreters and is the core of the notion of autopoiesis:

It is the circularity of its organisation that makes a living system a unit of interactions . . . and it is this circularity that it must maintain in order to remain a living system and to retain its identity through different interactions.

(ibid. p. 9)

51

Or again:

> Since cognition is traditionally defined as the process of knowing we must be able to describe it in terms of an organism's interactions with its environment . . . The specific phenomenon underlying the process of cognition is structural coupling . . . [A]n autopoietic system undergoes continual structural changes whilst preserving its web-like pattern of organisation. It couples to its environment *structurally*, i.e. through recurrent interactions, each of which triggers structural changes in the system. The living system is autonomous, however. The environment only triggers the changes; it does not specify them . . . By specifying which perturbations from the environment trigger its changes the system 'brings forth a world' . . . Cognition, then, is not a representation of an independently existing world but a continual *bringing forth* . . . to live is to know . . . cognition is embodied action.
>
> (Capra 1996: 261)

The key notion for Maturana and Varela, and especially Luhmann, is the persistence of a difference, stated in its most formal terms as inside/outside, system/environment. Spencer-Brown is the often credited influence but it would be more accurate to regard this distinction as the existential architecture of consciousness. Our first criticism of Maturana–Varela as a philosophical position, then, is that it is groundless in this specific sense: the establishment of the distinction, here of organism/environment, is entirely presupposed and fully operational. Their epistemology may describe what follows with some validity but there are grounds for concern as to the question of origin. Second, and closely related, the epistemology proceeds in a somewhat humanistic fashion: on the inside is 'the organism' and on the outside 'the environment'. The latter is another impossible set, unbounded like experience and reality. The former is also potentially impossible: does it denote any and every organism? Does it define 'organism'? The answer to all of these questions is 'well, sort of; perhaps not' and it is the inclusion of that vacillation that distinguishes the philosophy of complexity from traditional humanism. It is not the world brought forth by the organism that brings about the distinction in the first place. Instead, it is a concrete, situated and temporal ecology, a localised world, that brings about a viable distinction which we or other organisms may subsequently refer to, identify as, or eat in the form of an organism. In other words, 'autopoiesis' as *self*-structuring is massively misleading. Recall our earlier insistence on the rather more cumbersome concept auto-eco-organisation. Similarly, the world brought forth by the established organism is not a world at all but a nexus of relevant, that is part impression, part construction, experienced events. And the environment is not the abstract linguistic construction it purports to be: it too is localised, heterogeneous, radically temporal and is itself a collection of systems, some of which may be similar to the organism. On these grounds the whole concept of autopoiesis is up for re-inspection, especially where we press its use in the far less stable and analytically tenuous field of social systems.

In this context it is important to consider Maturana and Varela's distinction between autopoietic organisation and structure. The former is the constant, auto-organisational aspect of the organism, without which it would lose identity or become chaotic. The latter is the conditional state of that organism; conditional, that is, on the specific needs and demands of autopoiesis as recursive self-reproduction in relation to an environment which both enables and threatens it. At this stage we do not want to stress the need for recursive reproduction in the sense of 'correction' or conservation, the preoccupation of first-wave cybernetics, or of dynamic development, for example in the processes of human learning or immunity. Note, however, that homeostatic and homeodynamic processes work by responding to difference which they must cognise in some sense. These differences will be both internal and external, and perhaps somewhere in between. When our focus changes from organism to populations, including those specified by culture, this will become immensely important.

Whether we formulate our enterprise as sociology or as the philosophy of complexity, or both, we cannot, like theoretical physics, begin with a singularity – a big bang. We have to begin with a 'plurality' instead. The reader may think that merely another word for complexity but we want to emphasise that this is not a linguistic abstraction. It does not denote a plurality merely as opposed to a singularity nor merely a patterned field. It has colossal temporal and spatial dimensions at the same time as only presenting in this or that locality, massively multiplied, or in 'this' moment. We sample this little piece of it, knowing that its totality is as inaccessible to us as it is to itself. We, as part of that plurality, experience it as presence and loss, intimacy and massive estrangement. It is real in the sense that only a fraction of that reality is available to that reality. Language fails at this task, the sense is truly unrepresentable. Nevertheless, it can be sensed, carried in the heart, experienced as mortal burden, awe and ecstasy all at once. Perhaps Heidegger comes closest to this intimacy in his interplay of concealment and disclosure in the distinction between Being and *Dasein*. The colder names are possibility, likelihood, and immediately those names are mentioned it is clear that plurality not only means spatio-temporal structure in general but also particular local structures: auto-eco-organisations.

Think of auto-eco-organisation rather than autopoiesis as self-organisation. Experience this not as a speaker, not as a professional thinker beset by the usual hyper-formal idioms, but as the offspring of parents. You do not occur as an organism but as a human child. You do not make a difference in Spencer-Brown's sense but rather as an embryo set in a course of development and then a child with a limited amount of freedom and a great many needs. Millions of years ago, that occurrence would have been impossible: human children were not on the auto-eco-organisational menu. Important here is the auto-eco-organisation of the menu itself, or 'possibility', or better, 'likelihood', and so to emphasise that autopoiesis is equally a feature of what counts as organism and of what counts as environment. There is some modification of the environment/organism relationship in Maturana's and Varela's later work but the philosophy of complexity would never, have formulated such an absurdity as the organism bringing forth worlds without insisting that this is analytically identical to the world bringing forth organisms. If the former is absurd on grounds of auto-eco-organisation, the latter appears self-cancelling. Perhaps the fault lies with the saying rather than the sense.

Perhaps the weakness lies both in bi-polarity and formalism, that is organism *vis-à-vis* environment. Replace the analogy of the child with the more formal 'mutual-inter-dependence' and concede now that we may be speaking of any dissipative system, in Prigogine's sense,[2] including such things as organisms but also phenomena like customs or markets. The bifurcation, formerly organism/environment, is now much wider open. This should not be taken in any absolute sense: we are certainly not saying everything is contingent or could have been otherwise. We are speaking of mutual possibility, inter-dependence and therefore also mutually opposed or constituted identity. Absolute contingency (when we *really* mean 'could have been otherwise', without limit as opposed to open to limited variation) would be chaotic in the strict sense. Mutual inter-dependence would be impossible in such circumstances; it requires a measure of stasis. At this point we traverse the bipolarity of organism and environment and in truth meet multiple discrete and recursive interactions. Call this complex series of considerations simply a third dimension: that of the relation itself. It is singularly hard to characterise this relation. Is it heterogeneous? Certainly in its generality but not necessarily or significantly so in all particulars.

Consider an example of forced heterogeny: the customs that normally accompany the collection of the harvest suddenly facing a changed environment: war, famine, drought, disease. An example of the more enduring kind: the mother–child relationship in mammals. Nevertheless, if we cannot generalise or formalise the relation *per se*, it is still decidedly real: the elements involved have effects, they are attractors. They are essential components of auto-eco-organisation and will impinge on mutually dependent relationships as their organisational demands unfold. Take a non-living example: the use of fossil fuels implied one set of relations to the Earth as their source in the nineteenth century. In the second half of the twentieth and the beginning of this century the reduction of fuel stocks and global warming is forcing a different relationship to emerge. There is everything contingent and circumstantial in this but nothing unreal, chaotic or occult.

Yet when the example is living, apparently, the mysteries arrive. Now the relation is, at least in part, informational. With informatics all of the prejudices of humanism return. We have seen Maturana's emphasis: the self-organisation of the organism decides what counts as or in the environment. Varela's insistence is more interesting and more contradictory:

> information and information processing are in the same category as matter and energy . . . [yet] . . . Information, *sense strictu*, does not exist. Nor do, by the way, the laws of nature.
>
> (Hayles 1999: 155)

These informational relationships are reiterated adaptations, in Maturana called 'structural coupling'. Varela gradually stresses instead that information is embodied or enacted possibly more open-ended and transformative. Maturana's position is untenable as soon as 'eco' is attached to autopoiesis or as soon as 'structural coupling' is granted any ecological significance. So back to the contradiction; this time the philosophy of complexity insists on one, not both, positions: 'information and information processing *are* in the same category as matter and energy'. They are real, necessary in the sense of vital; and vital in the sense of the third relational term: 'given by' the ecology of organism and environment.

Before we explore the details of this counter-intuitive claim (counter, that is, to the idioms of humanism), let us stay with the general point. Information does exist, without qualification. It does not matter that it is information about and not the so-called thing in itself, any more than it matters that the Earth on which we stand is a bit of Earth and not the thing in itself. One cannot conclude on such grounds that the Earth does not really exist, though Kant, Maturana, Varela and many others will be tempted. Rather, the informational imperative is a direct, existential and ecological result of the distinction between the living organism and the environment. The non-identity of organism and environment of organisms is the unshakeable ground of an informational relationship as a condition and active participant in their ecology. Information is virtual in quite a different sense from the bit of Earth on which we stand, but both are caused by, what humanism insists are, the 'things-in-themselves'. 'Cause' and 'correspondence' are not the same thing; quite the contrary: it is because of the formal separation between organism and environment that the question of relationship, or structural coupling, emerges as a third ecological dimension. And because of the character of receptors and the architecture of the organism's mental and physical organisation that information-processing comes to have a species-specific, concrete character. This need, like other biological needs, does not somehow convert what is needed into sub-type or simulacrum any more than the need to eat simulates meat or vegetables. The informational relationship, or the simulacrum, is like the digestive process, inevitable, necessary and functionally transformational. Without it the organism could not exist.

It has been established that it is an error to pose an opposition between a realist and a constructionist epistemology: they are ecologically co-positing.

Nor does such opposition resolve questions of representational adequacy. It is rather the ontological, interactive or transformational basis from which we must begin. It may seem at first as though this proposition is without result, except to complicate matters, or with only negative results, but it nevertheless sketches the shape of paradigm change. The implications will become more apparent later in the text. For the moment we want to concentrate on where this leaves or rather transforms the Kantian subject. This is not a type of critical vindictiveness. Rather, Kant is credible not out of his idiosyncratic strengths or weaknesses, but out of our shared linguistic possibilities. In other words, this is the ecology of language-as-enaction reflecting upon itself, testing the measure of its constructions not because it is stuck with them in some Derridean poem of regret but precisely because it is alive and kicking. Language in this sense lives with us and yet displays its autonomy. It conceptualises and formalises yet displays both its unconscious depths and its raw concreteness.

Nowhere is this more apparent than in the transformation of the 'thing-in-itself', for Kant a pure beyond of thought; for us the very soil and sustenance of life. The 'thing-in-itself' re-thought in terms of auto-eco-organisation is precisely that other from which the energy requirement of a dissipative system is drawn. For the purely self-organising subject, Kant's transcendental subject, energy or capacity is presupposed, not unlike the Christian God which it resembles functionally and linguistically. We too must presuppose energy, theoretical physics is in the same boat. But where the prehistory of the transcendental subject is simply an earlier moment in the assembly of its necessary organisation, 'auto-eco-organisation' is a name for the gradual 'organisation of organisation'. It presupposes energy and also that this energy is packeted, dispersed or arranged such that some sort of tree of possibility and impossibility emerges. The 'thing-in-itself' is this energised emergence but of course must now be plural and manifold: 'things in themselves' connote available energy, fertility, manifestness, the propensity to interdependent structure. Similarly, the auto-eco-organisation of what has hitherto been called the subject authentically belongs to that tree of possibility whose branches are identified by no less important spaces of impossibility. The previous schism has functioned hitherto as our authorised ontology of something like error, or even sin, called appearances, deceptions, conventions, inauthenticity or what you will. The map has now changed: the certitudes of necessity, on the one hand, and contingency, on the other, have given way to a complex topology of mutually influenced possibility and impossibility.

How does this sense square up to the earlier formulation of the association of the thing in itself with agency? The key lies in the phrase, 'organisation of organisation'. Here we are describing the emergence of multiple, distributed agency characterised by degrees of mutual influence.

These rather dense formulations can be illuminated by examples. Maturana's autopoietic living systems are, viewed at the extreme, conceptually almost identical to the transcendental subject. Taken as purely homeostatic phenomena they simply have a history of coming into existence, of regular self-organisation until death by whatever cause that subverts that organisational competence. But we know they depend on available energy and that its availability to their organisational competence is 'evolved'. Maturana distinguishes between organisation and structure, the latter being the particular state of the organisation at any time. Death is post-organisation. But placed in a more ecological and evolutionary perspective the types of plants and animals that interact in a specific place might be regarded simply as the current structure of the ecosystem's wider organisation. The organism's operational closure is radically provisional.

Nor is that restricted to such populations as those. The current structure of the planetary ecosystem contains many humans and the outputs of their actions, such as cities and cultures. But one has only to contemplate any historical remnant, be it fossil or ruin, to see that this operational closure is poignantly provisional, however boldly it currently asserts its vitality. Similarly, it required scant knowledge of the Earth 'in-itself' to get inside itself sufficiently to mobilise the energy of agriculture, to say nothing of coal or oil. It is vacuous to say the vitality of humans and the spoils of their actions are conventional. That is too naïve, too sentimental, too much of an age of innocence when effects could be ignored. Similarly, the description of appearances is a gross affront to those on the receiving ends of the conventions of politics or economics. 'Things in themselves' far from being a pure beyond of thought are all around us, just as we too are 'things ourselves'. The fact that our knowledge is weak, incomplete or indeed non-existent is simply not relevant: the spider with little information-processing power still eats the fly because both are part of Being, not the estranged ghosts of Descartes', Kant's or Derrida's humanistic imagination. The human, however clever, well- or ill-paid, slave or master, still labours, thinks, eats and reproduces in reality, whether he knows it or not, because its authenticity only rests on what he thinks, to the extent that the thinking really matters. Operational closure is radically provisional, which is to say that the closure implied in thinking or positing about an external reality is entirely subject to the conditions of possibility and impossibility. These are mortal systems granted provisional vitality by the real opportunity in specific circumstances.

Maturana continued to stress the relative closure, despite structural coupling, implied in the first formulations of autopoiesis. This is the dominant position of what Hayles calls the second wave of cybernetics. Stress on interaction and implied layering of replication and innovation is characteristic of the third wave.[3] One might object that some of the criticism levelled above is made, so to speak, with the benefit of hindsight – of that third wave. However, like Kant, the kind of reflexive criticism outlined above follows from Maturana's own position. Hayles' comments come close to that position. The point is that Maturana's position is by no means superseded. On the contrary, it is regularly repeated; like Kant's usage it is not 'his' but a possible linguistic position. The immediate task then becomes to demonstrate his influence on epistemology and cybernetics, and in particular to show how that relates to social processes.

First-wave cybernetic devices did not construct themselves. Hayles' examples are, amongst others, electronic rats and thermostats. They hardly connote social structures. Autopoiesis, on the other hand, despite Varela's objections, is analogous to *sui-generic* social phenomena and even more so system-type recursive patterning. Here the ambiguities of Maturana's epistemology come decisively into play. On the one hand is the realism that describes the structure in the process of eco–auto-organisation. On the other, given the closure of the system on itself, the 'eco' part along with the 'exo' of reference, are threatened with assimilation. The organism, the culture, the member, and especially the observer, are massively compromised in their relations to the environment. Alterity becomes the most problematic notion, the most constructed, self-referential notion of all. Kant has returned. Embodied philosophy remains committed to, indeed celebrates, this position. For many fields the same conclusion is deeply frustrating: infertility and par- alysis through radical reflexivity. One does not have to read far in the literature of critical sociology and philosophy ever since to realise that, with few excep- tions, the more famous and respected names have added more persuasive and poignant detail to precisely that tragic impasse. Despite the promise of complexity and 'hybrid-network' theory, it is the intellectual obstacle that con- founds our epoch: its culture, its vitality, its beliefs and especially its political capacity. Part of the reason that political culture has come to despise sociology and philosophy is that it cannot possibly live with its conclusions. This is 'dramatised', by which we mean hidden from view, by partisan caricatures of positivists and insensitive politicians versus helpless pluralist-'moralists', which results in the complete impoverishment of any notion of preference. Where once that meant commitment on grounds of 'the better', now it means only consumer drift. Hayles (1999) cites:

> . . . Maturana's ideal is a human society in which one would, 'see all human beings as equivalent to oneself and to love them . . . without demanding from them a greater surrender of individuality or auton- omy than the measure one is willing to accept for oneself . . . Such a society is in its essence an anarchist society . . .'
>
> 'In man as a social being . . . all actions, however individual as expressions of preferences or rejections, constitutively affect the lives of other human beings and hence have ethical significance.'
>
> (p. 142)

This is the decisive point at which Maturana describes and departs from liberal, subjective humanism. His emphasis is on autonomy as the dignifying charac- teristic human beings cannot surrender without due thought and proper reciprocity. The human society that emerges from that requirement is anything but 'anarchic', or 'chaotic' in the narrow sense, but precisely ethical, that is complex, in the fuller sense. We define ethics as a *post*-human, emergent realm in the sense that it arises out of the interactions not simply of communities but, crucially, in relation to their need for resources or energy and in relation to other communities, including other species. Ethics is eco-auto-organisational and exo-auto-referential, whilst anarchy, like autopoiesis, like Kant's subject, is simply costless closure. It speaks of a being utterly on its own, the degraded godhood, the self-isolated *cogito*. But further, it is also recursive; it feeds back onto the presumption of autonomy: just as the *cogito* is revealed as the *computo*, so autonomy is revealed as opportunity, degrees of plasticity, eco-auto organisation. Or, autonomy rests like the 'thing in itself' on the ghost of the creator rather than the limited plasticity of mundane agency.

These points are crucial. The centrality of the humanist subject, whilst itself a decisively secularising act, still rests on something closely akin to 'man in the image of God', particularly with respect to the centrality of mind and autonomy. It is not surprising but unavoidable that the language of this metaphor results in the transcendental subject, the thing in itself. It is not surprising but unavoidable that this secular first step deteriorates into the modern form of radical reflexivity and the 'loss of faith' in the fecundity of moral agency. Despite the persistence of these metaphors, treated routinely as fact in everyday speech, including critical theory, a decisive intellectual event has authored their demise.

That event is the gradual incorporation of the notion of emergence in every intellectual field. Darwin may be taken as one of the first exemplars of the shock that dislocated the tight relationship of language and humanism. After Darwin there had to be a *pre*-humanism, a reform of such proportion that humans are the latest comers: not the constructors of time but beings of the last hours. And in the continual incorporation of emergence and interaction, complexity and feedback, there has to be a *post*-humanism consisting of restraints, attractors, effects and so forth that shouts plasticity in the face of autonomy. Alterity may still be a problem but instead of being the not-human, or indeed the not-I, it is the ecology from which our possibility – and perhaps our impossibility – is decided. The creator, our creator, is the planet, our spatio-temporal locality. Proper respect is long overdue.

This has not yet happened. The more common result of autopoietic theory is radical constructivism. Its premise is that the world only exists in and as my representations. Therefore in the book we have already cited (Schnitman and Schnitman 2002) – to which Prigogine and Morin are contributors! – von Foerster and von Glaserfeld (both influential figures in cybernetics) preach radical constructivism.[4] The former was cited by Morin and in turn by us (op. cit.); the latter cites Bishop Berkeley (1710). The book's title? *New Paradigms in Culture and Subjectivity*.

What is the alternative? The case for eco-auto-organisation seems evident, but it is by no means clear that exo-auto-reference is not beset by all the devils of radical reflexivity. It certainly cannot call out any of the apparatus of the traditional observer paradigm. All of this is fair and true, but we cannot graft our epistemology on the debris of humanism. We have to develop further sets of ontological foundations beforehand. The first of these, a branch of emergentism, is the contribution of evolutionary biology and psychology which will be our focus in the next chapter.

This chapter was intended as an introduction for readers unfamiliar with the work of Maturana and Varela. There is much more to say by way of developing understanding and criticism of their positions. We do, however, feel the need to explain a point to readers a little more familiar with their work, especially those used to hearing Maturana and Varela invoked in the cause of political pluralism, which they clearly support, and the epistemology of radical constuctivism. Such readers will probably be annoyed that we have suspended our discussion here and may be surprised at our treatment. On the first count, this is, as we said, an introduction. Development and critique will be resumed in due course. As to the second point, we must reply that the apparently 'liberal' connotations of organisms 'bringing forth worlds' does not and cannot occur at an individual level. The organism, so to speak, obeys its species: if the world is constructed or not pre-given, the specific characteristics of the species' autopoiesis certainly are, and so the brought forth world follows. This is, in sense, a kind of genetic determinism. We use that phrase with some reservations. There are many paradigms within genetic determinism, the most promising of which we shall discuss shortly. This does not lead to determinism of the type that talks about genes for character traits in humans. In Maturana and Varela is to be found the emergence of structure evolved, mediated and stabilised through genetic diversity. The emphasis on species as the ground of the specific organism, a relationship between homeostasis and homeodynamics at the very centre of autopoiesis. Other writers are apt to cite only the latter: it appears to be conceptually more friendly to a pluralist agenda. We share the same agenda, including its more naïve hopes, burdened by the guilt of its sometimes exclusive commitments. But the cause of pluralism and the desire for heterogeny are not furthered by ignoring their own specific homeostatic tendencies: a characteristic identity, or range or set of limits. That kind of ignorance is instead a prime cause of prejudice and conflict.

4

EMERGENTISM, EVOLUTIONARY PSYCHOLOGY AND CULTURE

The role of evolutionary psychology is both topical and controversial. Pinker (2002) and Dennett (2003) have released major studies for the non-specialist reader. Ridley and Baron-Cohen published in 2003; and at the time of writing Dawkins is about to publish. Pinker, Dennett and Dawkins, usually regarded, without justification, though Dawkins' wordings are sometimes deliberately provocative, as on the 'right' of the political split, have been widely trailed in the media. The traditionally, also mistakenly, regarded 'left' has responded, with particular hostility to Pinker. *The Sunday Times* had Steven Rose criticising Baron-Cohen's 'essentialism', but something of the real flavour of the debate can be sensed from this extract:

> He [Baron-Cohen] is beloved of mutually puffing evolutionary psychologists [in this case Steven Pinker and Helena Cronin] who specialise in placing hyperbolic praise on the book jackets of their friends. Evolutionary psychology is the school of thought that claims that human nature was 'fixed' during a so-called environment of evolutionary adaptation in the Stone Age.
>
> (*The Sunday Times*, 27th April 2003)

That is over-simplification to the point of propaganda. However, some of the 'nature' claims are bizarre (especially in relation to gender: men from Mars, women from Venus etc.), but on the whole, the so-called right-wingers do go for reasoned criticism; the 'left' for outrage. Anyway, the argument is hot enough to warrant regular media attention. We are definitely not going to offer a 'centrist' position. Our argument can be opened quite simply:

1. 'Emergence' is completely central and necessary to complexity theory.
2. 'Emergence' is not a formal description that could equally well be substituted for by 'varied', 'heterogeneous', certainly not randomly differentiated.
3. 'Emergence' is an observation about qualitative differentiations, patterned complexity with recognised, relatively durable, if dynamic qualities.
4. 'Emergent orders' as complex phenomena may depend on but are not

determined by preceding forms. Innovation and unpredictability are at least as important as initial previous conditions.

5. Human 'cultures' are emergent orders that depend on but are not determined by the 'initial' conditions of the evolution of human psychology.

6. Human culture also depends on the planet, its physical resources and its relationship to other living populations. There is a history, a present, and a future of ecological interaction with their own emergent consequences.

If the *cogito* is indubitable for Descartes, if the Transcendental Subject is unavoidable for Kant, Emergence is the absolute of complexity theory. Further, if complexity theory is understood correctly as a human representation, that absolute is bifurcated, just as it is for traditional philosophy, as an ontology of both material and informational dimensions, though the relationship is of course very different. Both of these dimensions mean that the evolution of embodied consciousness is a crucial topic. Therefore complexity theory as an ontology that includes human culture has to be neo-post-'quasi'-Darwinist. That is not to say that every aspect of culture has to be concretely understood with reference to Darwinian mechanisms. It is to say that such relationships are possible, even likely. That is, they shape the tree of possibility and the spaces of impossibility.

The traditional (left) objection to this observation is that it restricts human freedom. With some justification, it must be said, this conjures visions of a majority, or simply a more powerful or better-resourced, culture setting out to oppose relative minorities, non-standard orientations, the less well provided for, on the grounds that the opposition is natural, as opposed to artificial, or just part of the struggle for the survival of the fittest.

No one who is aware of the legacy of Nazism can possibly object to this left position. The question is: where is the objection to be placed?

The very idea of evolutionary emergence depends on ecology. It is precisely the same requirement seen in our earlier description of complexity, that the key is interaction. For the most extreme left position this does represent a limitation: human plasticity replaces freedom simply because it occurs within a world of interactions, a world of cost–benefit, possibility and impossibility. But to decry limitation is no more a left position than fundamental religiosity, the truly free human is simply another god. It is also one of the more naïve and ruthless prejudices of Modernist technicism. Nazism has its own savage interpretation. If one accepts, then, the analytic necessity of the limitation to plasticity that is to agree, tacitly or not, that the question of the improper restriction of freedom (e.g. of minorities) actually occurs at a much more concrete level. In other words, it happens when a specific type of cultural organisation runs up against another type and some sort of conflict is perceived, real or potential. And that question of propriety can be more fully, purposefully and reasonably addressed without making spurious claims to an exaggerated level of freedom that generates the counter-charge of irrationality.

Ecology and natural selection certainly assume and describe restrictions, e.g. animals depend on oxygen, but nevertheless generate massive numbers of differentiated species. The bottleneck of dependence here produces more variety than the ostensibly free human imagination ever has. Nevertheless, these species are ecologically interdependent. The richness and the tragedy of the situation is most manifest in the relation of prey and predator: it is ecologically likely and stable. But ecology does not care; instead it invests in weaponry, aggression, defensive systems, terror. Human society is not immune from this tragedy; as *eco* it goes with the riches of *auto* organisation.

Nevertheless, we do not mean to downplay structures. The corpus of emergentism and evolutionary psychology suggests structures in precisely the sense of attractors. Structures both enabling and disabling are presupposed. But these are not, or not yet, political structures. The contribution of emergentism and evolutionary psychology may be mapped as three overlapping areas:

1. Evolutionarily Stable Strategies (ESS) and associated ideas from game theory. Our main sources will be Dawkins, Dennett, Skyrms and Maynard Smith.
2. The criticism of what is called the 'standard social science model' (SSSM) drawn from Barkow, Cosmides and Tooby. This will introduce the controversial topics of evolutionary psychology and socio-biology. Further, the dependence of SSSM on generalised learning will be contrasted with specifically structured predispositions in the sense of evolved, content-dedicated mechanisms such as a language acquisition device in the Chomskian sense.
3. Views of consciousness, predisposition and the interplay of content-specific faculties in humans. Broadly, this is an objection to the 'blank slate' on the one hand and the priority of the serial *cogito* on the other. What emerges is the sense of a distributed parallelism of interactive processing that generates the phenomenon of a unified consciousness. Our main sources will be Damasio, Dawkins, Dennett, Pinker and Barkow *et al.*

These three overlap and present increasing degrees of complexity, especially from the point of view of the sociology of complex structure. The first describes strategies in almost mathematical or algebraic terms that are likely to be necessary to players in an evolving ecosystem or as supra-individual outcomes of their interactions.

The second seems ordinary enough, but in fact contains an altogether more radical set of implications. The criticism of SSSM is more than worthy of consideration on its own merits. Our view asserts that it contains a requirement of what we have elsewhere called a 'unified ontology' (see Smith and Jenks 2000) that underlies both the natural and the human 'sciences'. The ontology that currently supports and isolates sociology and its associated disciplines is so weak as be on the point of collapse. The resulting ontological synthesis makes demands on the traditional, both the 'natural' and 'cultural', disciplines.

It does not in any sense imply a return to the old authority of social-scientific certitude. Prigogine (1997) makes much the same argument from the direction of the science of thermodynamics. The impact on the concept of learning for sociology is fundamental.

The third examines claims ranging from architecture to nature in the human psyche. Again, without objection to architecture, we prefer the terms 'plasticity' and 'attractors' to anything approximating to nature. For example, we might say it is human nature to make images or use words. But to say that the tendencies to make visual images and to form verbal expressions are attractors that shape the diversity of human visual and verbal culture is a better description of both identity and within difference. This wording indicates an ontological and structural requirement of persistent importance: the current state of such an emergent system, or ecology of systems in this case, is not determined by but is in part founded upon a previous state of the system and a new layer of interactions. Emergentism means temporal structuring. Moreover, the human brain as an organ reflects this: far from being a generalised processor it consists of evolved content-specific structures in complex interaction. The total challenge for sociology is stark: the structure of learning in the sociology of knowledge has been largely ignored or treated as anathema, i.e. really a cultural variable, excused through a fundamentally outdated, simplistic and increasingly isolated ontology. Even a minimal concession to complexity theory consigns that ontology to occultism.

From the sociological point of view, we have made an important omission: the sociology of the emotions. For various reasons we have decided to postpone that series of considerations. At this stage, our intentions are more formal, foundational, more radically directed at, or limited by, ontology. However, given that focus we shall shortly offer a formal criticism of the social construction of the emotions. This could be taken as one of the tendencies in the sociology of the emotions (see, for example, Williams 2001), but we intend the term more narrowly at this stage.

Evolutionarily Stable Strategies (ESS) were first elucidated by John Maynard Smith (1972, 1974, 1976 a and b, 1982 and 1988). Perhaps his most famous example is the dove/hawk confrontation. These are not actual birds but strategies:

- Doves want the benefit of resources but they also want to avoid the costs of confrontation.
- Hawks want the benefit of resources and are always prepared to bear the costs of fighting for them.

The model assumes a level of resources such that there is competition, a position we shall have to qualify with respect to human action. On the basis of their preferred strategy, the doves will do better. On a given unit of resource, a pair of dove-competitors have an even chance of acquiring the resource.

Over time units are likely to be shared on a 50 per cent basis. There are no 'injury'-type costs, no expenditure of wasted energy, no wasted investment in weapons. A population of equal doves will, on average, gain a similar percentage of resources at no further costs. This looks like an optimum strategy. Indeed it is. It is not, however, an ESS.

A mutant hawk introduced into this population will be at such an advantage that it will gain a disproportionately large share of resources. The hawk strategy will therefore spread, either through reproduction or by the attraction of new hawk-like creatures to the setting. Would hawkism eventually take over from dovism? No, because it is at an obvious huge disadvantage: it gains no greater resources than those available but on top of that faces the costs in time, energy and investment involved in continually doing battle. Hawks, by their nature, are going to be less well off. Their strategy is inherently more wasteful. A given unit of resource will always support more doves than hawks.

Let us add a little more complexity. Suppose doves and hawks are strategies pursuable by a single individual such as a human or a less type-cast bird. Or, suppose that the resources in question are open to predation by both dovish and hawkish elements. An ESS will occur when the ratios of dovism to hawkism balance out each other's advantage and disadvantage. The ratio will be variable according to the precise actors' strategies but will over time produce something close to a normal state for those competitors. It is crucial to see that this arises entirely out of costs and benefits and is supra-individual. That is, the ESS will take the form of a ratio that decides what kind of actors make up the population. Nor will the ESS care that the stable solution is not the optimum solution of least cost.

Suppose we now humanise matters. Surely we should desire dovism on all grounds? If the answer to that is a resounding yes, then we have an equilibrium all right, but strictly in relation to desire. When it comes to the crunch, you don't know if you've 'doved out' on the very last meal in town. And even if your dove-luck was in, is that a hawk behind you? We have here another classic open versus closed set. The closed set is your/our desire: we know that we prefer shared optima. The open set is the environment in which the strategy takes place, which you cannot wholly know. Therefore the open set, the environment, extra-individual probabilities, is the arena in which strategy is decided on the basis of unknowability and it is the prime actor who decides the communal or ecological outcomes of our preferences. Nor will the ESS care if we are disappointed.

It will be noted that we have employed Kant's humanistic criterion, namely that experience teaches us that a thing is so and so but not that it cannot be otherwise, to reverse the terms. Alterity, the environment, is now the agent and the subject, humanity, is the patient. The outcome is the likelihood that dominant structure will persist in the face of weaker alternatives. The symmetry of all outcomes being equally likely, desirable, authentic, authoritative, vital means the implicit, also humanistic, assumption of post-structuralism is broken.

Skyrms (1996), operating from a purer games-theoretical perspective and with an eye on 'the evolution of the social contract' makes these observations. Whilst agreeing that an ESS 'is an attractor in [ ] replicator dynamics' (p. 52), '[it] only makes sense in the context of the random pairing assumption. It does not take correlation into account' (p. 54).

Correlation is a crucial concept in games theory and an instrument of common praxis. Understood in its simplest terms like is correlated with like. For example, doves could recognise or correlate with co-doves and by co-operative endeavour place the hawks at a disadvantage. The hawks' fitness, in the Darwinian sense, could be reduced. As Skyrms argues: 'We want a stability concept that gives correlation its due weight' (p. 54). A closely related concept is viscosity. Derived from Hamilton (1964) and discussed by Skyrms, this relates to 'non-dispersive or viscous populations where individuals living together are more likely to be related' (ibid. p. 58). Relatedness plays an important role in evolutionary theory as a, if not the, counterpoint to competition and, paradoxically, its intended goal. Hence Dawkins' (1976 and 1989) *The Selfish Gene*. A 'selfish' gene is, of course, out to have relatives, as many and as close as possible.

For the moment, we want to distance ourselves from the strictly genetic, biological and competitive relationships. Correlation and viscosity are also applicable at an aggregated social level. For example, the responses and strategies of those of correlated age are crucial structuring agents in social formations. Similarly, relations of gender are structure-forming at a number of levels. The same applies for relatedness of economic practice or interest, technological development, shared belief systems, and so on. The point we want to stress is that whether we assume randomised encounter or high levels of 'co-relation' in any sense (therefore also whatever scale of value we attach to competition) the outcome is the predominance of the more dynamically stable structures, not random variation. Where we add in, for example, the 'desired ideal' of co-operation, discussed above, and especially our ability to articulate our willingness to co-operate or not, for whatever reason, the propensity to structure or viscosity increases. This seems in a sense so obvious, why labour the point? Simply because it and its consequences are largely absent from naïve post-structuralist, post-modernist perspectives. Nor are they properly developed in sophisticated post-structuralism. The complex homeodynamic that follows from our positions approximates to human post-natal plasticity active in an ecological context. The lax pluralism of naïve post-modernism corresponds to the illusion of complete freedom and the absence of contexts and their costs.

The crucial point at this level is the consequence for the notion of sociology of rationality in the context of complex structures. How is the formal notion of rational action modified by the feedback loops of socio-ecology? This will have a distinct bearing on the proposition that cultural phenomena are so distinct as to require if not a different then a separated ontology. The issue is modelled by a simple ultimatum game.[1] Player one offers a proportion of a certain 'good'. Player two can only accept or reject. If they reach a deal, they get the money; if they don't, it's all forfeited. Here are the results that Skyrms reports:

> Supposing player two prefers more to less . . . she will not carry out the threat to refuse an offer less than 50% (or 40% or . . .). [So] the threat is not credible and player one . . . would do better asking for more. We are left with a subgame perfect equilibrium in which player one offers player two one pfennig and proposes to keep the rest [the total is five marks] . . . player two has the strategy of excepting one pfennig but rejecting an offer of nothing. But this modular-rational behaviour is not what the experimenters find.
>
> A round of twenty one games was played . . . The modular-rational equilibrium behaviour described above was not played in any of these games . . . [T]he most frequent offer was equal division . . . The mean demand was just under two thirds.
>
> (Skyrms 1996: 26)

A later re-run finds the ultimatum givers slightly more greedy, but the respondents also increased their rejection rate. Repetitions in a variety of cultures find a similar pattern. In lay terms, are the players acting irrationally or is fairness so desirable a goal as to outweigh the costs of refusing the ultimatum? Skyrms answers, more or less, by inverting his question: 'Why have norms of fairness not been eliminated by the process of evolution? [Because] an increase in income of real goods usually translates into an increase in evolutionary fitness. [Now the inversion]. How then could norms of fairness have *evolved*?' (ibid. p. 28, our emphasis).

We could come up with some fairly ordinary replies, most of which would stress that the predicted net gain over time in repeats of this game and countless other interactions with player one as analytic other is worth the cost of refusing to go along with an unfair offer in this instance. That prediction might be wrong, of course, player two may be destined to second-class status; player one might get such a taste for ultimata that he might set up a protection racket. These outcomes, along with levels of fairness, are of course observable, they have evolved. And we decline to answer Skyrms' question at a lower level of abstraction: their evolution asserts, however temporarily, a level of dominance or fitness that allows that particular complex to present itself. Thus writers in the field are apt to 'generalise' as follows:

> Political philosophy is a study of how societies might be organised. If possibility is construed generously we have utopian theory. Those who would deal with 'men as they are' need to work with a more restrictive sense of possibility. Concern with the interactive dynamics

of biological evolution, cultural evolution, and learning provides some interesting constraints.

When we investigate this interactive dynamics we find something quite different from the crude nineteenth-century determinism of the social Darwinists on the one hand and Hegel and Marx on the other. It is apparent . . . that the typical case is one in which there is not a unique preordained, but rather a profusion of possible equilibrium outcomes . . . Some are easy to upset. Others are robust.

(Skyrms 1996: 109)

Or:

The second feature that differentiates our approach from standard ones is the degree of rationality attributed to economic agents. In neoclassical economic theory . . . agents are assumed to be hyper-rational . . . This is a rather extravagant and implausible model for especially in the complex, dynamic environments that economic agents typically face.

Agents adapt – they are not devoid of rationality . . . they are recog-nisably human. Even in such 'low-rationality' environments one can say a good deal about the institutions (equilibria) that emerge over time. In fact these institutions are often precisely those predicted by high-rationality theories . . . [E]volutionary forces often *substitute* for high (and implausible) degrees of individuality when the adaptive process has time to unfold.

(Peyton Young 2001: 5)

It is essential to distinguish these generalised models of social outcomes from those promoted by naïve post-modernism. Skyrms, the liberal in this encounter, dismisses utopia but also limits heterotopia: the sense of possibility is more restrictive, the processes more constrained, the outcomes may or may not be robust. Peyton Young, playing conservative, decisively gives the ecological advantage to high-rationality equilibria even in low-rationality environments. How would that work out over time? Would it erode Skyrms' 'profusion'? Quite probably.

We want to suggest that the decision is less important than the idea that rationality remains one of the agent-attractors in the evolutionary dynamic. Contrasted with naïve post-modernism, in which rationality occurs on a spectrum which includes the absolutely elastic, the neurotic, repressed or just old-fashioned, rationality-as-attractor has a kind of constant identity and a perfectly respectable utility but is above all interactive. In the same way that economics rests on the universality of goods and game theory on the strategic parameters set by the game itself, so rationality requires a substance to work upon. It might be stretching the metaphor too far to see rationality as itself a sort of dissipative structure, but it is also clear that rationality lives on or by the materials upon which it acts by increasing the evolutionary fitness of its hosts, part of those materials being our needs and predispositions as hosts. In that sense, rationality is an emergent property of the evolutionary dynamic. Perhaps we could call it a virtual dissipative structure? If so, from where does it draw its virtual energy, its motivations?

However, the materials of rationality appear prior to its actions in organising or making them available for human purpose, just as rationality itself is with us, its hosts, the latecomer, if not the latest or last-comer, on the evolutionary scene. Hence evolutionary psychology insists that the operation of rationality, its equilibria, its knowledge, its institutions represent an ontology nested within a previous substrate of crucial importance. There are a number of ways in which this substrate, or these substrata, can be represented, each of them in explicit contradistinction with humanism. First, we might say that rationality finds a special or crucially illuminating form in the human host and from this we can detect its more rudimentary ancestors in older species. This is essentially the postulate of Morin's *computo*, described above. The ascription of human-type rationality to other species is rightly controversial. It also, in a sense, misses the point: the point is emphatically not a sort of neo-humanism, a converted homo-centrism. Information and ways of recognising and assessing it, such as consciousness, such as the *computo*, Maturana and Varela's 'internal worlds', are emergent properties of the evolution of the living.

Second and no less controversial is the insistence that human rationality and the consequent operations of modern social process are embedded in an older layer of evolved human psychology. Both the left and the right burn their fingers through the necessity of examining this area. From the left point of view, evolved predispositions threaten both freedom in the analytic sense and pluralism as a political preference. There are many notorious hot spots, ranging from issues of gender, faith, race, intelligence, inheritance, to name a few. But if the left wishes to dispose of predispositions, then it ends up promoting a notion of pure rationality, that is analytically as abhorrent as a pure race: if disposition is truly second to rationality, then it is only a matter of choice. This is the ultimate commodification of commitment of any kind. For those preferring a more philosophical exposition, Hegel argues that in order for Being to be manifest as 'beings' even God has to have a nature, that is to give life/birth/death to beings. From the right end of the spectrum, such as Peyton Smith's ostensible conservatism, the same problem arises: if low-rationality environments given evolutionary time can produce substitute equilibria that imitate high-rationality outcomes, then we are back in the same position: given enough time, the erosion of predisposition by rationalism is just as likely. Whilst the left needs disposition to save it from commodification or inaction, the right needs rationality to be disciplined by desire to prevent them threatening the extinction of each other. This of course is a caricature and nothing to do with right/left. We all require the relationship between the specifics of desire and the generality of rational assessment or they annihilate each other and, by the way, us. Economics is an impossible series of postulates without the assumptions of self-defining goods; sociology of any kind is impossible without desire. Or, more generally, there is no social process without desire and no assessment of its costs or benefits without the rational assessment, or better, imagination of alternatives. Nor should alternatives be understood in the humanistic or abstract sense: these are concrete alternatives, in the language of Skyrms constrained not infinite. In this sense, if rationality can be described as a virtual dissipative structure, desire is its power source and effectivity is its measure. If rationality is not effective in the strategy initiated by desire it will tend to become extinct in that 'game'. Or *vice versa*. Either way, it's decisive for humanity. As Jaggar says:

> [we must] rethink the relation between knowledge and emotion and construct conceptual models that demonstrate the mutually constitutive rather than oppositional relation between reason and emotion. Far from precluding the possibility of reliable knowledge, emotion as well as value must be shown as necessary . . .
>
> (Jaggar 1989: 157)

Damasio (1992), arguing from clinical examples, the structure of the brain as an organ and a notion of learning, adaptation and functional competence commensurate with complexity theory, similarly insists that the Cartesian separation of reason and emotion does not illuminate either. The result is instead the degeneration of the total personality.

Sociology is impossible without desire. Indeed, sociology is impossible without a fundamental concept of desire. A radical constructionism of the emotions, i.e. a sociology that insisted on the entire social construction of the emotions, is another postulate of creation *ex nihilo*. There is no substrate. For these reasons radical constructivism is not an option in relation to emotion any more than it was for cognition. Eco-auto-organisation and exo-auto-reference remain the mandatory components of the complexity paradigm. What constructivism, radical or not, leaves out is the analytic necessity of 'a' not 'the' previous state of the system. That is an awkward but necessary wording: it is not a concrete description but an ontological requirement. That is, we have to concede the ontological necessity of the previous state, the 'eco' and 'exo' in relation to the 'auto', as the ground in which the new state(s) of the system(s) take root. That is not to make a facile error of saying that contemporary tastes or prejudices consist of an old and a new component, the old being the explanation of the new. That is ordinary determinism. Here is a compelling case for considering the phenomenon of evolutionary adaptation which indeed stresses a 'past' state with which new conditions are interactive. A complexity perspective respects chronology but insists that causality is interdependent. Indeed, a ground must be presumed but that does not mean that the consequent cannot redefine, reconfigure, indeed annihilate, parts of its original substrate. That continuity-in-risk, that identity-in-difference, that co-determination, that fertilising and leaving behind, that cumulative-transformative movement is the essential complexity of evolutionary theory in both physical and cultural terms.

To say that emotions are socially constructed is fair enough – but at what level? Let us imagine a mythic past-time when the human first encountered itself. What do we find: time and space to choose, to construct, or do we find a situation seething with life's dangers and requirements? Does humanity decide what it wants or do what it can? Let's then fast-forward to a time like now. We now agree that emotions are actually socially constructed. By whom? Am I free to construct for myself? Am I free to construct for another, say a grieving parent perhaps whose child is ill? Is it feasible to consider enforcement if others object? If humanity does what it can, then we can conclude that socially constructed is a term that needs an awful lot of qualification, such as 'where possible' or 'very slowly' or 'at certain times'. This sense of social construction where circumstances permit throws us back to complexity and particularly to the terminology of fuzzy logic: where desire and emotion are socially constructed to a degree. Radical constructivism, where humans decide what they want, is ludicrously simple.

We have treated rationality as an emergent phenomenon, consequent on some notion of desire, emotion, perceived need. We should remember that life, let alone human life, is not necessary, except perhaps locally, from time to time. This might be presented instead as a mechanism, even an economic mechanism where any system does or does not meet its needs, with direct implications for its evolutionary stability. This is directly analogous to Prigogine's dissipative structures and von Foerster's dictum that every system demands energy from an environment. This is not to make a market of a general ontology. It is to say that a general ontology is directed by energy or resource – the human economic marketplace is just one example. The creatures or systems of this energy flow are themselves possibilities, shapes, destinies, temporary equilibria in its history.

A radical but not humanist historicism is premised here, again analogous with Prigogine's emphasis on the existential reality of time. In this sense, we ground the formal ontology and the formal idioms of complexity theory in this self-shaping flow of energy. By contrast, the formal idioms of humanism (e.g. experience teaches us etc.) are a misplaced formalism, gross simplification masquerading as reasonable categorisations.

The stress on the complexity of energy flows is a common characteristic of post-humanism and the physical sciences. At first glance, then, to place emphasis on evolutionary psychology seems a counter-movement, concerned precisely with human preoccupations and motivations and, moreover, at an individual level. After all, Durkheim famously distinguished psychological from sociological phenomena as the basis of the discipline sociology. Given our interdisciplinary stance, it is not unexpected that we reject or modify that distinction. Predictably also, evolutionary psychology rejects the notion of *sui-generic* social phenomena. But in evolutionary psychology, the relation between social and psychological structures is not simple nor deterministic. Rather, we see a landscape characterised by attractors with a variety of forces or compulsions and by equally variable plasticity in response or transformation. Keeping detail for the moment at the minimum, we are first interested in the formal complexity of interaction at an ontological level.

The old ontology of humanism, which is now beginning to emerge as a form of radical constructivism including Kant, Durkheim and all of the contemporary theorists who prioritise human language, human technology, humanity *sui generis*, invariably end with the problem of how the internal is related to the external. And, since we can't get out, there is finally nothing to say about the relation. There is no outside-text! How often is that stupid sentence echoed around the rooms of universities by teachers and students who can be alarmingly deterministic, and horribly realistic at other times. Prioritisation for complexity theory is no more than a declaration of neglect. It is part of the idiom of humanism to practise this neglect or to insist that more narrow or determined options only refer to the physical world. The idiom is itself not surprising. Humanism begins with the distinction between the necessary or determined and the *sui-generic*. What is truly strange is that we have found little systematic objection within contemporary criticism. Quite the reverse: the *sui-generic* is connoted with the progressive when it should be firmly associated with one of the oldest and most repressive dogma of all: creation *ex nihilo*, monotheism, what Dennett aptly calls 'skyhooks'.[2]

Complexity theory begins its ontology instead with emergence. As Byrne stresses, in the holism of emergence, where humanism acknowledges the emergence of estrangement between knowledge and being, complexity insists on the relation. Complexity theory, in other words, sees the emergence of difference as process, not simply between being and language but between being and a host of forms of responding, in fact the differentiated forms of Morin's *computo*. That is precisely why the natural tendency of complexity is toward evolution and evolutionary psychology rather than forms of constructivism, whatever kernel of sense they may finally contain. Constructivism finally requires time to be a construct, though it hedges that idea about with meek qualifications such as 'my reading of'. Only Kant is frank enough to say time is mine. For complexity, time represented most formally as the flow of energy is the source of structures, such as humans. Moreover, it is co-posited in that position that it belongs to the nature of energy-in-time to shape itself into structures and this is precisely Hegel's position. That 'shaping' is to break the symmetry of both the random and the uniform. We now find complexity, eco-auto-organisation, and with it, we find ways of relating, exo-auto-reference which also belong, no less authentically, to this notion of complex being. That sentence is unthinkable within humanism; it is blasphemy. For humanist phenomenology and hard science alike, being, the real and reference,

72

representation are placed in clear rank: the real opposed to the virtual. To connect the two is madness, hubris, Hegelian megalomania all over again.

But it is not madness or hubris, simply because the structures of response and representation are not primarily human and their efficacy is most certainly evolved. That is, the virtual is a structured outcome of eco-auto-organisation. So it is true that we finally have nothing to say about what lies outside representation, especially language, because Being has, so to speak, withheld that privilege. If we are prepared, however, to be provisional rather than final and realise that our language is only one small part of the ways in which being is represented to itself, we might still be able to get by. But the social sciences will feel a little different.

The central premise of *The Adapted Mind* (Barkow, Cosmides and Tooby 1992) is that there is a universal human nature, but this universality exists primarily at the level of evolved psychological mechanisms, not at the level of expressed cultural behaviours. On this view, cultural variability is not a challenge to claims of universality, but rather data that might give one insight into the structure of the psychological mechanisms that helped generate it. A second premise is that these evolved psychological mechanisms are adaptations constructed by natural selection over evolutionary time. A third assumption made by most of the contributors is that the evolved structure of the human mind is adapted to the way of life of Pleistocene hunter-gatherers, and not necessarily to our modern circumstances.

This, then, is the essentialism to which Rose and others object. But note that an essentialism of expressed cultural behaviours is explicitly rejected. Further, it is on the ground of the complexity of processes, that is, the difference between the slow processes of evolutionary time in human prehistory and the accelerated time of technologically assisted innovation, that an essential core or architecture is postulated. There is nothing unreasonable in this. It is akin to pointing out that the ability to drive a car rests on adaptations for bipedal locomotion. Yet the analogy can be taken much further: it is on the basis of bipedal adaptation with free hands as a universal assumption that car design is predicated. True, another set of technologies is grafted on – again widely separated in time – namely the invention of the wheel, stable roads and the internal combustion engine. But without the universal human characteristic of bipedalism (to say nothing of the wheel or the chemistry of petrol combustion) modern car design is either unthinkable or thinkable very differently. In the vernacular of complexity theory, *each* of these are attractors in their own right that, moreover, combine to form a multidimensional attractor of enormous variability. If cars, then trains, if utility then sport, if economical then lavish, and so on. It is merely propagandist to say this nature is fixed.

The converse argument is, if anything, more devastating for those opposed to evolutionary psychology. Suppose we concede that the residual nature of the human is so minimal that it can be ignored for all practical purposes. Or that it is so eroded by subsequent social constructs that it is vanishingly insignificant.

Take the car again. It is obvious that our multidimensional attractor comes nowhere near the mark of the actual complexity required. We have more or less left out the innate functions of sight and their capacity for training. The same applies for the innate sense of touch in the hands and feet, and for the ability to acquire language . . . and so on. Then the anti-evolutionists are demolished on three intersecting fronts:

1. Some level of innate function and functional similarity has to be presumed.
2. If so, but innate psychological structures are excluded, we have a mind/body schism of the oldest, most creationist, kind.
3. Even if everything is really socially constructed, it is still constrained by possibility, impossibility and interactions. Socially constructed, where possible, 'to a degree' is not an alternative position to evolutionary emergence: it is exactly the same thing.

Rose is of course, ironically, an evolutionist. He is a biologist and has to be. Gould, another objector to human nature, is a palaeontologist and an evolutionist with a different emphasis. The same applies to Lewontin,[3] and a host of others eager to soften the impact of evolution on our notion of humanity. This is an old, old story. All are afraid, rightly, that with human nature comes the political vices of totalitarianism, racism and contests for technological supremacy. If their objections do not constitute an alternative but an identical position, then this is a risk we shall have to live with and find better opposition from our own positions. We accept that this is the most serious responsibility.

The Psychological Foundations of Culture (Tooby and Cosmides 1992) is a long, important and detailed paper. Around half of it is a critique of SSSM on a step by step basis. For our immediate purposes, we shall have to reduce it to two central propositions:

1. For SSSM social reality is *sui-generic* and
2. An essential requirement for the member is the ability to learn the ways of the culture.

These propositions are hardly controversial for sociology. For evolutionary psychology (according to Tooby and Cosmides) and complexity theory, they are wrong. Here is the argument:

> For SSSM social reality is *sui generic* because: . . . 'Collective representations and tendencies are caused not by certain states of the consciousnesses of individuals but by the conditions in which the social group, in its totality, is placed. Such actions can. Of course, materialise only if the individual natures are not resistant to them; *but these individual natures are merely the indeterminate material that the social*

74

factor molds (sic) and transforms. Their contribution consists exclusively in very general attitudes, in vague and consequently plastic predispositions which, by themselves, if other agents did not intervene, could not take on the definite and complex forms which characterise the social phenomenon.'

(Durkheim 1895/1962: 105–6, cited in Tooby and Cosmides 1992: abbreviated but with the latter's added emphases)

Humans everywhere show striking patterns of local within-group similarity in their behaviour and though, accompanied by profound intergroup differences. [Yet] . . . infants from all groups have essentially the same basic human design and potential. Human genetic variation, which is now directly detectable with modern electrophoretic techniques is overwhelmingly sequestered into functionally *superficial biochemical differences*, leaving our complex functional design universal and species-typical. Also the bulk of the variation that does exist is overwhelmingly inter-individual and within-population, and *not between races or populations*.

(ibid. our emphases)

Their conclusion is strange if you have been reading anti-evolutionary psychology literature:

[Therefore G]enetic variation does not explain why human groups dramatically differ from one another in thought and behaviour . . . [T]his is the only feature of the SSSM that is correct.

(ibid.)

Charges of racism and nature fixing culture are therefore gross misunderstandings, or rather more to do with fear of the possible consequences of the analysis than its inherent reasonableness. In fact, the argument is a great deal more subtle. Because the variation in culture(s) cannot be explained by a constant, for example the relative similarity of infants, the SSSM is prone to treat the mental organisation of infants as rudimentary, but with a marked ability to learn. And the mental organisation infants eventually learn comes from 'the behaviour and public representations of other members of the local group' (see ibid. pp. 26-7). Whether we favour a strict socialisation model or a looser concept along the lines of the plurality of possible interpretations is largely irrelevant here. Both types of culture exist, as the recent collisions between fundamentalism and the liberal West painfully demonstrate. Both tendencies absolutely require 'the capacity for culture', whether to affirm or deny deviants or pluralists. And so:

Thus the central concept in psychology is learning. The prerequisite that a psychological theory must meet to participate in the SSSM is that any evolved component, process, or mechanism must be equipotential, content-free, content-independent, general purpose, domain-general . . . [T]hese mechanisms must be constructed in such a way that they can absorb any kind of cultural message or environmental input equally well.

(ibid. p. 29)

This, for Tooby and Cosmides, is the error: where the SSSM requires what amounts to a 'blank slate', despite its widespread opposition to the *tabula rasa* not so long ago, evolutionary psychology's model insists that completely plastic learning is an evolutionary impossibility and that the relatively plastic nature of human learning rests on an entire series of adaptive mental capabilities or mechanisms. Both like and unlike the a priorism of Kant, theses structures are necessarily content-specific and adapted to particular functions. Therefore the SSSM confuses the relative uniformity of the infant with structurelessness and the relative variety of cultures with infinite variability. Tooby and Cosmides take the opposite viewpoint.

Before we address the question of content-specific mechanisms, we want to relate this rather specific matter to the generality of complexity theory. For the moment let us say that an illustration of a content-specific, embedded mechanism is the ability to learn a language. Without that, not only would the infant have to learn a language but also would have to learn how to learn. A lifetime is too short but evolutionary time makes it feasible. From that unified antecedent the variety of human language is possible. It also follows that linguistic variety is not infinite and so Foucault's tale of Borges' Chinese categorical system[4] remains finally just a good joke, premised, ironically, on the very nature of language. Stated then in the more general terms of complexity theory, content-specific mechanisms are both attracted and are themselves attractors. They are attracted, they organise themselves on the basis of onto-ecological requirements. Thus, for example, the eye and corresponding visual systems have evolved independently and in a number of different forms over forty times in animal history (Mayr 1982; Tooby and Cosmides 1992: 57). The eye is recurrent because it confers advantages. Similarly, the recurrence of functional eyes is itself an attractor, it organises or influences its local environment in both the amount of brain structure dedicated to its mechanisms and to the amount of cultural resources dedicated to visual culture. Frankly, attraction is similar in meaning here to constraint, but we fail to grasp this as threatening in any way. Rather, we encounter a shift from infinite possibility and its cognate randomness to an enabling dynamic. What is enabled is, amongst other things, humanness and this is a nature of sorts. On that basis, it is possible to point also to inhumanness. The objectors to human nature also *ipso facto* rule out a concept of inhumanity or unnatural practices, or human rights. That is, if human possibility is infinite, political criticism is morally impossible. All that is left is the concrete dialectics of competing self-interest. That is precisely the conservative position outlined above: low rationality environments over time mimic high-rationality equilibria.

The SSSM confuses randomness with complexity;[5] that is, complexity describes at least broken symmetry and eventually structural emergence. Open possibility, on the other hand, is perfectly symmetrical, nothing is 'preferred' and, since it has no structure, it is chaotic in the ordinary sense. Of course, neither the observers nor the advocates of cultural pluralism actually mean this. As observers they mean moderately diverse but fail to say so. As advocates, they mean something much more like North American post-modern culture. But they do not say that. They do not even think it. But a lack of reflexivity about one's politics, which any faith community could soon expose, is no excuse, especially for professional politicians and academics. It is MacDonald-ism: cheap fast food, cheap fast thought: *junk*. Ironically, a great deal of French twentieth-century thought is responsible for its popularity.

The SSSM, therefore, is isolated by both political preference and ignorance. By insisting on maximum plasticity, reserved for humans, more or less as the only guarantee of their dignity, or their political preference, the ontology of unique humanness is separated from everything else. Isolation is the politically preferred option. But isolation is here synonymous with ignorance. What of the non-human? Is it simply the base setting for the human jewel? What of the politically committed of all persuasions: secular, leftist, theist, *anti*-theist, free traders, *laissez faire* economists, economic regulationists, mixed economies, privatisation, state ownership, environmentalists, nationalists, pacifists? Are they all part of the dark ages from which the light of radical pluralism will eventually dawn? Let's spare our own blushes, we are all party to this illusion to some degree, and say that post-modernism, post-structuralism, radical pluralism, in short, our version of political liberalism, has underestimated the complexity of its political stance. Something of that sort is currently being worked out in Iraq, Afghanistan, Israel, Syria, Pakistan, former Yugoslavia, Albania, Northern Ireland, etc., even between members of the European Community.

Just as maximal plasticity in culture is less a metaphor than an evasion, then the humanistic notion of maximally plastic consciousness is also an evasion, ever more clearly exposed by neuro-biology's ability to map both brain activity and structure. For humanism, the human mind is characterised by conscious-ness, for evolutionary psychology the brain is an organ, even a complex of organs. What follows from this is not the need for a detailed neuro-anatomy nor a concept of restriction. Rather:

> [C]ognitive psychology, evolutionary biology, artificial intelligence, developmental psychology, linguistics, and philosophy converge on the same conclusion: A psychological architecture that consisted of

nothing but . . . general purpose . . . content-free mechanisms could not successfully perform the tasks the human mind is asked to perform.

(ibid. p. 34)

And:

> The central premise of an opposition between the mind as an inflexible biological product and the mind as a malleable social product is ill-informed: the notion that inherited psychological structure constrains is the notion that without it we would be even more flexible or malleable or environmentally responsive than we are. This is not only false but absurd. Without this evolved structure we would have no competences or contingent environmental responsiveness whatsoever. Evolved mechanisms do not prevent, constrain or limit the system from doing things it otherwise would do in their absence . . . Evolved structure does not constrain; it creates or enables [an organised response to environmental inputs].

(ibid. pp. 38–9)

This is extremely close to Maturana and Varela's position in *Autopoiesis and Cognition* where organisms 'bring forth worlds'. Remember our counter-insistence: but worlds bring forth organisms. In this sense, the more radical agenda underlying content-specificity in the minds of humans as well as other species is that the world brings forth content-specificity and its information. This is not controversial for other species: the world engenders information in the form of instinct. The human situation is more complex. Thus what I see is 'mine' in the sense of 'my' image consequent on my position, my interests, my past, my future (at least in the sense of intention) and the functional state of my visual processing system. It might, for example, be limited by poor light or ill health, or aided by technology such as the magnifying lens or the camcorder. But in every sense these images are also 'ours'. True, there are the same limits 'outside-text' and 'outside-my-visual-perception'. Humanism stops here in despair: nothing is decidable. Post-humanism has a more reasonable position:

1. It is not necessary to 'get outside' in order to function. Evolution has come up with viable answers to this question. I do not have to scrutinise the minutiae of 'your' vision for us to know we looking at such and such an image (including this text). We both realise that ambiguities are possible, even likely, but we also exercise 'reasonable' judgement over what to do about it.
2. More radically, the separation between system (organism) and environment is impossible unless the latter is re-encoded in such a way that it may enter the former's field of mental consideration. Like the image before my eye,

this is necessarily virtual, as the condition of the organism/environment relationship. It is not necessary, nor is it possible to bridge this relationship. It merely matters that they are related and that the relation is functionally efficient.

3. Mental process and structure is thus species-specific, in the sense that it arises out of a persistent or recurrent auto-exo-relationship between the type of organism and its environment. Humanism and radical constructivism trivialise this by improper exaggeration on the individual.

4. This is where we play our scientific method card! Sorry, no. That just happens to be one very limited manifestation of the very necessary probing that is the physical outcome of bringing forth virtual worlds. This is common to all complex species and at times may well be fatal. So the scientific method gambit is as relevant or irrelevant as a cat playing with its prey.

Tooby and Cosmides spell out the consequences for the individual:

> [T]he behaviour of individual organisms is caused by the structure of their adaptations and the environmental input to them; it is not independently governed by fitness maximisation. Individual organisms are best thought of as adaptation-executors rather than as fitness-maximisers . . .
>
> Thus the biological notion of functionality differs from the folk notion of functionality as goal-seeking behaviour . . . [Biologists who see] humans as adaptation-executors (adaptationism) . . . [ask] What is the underlying panhuman psychological architecture that leads to this behaviour in certain specific circumstances?
>
> (ibid. pp. 54–5)

We can conclude our reading of *The Psychological Foundations of Culture* with two further observations. The first concerns the importance or effectivity of framing. Broadly consonant with content-specificity, framing is crucial in the ability of intelligence (human or artificial) to designate and complete its tasks. The alternative, a sort of general-purposeness, is seen to be hopelessly ineffective. This directly contravenes the notion that the malleability of humans is the key to their success. Indeed, it implies quite the opposite: that content-specific framing is multiply adapted, something like an excellent and well-maintained set of tools, and that the aptness of the 'kit' is the key to being able to survive in the face of environmental diversity.

Second, the paper concludes with the provocative title: *The Twilight of Learning as a Social Science Explanation*. It represents an important contribution to the complexity theory of mind:

> [Human] minds do a host of singularly useful things . . . they develop skill[s] . . . they change behaviour in impressively functional ways; they

reconstruct themselves in knowledge derived from others . . . Psycho-logists did not know what causal sequences brought these useful results about. They reified this unknown functionality imagining it to be a unitary process, and called it 'learning' . . . the unknown agent imagined to cause a large and heterogeneous set of functional out-comes. This name was (and is) then used as an explanation for results that remained in genuine need of explanation . . . Under closer inspection 'learning' is turning out to be a diverse set of processes, caused by a series of incredibly intricate, functionally organised cognitive adaptations . . .

(ibid. p. 123)

There is much more to be said on this and related matters. For the moment, we want to point to issues that influenced our choice of title: *Qualitative Complexity*. What is exposed in Tooby and Cosmides is a coherent theory of cognitive adaptation that is consistent, on the one hand, with Darwinian views of human evolution and, on the other, with relative cultural complexity. What emerges are patterns of recurrence: resemblances and differences between humans and other species but also patterns of recurrence in both the ground and outcomes of human behaviour. Also demonstrated in our view is the paucity of indeterminacy, constructivism, high-level plasticity as the ground of complexity, including human social complexity, but rather that complexity is itself emergent from the interaction of simpler components, such as the ability to see or to acquire language. Complexity is fundamentally qualitative, that is historical, ecological and apt to generate homodynamic structures, recurrences, limits, conflicts, alliances and so forth. That is not quite the view of complexity we see in much of the sociology that professes similar subject matter.

5

PRIGOGINE'S THERMODYNAMICS, ONTOLOGY AND SOCIOLOGY

In this chapter we address some of the most difficult accounts of complexity, so far as philosophers and sociologists are concerned, since they derive from various interfaces between physics, chemistry and maths. These disciplines benefit, and suffer, from an immense degree of independent specialisation and so at least part of the problem is the disentangling of important themes 'for us' from the specific history of dispute and emergence within these sciences. Here we shall use the work of Ilya Prigogine, winner of the Nobel Prize in 1977 for his work on the thermodynamics of non-equilibrium systems. This field massively overlaps, intervenes in and creates new relationships between physics, chemistry and biology. Prigogine, suggests that it is crucial for all systems involving evolution, whether, for example, of chemical processes, living organisms or societies. This challenge has been taken up by a number of authors important to our field, notably Reed and Harvey, Urry, Hayles, Byrne, Porush, Eve *et al.*, Douglas Keil and Elliott. For our purposes, Prigogine's significance lies precisely in thermodynamics, that is, in an ontology grounded in the actions of energy, whose products include human organisations. As such, it provides a key opposition to the ontologies associated with humanism. Another powerful source, this time informed by biology and maths, is Cohen and Stewart (1995), to whom we shall return later in this chapter.

Prigogine is an extremely difficult writer for several reasons. The most obvious is his predilection for equations, even in books written for the general reader. Some of his shorter papers are unintelligible on this account for readers without serious competence in mathematics. Second, he draws on debates in science and mathematics which require familiarity with the history of those disciplines. Third, the concepts he wants to work with are inherently difficult and enormously wide-ranging in their implications.

Equally difficult is the nature of Prigogine's preoccupations. The first of these is the irreversibility of time. It may seem strange to non-scientists that it is still the dominant view in physics that in Einstein's words, 'Time is an illusion'; even odder is the implication that time is 'introduced' by human perspectives or actions. The second is the focus on self-organisation. Or better, the reality of time and self-organisation are intrinsically co-dependent. The third is his interest in systems 'far from equilibrium'; driven by differential energy, they are the structures most likely to exhibit new patterns of self-organisation. This is both controversial and ubiquitous. Controversial in that it requires significant modification of the second law of thermodynamics; ubiquitous in the sense that Earth's life forms, amongst many other phenomena, are instances of self-organising phenomena in systems far from equilibrium. And so it is inevitably permeated by factionalism.[1] Let us begin with a non-specialist look at the second law of thermodynamics:

> The second law decrees that entropy . . . always tends to increase. In practical terms [this] means that in every real heat exchange, some heat is always lost to useful purposes. Lord Kelvin (William Thompson) called [this] 'a universal tendency toward dissipation . . . [I]f heat is constantly dissipated, the universe must eventually arrive at a point where no heat reserves will be left. The temperature would then stabilise slightly above absolute zero (−273 degrees centigrade) and life of any kind would be impossible . . . the so-called "heat death".'
>
> (Hayles 1991: 13)

This passage clearly illustrates the difference between equilibrium in normal and specialised usage. Ordinary usage suggests stability, 'business as usual', but in thermodynamics it is associated with entropy. 'Heat death' is a postulated, eventual equilibrium. Not so much 'business as usual' as 'end of business'. Let us suggest a sort of half-way usage: equilibrium occurs when what can happen has happened. By contrast, systems 'far from equilibrium' are, so to speak, in the course of evolution. Here we see emerging the constant theme of the difference between classical and evolutionary mechanisms.

Hayles continues:

> Prigogine and Stengers argue against this traditional view. They envision entropy as an engine driving the world towards increasing complexity rather than death. They calculate that in systems far from equilibrium, entropy production is so high that local decreases in entropy can occur without violating the second law. Under certain circumstances, this mechanism allows a system to engage in spontaneous self-organisation.
>
> (ibid.)

'They calculate' is a problem here. Can we? Are their calculations valid or accurate? This is not the traditional competence of sociology. However, we can draw on the convincing argument that living things 'excrete entropy', apart from plants, by consuming other living things. And we can further postulate that it is a characteristic of society, especially industrial society, to import energy on a vast scale, not for *depense*[2] but for reproduction. That is precisely a local decrease in entropy.

Porush (1991) writes:

> Norbert Wiener described the entropy vs. evolution problem in 1948 in his popularization of cybernetics, *The Human Use of Human Beings*: biology is an 'island of order in the universal entropic tide.' But this island metaphor doesn't communicate the dynamic, highly unstable growth (or morphology) of such orderly systems. Instead, to shift the metaphor, a dissipative structure is more of a *raft* which floats inexplicably but definitely upstream, *against the current* . . . Dissipative structures seem to have a mind of their own. They are self-organising systems that locally contradict the second law of thermodynamics.
>
> (Porush 1991: 57, original emphases)

The metaphors are wearing thin. The raft is an improvement but it is powered. This does mean that its course is entirely predictable. Dissipative structures in general do not have minds of their own: they are local effects of energy concentration, and their structures are part of the possibility of energy concentration, just as the living excretes entropy. The dissipative structures that form the class of higher animals do have minds of their own. Which way we should take this remains permanently in question.

The key generalisation is this:

> [Dissipative structures] represent *the spontaneous emergence of order out of disorder* – 'a self-organising system' . . . [these] are ubiquitous in the biosphere or the macroscopic world. Indeed the very fact of the biosphere – with its seething complexity and diversity and apparent tendency to evolve in the direction of increased differentiation and complexity is explained by Prigogine's theory of dissipative structures.
>
> (ibid. p. 56, original emphases)

They are not explained or even postulated by classical science, nor even adequately by neo-Darwinism. The key issue for us is that the process is driven by available energy, is itself structural and completely without moral motivation, surpluses, worldviews, judgement. It is *auto*-eco-organisational. That puts the 'selfish gene' in a more appropriate perspective.

Now let us try another view. As a précis it is one of the most accessible available:

> The Second Law . . . announces that every system contains temporally irreversible processes that force then to state of disorder called *thermodynamic equilibrium*. Thus, if left to itself, an isolated system would

evolve internally to the point where its energy would be distributed evenly throughout the system. In such a disorderly state all traces of structural differentiation would have disappeared. This increasing tendency toward the accumulation of disorder is called positive entropy.

(Reed and Harvey 1992: 361)

Again, we see this strange elision of equilibrium with disorder. Remember the phenomenon in question is a system, and our description 'end of business'. Disorder can then be seen as the end of systemic order: the system, so to speak, has become a 'lump', a cold coffee, a dead body. This is a delineated model, some would call it an arbitrarily delineated model. To put it another way, the dead body would lose its isolation or self-organisation; the cold coffee ends up in the sink, or more importantly it falls out of the isolating cup. They would re-enter the local ecology at the price of their identity. The 'lump' poses some more subtle problems: it is self-isolating through its very structure:

> [By contrast] dissipative systems are thermodynamically open. They are capable of assimilating large reserves of environmental energy and converting them into increasing structural complexity. The process . . . is irreversible . . . the system cannot return to its original state. Because of this irreversible increase in internal complexity, dissipative systems possess an evolutionary capacity which allows them to fend off thermal equilibrium. When speaking of these capacities, scientists refer to the ability of dissipative systems to transfer their positive entropy (i.e. the build up of internally generated disorder) to their immediate surroundings at a faster rate than they produced them . . . Hence the name 'dissipative structures'.
>
> (ibid. p. 362)

Metaphors are nicely absent from this passage, though it is still an abstraction, a reduced model. Let us inject some. A mouth is both a metaphor and a fact that opens (living) systems. You may not prefer the thermodynamic analogy but the function is clear. So is the opening at the other end. Put personally, you convert environment into you for as long as you can. You excrete 'entropy'. You are a negative-sum entropy machine, for as long as it lasts. Do you want to share your model, as a living being, or reserve your rights, as a *human* being? This question is becoming critical:

> Prigogine has shown that the complex array of thermodynamic phenomena can be organised in three fundamentally different ways: as equilibrated systems; near to equilibrium systems, or far from equilibrium systems.
>
> (ibid. p. 363)

84

The first of these corresponds with our 'lump':

> Structurally, they are non-evolving, stable entities [though] they can be
> destroyed physically . . . Internally the energy contained in these sys-
> tems can be treated as if they were dynamically frozen into the struc-
> ture itself. They are called linear or 'integrable' systems because they
> can be decomposed analytically and treated mathematically as though
> they were the mere sum of their parts. This means that equilibrated
> structures can be understood using the reductionist . . . schemes of
> Newtonian science.
>
> In contrast, near-to-equilibrium systems can assume a limited range
> of organisational states without losing their basic identity . . . [N]ot
> capable of sustained evolutionary behaviour, near to equilibrium
> systems can forestall their descent into thermal equilibrium . . . [They]
> are organised around a ground state to which they must periodically
> return [and] are able to dampen any oscillation which might perman-
> ently transform them. Such internal damping serves to homeostatically
> restore the system to its original state.
>
> (ibid. pp. 362–3)

Something like this type of structure seems to be the model for a large number
of systems approaches to the human sciences. In fact, Prigogine means something quite different: a tendency towards inertia:

> Linear thermodynamics . . . describes the stable, predictable behaviour
> of systems tending toward the minimum level of activity compatible
> with the fluxes that feed them. The fact that linear thermodynamics,
> like equilibrium thermodynamics may be described in terms of . . .
> entropy production implies that, both in evolution towards equi-
> librium and in evolution toward a steady state, initial conditions are
> forgotten. Whatever the initial conditions, the system will finally reach
> a state determined by the imposed boundary conditions.
>
> (Prigogine and Stengers 1984: 139)

Here we feel that the science is confounded by terminology which once might
have been useful. So, with due trepidation and apologies to any scientific toes
our ignorance might cause us to bruise, we shall attempt what we think is the
simple explanation. Equilibrated structures, at 'close of business', have a structural integrity which they will normally retain in that the strength of the
structure generally exceeds the energy required for disruption. Their stable
state is the most probable. Near to equilibrium systems have a degree of
environmental input that is not quite compatible with 'close of business' but
insufficient to generate any new business either. Both forget in initial conditions, albeit arbitrarily chosen, which can simply be translated as perturbations

because the tendency to stability is greater. In far from equilibrium systems the energy for change exceeds the tendency to stability, but new forms of more complex structural organisation may appear. We might say that *re*-organisations cope with the excess energy better. At this level the ideas seem quite simple, things will tend toward equilibrium unless more energy is supplied; then a more complex equilibrium or organisation will evolve. Can the matter be that simple? Unfortunately it has become very tangled in the contested history of science and its prejudices, but then, sociology is no better. The consequences are anything but simple. This is a crucial characteristic of complexity theory, especially in relation to self-organisation: if at least some of the basic process of self-organisation were not simple, it is singularly difficult to explain how complexity arises, how evolution begins at all.

In this sense it is clear that these simpler, i.e. equilibrated, near to equilibrium, systems form an essential continuity with their more complex counterparts. They are crucial to any notion of *eco*-auto-organisation, for without any stable, equilibrated identities, even in the form of a minimal ground state, a subsequent ecology of auto-organisational identities is indistinguishable from randomness. Those authors, then, who like to play up the buzzword-style 'whizzy' complexity as against these ostensibly more limited structures are in danger of merely reinventing a sort of post-modernism on the back of bad physics. Moreover, they too are ontologically crucial as the physical environment in which near-to and far-from equilibrium oscillations take place. In a number of cases, e.g. wood, coal, soil, they are wholly or in part composed of dead, defunct, former, far-from-equilibrium systems having eventually become equilibrated, present company eventually included. Does this mean we have forgotten our original conditions?

> Far from equilibrium systems differ from their near-to-equilibrium counterparts by being evolving entities. In addition to preserving a state of minimal entropy production, they can also increase in complexity, and, hence, increase their negative entropy production. Instead of being homeostatically constrained, their evolution is irreversible in time. As such they move naturally from one equilibrated state to another, often radically different, reference point. Furthermore, unlike conservative, far-from-equilibrium configurations are subject to spontaneous internal fluctuations. The fluctuations constantly probe and push the system beyond its boundaries . . . [mostly] for naught: In the absence of sufficient inputs of environmental energy, the systems falls back to its original dynamic state. In certain circumstances, however, the same system may be in such a state of flux that even the weakest perturbation can combine with the system's own peripatetic to send it spiralling into an hitherto unsuspected trajectory. In such circumstances the system's original symmetries are broken and a cascading series of self-feeding structural changes are set in motion.

Furthermore unlike . . . near-to-equilibrium systems, the evolutionary potential of far-from-equilibrium systems is limited chiefly by the relative energy richness of their environment . . .

These systems exhibit another crucial trait. They are *sensitive to original conditions* . . . the slightest lag or premature onset of a perturbation can send the system's evolution in to radically different channels.

(Reed and Harvey 1992: 363)

'Original' conditions simply means a chosen starting point. Now reconsider far-from-equilibrium systems. There seems to be a multi-dimensional equivocation here, which, whilst rarely stressed, is entirely crucial, especially in the field of the human sciences. An example of a far-from-equilibrium system is the Earth's climate. It falls, so to speak, right in the middle of the definition. It has terrific variety, turbulence; has evolved through quite different stages of gaseous composition; and yet it has a kind of identity. We know that the Sun's output has varied considerably relative to the dynamic constancy of the Earth's climate, and yet there have been periods of extreme change, such as ice ages. If environmental, in this case 'external', energy is the driving force, suppose the Sun provided too much energy, sufficient for the atmosphere to escape the gravitational field. In this extreme case, its identity, however dynamic, is literally lost. The Earth starts to look a bit like a nearer-to-equilibrium system with a limited degree of plasticity. Perhaps even a 'lump' that is physically exhausted. There is a kind of fuzzy continuity between the near-to and far-from equilibrium classification. But the Earth, especially the populated world of terrestrial ecology, shows this 'fuzz' not to be simply a question of degree, but also of structural interdependence. For example, the advent of oxygen-producers (plants) not only instigated a change in the evolutionary diversity of the climate but also set in chain a series of oxygen-dependent organisms. Stripped to its formal essentials, this means that a set of living systems, striving towards a kind of autopoietic stability (specific green plants) decisively added to, redefined, a far-from-equilibrium system (the climate) by drawing on such equilibrated substances as atmospheric nitrogen and carbon or other essential nutrient compounds. In this process they made possible the further evolution of the soil and subsequent dependent species. Green plants operate reconstructively at the interface between materials and energy. It may be, then, Prigogine's, or his interpreters', intention to show that Newtonian analyses are applicable only to 'integrable' systems and therefore to play up the difference. Dynamic systems are not thereby a separate class. On the contrary, interdependence, interaction and co-determination occur between all phenomena in the spectrum of thermal equilibria. Despite self-organisation, then, the eco-dimension remains crucial.

Prigogine constantly stresses interaction too, especially *within* far-from-equilibrium phenomena:

According to Poincare, a dynamical system is characterised in terms of the kinetic enrgy of its particles plus the potential energy due to their interaction. A simple example would be free noninteracting particle, where there is no potential energy and the calculation of trajectories is trivial. Such systems are by definition integrable. Poincare then asked the question: Can we choose suitable variables to eliminate potential energy? By showing that this was generally impossible, he proved that dynamical systems were largely *nonintegrable*.

(Prigogine 1997: 39, original emphases)

Recall Reed and Harvey's rather easier definition of 'integrable' as reducible to the mere sum of its parts. The danger, the implication of something like rank, is to see far-from-equilibrium systems as totally free agents, that is, composed of randomly related parts. This is an oxymoron. Randomness is not a relationship; a randomly structured system would have no identity, nothing which energy could transform. This is post-modernism revisited:

Suppose Poincare had proved that all systems were integrable. This would mean that all dynamical motions are isomorphic to free noninteracting particles. There would be no place for the arrow of time, for self organisation or life itself. Integrable systems describe a static deterministic world. Poincare not only demonstrated noningre-ability, but also identified the reason for it: *the existence of resonances between the degrees of freedom*.

(ibid., original emphases)

What is described here is not a random phenomenon but a new develop-ment arising from the interaction of specific components. It may be new, unexpected, non-linear or unpredictable, but it arises entirely out of the identity of the interacting components. Even when this new sphere of inter-action becomes important or dominant in its own right, that is when it threatens an evolutionary shift, it still has its ground in the components. As Prigogine puts it:

Near-equilibrium laws are universal, but when they are far from equilibrium, they become *mechanism dependent*. We therefore have to perceive the origin of variety in nature we observe around us. *Matter* acquires new properties when far from equilibrium in that fluctuations and instabilities become the norm. *Matter* becomes more 'active'.

(ibid. p. 64, our emphases)

This passage cannot describe randomness or infinite plasticity. The arrow of time, coupled with specific energies, instead describes a rooted tree of possibilities. This idea offers a better sense of what is meant by 'sensitivity to original conditions'. Prigogine's insistence that time, instead of being an illusion, especially one introduced by humans, is a real and active dimension of being equally requires a determinate or strong notion of matter. This is more often than not glossed in the emphasis on far-from-equilibrium systems; in particular on their capacity to evolve in unpredictable ways. Neo-Darwinism, because it places less emphasis on dissipative systems, supplies the corrective, which is that evolution is not possible without species. Species here corresponds with strong matter. It further implies a deep connection between equilibrated, near-to-equilibrium, and far-from-equilibrium behaviours. Crucially for sociology, it implies a strong version of equilibrated resources, strong near-to-equilibrium factors such as individuals or members, to successfully ground and energise further-from-equilibrium phenomena such as economies, technologies, social evolution. Post-structuralism is not even close to this requirement and consequently the many attempts to assimilate Prigogine's ideas to post-modernist heterology are entirely misplaced. In this sense, the use of autopoiesis in Maturana's sense or content-specific mechanisms in Tooby and Cosmides' sense, both of which stress identity or continuity, is intended to offset an emphasis on evolutionary homeodynamics that forget preconditions of relative homeostasis. This is close to Maturana's own criticisms of the emphases of evolutionary theory:

> [The] contradiction between the [Newtonian] thermodynamic and Darwinian cosmologies, between entropy and evolution has long been recognised . . . It has been left up to two disciplines to worry about the contradiction: philosophy and chemistry . . . first, chemistry shuttles between the orderliness of physics and the complexity of biology; and second, even in the early nineteenth century it was recognised that most chemical reactions were irreversible. And philosophy worried because of the metaphysical consequences of such an unresolved conflict.
>
> (Porush 1991: 58)

This straightforward description shows the relative self-isolation of the disciplines of physics and biology. Chemistry as the go-between, or rather Prigogine, re-energises the question of their relationship, for which he was awarded the Nobel Prize in 1997.

> Prigogine's model challenges classical science's assumptions about the locale of reality, it also indicts the insufficiency of classical science's discourse about reality. *As such it is part of post-modernism's three-pronged attack on classical scientific discourse.*
>
> (Porush 1991: 60, emphases reversed)

This is somewhat at variance with our position, and a detailed response is illuminating. The 'three prongs' are:

1. Quantum mechanics preaches the essentially . . . probabilistic nature of reality at the subatomic level.
2. Analysis . . . of the discourse of science by such writers as Kuhn, Feyerabend . . . show that normal science is itself vulnerable to irrational forces and trapped by the assumptions and language of its own discourse.
3. Prigogine's theory transfers the locus of reality from the microscopic world . . . to the macroscopic, where the influence is on complexity and time's arrow (the science of *becoming*) . . .

    [T]he fundamental question becomes a typically post-modern one: which level of description, which sort of discourse, is more universally applicable, more epistemologically potent?

    (ibid. original emphases)

First, there is a question of accuracy. Prigogine stresses explicit continuity between Newtonian and quantum mechanics, compared to his own:

As is well known, Newton's law has been superseded in the twentieth century by quantum mechanics and relativity. Still the basic characteristics of his laws – determinism and time symmetry – have survived. It is true that quantum mechanics no longer deals with trajectories but with wave functions . . . but it is important to see that the basic equation of quantum mechanics, Schrodinger's equation, is once again deterministic and time reversible.

(Prigogine 1996: 12)

He also devotes a significant amount of *Order Out of Chaos* to an attempt to ground a microscopic theory of time to complement its macroscopic tangibility. Porush's 'break advocacy' is seriously misleading. Like ordinary post-modernism, it is plagued by tacit or unconscious reductionism.

Second, Kuhn comments on the normality of science and Feyerabend on its willingness to bend the rules or invent new ones *ad hoc*. That does not ground the typically post-modern anti-scientific stance. All discourses exhibit reflexive self-dependence and all discourses depend on the viability of external referents to even recognise that fact, let alone manage it. Consequently, such observations do not contribute at all to the question of the quality of scientific discourse *vis-à-vis* any other.

Third, Prigogine's theory does not attack so much as supplement by pointing to the extra considerations presented by ensembles, interactions and evolutions. The key point is that processes occur due to interaction that could not occur at the level of non-interacting individual particles, as we noted above.

Fourth, Porush's fundamental question: *which level of description, which sort of discourse, is more universally applicable, more epistemologically potent?* is anything but a typically post-modern one. At least not one Lyotard could easily stomach. It is rather a question concerning the relative adequacy of specific discourses. Of course, Lyotard, who clearly preferred the adequacy of post-modern discourse to modernism's 'incredible' meta-narratives, could not then be a post-modernist either. Can we say instead that the strategy presented in each of the discourses has its different losses and gains and that elevation to the status of quasi-ontology (meta-narrative) produces meaninglessness? All discourses 'ignore'; they 'abstract', typify, stereotype, etc. We are claiming not to ignore but to topicalise this dimension reflexively as much as the positive assertions of a paradigm are emphasised. For example, there is a danger here that Prigogine's interpreters, especially in the human sciences, will make him simply a theorist of dissipative structure and make dissipative systems the grandest of grand theories. What would that tendency actively ignore? All of the components of the human being that exhibited the tendency to equilibrium. Evolutionary tendency would rank above specificity. To borrow from, but invert, Lyotard's sentiments: we have paid a high enough price for that sort of totalising simplicity.

What is emerging is a rather different, often glossed, relationship between chance and determinacy. On the one hand stands the Newtonian model of predictable cause and consequent event. The event has no choice. Einstein also says: God does not play dice. On the other stands the post-modern proposition of structurelessness; no constraint, no limit. Prigogine does not supply a middle course. He insists that both models fit only very limited sets of phenomena and hence have very limited validity. He is far closer to the possible or adaptive variation within limits that characterises Darwinian and ecological models.

It is crucial to see that Newtonian science models reality in a specific way. It provides an extreme idealisation of, for example, uniform motion, which is then modified by the action of such variables as friction. The universals count; the localised variables are either incidental or can be reincorporated into the general law. In our opening chapter we acknowledged that complexity is a problem. Newton's strategy is to maximise the constants, provide explanations, make control and prediction possible, to simplify. This does not remove the truth; it does imply possible limits to its validity. That situation is far more complex, more undecidable, than blanket declaration of anti-science, collapse of meta-narrative, science as conventional. Prigogine is acutely aware of the relationship between science and culture:

> Classical science was born in a culture dominated by the alliance between *man*, situated midway between the divine and the natural order and *God*, the rational and intelligible legislator, the sovereign architect we have conceived in our own image.
>
> (Prigogine and Stengers 1984: 51)

That could have come straight out of any critical sociology of science. Where else could any human collective construction be conceived except in the womb of culture? It does not follow, however, that science and culture are identical, nor does it settle the question of determination. As Prigogine says: 'it has outlived this moment of cultural consonance' (ibid.). In fact, the proposition that science 'is' culture, and is thus conventional, conceals a curiously Newtonian sense of causality, embedded within the rhetorics of randomness: cultural convention, ludicrously 'free' nevertheless, 'causes' science (which has no choice) to inhabit a corresponding straightjacket.

> It is not our intention to state, nor are we in any position to affirm, that religious discourse in any way determined the birth of theoretical science, or the 'world-view' that happened to develop in conjunction with experimental activity. By using the term *resonance* – that is mutual amplification of two discourses – we have deliberately chosen an expression that does not assume that whether it was theological discourse or the 'scientific myth' that came first and triggered the other.
>
> (ibid. p. 46)

The choice of 'resonance' is crucial and non-Newtonian. It implies a 'degree of freedom' between robust entities – in this case discourses, though it could equally well apply to matter, that are sufficiently grounded to exhibit vitality in the twin senses of self-sufficiency and ability to affect others. This is the strong sense of freedom, chance or chaos that underlies complexity theory and demands a strong sense of components. Non-integrability, that is the impossibility of treating a complex system as merely the sum of its parts, does not imply that the components are simply random contingencies. On the contrary, non-integration implies an increase in the possibility of re-organisation, given an already robust base. As Prigogine picturesquely says, 'hypnons' (sleep-walkers) become 'active'; particles begin to 'see'. Discourses as 'active particles' enter the material ecology of organisation precisely because they are not disposable, but vital simulations. It is truly strange that post-modernism always misses that imperative.

There is always a danger of dismissing determinism(s) by caricature, but this we think is apt:

> Western thought has always oscillated between the world as an automaton and a theology in which God governs the universe. This is what Needham calls the 'characteristic European schizophrenia.' In fact these visions are connected. An automaton needs an external God.
>
> (ibid. p 7)

Something of the scale of ambition that eco-auto-organisation represents is glimpsed here. Determinism literally expects causality to flow from precedent to consequent: the latter 'has no choice'. Deviations have to be accounted for in terms of modifications to what should be expected. God and the Devil, Newton and sublunar variants, Marx and the bourgeoisie, Parsons and deviance, globalisation and fundamentalism. Given the failure of reality to live up to what ought to happen, the post-modern response pitifully offers 'conventionality' and relegates the durable, repetitive or robust elements of Being to meta-narrative. Neither confront *self*-organisation: they comment on a paradoxical 'already there' finally devoid of reason or cause, except: God, language, human authorship. This is the meagre level of humanism's self-reflexivity.

Self-organisation, on the other hand, is at least collectively and at most ecologically organised: there is no way that *individual* particles, plants, animals, humans organise anything at all. Chance enters the picture precisely because we are now in the sphere of populations, of statistical probability that particles or individuals will occupy certain positions, have specific needs, death rates and so on. This is not a picture of randomness but of possible correlations and degrees of freedom. Even conventional assertion is only free 'to a degree'. The same can be said of the human imagination. But 'variation within limits' is perfectly capable of generating the complex ecology to which we belong. Differently put, in terms of ecology, the degree to which 'individuals' are sub-stitutable is increasingly limited. Any individual can substitute for any other and we can see that this way of working is a commonplace of political adminis-trations. It is, simply, 'quantification'. And its Newtonian characteristics are there for all to see. However, whether we want to treat our ecology at the level of the relations between species or the internal relations of one species, such as humans, substitution is limited by specificity. This is a small point with enormous ramifications. Note that quantification is equivalent to ran-domisation, as universal substitutability, and that post-modern versions of strict conventionality are precisely formal quantifications, whose Newtonian characteristics are there for all to see. Crucially, substitution, i.e. chance, is limited by specificity. This is also a commonplace of political, ethical and practical action; undeniably true, regularly ignored. The issue can be radicalised.

It is instructive to revise the components of Prigogine's position. The first is the availability of thermodynamic energy to drive systems 'far-from-equilibrium', to offset the probability of entropic equilibrium, to drive apart the stable structures of forms like crystals, all of which would otherwise be more probable outcomes. Second is the introduction of stochastic elements through the interaction of populations of particles or individuals, subject to specificity. We have not yet tackled in any depth: third, the dimension of time and irreversibility; nor fourth, the role of information within the system. It is with these last two factors that the position becomes radicalised – and radically important for critical sociology.

We said it was strange for the macroscopic sciences such as biology and sociology to realise that 'time' is a contentious issue for the microscopic sciences like particle physics and quantum mechanics. Nevertheless, this remains the case: for classical mechanics, time is reversible, for Einstein it is an illusion. Both of these decidedly odd positions are based on the idea that a simple formula or formulae, or sets of explanations, can provide a description of the universe independent of time. Hence the otherwise baffling conclusion that time is 'introduced by our ignorance'. Though it is still baffling why scientists persist with that perverse sort of wording. Many scientists, however, reject it.[3] The crucial issue is the relation between stochastic elements or probabilities and time:

> [Developing the theory of entropy] Boltzmann already understood that probability and irreversibility had to be closely related. Only when a system behaves in a sufficiently random way may the difference between past and future, and therefore irreversibility, enter into its description . . . The arrow of time is a manifestation of the fact that the future is not *given*.
>
> (ibid. p. 16, our emphasis)

One can quibble with the semantics, but the idea that randomness allows time to follow still echoes with the prejudices of physics. On the other hand, Prigogine will argue such a cosmology is viable. That is beyond our scope. The key is that the future is not given; it can only evolve, or happen. Again the point seems small. We are now committed to a macroscopic model, characterised by populations, probabilities and interactions where chance operates in limits given by specificity. Should we not, then, expect stability? Yes, in systems close to equilibrium, not in systems far from equilibrium.

> As soon as the system becomes large enough, the law of large numbers enables us to make a clear distinction between mean values and fluctuations, and the latter may be ignored.
>
> However, in nonequilibrium processes we may find just the opposite situation. Fluctuations determine the global outcome. We could say that instead of being corrections in the average values, fluctuations modify those averages.
>
> (ibid. p. 178)

Notice that the macroscopic dimension is fundamental. So is thermal energy: as Prigogine regularly reminds us, *Ignis mutat res*. But surely this allows reversibility?

No, that is increasingly impossible. This time the law of large numbers requires that, in order to reverse, the system must know and 'go back through' all of its previous positions. Given any degree of chance this is a practical impossibility that grows with the number of interactions. Then the punchline, if 'reversibility' is asserted then the storage of information must be presumed. Change reversibility to 'reproduction' and one can see just how far-reaching this small point is, it indicates the threshold of the living. Now *ignis mutat res* identifies the engine of evolution. We have in root form the common ontology of matter and information.

The transition from the 'physics and chemistry' of thermodynamics to the evolution of 'embodied cognition' is a crucial turn and this, then, is the place for summary and, where possible, simplification. Even here, our discipline has traditionally had no more than a scant working knowledge of the relationships between the biology of bodies and cognitive possibility. We still have a concept of human cognition which is disconnected with that of every other species and openly mysterious. The 'image of god' persists and any attempt to confront the materiality of information, especially when that means human knowledge, is met with an executioner's welcome. Theoretically speaking, we panic and run. Our freedom and pride are at stake. How far are we, still, from accepting the consequences of evolution? Moreover, we shall soon have to move from the establishment of a better working knowledge of relevant sciences to the massive complexity of our shared, traditional expertise in sociology and the revision that now seems necessary.

For our immediate purposes, the import of Prigogine can be reduced to the following emphases:

1. In contrast with classical mechanics and its deterministic relationships, he stresses complex re-organisation when systems are driven far from equilibrium by thermal energy.
2. This complexity typically takes place on a macro-scale, therefore involving large numbers of interactive particles.
3. Such interaction includes a level of randomness as well as probability and is therefore statistical in nature. Nevertheless, perturbations are not simply 'discountable' variations from the norm. Instead, they may reposition the average unexpectedly. Such reconstructions tend to demonstrate irreversibility.
4. This process does not ignore particles. On the contrary, they become collectively energised and extremely sensitive to small variables such as gravitational or electrical fields, which at equilibrium would be irrelevant.
5. Such processes are 'precursors to life' in a dual sense:
    (a) they describe the basis for the evolution of complex chemistry necessary for life, such as sensitivity and catalysis.
    (b) they show that eco-auto-'recursive' organisation, i.e. autopoiesis, requires the storage of information to combat the necessary onset of irreversibility.

The paradox is that increasing complexity, as Cohen and Stewart have it, is 'downhill' – or more prosaically, a probable outcome of thermodynamics. This is unexpected both in 'classical mechanics' and in Boltzmanns' model of increasing entropy. The further paradox we now have to confront is that the evolution of life indicates that the ability to respond to and store information – that is, cognition – is also downhill. Perhaps it would be more prudent to say that these apparent paradoxes are the result of our ignorance of, or prejudice against, the idea that cognition has to be grounded in the materiality of evolutionary processes. Is this a return to determinism? Of course not. It is a consequence precisely of the denial of determinism. Nevertheless, that denial rests upon a kind of materialism, or a materialism of information, and not on gods, humans in their image, or any other form of 'skyhook', to borrow Dennett's apt term. The radical version of self-organisation includes the self-organisation of cognition, which has a human variant. Here humanity uses and is 'put to use' by the ecology of cognition. Some (Dawkins, Dennett, Blackmore) go so far as to call it parasitisation.[4] Contrast this with the insular, assertive self-organisation of human knowledge that is the central characteristic of humanism in its Renaissance and post-modern forms.

Prigogine's studies lead us to a new conception of material probability. The microspcopic properties of matter, such as substance, particles, molecules, largely independent of each other at equilibrium levels, begin to act together at macroscopic levels at far-from-equilibrium conditions, charged by thermodynamics. This may be unexpected given the state of our knowledge, but it is not an occult phenomenon: *ignis mutat res* describes a material process. It opens a new sphere of material possibility. Time has become the crucial dimension since heat is temporally dissipated: its source and its consequences have materially, irreversibly changed and, given the element of randomness, only the storage of information allows the system to return to its original state, but at a subsequent point in time. This brief description concerns open systems; open in the sense of being subject to energy transfer. We now have to confront the class of systems which are relatively open, in the sense that they require environmental inputs, but depend on maintaining a homeostatic boundary or identity, such as a cell membrane, and therefore need to store information through DNA. This basic characteristic of the living is our embodied foundation and the origin of our social organisation. The degree to which the body and society are congruent will be constantly and increasingly placed in question. Here we are concerned with the rudiments of self-organisation on the grounds that, in the sociological tradition, it has been assumed rather than explored.

The concept of material probability must now be changed to accommodate both evolutionary and recursive tendencies. Also a new economic factor has entered the equation: information is not without cost. Especially so in a species such as ours that specialises in big-brain, information-saturated strategies. These costs occur in at least two forms: the physical cost to the biological system (20-25 per cent in energy/blood/oxygen supply, integrated systems for input/output, vulnerable points); and the cost of *re*-presentation. We choose the term carefully as it is congruent with Maturana and Varela's 'bringing forth worlds': the environment is *re*-presented by and for the organism. There is no ordinary 'correspondence' theory of truth/knowledge hiding here, recall this disjuncture: *re*-presentation. The cost and effect of representation will turn out to be crucial. However, this is still a materialistic explanation.

We are presented, then, with a twofold but integrated dialectic: on the one hand, and ontologically the most dominant, the drive to diversity, represented in nature by the complexity of different species, in society by the heterogeny of culture and behaviour. On the other, by the drive to reproductive identity, represented no less by self-maintenance, such as hunger, fear of death, and sexual drive than by the human desire to stabilise the knowledge and indeed the contents of the environment. The first is clearly the ground of the second. There is no need for humans. Life, on the other hand, seems likely.

Complexity and diversity are not givens, they need to be explained. Nor are they the same. Complexity may be grasped, on Prigogine's authority, as a likely or 'forced' outcome of thermodynamics. It may be that life and cognition are 'downhill' to thermodynamic complexity, even 'highly likely'. But diversity is a fundamentally ecological concept: it refers to a differentiated field and, especially in the case of the living, it refers to adaptation, to an environment that is differentiated and potentially contains other life forms. Possibility is therefore structured. And the first constraint is energy; again a thermodynamic engine.

> [Malthus's] central point is that an exponentially expanding population (one that multiplies by a fixed amount at each generation) will outgrow its linearly growing food supply(one that adds a fixed amount each generation) . . .

> But there was a deeper message for Darwin . . . [N]ature's rules, even simple rules like the one dictating that exponential growth will outstrip linear growth, bind human plans and desires into inevitable patterns.

> Darwin did not simply declare that natural selection had occurred, he set up an argument that makes sense of the hierarchical classification of animals, because natural selection has *driven them to diverge*. Similar animals have common ancestors in the recent (by geological time scales) past; different animals have more remote common ancestors. And what drove the two apart, making them recognisably different, is that they specialized toward different ways of competing for the same resource. Then their specialisation began to free them from competition.
>
> (Cohen and Stewart 1995, 2000: 107–8)

This is an elementary explanation in evolutionary theory. The problem is, contemporary 'critical' sociology seems to have forgotten about it. Further, we argue that sociology has routinely given scant attention to its implications. True, a similar argument underlies Durkheim's rationale for the growth of organic solidarity and economics is 'the science of scarce resources', but that's about it. Let's try to tease out the implications a little further. First, it emphasises what is implied but concealed in that phrase: sensitivity to initial conditions. Biological and social systems have a past. This is not to be understood as recourse to a simple, linear determinism but again it is material. In other words, the past and the current status of the organism, system, or social system is the condition of its own possible revisions. Self-organisation is fundamentally self-reflexive. Second, as auto–eco–organisation the past and current state represents a viable possibility; or its relative permanence represents a sustainable adaptation. As such it 'contains' possibly facts, physical responses, information, ways of dealing which cannot be dismissed with the snap of a finger or a change of will. Or again: self-organisation is fundamentally reflexive or adaptive *vis-à-vis* its environment. This means that the probability of change will lie in the direction of further adaptation: it will tend to be additive. This is what is meant by 'driven to diverge'. There is just the trace of a narrowing here. It is easy to counter.

We are not describing a homeostatic state but rather an ontological spread of possibility. Analogy with evolution demonstrates the difference clearly. Homeostasis is certainly feasible; it corresponds to a distinct species which may maintain its viability, or become extinct. But the drift implied in 'driven to diverge' is observable without doubt as a massive source of complexity, the range of terrestrial species, which nevertheless has common structural relations and limits. Moreover, there is always the possibility of catastrophic bifurcations within or between species and environments that shut off what once seemed possible and insisted upon a different future. Add to this the variable dimension of chance, even within limited change, and the simpler homeostatic models demonstrate their limitations: 'limited' homeostasis indicates one amongst many possible attractors. However, chance is a structural component amongst other determinants and not a totalising description: the number of attractors is finite.

Another, certainly less technical way of saying this is: life is sticky. Compared with the clean abstractions of the *cogito*, the absurd, heroic, delusional self-creation of the transcendental subject, the *sui-generic* authority of modernistic sociology or the entirely presumed ability to 'bracket out' that socio-phenomenology requires, mundane life is heavy with the traces of primeval ooze. Maternity and childrearing are still palpably mammalian. Competition for food, sexual partners, prestige, freedom from want or danger, still permeate our praxes.

> The main evidence that mind is a process carried out by brains is that there are clear links between particular physical regions of the brain and particular aspects and functions of the mind. If the mind were

simply a mystical add-on, there would be no reason to associate various bits of it with bits and pieces of the totally different material brain. But in fact the brain divides quite naturally into quite different structures and functions.

(Cohen and Stewart 1995, 2000: 170)

We are back with Tooby and Cosmides' content-specific structures, but this time the adaptive history is somewhat longer in its perspective and different in its character. Cohen and Stewart are more disposed to stress the ancient 'arms race' for food as the basis of the brain's development but the central point – the sticky history – remains the same: new is overlaid on old. The regions may be reorganised but the history sticks. The most recognition reflexive sociology concedes is the recognition of the 'observer in the observation'. What about the sexually active, the frustrated, the once-active, the hungry, the driven by anger, the insular, the very young or old, the schisms of gender, the mentally limited (all of us in one way or another), to say nothing of the levels of brain function that are below the levels of consciousness? What is abstracted in that innocent observer? The answer to that question, if complex, is also clearly indicated:

1. The evolution of human cognition.
2. All those aspects of mind that fall outside the normal range of the humanities, including low or subconscious functions.
3. The fact that the mind cannot have enough 'bits' to encode the universe of its own operations; let alone others' operations or subconscious operations.
4. The extent to which the mind is variously free from or dependent upon the 'sticky stuff' of its development.
5. The extent to which the 'collective' mind is subject to the same ancestry or redefinitional capability.

Having spent much of the work so far (and much of this chapter) analysing the limits of linear determinism, it would be something of a disaster if readers were to misunderstand the upshot of the role of DNA and the implications of evolved mental adaptations. We are not trying to replace linear determinism with an argument asserting a better, more complex blueprint. This would completely miss the point of *self*-organisation and the tendency toward increasing complexity.

It must be conceded that the DNA 'blueprint' is better, more complex or whatever. The real problem is: it isn't a blueprint and in several senses. The mechanical analogy is misleading: DNA is not a set of instructions for making a machine. Instead, we are talking of something far more like an attractor. Correspondingly, the living organism, unlike a machine, but arguably like social structures, is an open system with respect to a constantly changing environment. DNA flexibly manages what can be treated as 'forces to differ' to recreate constantly the identity and the components of the living system. This is precisely what is meant by autopoiesis. This relationship roundly condemns the simpler forms of radical constructivism: echoing Maturana and Varela, the organism can only 'bring forth worlds' or 'decide what counts as environment' by a viable or realistic process of adaptation. Notice that realistic is here a truth hammered out by interaction. It is not primarily or necessarily a mental construct. Moreover, as Cohen and Stewart constantly point out: this relationship itself evolves. Consequently we are talking of multiple, branching organisations, not organisms but varied species. In other words, the ecology of the environment evolves as well. Given this non-equilibrium situation, blueprints are inadequate or redundant.

There is also the problem of internal genetic mutation within the DNA code. Contrary to popular belief, there are not 'genes for' but interactive propensities. Also DNA contains lots of 'junk' with no, or only superseded, functions. Mutation is possible but most mutation will not confer advantage and will tend to die out. Some will confer a reproductive advantage and persist. If mutation is related to environment, there must be a sort of buffering relationship to maintain the identity of the organism against the possibility of genetic 'drift'. Waddington called this 'canalisation'.[5] Such mechanisms are crucial in species that are open, for example, to environmental temperature variation. The crucial point for complexity theory is the ability not only to 'instruct' but to flexibly interact. Some of the outcomes of this interaction will be new or increased complexity: the canals are bridged.

> If the point of DNA is to offer a series of adapted and adaptable survival kits then there are clearly limits to how much of the environment it can 'picture' in advance or by sensitised recognition mechanisms. The development of brainpower eases the problem by offering non-genetic routes that can be 'learnt' from the manner in which environment presents itself and stored, where appropriate, in cultures (however rudimentary).
>
> These routes can be far more adaptable than DNA chemistry; by the same token, they are not always as stable . . . [F]or creatures as complex as us privileged apes, the *direct* DNA route [i.e. pre-specification] isn't even available: There are more neural connections than there are DNA bases . . . Humans . . . are the extreme case of nongenetic transfer between generations. Much of what we need to be human is genuinely transmitted to us through a message . . . Language is the key example.
>
> (ibid. p. 350)

Think of Tooby and Cosmides' argument against the overemphasis on learning: adaptation is at least as important for the generation of content. In other words, a hard-wired language would not have to be learned but would be rudimentary and incapable of versatile development. It would be analogous to a series of reflexes. On the other hand, faculties without content-specific adaptation would have to spend their active life learning what they might, or might not, be 'for'. Both positions are manifestly unviable. Moreover, and by definition, non-genetic transfer in this model is fundamentally collective. There is, therefore, an 'ethics' of variation in the sense that it bears relations of responsibility, reciprocity and variously grounded modes of viable behaviour. It bears scant relation to the God-given or its degraded form, the conventional notion of behavioural ethics of religious or post-religious humanism. We recognise the political challenge and responsibility that formulation presents. It lies at the centre of democracy, we argue, and is clearly unacceptable to fundamentalism of all kinds. We shall address that question in the second and third sections of this book.

Part II

CRITICAL
DEVELOPMENTS

6

MODERNISM AND DETERMINISM
Linear expectations and qualitative complexity analyses

In the early stages we considered minimising this chapter because our response to various kinds of linear determinism was so relentlessly negative. We were wrong. That may come as a surprise. The reasons for our revised opinion come in two forms, which might be provisionally described as the negative and the positive. We shall shortly revise that as well. It is impossible to treat linear determinism minimally because it is so pervasive in its social effects. Taking that view, as all complexity theorists must do, explicitly or not, puts one in a camp of the 'wise' (so to speak) with the 'less wise' on the other side. This is yet another example of the old 'cultural dope' argument. Since the gathering of dopes so defined by the complexity turn itself includes a vast number of humans, an entire tradition of explanation, not to mention one Isaac Newton, and a host of eminent scientists and thinkers from other critical disciplines, the wicket begins to look decidedly sticky. Remember how we handled 'stickiness' in Part I? Would it not be more prudent, and certainly more consistent, to insist that linear determinism is a powerful attractor in human thought, and often for sound practical reasons? This is the positive formulation. We belong to the same camp (the dopes if you insist) and only move out when the setting gets unbearably uncomfortable. A more formal way to say this is to concede that the linear attractor is ecologically viable, an instance of what Tooby and Cosmides would call 'adaptation enaction'. Only where its viability is physically, i.e. existentially, compromised does the notion of complexity arise as an emergent re-adaptation. The rational point of complexity theory is to discover patterned or self-organising structures. We are not operating with Lyotard's old theology of the celebration of the 'incommensurate', otherwise known as 'chaos'; this is not post-modernism revisited. Post-modernism? Determinism? We must avoid complexity-ism. The problem is not the viability of the various theoretic stances as conceptual strategies but as ideological prescriptions. This, like Kant's criterion, is misplaced universality. More ominously, it is an attempt to coerce the character of understanding as a whole. But prescription can only be viable in the face of invariance. It is not then wrong but limited.

The wise versus the cultural dopes might be better represented, then, as the distinction between pragmatic strategists and ideologists. If modernists prefer order, the post-modernists prefer disorder and we risk vacillation, then that is a series of camps and hierarchies we can live with. We are claiming a better sort of adaptable and adapted rationale on the grounds of environmental dynamics.

Despite giving linear determinism the respect it deserves, we nevertheless have to formulate some tough definitions. Following both the supporters and critics of linearity, it may be defined as the expectation, which sometimes amounts to certainty, that given an understanding of a current state of affairs its future and its past condition can be deduced. The information indicated *now* is sufficient to define the situation *then*. Typically such statements involve things like planetary positions and landing spacecraft: the stuff of Newtonian mechanics. This is the part that tends to get elevated, that has Newton as the Moses of his time and determinism as ideological prescription. More mundane examples are usually glossed, though they are the very stuff of sociology: Mother rings on Sundays. Back to work on Monday. The Boss is bad-tempered. This is hard to elevate. It is not hard to see, though constantly over-looked, that all of these mundanities are irreducibly complex, unlike the orbit of Mars – that we do not, cannot, and do not want, to make ideological-type elevations because we hedge such judgements about with practical limitations, such as: Mother is away for the day; the bad-tempered Boss sells up and you are redundant. Philosophy's desire for order sometimes robs it of that practical intelligence.

Why should that be? Without revisiting Prigogine and Stengers' lengthy and excellent analysis of the relationships between Newton's and religious culture[1], an excellent study in the sociology of science, part of the reason just might be humans' cultural ambition to realise their relation to God in the Platonic-Christian and Judaic senses. Others might call it hubris. Put more ordinarily, inclusively and structurally, it turns on the old and valuable distinctions between essence and appearance, ground and consequent, Being and becoming and so on. The generic characteristic is a reductionism based on something akin to the non-authenticity, or irrelevance, or ignorability of second-order or trivial mediations; that is, this further level of complexity is covered, or managed, by a routine and extensive ascription of contingency. Let us consider Luhmann's definition: 'Something is contingent insofar as it is neither neces-sary nor impossible; it is just what it is (or was or will be) though it could also be otherwise' (Luhmann 1995: 106).

Stripped of its Platonic-Christian overtones, nevertheless the ghost of Kant can be glimpsed and Luhmann's usage is haunted (to the point of possession) by the problem, as we shall argue below. It is an extremely odd definition even though in the text it is copiously referenced to show its lineage and acceptability.[2] It is the norm. Yet it bears no trace of eco-auto-organisation, and finally no adequate conception of chance either: chance is merely understood formally. It bears no sense of ecological possibility. Chance is not seen as a dynamic or qualitative phenomenon arising out of interactive relationships but as a general or pervasive environment that stands alone – not unlike time or space in Newtonian physics. As fuzzy logic might put it, the necessary and the impossible are not well understood as 'either/or' dimensions but better understood as questions of degree. Similarly the contrast 'as it is' and 'could have been otherwise', also matters of degree, are overlooked or over-formalised. Humans and dodos are both contingent, neither 'can be otherwise' to any great degree as the prospect of extinction sharply underscores. Neither are necessary nor impossible but that hardly describes their real ecological possibility or impossibility. 'Not necessary not impossible' says practically nothing more than the statement: they are not green. Both are true by default, by almost complete irrelevance: they say nothing. That would equate with the early Wittgenstein's concept of 'literally nonsense'.

This nothing, this absence, is crucial. The kind of determinism on which the ideological inflation of Newton is based is this absence. This point is not new, it is essentially a variant on Hegel's bad infinity. If God, Being, the ground, the essence indicate 'what matters', why does He, why do *they* (never mind *us*) bother with creation, beings, appearances, second-order manifestations? Hegel's answer is that it belongs to the nature of God or Spirit to differentiate Him/Its self. Slightly more sophisticated than ordinary determinism, this is still no more than an assertion of fate. Others, for example Plato, the authors of Genesis and Kant, rest, respectively, on a degenerative process, a kind of cosmic con-trick, creation *ex nihilo* that is somehow bound to be betrayed. In every case, not unlike Luhmann's objection to Parsons, the past matters most. Causality flows through time in a linear fashion, though not without excuses and apologies for mistakes such as *anamnesis* or original sin. As Einstein says, 'God does not play dice' – or *shouldn't*. Quantum mechanics does not agree. And our position, indeed complexity theory's sometimes implicit position, is very different.

A brief excursion into cosmology: first there was the big bang. This may or may not be the case but that is not the point. At some time we have to accept that there is a planetary system orbiting the sun. The universe, the product of the big bang, contains the solar system. The past still looks decidedly primal but was it fated to have our solar system or is something else possible or even more likely? Now consider the Earth. Here the position changes decisively. There is no need to invoke Lovelock's *Gaia*[3] in full to see that events subsequent to Earth's formation are reciprocally causal to its current identity. Earth, the living and non-living systems that permeate it, are reciprocally causal; cause and chronology and are no longer the simple unity that religion, linear determinism or even the Hegelian reform envisaged. The same may be true of the universe. We are not qualified to argue the point, but the effect on reductionism is clear, if true, even to a slight degree, the result is fatal. It is in this sense that the question of chance can be raised. It is not a formal assumption nor is it a dimension of uniform quality or distribution, as it appears in post-modernism. Its 'shape' or function, influence, degree, magnitude, is also reciprocally caused and causal. Taken together, these transform the notion of contingency: not necessary, nor impossible; as it is, but could be otherwise. Well yes and no: possibly. True to a degree? Possibly. Relevant? Perhaps. This is the 'nothing', the absence or suppressed equivocation that infects ideological linear determination. Its positive reciprocal is eco-auto-organisation. Just in case we are tempted to raise that to ideological status, it is itself contingent but in the revised sense. In other words, its being neither necessary nor impossible is a dynamic matter of degree, position, circumstance, inter-relationship.

It is crucial to consider the status of information in this idea of ecological or reciprocal causality. We have seen that recursive or autopoietic structures require information to, literally, re-produce themselves through time. This was because of the operations of chance and/or their being typically open systems; that is, open to complexity and variation. Information in the humanist and positivist tradition is neutral, transparent, or its media are unimportant. They can be safely ignored. For complexity theory, this is just another instance of ignoring the complex dimensions of second-order mediation. Then DNA is not a neutral substrate but one specific structure necessary to the evolution of the biosphere. Evolution here is precisely congruent with reciprocal causality. Therefore DNA cannot be the author but only the precursor of the diversity to which its presence contributes. It is a necessary but not the sufficient condition. We shall return to this point in the closing section of this chapter when we discuss the limits of genetic determinism. For the moment, our more general point is that when we consider the diverse materials of human cultures of information, they also are not neutral. They are enmeshed with the dynamic systems of reciprocal causality, a point amply demonstrated by the sociology of the media.

'Media' and 'mediation' catch some of the senses we want to convey. Media implies a rather neutral transfer process as though the same item of information can be translated from one to another without loss, distortion or transform-ation. But given the generally conceded view of the constitutive role of media and in particular the examples we want to discuss below, namely the verbal analysis of visual art, this assumption is misplaced formalism. Words and images cannot deal with information in the same way; the substrates are not neutral. In many senses, one substrate deals with information that is almost impossible to convey in the other. Rather than translate they only overlap to a degree, fuzziness again. Their actions are more like substitutions. Mediation catches a little of this but, for us, it is still too neutral. We want something more like DNA, more like genes that make bodies possible, allow variations, allow evo-lutionary bridges to be crossed, allow eco-auto-organisation to occur, but in the cultural sphere. Happily, the solution is ready made not as genes but as 'memes'. It resonates nicely with the French term *meme* (the same) and with mediation. Crucially, it also resonates with *mem*bership and this implies for us at least two major sets of considerations. First, membership, for humans, is an ecological imperative; it is a requirement, a drive, an unavoidable condition.

Second, the instruments of membership are not neutral substrates or catchable in formal descriptions. On the contrary, they are built on such issues as environment, age or gender and expressed in materials as diverse as words, dance or body modification. Some caution is required, however, because the inventor of this term is Richard Dawkins, author of *The Selfish Gene*, the hardest of neo-Darwinists, much detested by the proponents of human ultraplasticity. We take it as a convenient shorthand for eco-auto-organisational structures in cultural reproduction. We stress structures to denote evolved, qualitative differences.

Memes or memetics might be understood as a radicalisation of an earlier notion, that of iteration. Derrida (1982: 315) says:

> The possibility of repeating, and therefore identifying, marks is implied in every code, making of it a communicable, transmittable and decipherable grid that is iterable for a third party . . .

Crowther's simpler defintion is:

> the iterability of a sign or group of signs is their capacity to be recognised and repeated across many different contexts of use. Iterability is that *stable* dimension of meaning . . . *independent* of any one specific context of employment.
>
> (Crowther 1997: 10)

Earlier Crowther argues '[this definition] is actually partly destructive of post-structuralism'. It certainly is, insofar as post-structuralism is characterised by 'scepticism about the fixity of meaning, categories and, indeed, the stability of the self' (ibid).[4] But look at the wording that forces itself on Crowther: 'destructive of post-structuralism', a telling phrase in which language is forced to whisper absurdities that indicate the weakness of the Derridean position. Let us now say that a reiterable meaning or cluster or pattern is presupposed. We shall refrain from any spurious measure of its (in)stability, though Derrida would clearly prefer instability, but insist that it takes place within a social setting and not in an abstract or formal intellectual space. Then it is easy to see that the relative (in)stability is radically undecidable. The expectation of a general measure of instability is only a persistent idiomatic trait or, if you like, Derrida's style. Actual (in)stability would rest on a complex of issues or eco-auto-organisational possibility. Remember this cuts both ways: it will not decide in general between stability and instability; it simply reinforces the possibility of circumstantial continuities and discontinuities. In sum 'iterability' seems to be presupposed but problematic. Let us now turn to memes.

Some of Dawkins' wordings are polemical or plain misleading. The classic case is the 'selfish' gene, but memes really hits the jackpot. Rather like the 'iterable unit' it is presupposed but, through its relationship on the one hand to stability (the gene or the French *meme*) and on the other to shifting phenomenology of members, membership, memory, re-membering, it soon takes on a life of its own that challenges pre-definition. Radically autopoietic, its existence rests on members' judgement that 'it', a meme, exists. It is, then, the ability to assert patterned complexity and have the asserted pattern recognised by another member. We have a fine state of affairs now: Dawkins the disciple of Darwin is radically less deterministic than Derrida. There is one further twist in the tale. Derrida is fond of metaphors of parastisation where the main work (the *ergon*) is permeated by supposedly subsidiary concerns (the *parergon*) such that the boundaries are always undecidable, a 'parasitised economy' (Derrida 1987). So with memes. Dawkins (1976), Dennett (1991), Blackmore (1999) formulate the human mind as parasitised by memes, the host of memetic reproduction. We prefer the causality to run reciprocally: cultural memetics and the human mind presuppose and reproduce each other. Reproduction is understood here as co-evolutionary, homeostatic and homeodynamic. This in no way diminishes Tooby and Cosmides' notion of adaptation-enacting, contrasted with learning, indeed they refer to the homeostasis of content-specific adaptations to ground the homeodynamics of the human mind in culture-specific locations.

Another way to understand this would be to portray memes as attractors within attractors. Suppose we take the attractors to be macroscopic. Examples might be the tendency to differentiate between genders, the propensity to record in pictorial forms. Then memes might be understood on the level of nuances in the design of skirts or shoes. Or again, as the disciplined but contested relationships between painting, photography, film. It is at this level of diversity and differentiation, in the active sense, played in the environment of the eco–auto–organisation and exo–auto–reference of membership that linear determinism, the ideology, not the attractor, shows its limits. In contrast, the spheres of memetic processes are through and through qualitative in their operations, for example fashion, film etc. We suppose that a doctrine of memeticism is conceivable but it would be singularly hard to see what difference that would make between entangled analyses and formal principles. Determinism implies, however tacitly, that a series of relationships can be stated a priori, that one can expect a relation of ground-and-consequent and that the impacts of causal reciprocity can be minimised.

Similarly, the philosophical debate stemming from Habermas and Lyotard on the possible consensus of rationality, morality and justice is typically argued without reference to qualitative considerations. How could one possibly object to a formal consensus? It presents no costs or restrictions. However, we are all aware of its qualitative counterparts, such as bargains, agreements, settlements, treaties, which exist entirely on the basis of previous dispute. For this reason, we have chosen an entirely qualitative consideration of a possible consensus about the social relationships, processes and the ostensible essence of visual art: in this instance, painting.

One of the classic areas in which determinism fights a rearguard action against the complexity of further mediation is the sociology of art. Frankly, much of this is crude and stupid: art reflects society. Could the desire for substrate neutrality be more clearly, and hopelessly, announced? The desire to contest genius and stress the collective production of art,[5] appears as a doctrinal requirement laid upon (and concealing) a fear of complex differentiation, especially questions of rank and quality. Of course, art is related to society and genius is generally a lot less lonely than its publicists would care to admit. But what kind of rationale is at work when a considerable publication industry and an awful lot of university departments' prestige and students' time is devoted to denying the importance of the difference exemplified in the visual of visual art, as opposed to words, and the exceptional artist, as opposed to the more ordinary one? It used to be called 'the new art history', now rather aging. It ought to be called the history of ideology illustrated by art. Such a formulation would expose its paucity as a history of either art or ideology. What is gained by treating the British painter Turner's amazing inventiveness as a collective or ideological product? Probably the transformation that insists conceptual, that is, verbal art is more important. Hence the fracture instituted by Duchamp and constantly repeated by contemporary art and art education for the best part of a century – though they call it innovation. That truly is a social, or better, institutionalised phenomenon. We have instead chosen a quite closely related but rather better, well-reasoned and certainly well-written, indeed persuasive, piece of determinism: Tim Clark's analysis of Manet's *Olympia*.

To set the scene: *Olympia* was painted in Paris in 1863. Intended as a picture of a prostitute, it chimes (and was seen to chime) with Baudelaire's and Zola's literary explorations of similar themes. Locally speaking, this is the time of Haussmann's rebuilding of Paris. Globally it is the time in which commodity capitalism was variously emerging and consolidating. It is the vociferous opening of the ideology of Modernism in commerce, culture and industrial production. Here are some samples of the public response:

> A sort of female gorilla, a grotesque in india rubber;
> Her body has the livid tint of a cadaver displayed in the morgue;
> She is a coal lady . . . never outraged by water;
> The little faubourienne, woman of the night from Paul Niquet's
>   [a bar/brothel]
>
> (Clark 1985: 96)

The picture actually portrays a reclining nude, wearing quite a forceful expression, looking 'you' straight in the eye. She's very obviously on display on a raised and sumptuous bed with her hand clutched provocatively, covering her genitalia: definitely alluring. She is attended by an Afro-Caribbean maid, bringing her flowers and a black cat is on the bed. The implication is that she is doing quite well (in whatever sense) from prostitution, though the underlying mood is ambiguously tragic or threatening. Both the model and the maid were identifiable members of the ambiguous scene that included modelling and prostitution. Manet is also a cerebral painter who enjoys the play of references. This time the pose is based on Titian's *Venus of Urbino*, also deliberately erotic but quite without the sharp candour of Manet's portrayal – so much so that the critics missed the parallel. Clark sums up:

> It was as if the work of negation in Olympia – and some such work was surely intended, some kind of dissonant modernisation of the nude, some pitting of Baudelaire against Titian – were finally done but done somewhat too well. The new *Dona Olympia* was too much the opposite of Titian's for the opposition to signify much, and the critics were able to overlook those features the two pictures had in common.

> What the writers saw instead was some kind of indeterminacy in the image: a body on a bed, evidently sexed and sexual, but whose appearance was hard to make out in any steady way . . . sexuality did appear in the critic's writing but mostly in displaced form: they talked of violence . . . uncleanliness . . . a general air of death and decomposition.

> (ibid. p 96)

In the context of Clark's writing, the terms 'modernisation' and 'indeterminacy' are crucial. They indicate his notion of the connection between the substantial but incomplete, not fully intelligible, reform of social relations, and of painting. His argument is massively detailed, but for our purposes can be reduced, approximately, to the assertion that Paris, its physical and social topography, became one concrete and important occasion; perhaps the most visible one, of active reform in the name and interest of commodity capitalism:

> The essential separation of public life from private, and the thorough invasion of both by capital, has (had) not yet been effected. The public idiom is not standardised satisfactorily, not yet available to everyone with the price of a newspaper or this season's hat. In this sense, the 1860s are notably an epoch of transition. The great categories of collective life – for instance, class, city, neighbourhood, sex, nation, place on the 'occupational ladder' have not yet been made into commodity form, though the effort to do so is impressive. And therefore the spectacle is disorganised, almost hybrid: it is too often mixed up with older, more particular forms of sociability and too likely to lapse back into them. It lacks its own machinery; its structures look flimsy alongside the orders and means of representation they are trying to replace.

> (ibid. p. 64)

Thus his corresponding reading of *Olympia* which:

> makes hay with our assumptions as spectators . . . but this negation is
> pictured as something produced in the social order, happening as part
> of an ordinary exchange of goods and services. The painting insists on
> its own materiality, but does so in and through a prostitute's stare, a
> professional and standardised attentiveness.
>
> (ibid. p. 80)

Yet in a telling endnote we find:

> The value of a work of art cannot ultimately turn on the more or less
> of its subservience to ideology; for painting can be grandly subservient
> to the half-truths of the moment, doggedly servile and yet be no less
> intense. How the last fact affects the general business of criticism is not
> clear.
>
> (ibid. p. 78)[6]

But of course one is clear: *Olympia* is matched as 'a picture of modern life in
Paris in the 1860s' by all manner of written and visual documentation. It
will easily fit in the set of 'images of Paris 1860–70'. The problem is: its co-
members will fit in the set of 'important works in art history'. Even more
problematic are the members of the first set that choose to be pictorial rather
than verbal. And yet more so all those artists and writers who are also ostensibly
determined by the social conditions but produce extraordinarily different
stuff, sweeter and less frank than Titian could ever be: practically the whole of
the French *Académie* – which is why Manet stuck out so much. So determinism
determines some, but not others. In this case only the minority gets determined. The usual response is to distinguish between progressives and reactionaries. And, by the way, you are a reactionary if you do not now subscribe to the
truth, that really Manet's *Olympia* is not so much an extraordinary painting but
an unusually sensitive antenna for the social changes then in process. Here the
substrate is subtly but decisively neutralised: it is 'sensitive'. The reactionaries
are 'not sensitive' or they are blinded by ideology. This is classic positivism.

Let us play the devil's advocate. Surely Clark is right. This was a time of
enormous upheaval. Manet has a tradition, a discipline, at worst a convention.
The changes force him to modify his expected subject matter. Drawing his
motif from the urgency of his new surroundings, he modifies his content: he
refuses idealisation and describes frankly, even brutally. He changes his method
too: the space is more flattened; his handling is startlingly more visible. Some
critics would say his method is more honest too; but others may cite an old,
well-worn, even widespread tradition of virtuoso or bravura handling, like
Hals, or Goya, or Velázquez – hardly modernistic. Surely this is a manifestly
causal relationship where changes in the economic order force corresponding

changes in the cultural order? Yes, of course that is plausible; but that's exactly when the problems start.

Now *Olympia* is itself in the public domain. Even if we concede that it has been caused, it is now part of the causal mechanisms of the economy and culture. One of the things it causes, or perhaps influences, is the demise of the *Académie* and the rise of impressionism, post-impressionism, the advent of Duchamp, the possibility of abstraction. These are economically and culturally significant events, to say the very least. They still make fortunes and headlines. Ironically, Manet is actually received into Modernist art history as the precursor of critical formal abstraction through his handling and through Zola's critical presentation of his formalism.[7] Clark has to insist this is wrong. Indeed, his entire project might be understood as restoring the image (in this case *Olympia*) to the true and proper conditions of its production; to clear up the ill-informed views of late Modernism.

What a dire position for linear determinism. Having seen the consequent wrest itself almost entirely free from its first cause, Clark is stuck with the analytic task of getting it back. Is it stretching the point too far to point out the structural similarity between this 'remembering' and *anamnesis*, the return to essence rather than appearance, Hegel's post-historical exemplifying its own negativity, Judeo-Christianity's need for an accident caused by the Devil and its scriptural documentation, even the afterlife as a solution to the problem of mundane life, a problem God created? All of these varied metaphors, and note their universality which makes them rather more than literary tropes, feel bound to deny the complexity their own images of cause somehow come to be burdened by. The parent denies their children; the children deny theirs. Thus determinism cannot recognise the limits of parentage. Children are not clones. Parents are precursors, necessary but not sufficient conditions. Consequences are not reproductions of their causes. And so Clark's restoring to the original conditions of production, as though it were in some sense privileged, is both ordinary and absurd. Let us not take this too sentimentally. Remove the privileges of origin and what might happen to *Olympia*? Shall we continue to revere it? Can we rule out its condemnation as degenerate for political or religious reasons? Can we rule out its destruction when other priorities allow or demand it, or elect to ignore that possibility? Can we guarantee that it won't get chopped up for firewood *in extremis*? Of course not. That is why determinism looks more acceptable and why we are less prone to enquire after the more awkward ramifications of complexity theory. It is also clear that we do, and in many senses should, attach greater formal priority to precedents, 'first' and ultimate causes. The problem is that this strategy is not always viable in the face of qualitative complexity.

In many senses the more chaotic outcomes are attached to *Olympia* as a work. As a painting it does not carry instructions for viewing such as: this is a picture of a prostitute – and though the history of the work is widely disseminated, it is entirely possible to forget or ignore it. Sociology is not viable simply as a view of what the well-informed might do. Moreover, some of the well-informed, be they art critics or critics of the West, may come to quite different conclusions. Despite the apparent reasonableness of some aspects of Clark's deterministic position, the substrate painting is not neutral, nor simply a medium, but a mediation. What is savagely underscored here is the unpredictability of the course of that mediation *qua* painting from the entirely reasonable account in Clark's writing. We do not intend this in an exclusively formalistic sense: painting is as much defined by its procedures and beliefs as its materials. Similarly Clark's writing does not suggest a formal homogeneity as our critique amply demonstrates. Many quite different writings are conceivable.

Another way to understand this is to radicalise the status of the object called *Olympia*. Barthes' distinction *From Work to Text* (1971) offers a half-way stage to grasping its complexity. The work may have a physical being, a site, a proprietor, a legal status. Then Barthes recognises the text as the infinity of possible interpretations. Now we disagree. Barthes is back in the abstract world of formal contingency; though he intends it liberally, any interpretation is possible; every one could have been otherwise; necessity is excluded. You also are expected to take this liberally. There is no place for the religious fundamentalist who insists *Olympia* should be destroyed on grounds of public decency. Take Hitler's charge of degeneracy directed toward the Modernist work Manet ostensibly sets in motion; it is simply madness, not to be expected, and can safely be ignored. Such aberrations are freaky. This is the routine dismissal of difference as trivial contingency, this time ironically folded within a position that contingency is authentic and not-ignorable and non-trivial. What price have we paid and continue to pay for this principled ignorance? More subtly, there is rather more room for the radical artist who insists that painting is over, on several artistic-theoretical grounds, and so the former status we gave to Manet is misplaced. A bit like the way in which astrology is now tolerated but only as entertainment. So Barthes is perhaps a little too sentimental, polite and unimaginative, compared with the vigorous and vicious dimensions of cool, uncool and destructive processes of concrete social worlds.

Think instead of attractors and memes. Painting may be seen as a kind of attractor, a subset in the broader functional attractor that is the need for humans to make visual representations. Dwell on this need as opposed to Barthes' or Luhmann's or conventionally ascribed contingency. It describes a survival requirement. Layered over this more fundamentally qualitative substrate are the more nuanced memetics of what is involved in the traditional discipline of painting a female nude. These may be taken as more conventional but remember: earnings, status, culture are at stake. If the female nude as a meme is truly conventional, then so are the phenomena that rest on it. Try that out in practice. Tell the National Gallery that its Velázquez painting *Rokeby Venus* is really and truly conventional; along with that its price, status, security arrangements. After all, that is what contemporary art says: look at Duchamp's *Fountain* (a urinal); or Emin's *My Bed*; or even critical Modernism; even some branches of feminism; certainly radical Marxism. The proposition is simple enough, figurative painting, especially of the female nude, is as surpassed as the discipline of the castrati or the astrologer. One cannot see the National Gallery agreeing. Perhaps they are right in a deeper sense than sociology usually concedes. Perhaps it would be more reasonable for sociology to conclude that it is not a question of convention at all. That was just a formal possibility that Barthes imagined. Did Luhmann not show that his definition of contingency was the norm? It doesn't stop them being wrong.

In memetic terms, Manet gets hold of the *meme*, 'the reclining nude', strips it of its older associations of eternal or idealised forms and frankly asks: Why would you be looking at a female nude? Could it be a matter of eroticism? Is this necessary? It is not. Neither the *Académie* nor the public thought so. On the other hand, as a matter of fact, apart from the 'new' art history, nobody else has cared very much about the prostitution, though they have certainly cared about the painting in a quite different sense. Then is it contingent or conventional? Not if the National Gallery's reaction to your assessment of Velázquez is as we expect. The French National Collection would be equally adamant that *Olympia* is crucial. Might we not try the fuzzy way out of this impasse? Shall we say instead that the *meme* 'the female nude' is vital in the sense of having vitality? In the sense of being able to interest artists, to persuade collectors to part with their money, to engage critics on questions of quality and meaning, to engage even determinists to decipher the enigma, to still fascinate the sociology of art? Then all of those consequents, the money, the status, the monographs, suddenly look rather more vital too, that is, part of the process by which the meme sustains itself. Though, of course, this particular meme is less healthy these days, Lucien Freud still makes a good living, but the Medicis have become the Saatchis and taste is changing. Perhaps you might care to run the *Rockeby Venus* experiment over at the Saatchi Gallery and *My Bed*. Vital? Certainly more vital than conventional. Necessary? Certainly not. Perhaps we should understand necessity in terms of the need to make a living, in terms of the need to assert status, or grasp security. All of these generate social structures of varying robustness. Set that kind of animated necessity against Kant's spectral concept.

In fact, the story of *Olympia* and Manet's related paintings is staggeringly convoluted in its various courses, both verbal and visual, and fortunately, richly documented. Let us now consider the formalist version. Clement Greenberg was one of the most influential art critics of post-war America. The time was politically and critically ripe. Both political policy[8] and cultural momentum resulted in the promotion of American abstract painting. Despite being perceived as 'critically difficult', its international appeal was taken as outweighing the provincialism of American figurative painting. Greenberg was its critical philosopher. And Manet was cited by him as the precursor: 'Manet's paintings became the first Modernist ones by virtue of the frankness with which they declared the surfaces on which they were painted' (Greenberg in Harrison and Wood 1992: 756).

Frankness, yes, but not a word about prostitution or even eroticism. Even Cézanne contemporaneously painted *A Modern Olympia* whose ironic title and vastly emphasised brushwork suggested also that surfaces might be the key and in fact Manet might be the one making the mistake. Zola defended the nude woman surrounded by clothed men, the same model, in Manet's *Dejeuner sur l'herbe* on formal grounds, namely that colour and shape were there entirely for pictorial or compositional reasons. Soon Maurice Denis had asserted that a painting was essentially colours assembled on a surface in a certain order. More to the point, the meme has mutated. By Greenberg's time it was a mixture of abstract painting and ostensibly critical justification that held sway. Not sex but surface. Even the fundamental attractor, the need to make pictorial representations, had passed to the spheres of photography, film and television. At the same time this formalism is quite different from Habermas' formal consensus.

Greenberg writes:

> I identify Modernism with the intensification, almost the exacerbation, of this self-critical tendency that began with the philosopher Kant. Because he was the first to criticise the means itself of criticism, I conceive of Kant as the first real Modernist.

> The essence of Modernism lies as I see it in the use of the characteristic methods of a discipline to criticise the discipline itself – not in order to subvert it, but to entrench it more firmly in its area of competence.
>
> (ibid. p. 755)

Notice the urgency of the task: 'Modernism . . . includes almost the whole of what is truly alive in our culture' (ibid.) and 'a more rational justification had begun to be demanded of every formal social activity; and Kantian self-criticism was called on eventually to meet and interpret this demand . . .' (ibid.). Notice the imperious form of 'more rational justification *had begun to be demanded*', by some sort of critical rationalism. As idiom or as convenient cultural peg, rationality justifies the urge and the demand. It is by no means clear, however, whether this explains or instead covers a massive autopoietic demand whose fierce desire to replicate is often conveniently ignored when perhaps it should be regarded with prudent suspicion. Think of this urgent dynamic as an emergent property of the memetic field in which membership is enacted.

There is no separate space outside the complexity of social *memes* in which free, formal or asocial subjects roam. Membership and the specificity of memes presuppose each other. There is no different, other sphere in which membership is undisciplined. This looks like an advantage to the pro-determinist case, but in this case the determinant force is not so much economic but rational. In Greenberg's imagery, humanity as the rational animal, so to speak, is a fundamental attractor, an emergent requirement even in traditionally creative fields such as art, especially when modern developments in the economy, technology and culture of visual representation have questioned its continued function.

But just as something like a rationalist meta-narrative that justifies the critique and redirection of a consequently determined or subordinate field seems to be gaining the upper hand, its absurdity becomes clear.

> What had to be exhibited and made explicit was that which was unique and irreducible not only in art in general, but also in each particular art. Each art had to determine. Through the operations peculiar to itself the effects peculiar and exclusive to itself. By doing this each art would, to be sure, narrow its area of competence, but at the same time it would make its possession of this area all the more secure.
>
> It quickly turned out that the unique and proper area of competence of each art coincided with all that was unique to the nature of its medium.
>
> (ibid.)

In social time the change was almost instantaneous. Flat, formal abstraction was in and everything else was out. What is it that makes painting, reduced from its traditional representational role but still confined to its re-presentative media, rational? Nothing. If anything that is less rational. And so Greenberg is bound to fail precisely at the borderline between painting and non-painting, for example conceptual art. All he does is mistake rationality for materiality; the procedures of painting are supplanted by the material components connoted by the noun 'painting'. Why did he choose Kant and rationality when it was so utterly inappropriate? Perhaps because it had become customary. And in that sense it is not so much Greenberg's problem but a structural deficit of our own memetic *habitus*. At best, Greenberg documents the requirements of an attractor and at worst repeats the memetic structures of rationalism in the debased form of idiom. This is not the critic's insight but the bureaucrat's requirement of a guarantee. Perhaps a critic looking for status and the rewards that go with it, repeats the old mantra (meme) with a slightly new twist?

The vitality of memetic-complexes is eco-auto-organisational. Indeed, the vitality of this or that memetic complex is decided by its ability to iterate in a context of other replicative systems in the widest possible sense. This has very little to do with rational justifications which, if anything, only serve to confuse the ontological with the moral. It's more akin to the question of survival. It is clear, then, that the foundations of Greenberg's enterprise stand upon an ever-widening contradiction in which the memetic form called the discipline is to be preserved in its competence by destroying its plasticity.

We repudiate entirely the habitual reference to Kant as a sign of criticalness. There is no necessity, in the Kantian sense, attached to painting. Painting is not a subdivision of the a priori, nor is the a priori critically sustainable. It is important to concede that our 'subjecticity' takes place in a qualitatively different field. Membership and formal subjecticity have nothing in common. Membership is already a concretely patterned complexity and a dynamic in which we are complicit: we have no 'formal' life. It is our immediate *habitus* but also our responsibility to mediate. This is where the crucial schism takes place. It is customary to reflect upon that *habitus* and ask, 'what is necessary?' Kant asks that question of reason; Greenberg of painting; sociologists of society. For them, the answers take the form of essentials, corrections, limitations. For us, the complexity is necessary. The direction of each ontology is fundamentally opposed.

Evelyn Waugh challenges the orthodoxy of Modernist/rationalist determinism with customary wit:

> The whole argument about significant form stands or falls by volume. If you allow Cézanne to represent a third dimension on his two-dimensional canvas, then you must allow Landseer his gleam of loyalty in the spaniel's eye.[9]

Both are precisely identified memetic devices, but Greenberg, of course, could allow neither:

> Cézanne sacrificed verisimilitude, or correctness, in order to fit draw-ing and design more explicitly to the rectangular shape of the canvas. It was . . ., however, the ineluctable flatness of the support that remained most fundamental . . . under Modernism. Flatness, two-dimensionality was the only condition painting shared with no other art and so Modernist painting oriented itself to flatness as it did to nothing else.
> (Greenberg in Harrsion and Wood 1992: 756)

Then Greenberg's memetic imperatives boil down to a choice: either he can act so as to guarantee the stability of the category by making a concrete stipulation and excluding everything else, or he can admit no common property, no basis of stability, no rational justification, not even a principle of non-contradiction. Clearly he chooses the former: the most binding category but also the simplest and apparently least controversial. With immense care and knowledge of his responsibilities, he takes proper account of custom: he picks up a dictionary and finds that a painting is a two-dimensional art form. Green-berg, aided and abetted by ordinary usage, has made the habitual, widespread and destructive linguistic error of confusing the essential with the simple and its converse, confusing complexity with unnecessary, contingent elaboration.

To summarise, we have discussed two of the most commonly cited 'universal' determinants, being economy and rationality, associated in the sociological tradition with Marx and Weber respectively. Painting, as demonstrated, escapes their proposed control and describes its own independence. That was simply a matter of personal inclination and research interest, other phenomena could have been treated similarly. We could have chosen another ostensible determinator, such as gender. The key general characteristic is the expectation that cause A will necessarily bring about effect B and not C or 'sort of B', or that a different cause D will intervene before B happens. This is an extraordinarily restricted notion of cause. It is more appropriate to the relationship of creator and creature: what creator would invent both its intended creature and a bunch of accidents that it both does and does not control? Suppose you say: 'What a caricature. Determinism is nothing like as simple as that.' The reply is, then it is *not* determinism. The loose version instead describes an attractor. There is room for unintended or unpredictable effects, for degrees of probability. Determinism is not to be saved by pretending 'we didn't really mean that'. Ordinary usage colluded in making Greenberg's definition of painting's competence. When it is said that painting is essentially a flat plane, a two-dimensional rectangle or square, a fixed thing, not an active series of loosely related practices, are we about to make the same protest? 'We didn't really mean that.' Then similarly we must reply that the implied relation between definition, or category, and instance is also extraordinarily restricted, as though God was at work guaranteeing the match between essence and instance. Our memetic *habitus* seems more ridden by creationist onto-theology than we are prepared to recognise. Perhaps it is necessary to look again at cause; in particular, cause as eco-auto-organisation.

Kant's humanism is again responsible for the philosophical proof that every event has a cause, even if only in the restricted sense as a condition of human cognition. This means that even if you allow the proposition only phenomenological status, you still cannot possibly escape its truth. Well, single events can have single causes, but they can also have multiple, concerted, variable, mutually influencing causes. Kant's proof is another piece of humanism's truth by default, like the normal definition of contingency. It says nothing more than 'events happen' or 'things change'. Perhaps that does not amount to literal nonsense in Wittgenstein's sense, but it's close. It is an extremely formal expression, highly characteristic of humanism, and there is nothing necessary about formalism. On the contrary, it promotes falsehoods of considerable importance when its simplicity is taken as a reliable substitute for a massively complex reality. In this sense, it does not so much describe the condition of consciousness but the habits of humanist philosophy. Let us think in images for a change.

One of the illustrations we considered to show the import of complexity goes like this. Imagine a large room. In the centre, high up, a net is suspended. A series of materials are placed in this net then released. Their final positions on the floor below are mapped. The first material is a number of soft clay balls of equal weight. The second is a number of practically identical ball bearings. The third is ping-pong balls. We couldn't quite think of the last one, which is why we abandoned the illustration as a practical possibility. The nearest we got was small spherical balloons or perhaps even lighter ping-pong balls – anyway anything light enough to be influenced by air currents. These imaginary materials will 'do' for our thought experiment. Imagine what happens. The clay balls will be inelastic, they ought to stay close to where they land. The spread will be due to factors such as their consistency, their position in the net or collisions. The ball bearings will collide and bounce far more, having several attempts at finding a final place. The ping-pong balls will operate similarly but their elasticity will be different. Their lighter mass will alter the impact of collision or may make them subject to air currents. The imagined final lighter materials will be far more influenced by air, perhaps so much so that the attempt to measure their position may cause further movement. In the terms used earlier and more generally by Prigogine, Dennett, physics, philosophy, these effects on final positions are due to chance. But surely, chance is the factor for all practical purpose? On the other hand, did we not deliberately build in causal factors in the different weights and elasticities of the chosen materials? Not chance at all, then but multiple, co-influencing causes, even though chance is the more practical formulation. What it says in practice is that it is more economical to call this chance, *even though we know it isn't*. As with all rough approximations, this may turn out to be costly.

Now suppose we make an experiment that might conceivably take place within conceptual art; indeed Richter might have done something similar. A painter has two colours. One colour can be applied in separated brushstrokes for three minutes. Now the other colour is applied for the same time. The process is repeated until an alarm goes off, set by someone else. Several painters carry out the task on several canvases. Times may be varied. The results are exhibited. Again we have deliberately restricted the arena. We have 'caused' it. But the actual distribution of the marks is far more radically determined by chance than any of the position distributions in the previous illustration. Each painter is 'free' if only to a restricted degree. The nature of cause is radically changed. According to quantum mechanics, particles are also free in a similar sense. But once the painter or the particle 'decide' a part of existence has been, as it were, laid down in time, this is Prigogine's thesis again. It is part of the environment and a potential or actual dimension in the causes of the final outcome. Their freedom has been curtailed and their action or causal potential is dependent entirely on what follows – which, if any, mark is overlaid; which, if any, particle interacts. Cause is reciprocating, each 'cause' has, or depends on, a subsequent event.

Let us run that over the previously discussed Clark-Manet-Greenberg relationship. Somehow *Olympia* and *Dejeuner sur l'herbe* are caused. According to Clark and to the dominant perspectives in sociology, we should not forget that the surrounding social and economic causes are dominant. The work's 'reality' for those perspectives lies in its original conditions of production. Our counter-argument, following the thought experiment above, says that this is not rational at all. It is rather an habitual or stylistic attachment of privilege to the original conditions of production over and above the subsequent processes of reproduction. Put in the terms of our experiment, if blue brushmarks are overlaid wholly or partly by yellow ones, it makes no sense to insist that the resulting spectrum of blue-green-yellow is 'really' blue. It is also essential to realise that the error is as gross as that.

And further, the epistemology of humanism as exemplified in Kant, and to a singular degree in ordinary 'categorial' usage, as we have seen, routinely makes that gross error seem reasonable. That is the linguistic inheritance the sociology of complexity has to face as its own – a most unenviable task.

A further linguistic inheritance, an idiom, limits the discussion of chance or contingency. Recall Luhmann's normative definition: not impossible but not necessary; could have been otherwise. How is something both dependent on chance and at the same time contingent upon some event? Let's suppose the event is a fatal road accident. In this case the causal chain that places the victim at the scene and the causal chain that ends in the vehicle hitting him are independent variables. The causal chains collide so that their mutual separation is entirely superseded by a chance encounter which now binds them. This is not unlike the Copenhagen Interpretation[10] in quantum mechanics, or at least Cohen and Stewart's (1995: chapter 8) presentation of it, in which the future is less determinate than the past, because the latter has 'happened'. This 'happen-ing' is routinely confused with 'being observed' – even by Cohen and Stewart (see p. 276). On the basis of this muddle Schrödinger's famous cat is 'alive or dead' until someone opens the box in which it is hidden and 'observes'. How-ever, both opening and observation mean event: *determination*. Before that both states are possible, but not after. This has no more to do with the observer than the witness is responsible for the road accident.

In this sense, our thought experiments may be said to deal not so much with randomness but pseudo-randomness. The events within them cannot be genuinely random because there is too much control. Even the painters might have their free will contained, even subconsciously, by what a painting comes out looking like. Then there comes a moment of clarity. In dealing with events randomness is always bound up with the circumstances, the materials, the timings – the traditional fact of the painting, the vulnerability of the victim as opposed to the vehicle in the car accident. In fact it is quite the other way round, pseudo and authentic randomness will have to swap places. The formal abstraction 'randomness' is pseudo-random. Authentic random-ness, in events, is always 'compromised' by the tissue of circumstance, it is truly contingent upon and so cannot easily be otherwise. Randomness as a formal concept, however, is compromised precisely by its formalism, the trammels of its reductive idiom. It is wrong, it is just the stylistic counterpart to something like Kant's formal subject or the simplistic notion of cause. How far, then, does the notion of conventionality in relation to social phenomena, especially culture, turn on randomness in the simplistic sense? This is the pervasive pseudo-randomness that infects sociology as a user of the normative concept of contingency. It is a truly far-reaching problem. Science has a neat description for the issue, namely the 'hidden variable' hypothesis leading to the ascription of apparent contingency. This is sometimes placed as the alternative to the 'Copenhagen Interpretation' which stresses actual randomness at the quantum level. Which is the more likely position at the classical level of social processes?

Laplace's demon[11]

It is a painful embarrassment to linear determinism that things just do not turn out as they should as often as they should. In the political arena the common result is a high level of casualties, for left, right and centre. The conventional, linear response is to blame insufficient data or understanding: if we knew enough we could predict better. An apt, if monstrous metaphor captures this sense: Laplace's 'demon'. It works like this.

We predict that so and so will happen. It does not happen. According to Popper, this means we are wrong. But this 'falsificationism' is more often treated as simplistic. The more practical conclusion, especially when our predictions are partly correct, would be to say that our predictions were not so much plain wrong, more likely they were based on 'incomplete' understandings, data, or whatever. The demon is implicit in that response, if we had sufficient data, understanding, observation, our predictions would be better. Further, a demon that was infinitely wise, open to observation, could store a big enough data bank, could do millions of calculations per millisecond, would be able to predict the future course of, well, just about everything. This can be both dizzyingly mad and irritatingly sane. Astronomers have calculated the forward orbits of the planets for millions of years (Cohen and Stewart 1998). On the other hand, we can, with sufficient expertise (demonic capacity), control quite a lot of things it would be hard to call 'simple'. There are still problems of course: leaves on the line, the wrong kind of snow, adolescents.

We identify two classes of objection which are rarely made quite specific enough in other critiques.

1. *The universe of possibility is probablistic.* This is neatly illustrated from evolution. The Earth possesses an atmosphere that is a necessary but not a sufficient condition for the actual phenomena of flight. That is, flight in the senses used by birds or by aircraft might never have evolved. Or, it could have evolved differently through something along the lines of balloons or flotation devices such as fish use (see Cohen and Stewart op. cit.). Moreover, as soon as one possibility has evolved, say bird flight, it will operate interactively in the shaping of subsequent possibility. This is the positive feedback and mutual causality we referred to earlier. Laplace's demon would not only have to know all possibilities but the histories and interactions of the ones that do and do not 'make it'. Another way of saying this

is that you cannot tell until it happens. Neither can the demon. So its fortune-telling days are over.

2. *Reductionism has an existential limit.* Demons who want to keep their fortune-telling business intact will distinguish between demons and mere mortals. Whilst mortals go for 'coarse-grained' (that is loose, approximate, analogous) explanations, demons go the heart of the matter; uncannily like physicists. With a proper understanding of the fundamentals, at a quantum or sub-quantum level, you could predict the laws of the universe and with enough calculating power, 'prove' that bird-type flight has a higher probability than whatever else. This is Hawking's position, a theory of everything; to know the mind of God. Someone might have told him that precisely on these grounds God is not viable, nor are demon substitutes, and certainly not ordinary physicists claiming to be nearly as good. In other words, the demon is just an ordinary reductionist whose more preposterous claims would require such computational power as to form an alternative universe (which in turn would affect this universe etc.). To say nothing of the size of such a beast! Presumably it still has some extent? The demon is absurdly uneconomic in precisely the reverse sense that genuine limited knowledge is economic. Knowledge is a kind of modelling, a kind of compression, a set of approximating and estimating rules and, above all, containable within a variety of assorted, small heads. Even the most extensive and complex human culture must respect this requirement: if not exactly 'contained', then in some practical way it must be socially accessible. For those beings (human or not) blessed or cursed with simpler or different minds, knowledge of this complexity simply does not exist. For those of us in areas like academic research, it's a messy, provisional sort of existence. Either way, Laplace's demon has far more credibility as a last gasp of the God-creator metaphor than as an analytic device.

If Hawking aspires to know the mind of God, we better be sure what kind of God. This is not the omnipresent creator and controller but rather someone who chooses an algorithmic rule, starts the programme and absents himself from the scene. Perhaps 'light the blue touch paper and stand clear' catches the sense better. It is complexity theory's 'butterfly effect' taking revenge for being so persistently ignored. We may know a great deal about arbitrarily chosen initial conditions, or believe that nothing is impossible or uncontrollable if you throw enough resources at it, but all of those statements depend on absolutely rigid continuity between initial and future conditions. This is philosophically unsustainable.

More importantly, it is also ecologically unsustainable. 'Not economic' is exactly the same as 'not ecologically viable'. Put differently, the planetary ecosystem has invested in immensely localised and developed expertise. One only needs to think how the limited processing power of an insect brain can organise a phenomenon so interactive and complex as flight. The error, the human illusion, is that a projection of its wide-ranging but finite intelligence into the infinite intelligence of God, demons, world governments, command economies or whatever, will produce a more effective or supra-human intelligence. In fact, it produces a being unaware of its own blindness or that refuses to acknowledge any limitation. This is not to denigrate the aggregation of knowledge through cultural and technological collaboration. On the contrary, that is the essence of humans' practical effectiveness. It is, however, to insist on the ecology of knowledge. Somewhat like the inversion of true and pseudo-randomness, divine, Laplacean or infinite knowledge is actually pseudo-knowledge, an abstraction, an over-imagination. The more limited, rooted kind of knowledge is the authentic phenomenon. Crucially, this is not a post-Heideggerian turn, a sort of anti-scientism, or a plea for return to the true soil. That is more likely to result in intellectual fascism. No, we are saying something quite different: the limitation of knowledge is more accurate, more scientific, more reasonable and more likely to lead to practical success than dreams of infinite extension.

All of this seems rather formal and esoteric. On the contrary, however, the expectation that outcomes could be determined and 'disappointment' in the face of unintended consequences lies behind the most profound political upheaval and waste:

> The roots of the Soviet system were rooted in the Enlightenment's most utopian dreams . . . Marx's conception of communism presupposes that the chief source of conflict is the division of society into classes.
>
> In reality the roots of human conflict are more deeply tangled . . . Ethnic and religious differences, the scarcity of natural resources and the collision of rival values are permanent sources of division. Such conflicts cannot be overcome, only moderated.
>
> (Gray 2003: 9)

Or again:

> We have embarked on something – something grandiose and gigantic beyond imagination. There are no more impossibilities for man now. (ibid. 13)

This time the words belong to a philosophising Nazi diplomat from Koestler's *Arrival and Departure*.

In a sense our response to determinism brings us back where we started from and thought we had left behind: Kant's criterion. Experience, the reality of unintended consequences, teaches us that a thing is so and so but not that it cannot be otherwise. Nevertheless, the limits we placed earlier remain appropriate. The criterion is true 'to a degree' but the degree is a priori undecidable. As common sense has it: there is no alternative but to wait and see. The least we can do is try not to make simplistic assumptions about either the present or the future. Some may respond that this amounts to a council of despair: whatever we propose is likely to have unforeseen, possibly disastrous, consequences. In due course we shall argue that action and reaction are existentially unavoidable. But our concern at the moment is to explore further the notions of causality and time that will have to inform our theoretical modelling.

It is possible to perform a preliminary sharpening of the lessons taught by the demise of Laplace's demon. Perhaps the most drastic is the limitation of knowledge to what may be called modelling. This is economic in two senses: it saves us the universe of cost, space and energy resources of maintaining this vast correspondential oracle; second, it means that we can compress knowledge *vis-à-vis* fact. Instead of knowing the Earth specified in infinite corresponding detail, we can regard it as a uniform sphere, for certain practical purposes, as flat, for the simpler conceptions of locality. To take a simpler example, my car is a vastly different model for me compared to a mechanic, a marketing man or an environmentalist. In other words, 'the Earth', 'humankind', even 'my car' indicate a heterodoxy of position and intention, not a correspondential mapping of object space and information space. To say that the 'model' (image, representation, description) is 'virtual' relative to some sort of reality is to miss the point (or to drop it in the theoretical vacuum of post-modernism).[12]

As we argued in Chapter 2, humanism routinely blocks out the complex pragmatics of exo-auto-reference on weak grounds of principle: its outcomes are seen as too contingent, not 'necessary enough'. But its outcomes do not have to be 'correct', broadly or absolutely; narrowly and practically will do. They only have to work ecologically. An earlier example was that birds know nothing about trees in the human sense. That does not stop them making use of their accessible-to-birds properties. The aspirations of humanism insist that because we cannot know the thing-in-itself (the tree), an intellectual barrier has been erected: exo-reference is placed wholly and absolutely in doubt. There is no way 'out'. The evidence of life suggests there are thousands of ways out. True, none of these are certain but perhaps it is strategically viable to do without that type of certainty? Re-think the certain and the necessary as the vital?

We are not back with Kant's criterion nor with the thing-in-itself set against the contingencies of representation. Rather, if reality is capable of sustaining distinct organisms, then it must also sustain representation, at all the levels of *computo* or *cogito* for that organism. This is the lesson of Tooby and Cosmides' 'adaptations' and Maturana and Varela's 'bringing forth worlds'. The clear upshot is that possibility and impossibility belong equally to organism and representations. This is an important difference with naïve post-modernism: 'anything goes' set against 'some things go' and some do not. In this sense, realities, things in themselves, are radically open to organisms but auto-eco-organisation limits still arise. If they did not, the result would be chaos, not post-modern plurality.

For the moment, however, we are still with Modernism. Lyotard (1973) famously identified the beginnings of post-modernism in the collapse of belief in 'meta-narratives' by which he meant the 'unifying' discourses that legitimise the Modernist project. Yet why is unification necessary? Because modernisers *know* that humankind is actually grossly divided. It is tempting to lay this accusation at the door of Marxism, which was also too simplistic, or to point to Hitler, Stalin, Mao, Pol Pot whose answer to 'pluralism' was to kill it. This would imply that meta-narratives are 'only' tyrants' fictions. Also, Lyotard was a complacent thinker, meta-narratives are too entrenched to be despatched so easily.

Gray (2003: 39) cites Saint-Simon: '. . . the universe is ruled by a single immutable law. All the systems of application, . . . religion, politics and civil law will be placed in harmony with the new system of knowledge.' Or Comte, '. . . all phenomena [are] subjected to invariable natural laws. Our business is . . . to pursue an accurate discovery . . . with a view to reducing them to the smallest possible number.'

These reek of an old demon we have met before. But it comes as rather more of a shock to read:

> US policies were based on the belief that cultural differences are surface manifestations of economic forces that will disappear, or else shrink into insignificance, with the advance of knowledge and technology – a view strikingly reminiscent of Marxian determinism. As Liah Greenfield has observed: 'Curiously, Marxism . . . is remarkably similar to the Anglo-American view of the world.'
>
> (ibid. p. 57)

How many are we likely to kill (with the best possible intentions) in the name of unity? This is no longer an idle question. According to some viewpoints, recent events have put it more like this: How many can we afford not to kill for the sake of 'our' unity? Less starkly perhaps, conflict is not a property of the right, or the left, or the centre. Everyone knows that humankind is grossly divided. Every social theory is complicit in that contested dynamic, even the aspiration to value-freedom.

The dimensions of (Anglo-American, Marxian, etc.) determinism now become more explicit. Along with the belief that certain phenomena, broadly economic ones, carry far greater weight or significance, there arises the possibility of a formal analysis of a very specific character. It distinguishes between the determinants and the determined, a classic 'essence and appearance' scenario. Theory and policy will then proceed hand in hand as the rationalisation, legitimation and enforcement of this chosen hierarchy. Whatever fails to be determined can now be viewed as aberrant, whilst every investment is made for the advancement of the 'authentic' core of social solidarity. Of course, it is absurd to suggest that on these grounds there is no substantive difference between the 'authenticity' of liberal-democratic capitalism and that of Stalinism or Nazism. Yet there is plainly an analytic parallel we have been at pains to deny and which must be factored in to our assessments. Innocence is no longer credible either for global *realpolitik* or complexity theory. At the same time, the tactical remedy offered by complexity theory is simple and elegant: rethink determinism as the play of attractors. In this sense, economic-technological determinism becomes an attractor that can bear the play of differences gathered around it. Its influence, its weight, its magnitude, will be variable, not a doctrinaire 'constant'. Where it 'wobbles' we need not predict catastrophe, it is not the end of the West as we know it. It is rather the advent of a countermanding force. Such episodes were hardly rare throughout the twentieth century, even at the height of Modernist expectation.

7

COMPLEXITY THEORY AS A CRITIQUE OF POST-MODERNISM

Part I was necessarily dominated by the re-appropriation of the structures of consciousness for complexity theory. The humanist paradigm is obsessed with epistemology and it is likely that its critique must begin from an epistemological revision. Part II has so far considered the limits of linear expectation in the face of the complexity of social phenomena. We now turn to the emergence of collective structures. The association of post-modernism, post-structuralism and ostensibly 'progressive' political pluralism will guarantee something of a question here. However, we are not re-inventing constraints, fixed roles, the hegemony of the normal, rather we are entirely centred on eco-auto-organisation.

We have established that complex, qualitative structures are likely to arise from the dynamics of eco-auto-organisation and exo-auto-reference. This was seen in the context of the conceptual shifts and interdisciplinary considerations that such understanding might entail for sociology. This is not a surprising development, contemporary thought is characteristically made up from hybrid specialisations, from the most theoretic of the sciences to the most practical aspects of design, engineering and materials technology.

However, such assimilation is not without cost or disruption. That is the topic of this section, how complexity theory, the dynamics of eco-auto-organisation and exo-auto-reference impinges on, especially, contemporary 'critical' sociology. We want to define *humanistic* sociology as a discipline that begins with Modernism and ends in post-modernism. That is rather too clear a delineation for writers who praise fuzzy logic, and we shall qualify that in due course. For the moment, it allows us to continue to focus on the modifications to the notion of causality that follow from the complexity or post-humanist shift in sociology. There are six key points that will be developed in detail:

1. Modernism is fundamentally linked to linear causality.
2. Post-modernism does not ground a fundamentally different theory of complex, plural outcomes in anything but a corresponding model of complex, plural cause. This is usually grounded in, or at least emphasises, the

heterogeneity of human culture; that is, in the processes of interpretation: the locatedness of observations, their permeation with the idioms of culture, speech, text.

3. Therefore the latter tends to lose the materialism of the former. But that is unnecessary. Moreover, it is at least as important to see the evolution of complexity becomes occluded. Cultural-technological complexity, both by action and default, is presupposed as the ground of the further apparent complexity of the perceived-produced material world.

4. The idea that complexity can, indeed must, develop from simple beginnings is not, therefore, treated seriously. There is, then, a *de facto* separation between the ontologies of the 'simple', the non-human, and the complex human. At best, the non-human is reincorporated as the known – as to some extent conceptualised.[1] This is distinctly logo-centric; it exemplifies the Cartesian and Kantian prejudice of conceptualising humanity not 'as' but 'is' knowledge; knowledge, of course, of a highly specific and unconsciously idiomatic kind.

5. Neither generates a notion of causality that links energy in the formal sense, with actors in the specific senses of singular or collective human endeavour, nor the outcomes of action.

6. The possibility of writing a formal sociological description demands distinctly different and contradicting grounds for Modernism, postmodernism, and complexity-influenced sociology.

These statements may appear cryptic; they are in fact schematic. We are dealing with those theories in post-modernism and post-structuralism that stress the primacy of language; the construction of worlds in language. Our critics have argued that post-structuralism has moved on. This is a fair point. A great deal of work that calls itself post-structural and continues to cite, say, Foucault or Deleuze, is properly engaged with the material world of political effects, and environmental consequences of human culture. We shall reconsider such work in Part III. Much of that work at the interface between post-structuralism and complexity theory, has not so much 'moved on' as become trapped in painful transition. The aim of this work is to make the difference decisive. We do not accept the response that implies that we have invented the obsession with and prioritisation of language and so over-simplified the post-modern and post-structuralist stance.[2] As Law so clearly puts it:

> [D]ivisions and distinctions are understood as *effects or outcomes*. They are not given in the order of things . . . [A]ctor-network theory may be understood as a semiotics of materiality. It takes the semiotic insight, that of the relationality of entities, the notion that they are produced in relations, and this applies ruthlessly to all materials and not simply to those that are linguistic. This suggests: first, that it shares something important with Michel Foucault's work; second that it may usefully

distinguished from those versions of post-structuralism that attend to language and to language alone.

(Law 1999: 3–4)

Is, then, the semiotics of materiality a reductive expression or the declaration of an intention to confront qualitatively different phenomena? The matter remains equivocal and crucially in transition. Instead of a semiotics of materiality we prefer the notion of an ecology that includes the possibility of the semiotic, however much we as humans might put that first in practice. Our topic here is not 'those versions of post-structuralism that attend to language and to language alone' but more precisely, those versions that following humanistic preoccupations prioritise language. It is disingenuous to call this 'naïve' post-structuralism or post-modernism because it rests upon and develops a very specific and powerful theme in the philosophy of idealism. Its roots are at least as old as Plato, it draws explicitly on philosophers such as Kant and Nietzsche, it detests Hegel and has absorbed the significance of Heidegger's criticisms. This is hardly naïve but knowing; both persuasive and persuasion. Those who express surprise at the prioritisation of language and claim to have moved on are in danger of falsifying history.

Modernism and post-modernism are beset by two interlinked, different and conflicting senses of human agency. Both intertwine, break surface and persist in a variety of forms in contemporary critical theory. The first and by far the older is the notion of individual, often aristocratic sovereignty, articulated in such writers as Sade, Nietzsche and Bataille, whose contemporary significance is considerable. The second is fundamentally collective and technocratic, from the notion of human self-appropriation in Marx and the ethics of economic rationalism in Weber to the emergent organic solidarity of Durkheim. Reading Gray (2003), it is instructive to look at the concrete history as well as the formal expression, of these theories. The effects of Stalinism, Maoism, Nazism, Imperialism (nineteenth- and twentieth-century versions), to say nothing of the costs of capitalism, ought to underscore that social theory put into action is a dangerous business – at least as dangerous as the arms trade. Some of the key writers of Modernism and post-modernism have disastrously failed to take that onto account.

Sade and Nietzsche are extremely ironic choices for the voices of sovereignty. The former seems ridiculously limited to countless variations on the same old theme. His aristocracy is rather more to the point: he seemed to be in the economic position to do what he wanted. As it turned out, of course, he was not quite as free as he imagined. His imprisonment in sexual variation turned out to be enacted in a more mundane fashion. He enters French literature and thought, then, both as a curiously important and ironically impotent figure, as though the difference between the free agent and the prisoner had become unintelligible. Nietzsche is even more improbable. 'God is dead,' he proclaims. The age of human sovereignty is about to begin! Unfortunately

131

disease and madness did not pass away with God. They killed Nietzsche instead.

Nevertheless, Nietzsche's spirit lives in the aspiration to human freedom. Modernism and post-modernism are shot through with praise for that. In formal terms it does look innocuous, even desirable. But concretely, we need to ask: freedom *from* what, freedom to *do* what, *to* whom? It is essential to see that the innocent lies on a continuum with the guilty. Freedom from hunger is just as able to bring forth death as political self-expression is able to seed the Holocaust. Perhaps we were remiss in blaming the writers. Rather, it is the aspiration to human freedom, the twin of the darker 'will to power' that is the real culprit; the writers simply its means of expression. In other words, risk and price and consequence enter our considerations as they rarely did for Modernism or post-modernism and largely because of the dissonance between their articulation and their history. The course of events was supposed, presumed, to be, if not linear, then not impossibly convoluted. But it was not and we cannot now remain innocent of unintended consequences.

Those who object to something akin to a human nature or condition, moderately plastic but in some sense iterated, and find this repressive had better be clear what is at stake. No one in Europe has sovereignty enough to say that Nazism had some of the right sort of ideas about human freedom, perhaps derived from Nietzsche, but got it wrong in practice. Elsewhere, that may still be possible. Saddam Hussein, for example, constructed a Stalinist state and practised mass murder for the sake of God, activities unthinkable even twenty years ago yet now commonplace. However, Europe (especially its academics) is still inclined to give credence to Marxism as morally and intellectually well founded but problematic in practice. Could it be instead that Nazism and Marxism, as extremes, and many of our more moderate policies, do not take into account sufficiently the dimension of human need, which implies nature, and the variable outcomes this may generate, which implies plasticity?

Functionalist determinism offers a variation on the theme:

> . . . the fact remains that all social action is normatively oriented, and that the value-orientations embodied in these norms must to a degree be common to the actors in an institutionally integrated interactive system. It is this circumstance which makes the problem of conformity and deviance a major axis of the analysis of social systems.
>
> (Parsons 1951: 251)

This image, what O'Neill (1995) refers to as the 'social production of a docile citizenry', offers a cybernetic rather than a determinist structure, yet still requires a parallel distinction between the normative and the deviant. That contested space is ostensibly pacified through docility, but who can now give that credence? It simply postulates the absence of real conflict, the absence of any analytic attention to that particular problem. Such a stance may be pragmatic in times without distress, but it hardly passes for theoretic rigour.

The spectrum in which we are all complicit seems to have moved from, 'it shouldn't be much of a problem' (economic determinism) to 'kill it if it is' (totalitarian politics) to 'what problem?' (functionalism).

> In Parsons' social system the social norms are the source of ' . . . identity because they diminish the potential distinction between the self and the collectivity. It is through this basic identification that individuals become committed to the social system, that they become claimed as members and, significantly, that their behaviours cohere.'
>
> (Jenks 2003: 39)

In this sense, distress, conflict, difference are seen as non-phenomena, dysfunctional, pathological. It is only a difference of degree to give this a totalitarian twist: non-phenomena become non-people. And only another degree to find divergence from the Anglo-American economic norm 'outdated'. We are not offering a 'meta-move' to leave us free of the problem. Instead, complexity theory says it will persist. This is just another way of emphasising the real-time upshot of eco-auto-organisation. It has requirements and consequences. It is also just another way of saying that if your causal models are linear, your predictions will be unviable.

There is a paradox that arises from the more radical areas of social constructionism that we must consider.

> Behaviour is not a manifestation of hereditary factors, nor can it be explained in terms of heredity. '[It is] a passive and forced movement mechanically and solely determined by the structural pattern of the organism and the nature of environmental forces . . . All our sexual appetites are the result of social stimulation. The organism possesses no ready-made reaction to the other sex, any more than it possesses innate ideas.'
>
> (Kuo 1929, cited in Pinker 2002: 20)

Or let us take a similar, more 'modern' position:

> [Gender feminism holds that] bisexual infants are transformed into male and female gender personalities, the one destined to command, the other to obey.
>
> (Sommers 1994, also in Pinker 2002: 341)

These positions are absurd. Critics rarely take the time to dismiss them properly. Both are treated circumspectly on the grounds that they ostensibly help liberal policies on sexual orientation. Actually they do nothing of the kind. For example, the first passage simply disregards everything that could potentially contribute to sexuality. All our sexual appetites are the result of social stimulation. Several paradoxes arise, like: why then do animals display sexual characteristics? Why do we have residual sexual physiology? Why do we then use society to copy animal sexuality? Why does society feel inclined to sexualise us with animal imagery? Either there is a continuity, which Darwin called evolution, or there is not. If not, why are we not attracted by inanimate objects, or animals? All of this, remember, is 'passive and forced'. If you find the selfish gene a bit too ill-mannered or right-wing, what is the auto-organisational logic here? What is the advantage; what is the mechanism? Perhaps the source is society itself, society as a source of evil? How can such a position claim the authority to protect liberal policies on sexual orientation?

The second passage occupies the same peculiar theoretical dimensions. If all infants are naturally bisexual, why is nature so paradoxically minded as to forget and give us only one set of sexual organs each? Here is a familiar demonography, namely that nature and society both found and failed us. They both give the scope for self-sovereignty at the same time as making it as hard as possible to exercise. For all that comes out of this sovereignty is a surprisingly limited set of sexual options. You are either hetero-, homo- or bi-sexual. And into this groundless limitation is poured the apparatus of power, the equally groundless relations of command and obedience. Paradoxical mimicry again, this time of animality and political convention. The probability of these incoherent positions being in some sense true is vanishingly small. They are also manifestly ignorant of the functional evolution of sexuality which is necessary to self-organisation in the sense both of reproduction and of avoiding the inevitable degeneration of copies.[3]

These are not exhaustive but characteristic features of humanist sociology of the Modern and post-modern periods. They represent a spectrum with economic determinism at one extreme, predicting a gradual homogenisation of 'second-order' phenonomena, a monolithic form of society, as a reality *sui-generis*, 'producing' its members. At the other end of the spectrum, and more usually associated with post-modernism, is an extremely 'plastic' conception of the space of membership which ends in a paradox of limited mimicry. The last, of course, is no more than an extension of the second. So we have two models, the first deterministic and unable to explain the persistence of difference, and the second 'constructivist' and equally unable to explain the converse, that is, persistently limited variation. Somewhere near the centre lies functionalism, unable to decide whether it is radically 'economist' or 'constructivist'. As such, it shares both dilemmas, which in turn are the echoes of collective-technocratic and 'aristocratic' sovereignty we identified at the outset.

The weakness in the humanist model can now be more explicitly identified. There is no coherent relation between individual and collective action. Correspondingly, except in the important work of Wolfe, Cilliers and others, there is little coherent analysis of the ecology of the human-social and its 'alter' environment. Perhaps this was forgivable in the days of heavy industrialisation when everything seemed possible, but now it is absurd. Because no credible theory of the ecology of the human-social and its alter-environment is offered, (post-)modernism is unable to provide a coherent account of the relations between individual and collectivity. This is simply because of, or despite, Sade and Nietzsche, the (post-)modern individual entirely signifies plasticity. Pinker rightly calls it 'silly putty'.

This is not the preparatory to an argument for genetic determinism. That can be dispensed with immediately:

> The human genome does not specify the entire structure of the brain. There are not enough genes available to determine the precise structure and place of everything in our organisms, least of all the brain, where billions of neurons form their synaptic contacts. The dispro-portion is not subtle: we carry about 10^5(100,000) genes but 10^{15} (10 trillion) synapses in our brains.
>
> (Damasio 1994: 108)

Consequently, genetic determination of the mind is not unlikely; it is impos-sible. Instead, we are arguing for something like a 'content-specific' mechanism in Tooby and Cosmides' sense. To put it another way, unless the individual has something more than a formal identity (silly putty), it cannot enter into the socio-ecology envisaged by complexity theory at either the environmental or the social gateway. Formality, total plasticity, silly putty, the (post-)modern individual, all signify only this impossibility.

In contrast, complexity theory, in the context of social eco-auto-organisation, insists that intelligible structure arises only on the basis of inter-action. An interaction between individual plasticity-shaped content-specific adaptations (if not 'nature' then 'dispositions') and a context rich in both enabling and disabling structures. Content and context, then, have evolved together: fundamentally they share the same unique ontology. Laplace's demon, that is reductionists of any kind, physicists, geneticists, creationists, constructionists, may aim to know everything about the content, but this specifies nothing about the probabilistic contexts of interaction. The unique ontology is fundamentally one of outcome, one that belongs to outcome, not a generalisable rule of procedure.

Post-modernism cannot be a full-blown doctrine which says: 'meta-narratives have lost their credibility'. It would be less contradictory and cer-tainly more accurate to say that post-modernism holds sway in the social spaces where meta-narratives are disbelieved. These spaces may be large or consti-tute the majority outlook, for example, in the study of culture by European scholars. Or it may be little more than peripheral variation. This is usually overlooked by academics and is one reason why the scant resemblance of post-modernism to complexity theory is entirely illusory. The possibility of a transformation from post-modernism to complexity theory is open, but so long as post-modernism is academically promoted as a general theory and not just a reaction to Modernism, it remains just another over-simplified meta-narrative which in turn lacks credibility. Post-modernism looks like liberal democracy's best bet, and it probably was. However, that age of innocence is over. Determinism cannot concede difference as significant. Despite the illusion, neither can post-modernism; it can only tolerate similar or compatible difference.

The illusion is aural; it depends entirely on this gross simplification: society, human being-in-the-world, culture is primarily constituted in language. This is another version of human as content-free, the paradigm in which nothing is known and everything literally is learnable. It is truly strange, then, that academic post-modernism rarely risks the surrealism or magical realism it resembles in the arts. We rarely hear of fantastic animals, transformations, the living dead or more prosaically 'light weights that are heavy', not even funny goings-on at the subatomic level. All of these are 'learnable'. Academic post-modernism is staggeringly polite and unadventurous and so conceals a deep seam of literal nonsense. On the other hand, its evangelism is quite overt. Of course, this does not prevent post-modernism being true 'to a degree'. Incidentally, that redefines information completely, information and learnability become subject to possibility. The 'materiality of informatics', to use Hayles' term, enters the centre of critical consideration.

It is instructive to see how relatively simple reforms of modern and post-modern positions produce the vastly different emphases of complexity theory. If, for example, economic determinism were instead understood as an attractor, amongst others, the diversity of economic and other imperatives might not produce such shock and despair amongst 'modernists'. Nor would it require the wholesale dismantling of their conceptual apparatus. So far as post-modernism insists on the conventionality of iterated structure, that is, iteration is cultural, linguistic or learned and only appears stable, it is tantamount to a description of structure, through the rubrics of radical constructivism as 'really' or at base, random. Now it becomes possible to level every structure by virtue of common randomness, or be-spoken-ness. There is a great danger that complexity theory will fall into the same trap: complexity will become the new randomness; the buzzword 'complex', like 'conventional', will authorise a manner of description every bit as repetitive and trivial as the worst naïve post-modern dogmatism. In fact, 'complexity' implies relations between relative simplicity and relative complexity, relative order and disorder, in short, inter-activity, possibility, robust and not so robust materiality. We are then at something of an impasse. We might say that complexity theory is so different from post-modernism that we need not dwell on formulations of post-modernism. This is more or less the position of complexity theory from the harder disciplines. However, sociology and critical theory have become so dominated by the critical idioms of post-modernism that it seems important to explain the difference. This is not the place to offer yet another extended essay on post-modernism, consequently we provide a brief view of:

1. The influence of Heidegger and Nietzsche.
2. Disruption and deconstruction in Lyotard and Derrida.
3. The possibility of critical theory in Foucault.
4. Bataille, excess, transgression.
5. Foucault reconsidered as a possible critical materialist.

Some readers will be disappointed that we have not addressed the post-modern embrace of complexity theory, best expressed for us in Wolfe's (1998) *Critical Environments: Post-Modern Theory and the Pragmatics of the 'Outside'*. This is an important book and those familiar with it, and also those influenced by Foucault as a social critic, might be disappointed with our negative position in this chapter. However, Wolfe's key chapter *Systems Theory: Maturana and Varela with Luhmann* requires significant development of our critique of those writers. Consequently, we shall develop the theme of post-modernism's (ostensible) 'complexity turn' in Part III of this book. We shall, however, give some consideration to readings of Foucault that stress his possible materialism here.

We will summarise and then contrast the five themes listed above with their counterpart in complexity theory, that is, 'far-from-equilibrium dynamics'. Drawing on the work of Prigogine, Cohen and Stewart, Cilliers, Hayles, amongst others, we shall argue for a much-modified notion of interactive causality and a model of plural outcome that can be grounded in both the traditional materialism of science and the interpretative-linguisitic turn of contemporary critical theory.

Humanist sociology in its Modernist form characteristically fell back on two notions of sovereignty: the first associated with individual freedom; the second with collective, political and technologically saturated solutions to current material limitations. The latter is not simply collective but monolithic; it demands consensus to tip the balance of material conditions from the actual to the desired. As such, a totalitarian impulse is never far below the surface (hence the resemblance Gray notes, cited in the previous chapter, between Marx and Anglo-American 'economism'). Otherwise, the available energy and resources could not be marshalled. Lyotard's identification of the post-modern with the growing disbelief in meta-narratives partly attends to the dissatisfaction in the relationship between collective and individual, or more precisely, between monolithic culture and subgroup identity or aspiration. Lyotard partly attends to and partly glosses this disparity. According to Modernism, it simply should not be there. It does not accord with economic determinism, nor with the view that societies create their members. Of course, Lyotard is no functionalist, but neither does he address this contradiction frankly. If membership is constituted in cultural practice, especially in language, what is it that grounds *difference?* This may be expressed in the form of the following contradictions.

If culture is regarded as conventional, the concept of value cannot genuinely arise. If, on the other hand, values are real, or even treated as real, then culture is not or cannot be treated as conventional. If cultural (re)production is random, there is no basis for its apparent, differentiated structures and certainly no basis for its reproduction. If differentiated structures are real enough, sufficiently robust auto-organisations for pluralism to be philosophically or politically desirable, then they cannot be random. If these contradictions remain buried, their consequence, eco-auto-organisation, is not even conceived. Predictably, the result is a retreat that confuses post-modern with pre-modern. Hence, in turn, the perverse influence of Nietzsche.

> [With Nietzsche] the new historical focus falls upon the action of the person, the conduct of the self – *mea culpa* – the world is built in my image. Beyond this, the alarmingly analytic, if God is dead then infinity is released upon the universe, upon humankind and upon the individual consciousness . . . This is the new dawn of epistemology and ontology, there is an existentialism here, a seismic shift and the seeds of the post-modern. In many senses, transgression of the foundations of Western life has become a necessity.
>
> (Jenks 2003: 69)

Those, however, may be simply the conditions for post-modernity or for those in some sense 'shocked' by the death of God. For a more obstinately secular reading, the death of an illusion might make no difference. For modern others, including Marx, it becomes a critical lever that exposes levels of authenticity and inauthenticity in human collectivity and the critical response is not individualistic but collective. For others, such as Durkheim, it marks a shift to a reflexive consciousness in which society grasps itself as a reality *sui generis*. Post-modern readings tend towards the 'anarchic' reading with scant attention given to the point that this is by no means necessary.

Perhaps the readiness to embrace so willingly the arbitrary or nihilistic upshot of Nietzsche is partly due to Heidegger's compounded influence. Heidegger's line on the randomness or thrown-ness of human culture or *Dasein* is vastly more inclusive and so, apparently, more necessary. According to him, metaphysics 'belongs to the nature of man' but at the same time limits him to a kind of inauthenticity. This is Levin's interpretation (1988: 45):

> Thinking which merely re-presents . . . is metaphysical thinking . . . Our particular concern is with vision insofar as it either embodies or is capable of *freeing itself* from that body of thinking . . . It is important to bear in mind the inherent *aversive and aggressive character* of re-presentation. As the prefix itself informs us, representation is a

repetition: a process of delaying, or deferring, that which visibly presences. It is a way of *positing at a distance*, so that vision can 'again' take up what presences – but this time on ego's terms.

The crucial concept here is 'enframing'. Allied to and influencing Derrida's notion of 'framing' and Foucault's 'scopic regime' – a kind of placing under strict control. In characteristically exalted language, Heidegger puts it like this.

> Enframing blocks the shining-forth and holding sway of truth . . .
> The rule of enframing threatens man with the possibility that it could
> be denied to him to enter into a more original revealing and hence to
> experience the call of a more primordial truth.
>
> (1978: 332)

Heidegger, then, confirms Nietzsche in the sense of pointing to the, if not arbitrary, then inauthentic mode of mundane representations. Of course, for Heidegger, Nietzsche is still fundamentally nihilistic, trapped within the spaces of metaphysics. This extra, quasi-religious turn is a crucial opening for post-modernism, one that licenses a seam of irrationality to be *concealed from itself* in a manner Nietzsche alone cannot ground. The demand for '. . . polysemy, the many voices within a culture waiting to be heard, all with an equivalence and with a right' (Jenks 2003: 74) rests on this curious interplay.

Lyotard, for example, is for us unequivocal in his ranking of disruption over polysemy. He speaks of 'the answer', of war waged against totality, of the dissolution of the 'nostalgic' modern aesthetics, of the sublime, as:

> . . . that which denies itself the solace of good forms, the consensus of a
> taste which would make it possible to share collectively the nostalgia
> for the unattainable; of that which searches for new presentations . . . in
> order to impart a stronger sense of the unpresentable.

Or again:

> We have paid a high enough price for the nostalgia of the whole and
> the one, for the reconciliation of the concept and the sensible . . .

These sentiments, the denial of the solace of good forms and 'we have paid a high enough price', mark out the complex relationship in Lyotard's thought between the aesthetic and the political. Both are destined:

> to have to furnish a presentation of the unrepresentable . . . The
> aesthetic supplements the historical-political and the theoretical in
> general . . . as a means of pushing the theoretical beyond itself in
> pursuit of what it cannot capture or present, [or] conceptualise.
>
> (Lyotard 1984: 81–2)

The aesthetic, in effect, models an image of how the theoretical-political ought to function: in contrast to totalising and totalitarian impulses, the aesthetic shows how the task, the 'destination', is not consensus, whether imposed or 'freely' elected, but rather that of keeping the critical tasks unresolved; 'finding ways to phrase *differends*'. This is a pale approximation of polysemy, the reduction to the formal concept of difference. For what? For the sake of the post-modern 'sublime', the unpresentable. The aesthetic is the higher plane before which the political is subject, dissolved, deconstructed, made merely concrete, humbled. It is no more polysemic in its intentions than Heidegger, whose later preference for silence is better known than his early vocal support for Hitler:

> Before he speaks man must let himself be claimed by Being, taking the risk that under this claim he will seldom have much to say.
>
> (Heidegger 1978: 223)

With the greatest respect, that is not the lesson we need to learn.

The limitations of Lyotard's position can also be demonstrated more concretely. Phrasing '*differends*' would be of little appeal to Al Qaeda, or Bush, many non-governmental agencies working for humanitarian relief, to say nothing of the urgent need for water, oil and other scarce but essential resources. His position is remarkably insular, or naïve, or narrowly Western. It has the ring of, 'Let them eat cake.' It would seem that now politics (Marxism) has failed, aesthetics, the sublime, must do instead.

Perhaps, too, Heidegger's background influence is less important than the concrete perceptions of Lyotard's post-modernism, which says, in effect, consensus is, and has been, the root of repression. Polysemy, heterotopia are by contrast the way forward:

> . . . consensus does violence to the heterogeneity of language games. And invention is always born of dissension. Post-modern knowledge is not simply a tool of the authorities; it refines out sensitivity to differences and reinforces our ability to tolerate the incommensurable. Its principle is not the expert's homology but the inventor's parology.
>
> (Lyotard 1984: xxiv–v)

Is it conceivable that we thought no true conflict, far less that nothing 'evil', could be spawned by 'the inventor's parology'? There are few other credible explanations for what amounts to blind faith, not even the slightest suspicion; and so soon after Hitler? Perhaps we thought the final war had been won. We recall sentiments of this kind being around in the culture of the 1960s and 1970s. Are we not yet fully disabused?

What is exposed here as the 'form of life', and in one sense the fundamental ethics of philosophical-critical praxis, is a penchant for a particular kind of 'spectatorial' role. In Heidegger's work that is grounded in the destruction of metaphysics or 'representational thinking' and the 'release' of thinking as a 'thanking' open to the 'shining forth' of Being. The political problem exposed by this ethic is the description of mundane society (or *Sasein*) as somehow 'fated'. This not only absolves the philosopher of responsibility but detaches the concrete work of mundane social reproduction as something inauthentic; a series of phenomena whose inauthenticity is part of the spectacle. If it marches to its death in a catastrophic world war and the most systematic genocide ever organised, so be it. There is an uncanny resemblance to a certain person's remark when challenged about his political aspirations: 'Render unto Caesar . . .' The ethical resemblance rests on a structural-epistemic common ground, the discontinuity between Being and beings, truth and untruth, authenticity and inauthenticity. The familiar term deconstruction is embedded in the same epistemic-ethical stance. As a strategy it is not objectionable, it marks out an analytic stance.[4] As an ethic it is far too willing to risk de(con)-struction, a risk underwritten by the assumption of inauthenticity and its cognates randomness, disorder, conventionality, radical contingency.

Derrida's thought seems more informed by the mood of pessimism than it is by Lyotard's disruptive drives or Heidegger's piety. Here he is talking about representation not in the sense of metaphysics or technology's mode of enframing but of the frame (literal and otherwise) that marks out Cézanne's painting.

> For Derrida, the act of drawing itself necessitates a moment of non-seeing in which the artist depicts the ruins of a previous vision. Or rather, there is no initial vision that is not already a ruin (a visual analogy to his familiar argument that there is no original word or thing prior to its representation).
>
> (Jay 1993: 522)

Derrida's own voice is characteristically complex. He begins:

> 'Cézanne had promised to pay up: "I OWE YOU THE TRUTH IN PAINTING AND I WILL TELL IT TO YOU"'
>
> (Derrida 1987: 2, as original)

He distinguishes four senses this truth might imply. First, the truth of the thing in itself, unmediated, but indicating the contradiction that it is also represented. Second, (therefore) truth 'doubled' in its representation, in its 'likeness' in painting. Taken together, these two senses:

> . . . presentation or representation, unveiling or adequation, Cézanne's stroke [trait] . . . opens up the abyss.
>
> (ibid. p. 5)

Third:

> Truth could be presented or represented quite otherwise, according to
> other modes. Here it is done in *painting*: and not in discourse . . .

(ibid. p. 6)

But this separation is immediately undone:

> But that is what an idiom (painting) is . . . It does not merely fix the
> economic propriety of a 'focus' but regulates the possibility of play, of
> divergences, of the equivocal – a whole economy, precisely, of the trait.
> This economy parasitizes itself.

(ibid. p. 6)

And fourth: 'the truth in painting' understood as truth or knowledge 'on *the
subject* of painting' (ibid. p. 7). With cryptic exactness Derrida says:

> . . . I owe you the truth about the truth and I will tell it to you. In
> letting itself be parasitized the system of the language as a system of the
> idiom has perhaps parasitized the system of painting; more precisely,
> it will have shown up, by analogy, the essential parasitizing which
> opens every system to its outside and divides the unity of the line [trait]
> which purports to mark its edges.

(ibid. p. 7)

With contrasting, brief clarity, Jay summarises:

> Arguing against the integrity of the work of art (the *ergon*) he
> [Derrida] showed that it is always polluted by its framing contexts
> (the *parergon*), so that any purely aesthetic discourse cannot itself avoid
> intermingling with those it tries to exclude – ethical, cognitive, or
> whatever . . . Cézanne's pledge . . . is, doomed to be betrayed. For what
> is inside and outside a picture is undecidable.

(Jay 1993: 516)

These remarks are directed against what might be called Cézanne's claim to
'authenticity', or rather that claim made on his behalf by Merleau-Ponty for
an autonomous, uncorrupted access to a more primordial reality.[5] In turn,
Derrida's position is situated in Jay's (1993) discussion of the denigration of
vision as a general characteristic of French twentieth-century thought. It is
important to make clear that complexity theory gives no credence to Merleau-
Ponty's, or indeed other, claims to primordiality. The visual system, on the
contrary, is intensely integrated with other neural circuits, including, and perhaps especially, those involved with language. There is, therefore, no 'outside',

142

for everything is mediated through the systems of perception and cognition. But we say 'mediated' rather than parasitised; 'content-specific' rather than 'ruin based upon ruin'; 'adaptation' rather than 'abyss'; 'counterposed' rather than 'betrayed'. Which of these emphases is the more probable?

The crucial point is not an argument against what in Derridean terminology would be corruption, nor content-free innocence. We might agree that 'there is no outside-text' or that the thing in itself is 'a pure beyond of thought' but that is still to mistake the nature of perceptions and cognitions. They are not, as humanism even in its contemporary form insists, creations imposed for good or ill on a mystical ('ruined') environment, but outcomes of environmental and organic interactions. The role of thought, perception, or cognition, is to differ from environment not as a mark of estrangement but as a matter of structural necessity. And as a similar matter of evolved necessity, perception or cognition is also differentiated within itself. This does not preclude but rather demands the integration, that is the 'parasitising', of content-specific structures. The well-aired term *différance* does not address such relationships or differentiation but rather prescribes dislocation. This is already an unacceptable ethical limitation.

In one sense, the conceptual shift seems small, reasonable and easily managed. Apparently, all we need to move from the post-modern to the complex is a shift from relative isolation to relative interaction. In that way, much of the critical insight of post-modernism could be conserved, though its directions and interests would inevitably change. Yet this seems to be prevented by what we can only call an idiom of lamentation that says, 'truth is not unproblematically open; the possibility of "correspondence" is denied'. But that is no further than Kant; and moreover a lament for a kind of positivism that is at the same time ridiculed. Like Nietzsche, the death of a fictional God has profoundly strange consequences, none of them necessary; all of them drawing on an ancient and oppressive past.

Foucault's position is at first more promising. Rather than lament the passing of a fiction that used to order and centre us, he confronts the powerful spectacle of self-organisation. True, there are traces of this in Derrida but, for us, buried under the suffocating weight of ruined 'writings upon writings', 'images on images'. Foucault's followers, on the other hand, see in him the critical confrontation of knowledge and power, huge and active, not at all a Derridean ruin. He is therefore seen as an 'emancipatory' theorist, or better, critic; and not beset by either the monoliths of traditional Marxism or the Enlightenment's 'subject'. This faith is misplaced; he falls back into precisely the self-constituting subject he is at pains to avoid and fails precisely where he promises most, namely in the analysis of power. One cannot easily recognise a subject that constitutes itself *ex nihilo*, but in Foucault, there is always 'the abyss'.

> . . . certain texts and paintings are self-reflexive, that they represent or mirror their own image of themselves and explicitly reflect how they are constructed and how they function. Less clear is whether this

mechanism of self-reflection (the *mise en abyme*) – which suggests an infinite process of doubling and regression up to and into the 'abyss' – has metaphysical, aesthetical, aesthetic, or critical implications.

(Carroll 1983: 53)

Foucault never seems to grow tired of describing this movement of language towards its own disappearance, one could conclude that much is at stake for his own theoretical position (ibid. p. 73).

This obsession is characteristic of critical phenomenology from Kant, through Husserl, Heidegger and Foucault. Drefus and Rabinow (1982: 87) describe Foucault as a 'metaphenomenologist' in the course of a lengthy critique of his methodology. If this stems from or bears residual traces of Kant's postulation of the transcendental subject or more generally from the radical construction of 'one's own' world, it is extremely difficult to square with intersubjectivity. Kant immediately concedes this, though it was not his problem. For Foucault, whose very topic is intersubjectivity, it ought to be a greater problem.

Instead, the phenomenological attitude becomes imperative. It consists in the 'placing in groundlessness', putting in the abyss, suspension, bracketing, that is, in treating social phenomena as if groundless. This practice is merely a discursive procedure, not a matter of logic, reason or necessity, it is idiomatic. Carroll is right in saying this tendency 'never tires'. It is repetitively active in the supposedly self-reflexive arts of the late twentieth century, especially in its most sterile formalisms. It is most firmly entrenched the moment; representation, culture and language enter the scene, primarily because it is still the SSSM's conventional position to exclude all such phenomena from *eco-auto-organisation*. They are still treated as auto-organisation *ex nihilo*. If this is the point from which SSSM begins, and here we include Foucault as a fully paid-up member of the convention, it is hardly surprising that this is also where it reflexively ends. More precisely, the only surprise is the designation 'reflexive'.

It is no part of our remit to insist that every interpretation, every speech-act, all cultural practices are firmly grounded. It is singularly easy to find chains of invention, Baudrillard would call them simulacra, then depend only on their own precedents. On that reading, the most 'fictitious' of all human activity, the fictive arts, is simply an arbitrary series of formal acts. Duchamp's art might be taken as an exemplification. Then why bother, why repeat, why reproduce with improvements, nuances, new directions? It would be more credible to suggest that some kind of attractor(s) is at work here? If so, 'groundlessness' and 'simulacra' are absurd descriptions and the gross formalism on which they depend is revealed as a completely sterile idiom.

Foucault writes:

> What, in short, we wish to do is dispense with 'things'. To 'depresentify' them . . . To substitute for the enigmatic treasure of 'things'

anterior to discourse, the regular formation of objects that emerge only in discourse. To define those *objects* without reference to the *ground*, the *foundation of things*, but by relating them to the body of rules that enable them to form as objects of a discourse and thus constitute the conditions of their historical appearance. To write a history of discursive objects that does not plunge them into the common depth of a primal soil, but deploys the nexus of regularities that govern their dispersion.

(Foucault 1972: 47–8 original emphases)

This fits neatly with the view that 'Foucault shares the post-modern penchant for seeing the social world as more or less linguistically constructed' (Price 1997: 5). Yet there are several equivocations:

However, to suppress the stage of 'things in themselves' is not necessarily to return to the linguistic analysis of meaning . . .

A task that consists not – of no longer – treating discourses as groups of signs . . . but as practices that systematically form the objects of which they speak. Of course, discourses are composed of signs; but what they do is more than use these signs to designate things. It is this *more* that renders them irreducible to the language . . . and to speech. It is this 'more' we must reveal and describe.

(Foucault 1972: 49)

And perhaps because of this:

'Pure representation' . . . reaches a limit as it approaches the void on which it rests; in order to be itself and only itself, representation has had to displace any subject that could serve as its foundation or referent.

(Carroll 1987: 66)

On the other hand, we find the dissident:

Maybe the target nowadays is not to discover who we are, but to refuse what we are. We have to imagine and build up what we could be to get rid of a political 'double bind' which is the simultaneous individualization and totalization of modern power structures. The conclusion would be . . . to liberate us both from the state and the type of individualization that is linked to the state. We have to promote new forms of subjectivity through refusal of this kind of individuality that has been imposed on us for several centuries.

(Wolfe 1998: 99)

This might be taken, indeed is generally taken, as a statement of critical opposition to modern forms of power. This is unconvincing in view of remarks such as:

> What can be the ethic of an intellectual if not that: to render oneself permanently capable of getting free of oneself?
>
> (ibid. 99)

> For Jameson this and similar sentiments mark 'one of the great ethical fantasy images of the post-modern.'
>
> (ibid. 101)

To what genre does this image belong? Is it an image of the self that accords with adaptationist positions of Tooby and Cosmides or the autonomous subject of Kantian humanism? Does it include or preclude possible reference to content-specific structures? If the former, the wording is unhelpful. If the latter, the wording is 'spot on'. Does it connote the infinite plasticity of the self-authoring subject or the more modest proposition of a certain degree of post-natal plasticity? Either the expression is perverse or else that Foucault intends a 'self' even less grounded than Kant's transcendental subject in that the latter recognizes its own structural inescapability. Is Foucault's 'self' then specific at all in the sense of bounded or even mortal? If not, then it is clearly Subject and not self; formal and not bounded by circumstance or intersubjectivity. This seems nonsensical; how could it not be bounded? Precisely because of the formality of the chosen idiom. The idiom precisely excludes all of those dimensions, all of that usage that would describe the manner of its embeddedness; all that would show that 'permanently getting free of oneself' is a negligent aspiration. Put them in, of course, all of those mundane connections that show not a Subject but a very ordinary self of limited opportunity, then there is only one time when permanent freedom from oneself is possible: death – or should we indicate the semantic continuity of the ethical fantasy by calling it, not death, but the afterlife?

This reading may be disputed, but then we must re-pose the question, 'what does the self in Foucault most resemble?' Is it the self-constituting subject, the formal and infinitely transformable being that inhabits European philosophy from Plato to Nietzsche? What is the source of this absolute malleability, is it self-creation because we stand in God's image; or equally derivative, *because of* His death? Does it in any sense resemble the self of complexity theory? Here the self belongs distinctively to a species and an epoch where it meets a developed ecology of material, biological, social and technological self-organisation to which its own organisation must adapt. Is Foucault's self then post-modern or a regression even older than Marx? Is this a social self or simply the idiomatic self of logocentrism?

146

How far, then, does Foucault's 'self' concur with the ethics of dislocation exemplified by Heidegger's 'man' that seldom has much to say?

> 'For a long time it was thought that language, had mastery over time, that it acted both of the future bond of the promise and as memory and narrative . . . In fact it is only a formless rumbling, a streaming; its power resides in its dissimulation. That is why it is one with the erosion of time . . .' to submit discourse to the challenge of the outside, then, involves 'a listening less to what is articulated in language, than to the void circulating between its words, to the murmur that is forever taking it apart' to the 'non-discourse of all language' steadily, erosively at work 'in the invisible space in which it works'.
>
> (Foucault, Massumi trans., in Wolf 1998: 115)

The poetics are intense, just as are those of Heidegger. The question Foucault himself instructs us to ask is: what forms of power and ethics do they serve? Do they interest us at the moment of aesthetic reflection or at the point of political decision? The sentiments expressed are not intrinsically culpable, nor are Heidegger's, but neither are they innocently without effect, especially when concretely misplaced as Heidegger's undoubtedly were.

It could be argued that these criticisms are more appropriate to the early archaeologically centred analyses which are concerned with the self-organisation and mutual exclusion of epistemes. This is, to say the least, a vastly ambitious project; an ambition largely glossed over. Its methodological ambition, shortcomings and its destiny to self-relativisation is discussed at length in Dreyfus and Rabinov (1982: chapter 4). Typically, it remains unnoticed that the tendency to relativise others' discourses, inevitably rebounding on one's own, is not a suspension or a genuine criticism of archaeological-type practices, merely a repetition: 'all discourse is relativistic, contingent, constitutive etc.'. As we have already argued, this is not so much true, or grounded, as idiomatic and consequent on taking all discourse at the same, maximum level of formality. It does not seem to occur to post-modernity as a whole that some discourses are truer, more likely, simpler, more credible than others. Certainty is sometimes a quite ordinary matter. At the same time, some cultural or discursive practices, seemingly groundless in their developed complexity, may well be responding to some deep attractor that does not so much determine or collect but energises processes of correlated difference.

Perhaps the clearest, and certainly the least reflexive, indication of this conceptual confusion occurs in Barthes' *From Work to Text*, though it might equally apply to Derrida's endless deferrals of meaning. Barthes' clear intention is to theorise the structural distinction between work and text, but the commitment to linguistic priority utterly thwarts this. The work may be situated somewhere, made at a certain date, concede ownership, copyrights, originality and so forth, but 'text':

is a methodological field;

is experienced only as an act of production;

practices the infinite deferment of the signified;

is plural; which is not to say that it as several meanings: [it is an]
    irreducible plural;

and so on.

What texts might these be? A ticket? A political pamphlet? A set of instructions? The proof of a mathematical theorem? *The Life of Brian, Mein Kampf*? Every word Barthes utters specifies a kind of limit on readership and is affiliated to a series of clearly recognised practices of deconstruction. But all he does, in effect, is to distinguish between the most concrete, this work, and 'text' at its ostensibly most formal. Of course, it is not formal at all, it is simply a general exclusion of those instances that do not fit the form. Complexity theory has to point this out. Barthes' position is not a view, a way of working, a methodological field, but a clear breach of adequate reasoning found throughout post-modernism in particular and humanism in general. It consists in the idiomatic refusal to allow the diversity of types.

The humanist canon, in its most formal expression, consists in the relentless categorisation of categorisation, the pursuit of the most universal set. Russell has shown this is ultimately impossible. Nevertheless, something approaching it is conceivable, where all phenomena are reduced to 'instances'. That statement is an example. We need to be sure what this process is and usually we are not. It is nothing more than the reduction of specific characteristics to 'objects that can be classed together'. There is nothing wrong with this in principle. It is a characteristic economy of human judgement. If Maturana's story of the frog is credible, it seems to suggest a widespread phenomenon. In practice, however, we are free-er (more plastic) than the frog and so the pragmatics of this kind of reduction come into play. Is the categorical economy worth it, or does it reduce to inaccuracy, then meaninglessness? Does the 'classing together' work? At a certain level it does not, where the loss of specific information outweighs the advantage of simplification. This is the 'breach of adequate reason', where reduction of specificity becomes excessive purely on practical grounds. It has no a priori limit. The idioms of post-modernism are well into the area of pragmatic deficit. In particular, differences of 'type', for example, of representation or discourse, are reduced to the quantitative measure of instance or unit. Their qualitative actions are rendered absent or obsolete for post-modernism. Further, if the diversity of types is made invisible or unspeakable through excessive formalism, so is the manifold character of their possible manifestations, developments and history swept from view. Let us look again at 'painting'. Think of an analysis from the point of view of extreme compression: What is painting? How will you answer? Something along the lines of Greenberg? Now think of a less compressed question: How does the work of Cézanne differ from Velàzquez's? How does your answer change? The former represents simple quantitative formality; the latter, the interplay of complex qualitative attractors.

It is instructive to put this more formally, to play formalism at its own game, by using fuzzy set theory. Ordinary set theory says that, for example, apples and oranges belong to the category fruit. A Venn diagram would have them wholly contained with the set labelled fruit. Fuzzy set theory has them belong to that set 'to a degree' in this sense, it is only by revoking their specificity that they belong to the set fruit at all. The set is therefore provisional, strategic, representational; a contradiction lies at its heart even in this simple case. The logic, or illogic, is therefore contingent on the circumstances and never without effect or cost. If that is true for so simple an example, how much more will its devastating provisionality intrude into areas as complex as social phenomena?

Foucault's later 'genealogical' approach is rather different. Whilst Neitzsche laments:

> 'What if God himself . . . turns out to be our *longest* lie?' Foucault the genealogist [in the sense we noted above] is no longer outraged . . . the task of the genealogist is to destroy the primacy of origins . . . he looks to the play of wills. Subjection, domination and combat are found wherever he looks . . . [W]hereas Nietzsche often seems to ground morality and institutions in the tactics of individual actors, Foucault totally depsychologises this approach and sees all psychological motivation not as the source but as the result of strategies without strategists . . . force relations working themselves out. [Power's] effects and dominations are attributed . . . to dispositions, maneuvers, tactics, techniques . . . a network of relations constantly in tension, in activity . . .
>
> (Dreyfus and Rabinow 1982: 108–9)

That position, if promising, remains chaotic rather than complex, precisely because 'the primacy of origins' must be destroyed or denied. A subtle reading shows this to be close to the characteristics of Barthes' position. Can 'origins' be dealt with more concretely? Like 'text' these are not of a uniformly complex character. And surely 'initial conditions' can be chosen and justified for certain theoretic procedures? But of course, the echo of Neitzsche's (humanism's) lament still rings through the writing. *The Origin* has absented itself and there is no conceivable way that post-modernism, that is, humanism in its late form, can feel anything but betrayed, ruined, parasitised, contingent. It cannot revert to an eco-auto-organised 'choice' of initial conditions because its notion of causality is fundamentally linear. Surely if the first cause goes, everything falls. Foucault is as wedded to that as Nietzsche. Post-modernism's lament, if not for God, is for a Laplacean substitute. So, we still belong to God so far as our epistemology is derived from His death. Complexity theory, of which Darwin is one exemplar, offers a completely different account of the origins of

149

organisation. It is truly strange that we still have to point this out to ourselves. If Nietzsche or Foucault accept that God is dead, complexity insists that philosophy is immeasurably different if He never was alive.

We read Foucault's position as a double-edged refusal; epistemes or conventions without ground; strategies without strategists. If the immediate 'cause' of this position lies partly in the idioms of phenomenology, partly in a fairly weak politics that equates convention with repression and plurality with freedom, the result is the spectacle of a dynamic of power that is itself without cause. Why should this demonic tendency arise? Is it speech's 'destiny' to fertilise these contests? Or are we back with SSSM's limited notion of causality: material causes are constant, therefore complexity must be caused by complexity? Then the circle is closed: in Foucault the groundlessness of culture is not simply the cause of complexity; it is identical with it.

Nowhere is that more obvious than in 'strategies without strategists'. Again it is groundless, but also, crucially, agentless. At first it looked promising; it seemed to present a post-humanist point of departure. However, a simple example can demonstrate that this cannot be the case. 'Fossil fuels', especially oil, are potentially a strategy without strategists. They cannot become strategic until humankind comes along and discovers their latent energies. At this point, they enter the possibility of being strategic, and eventually the object of strategists' attentions. Now, along with water, they are arguably the most important strategic considerations. Take another non-human energy source, sunlight. It enters the theatre of the strategic, probably many times, but decisively with the evolution of green plants. At this point, its strategic import explodes into hitherto impossible forms of evolution, food chains, ecological interdependency. Now if we obey Foucault's prescription, we destroy the primacy of origins, we ditch the strategists (the plants), then the result is that there is nothing, no evolution, just a barren rock near a small star.

Now the scale of post-modernism's and Foucault's refusal becomes clear. The groundless episteme, the strategy without strategist, is simply an 'energised' reworking of something startlingly close to Kant's self-constituting subject, but this time on a collective scale. Meanwhile, the whole Kantian edifice of certainties and contingencies has simply slipped out of focus. It would be simpler to say that in Foucault there are no grounds, no consequences, no actors, no action, and finally no power. Their presence, so to speak, is an aural illusion, a left-over, a kind of fall-out from a previously collapsed episteme in which the reality of contested positions was believed in implicitly. What was asserted is now counter-asserted, the classic deconstructionist position. Just as the death of God still binds to lament, deconstruction remains the hopelessly derivative counterpart to what was previously constructed. To call this predatory or parasitic is to miss the point; it is far less ambitious. If the predator and the parasite demonstrate their opposition to entropy, as self-reproduction, deconstruction is simply equilibration; entropic decay, the most lifeless, the least ambitious of all voicings. Of course, when God was alive in the

Renaissance of Michelangelo, Cennini or Augustine, deconstruction of the mundane-inauthentic, the sublunar, was a principled position.

If fossil fuels and sunlight can destroy Foucault's arguments, then is not his position simply misplaced formalism? Surely power, not to mention representation and a host of others, cannot exert itself formally. It has to have concrete, that is, eco-auto-organisational, opportunity. This entire dimension is absent from Foucault primarily because he writes at a level of formality that precludes it. This is a linguistic error of enormous scale, analytically close to Kant's over-formalisation of experience and entirely characteristic of European philosophy. Here, it is tantamount to refusing the differentiation in ecology by forbidding all specific terms and insisting on the generic 'living things'. Hence living things cannot fly, have roots, have adapted locomotion and so forth because that level of specificity is disallowed. Kant's criterion rests precisely on 'disallowed specificity'.

It is crucial to see that this is not simply a problem for Foucault, for post-modernism, or for 'critically oriented' discourse. On the contrary, it is a possibility latent within language that he, amongst others, constantly risks actualising. Formal discourses propose to ignore certain levels of specificity. Every linguistic category operates on the same basis and with the same risk. Recognising this, operating within its implications, constitutes the task, the very identity, of complexity theory. Yet complexity theory can be contrasted with humanism, however much their language and analytic ambition overlap. Modernist humanism, especially in its political forms, is confounded by the complexity of outcome. Post-modernism equates this complexity with the open horizon of interpretation and so diminishes material cause to the point of insignificance. Complexity theory resolves this within non-linear, interactive causality in the specific form of auto-eco-organisation. This is not an answer but rather a general condition for framing inquiry. From now on we must ask: Is the model complex enough? But this is not the same thing as saying complex outcomes only stem from complex causes. That is post-modernism's mistake.

Modernism's concept of determinism is simplistically linear and so cannot predict or formulate heterogeny. Post-modernism resolves this obvious failure by postulating complex causes leading to complex outcomes. But because there is no way to match complex outcomes to complex causes, the causes themselves are conceptualised as infinitely conventional, realised entirely through cultural, if not linguistic, production. For all analytic purposes, that amounts to an assertion of randomness. It is easy to see that any act of iteration, reproduction, reciprocal response, drastically reduces open possibility, randomness and so undermines strict conventionality. This critique can be summarised as two propositions:

1. It is not analytically necessary to propose complex causes to generate complex outcomes. All that is needed is a degree of freedom, marginal

differences, interactive consequences for quite ordinary determinism to transform itself into a dynamic ground of newly emergent phenomena.

2. Conversely, one does not need infinite conventionality to ground the relative complexity of eco-auto-organisation: indeed, the two are completely antithetical. The first condition of complexity is the reduction of randomness.

Derrida, following Heidegger, describes the importance of (en)framing. In their hands the concept is coarse, permeated by metaphors of loss, deception and wilfulness, taken in the sense of 'sin' rather than purpose. For Tooby and Cosmides, the concept is elaborate, it denotes a complex, integrated apparatus of content-specific (i.e. focused, framed, selective) structures in human cognitive and perceptual adaptations. Conversely, the framing employed by Derrida, Foucault and similar critics is the idiomatic practice of *mise en abyme* which allows every specific content, however generated, to be treated as conventional and contingent in Kant's sense of 'could have been otherwise'. It is impossible to forge links between this radical conventionality and the type of adaptive 'framing' seen in Maturana's frog, a cat 'locking on' to movement, in other words any kind of instinctive response. This is why human sexuality comes out looking so decidedly odd, caught in the strange interplay between human freedom or sovereignty and animal mimicry. Framing of the *mise en abyme* variety cannot square with even the most general theory of evolution. Take this how you will, argue for a decisive structural break or conclude that at least one of those doctrines is false. Let us take it as a matter of fuzzy logic, breaks and continuities 'to a degree', dispersed, overlapping, mutually influencing, often an open question. This is what 'phrasing *differends*' ought to mean.

By contrast, the postulate of radical conventionality imposes an invariant structure on the present, the future imagination and the memory. No wonder Foucault 'never tires'; he has no alternative. There is one figure, however, in the otherwise rather insular collection of Foucault's folk heroes that can save him from willed conventionality in either the Nietzschean or its bizarre collective form, that is Bataille.

Foucault is fond of transgressive poets and writers. There are at least two questions here. What is the reason for Foucault's fond interest? Why does Bataille fit the specification? There is something of a tension between the two responses.

Foucault's reasons can be presented as twofold, and of course they are intertwined. The first argument concerns what Foucault calls the 'tragic or cosmic experience of madness' which the rules of rational discourse exclude from literature. It is kept alive, in view, presented back to us in transgressive literature and art: Bosch, Goya, Nietzsche, Roussell, Bataille. The second is the more familiar argument that such work points back to the instability and disorder at the heart of being.

The poet and the madman thus share the same dwelling and the same proximity to being in Foucault's work; they both dwell not so much 'poetically in the house of being' as Heidegger would have it but in or over the empty cellar or abyss under the house of language.

(Carroll 1989: 116)

Bataille fits the description through his penchant for trangression:

Transgression . . . is not related to the limit as black is to white, the prohibited to the lawful, the outside to the inside, or as the open area of a building to its enclosed spaces. Rather their relationship takes the form of a spiral which no simple infraction can exhaust. Perhaps it like a flash of lightning in the night which, from the beginning of time, gives a dense and black intensity to the night it denies, which lights up the night from the inside, from top to bottom; and yet owes to the dark the stark clarity of its manifestation, its harrowing and poised singularity; the flash loses itself in this space it marks with its sovereignty and become silent now that it has given a name to obscurity.

(Foucault 1977a: 35; see also Jenks 2003: 91)

This talk of sovereignty, which we associated with mimicry above, is extremely equivocal. On the one hand, trangressors 'authorise' themselves but only by reference to and crossing an agreed demarcation. Sovereignty and subjugation belong, like the night and the lightning, in a binding embrace. It is no surprise, then, that Bataille associates sovereignty with the will to self-loss and death (Pefanis 1992: 47-9). Transgression, then, especially in its erotic forms, is double-edged, it is attracted, driven, subjugated, trammelled, obsessed but bound to break the recognised limits of its subordination.

One of Bataille's most revolting enthusiasms was the 'sacred monster' Gilles de Rais.

We must picture these sacrifices of dead children, which kept on multiplying . . . His crimes arose from the immense disorder that was unwinding him . . . [H]e would sit on the belly of his victim . . . masturbating, come on the dying body; what mattered to him was less the sexual enjoyment than to see death at work. He liked to watch. He had the body cut open, the throat cut etc.

(Bataille 1991: 10; see also Jenks 2003: 99)

This deep association of cruelty, pleasure, waste and disregard is characteristic of the philosophy of eroticism which in turn is sometimes (e.g. Suleiman 1999) associated with religious ecstasy and the sacred, hence the sacred monster. However, the issue can be understood in a more radical form. The fascination of Foucault with Bataille, to say nothing of the consumers of media images, stories, songs, histories of excess, consists in the exposure of the 'void' (abyss, madness, misrule, mischief) through the transgression of taboo. The rather ordinary point consists in taking the act of transgression asocially. In other words, the rules of collectivity are exceeded by something akin to the aristocratic, unbound individual's pleasure without concern for suffering or retribution. What is transgressed, then, is the normal state of social relations. For Foucault the normal is finally conventional. For Durkheim it is moral. For Marxism, depending whether bourgeois or socialist norms of collectivity are broken, it would be revolutionary or reactionary. All of these juxtapositions merely reflect the humanist position, for Kant there is nothing outside of the transcendental subject. For humanist social philosophy, more rational but less consistent, there is nothing outside society. This is simply an ontology that begins and ends with the human form of 'being as things'. Heidegger despised it too but for other reasons.

'Our' notion of ontology, grounded in *general* eco-auto-organisation and in auto-exo-reference, insists instead that the human form of such organisation and reference (our sense of being) is decisively continuous with the general ontology-ecology whilst being a discrete and distinct 'latecomer'. No sense of rank need be read into this. It follows that what is transgressed by figures such as Bataille (in literature), by film-makers (in film), by neither in reality, *is* simply a break of convention, to the extent that it is contained in the relatively harmless conventions of story-telling. But when Gilles de Rais (or Hitler, the Wests, the Krays) act *in reality*, a much deeper universal is violated: *Life* itself and not simply human life. This point is crucial, so we shall set it out another way.

Before, and even after, Darwin, ontology was a branch of philosophy concerned with 'Being' and generally, despite Heidegger, that meant Being-*for-humans*. For evolution theory, ontology is shared with the yeasts and the birds and the plants. The upshot is only just becoming apparent – in complexity theory. General ontology, in this sense, has to concern itself with embodied cognition or the 'organisation of the living' in Maturana and Varela's sense. Human being, or ontology practised for the sake of human understanding, is only part of embodied cognition, despite it being the medium in which the question of the general 'organisation of the living' can be formulated. Again, this speaks not of rank but inclusivity, an ecologically possible phenomenon. In more exalted language, a gift from Being.

One of the distinctive phenomena of human embodied cognition is the telling of stories. Not all of these, but very many, and many of the most entertaining, concern the pursuit of and resistance to vast categories of transgression. The central feature of all of these is the risk of life, usually human life, in the pursuit of obsessions. Bataille describes this as the processes of disorder, or 'unwinding'. We want to emphasise order and disorder, interest and conflict. Such stories conventionally permit the 'distanced' experience of gross forms of violent transgression, real or imagined. In recent films, Spielberg's *Schindler's*

List is an example of the former, Copola's *Dracula* an example of the latter, both transcriptions of famous literary precedents. Bataille and Foucault are firmly and ordinarily located within the self-'reflexive' academic dimensions of this genre. Hitler is equally grounded in culture, if anything in a more elaborate mythology of Aryan identity, resentment and ambition. He too is a writer (of sorts) and a skilful user of the mass media. But Nazism is not confined to representations. The transgression is of an entirely different kind, quite apart from its magnitude. Gilles de Rais is a minor representative of the 'more than represented' category of violation.

What is it that distinguishes the genre of transgressive representation from the class of physical perpetration? Nothing but cost, and cost sharply focused: cost that impinges upon other humans. The extermination camps cannot be equated with abattoirs. This exposes a degree of human bigotry; it is less acceptable to kill humans than animals, though the distinction was not (and sometimes is not) always so clear cut. Also a degree of pragmatism, that is, humans are more capable of reprisals, but this too was not also clear cut. This complexity ought to show that 'cost' is not simply equated with physical effects. Perceived cost, real or imagined, is still cost. Much the same result came from our discussion of game theory. That observation is enough to convert the two classes of trangression in question here into fuzzy sets, one shades into the other. No 'rational' scale of 'real' cost is implied here. Costs of any kind constitute barriers or taboos that cannot be easily undone or transgressed. It is crucial to see that this is not simply conventional or simply 'physical' matter. It is always both, but to unspecifiable degrees. Consequently, transgression does not merely cut across convention but also eco–auto–organisation and, especially, embodied cognition. Humanism, even in its most fashionable post-modern form, always glosses this and essentially becomes part of the speech idioms of humanism: there is nothing 'outside' text, society, belief, convention *et al.*

In this sense, Suleiman's talk of the sacred bears closer inspection. Clearly, whatever was intended, we cannot take the sacred as a domain detached from material concern, certainly not a convention. Crucially, we cannot take it in the Durkheimian sense either, as a structural product of *sui-generic* social processes. Rather, the issue of transgression cuts into the bone of the body of the believer, not simply into the corpus of belief. Again, this must be understood with proper complexity or fuzziness: both bodies, the corporeal and the cultural, are involved but to unspecifiable degrees. The consequences of that position are important: the rejection of Nazism, the Wests, the Krays, Al Qaeda, may not be moral absolutes but neither are they conventional. They are instead not acceptable; a conflict of interest will eventually arise. We therefore understand the possibility of the sacred, of moral systems, or looser definitions of what is tolerable, as rooted within this soil of representation–saturated reality.

In this sense, Bataille's image of de Rais ironically exposes a universal taboo. Moreover, the wasted child, the horror of the means of disposal and the

155

conflation of insult, contempt and self-interest shown in the masturbation and ejaculation, is a brutality 'designed for' but not entirely restricted to humanity. Rather, it is an agony common to many sentient beings, which is entirely why it could be just as easily or effectively perpetrated on animals. Otherwise, animal sacrifice would be entirely meaningless. Nobody cooks a potato to placate the gods. For all Foucault's talk of the abyss, Bataille has hit a fundamentum here: a substrate, a foundation, an undeniable condition of embodiment, a meeting place for many kinds of embodied cognition. And in turn it is recognised in our animality, associated with the mute urgency of the reproductive drive, the prelinguistic voicing of orgasm. How different these widespread fundamentals seem from Kant's brittle, restricted notion of necessity.

Bataille recognises this, which is why we place him 'with' Foucault, but in a relation of (latent) opposition:

> There is no prohibition that cannot be transgressed . . . But the taboos on which the world of reason are founded are not rational for all that. To begin with a calm opposite to violence would not suffice to draw a clear line between the two worlds. If the opposition did not itself draw upon violence in some way, if some violent negative emotion did not make violence horrible for everyone, reason alone could not define these shifting limits authoritatively enough. Only unreasoning dread and terror could survive in the teeth of the forces set loose. This is the nature of the taboo which makes a world of calm reason possible but is itself basically a shudder appealing not to reason but to feeling, just as violence is.
>
> (Bataille 2001: 63–4; Jenks 2003: 96)

But for all Bataille's obsessive interest in blood, bone, viscera, there is still an evasion.

> [Bataille is] concerned to eroticism at the very centre of life but to do so by stressing its relationship to death as the moment at which our individual existence breaches the confines of the body to join the undifferentiated continuity of existence.
>
> (McCabe 2001: x; Jenks 2003: 94)

If this is fair comment on Bataille as he is currently understood, it bears detailed exegesis aimed to distinguish post-modern from complexity theory. To see 'death as the moment at which our individual existence breaches the confines of the body' and imply this is the only and final moment at which the confines of the body are broken is typical of this model's simplistic concept of the relation 'inside/outside'. It is conceptually parallel to Kant's imprisonment of human being in the transcendental subject or the bottleneck of Descartes' *cogito*. Complexity theory, by contrast, insists that eco–auto–organisation precedes the specific structural organisation of the body as its condition and persists as the environment from which its resources are drawn. In other words, the relation of organism and environment is a perpetual constant but a homeo-dynamic one. In this sense, the stressed relationship of eroticism to death is a decisive narrowing; a programmatic but unconscious ignore-ance. Eroticism is intensely more varied than that; intensely more complex. Then we come to that staggering phrase that so encapsulates this ignore-ance: the undiffer-entiated continuity of existence. Existence, especially on Earth, is massively differentiated. Again, we find that idiomatic formalism where one set of charac-teristics or relationships 'stands for' heterogeny. It ignores heterogeny almost totally, yet post-modernism is supposed to be about heterogeny. There is a conceptual inadequacy here. At its core lies the humanistic supposition that 'being' can be equated with being 'for humans' and then of a very restricted kind: the subject, the *cogito* and so forth. The idioms of McCabe's comment proceed as though Bataille's resonant eroticism had never found utterance.

There is another count on which Bataille resembles the complexity of eco–auto–organisation, namely his prioritisation of energy. However energy drives excess it remains a very humanistic concept with roots in the mean morality of Marx's 'use value' and 'surplus value'. The two are about to collide (or collude) in over-simplification.

Bataille's model for the 'gift' of energy is the Sun. Terrestrial ecology also depends on solar energy, with further inputs and more active regulatory func-tions for the Earth (especially in Lovelock). Bataille's 'Sun' is characteristically humanised, it dispenses energy 'without return'; it is 'selfless'. You can see where the idiom wants to lead us. It also generates *surplus* energy. This too is a humanisation; also a questionable empirical statement.

> Bataille's argument for the necessity of luxury goes as follows: any circumscribed system receives more 'energy' from its surrounding milieu than it can possibly use up in simply maintaining its existence. Part of the excess, (the 'luxury' with respect to what is strictly necessary), can be used in the growth of that system, but when that growth reaches its limit . . . then the excess must be lost or destroyed or consumed without profit. The premise of this argument, and it is clearly an empirical premise, is that there clearly is such an excess.
>
> (Bennington 1995: 48; Jenks 2003: 102)

> This ecology . . . is neither stable nor homeostatic, it does not balance itself, it has no stasis, it is without peace. This general economy is driven to, and by, acts of violence, it is dedicated to transgression as a way of its energy; thus we have war, murder, cruelty, sacrifice, torture . . .
>
> (Jenks 2003: 102–3)

It is important to unpick this argument in stages. We can dispense with the Sun being 'selfless': yes it is, but in quite the opposite sense. Nevertheless, it has an identity and so does the Earth: from our point of view a highly differentiated identity. We need not dwell on the details here except to say that energy is, consequently, differentially available. That is altogether different from 'surplus'. The counter example of a hot desert springs to mind. The energy is there, in abundance, but without water it is not readily accessible to life, human or otherwise. From the empirical point of view, then, Bataille is talking nonsense, though it might be more polite and certainly more accurate to say he has oversimplified: surplus energy is a possibility; he could be right 'to a degree'.

Next comes the classic Marxian, narrow moralism: the question of 'surplus' value. True, you cannot argue for the redistribution of wealth without in some sense saying that someone (some class) has 'an excess'. But that also rather ties your hands. 'Surplus' may be relatively defined in terms of inequality. But now it becomes difficult to argue that greater wealth is undesirable, you end up sanctioning individual acquisition and ever greater demands on collective welfare provision. New Labour has the same problem. It has to say 'enough is enough' at the individual and the collective scale. Of course, ecology does not have that problem. It will not be driven to 'dispense' with its surplus but to produce ever new states of the system. That is the essential difference between complexity theory's, or more precisely Prigogine's, 'systems far from equilibrium' and Marx's, Bataille's, or New Labour's 'surplus'. Ironically, the latter, finally, are clearly proponents of homeostasis, Bataille included. That is what the 'luxury with respect to what is strictly necessary' really implies.

Finally comes the requirement of destruction, war and so on. But reconstruction, renewal, development, experimentation, 'not-necessary pursuits' are equally possible. However, so long as you are bedevilled with notions of 'surplus value', all such practices seem indistinguishable from chaos or negativity. This is exactly the obstacle that confronts homeostatic functionalism, Bataille's included.

Prigogine, in contrast, offers a 'post-' or non-humanist conception of agency: available energy. Driving the atmosphere, the biosphere and human evolution, and the planet according to Lovelock, it is not beset by human tendencies, like war, or concepts of surplus. Dissipative structures exhibit energy-driven emergence of order out of disorder, 'recklessly' without thought or compunction driving the biosphere toward increased differentiation and complexity. These processes are not explained or even postulated by classical science, nor adequately by neo-Darwinism.

In the specific context of human social phenomena, one agent is clearly humanity itself and its nearness to equilibrium is massively contested, in one direction by requirements linked to evolutionary development of *homo sapiens*; in the other by the technological action of *homo laborans*, becoming . . . who knows what? That multi-directional dynamic is dependent on equilibrated structures of immense variety that can yield such things as energy, transformable structures, cutting tools, recording devices. Always remembering that humankind is the latecomer of terrestrial ecology and evolution itself. What we want to stress, along with Bataille, is that solar energy is the major driving force at least of our current evolutionary state. But we think Batialle's picture is too humanised and strangely unimaginative. We also want to agree with Prigogine on the crucial function of thermodynamics, especially 'minimised entropy production', but we are less interested in the contrast of the limits of 'linear' scientific modelling or in categorisation than in the dynamics of inter-action.

We began with Foucault's abyss at the heart of language and formulated as a programme that confined itself to the horizons of being expressed, almost exclusively, within the confines of human language. As a limited strategy this is not objectionable, indeed every 'putting in question' involves something of the sort so far as language is at all involved. As a general doctrine or worldview it becomes at best an idiom used by certain classes of people about certain classes of phenomena, and at worst simply ludicrous. It is easy to find both positions regularly expressed in the academy, politics, the media, chatter.

The 'abyss' underlying Bataille's eroticism invoked a rather more concrete series of drives, taboos and intelligibilities of fundamental, possibly universal proportions, at least for the so-called higher animals. The abyss became the planet, the motivations, pain and risk inextricably linked to its ecology. The abyss declared itself as a different, complex reality that could not be subsumed under the rhetoric or prejudices of humanism. What emerged from this relationship of 'mimicry and creativity' was a reinforcement of the concept of relative plasticity that has reappeared throughout this discourse, from mental to evolutionary processes, from discussion of probability and strategy, in short from eco-auto-organisation.

Finally we examined the generalised concept of thermodynamic cause, contrasting Bataille's story of solar gift and human 'excess' with the notion of increasing complexity in dissipative systems as negative entropy 'machines'. These processes are still bound by limits given by the availability of external useful energy and by interaction between components. In the sphere of the human sciences, this especially requires a strong or content-specific or adaptive notion of human nature (or need, or history, or motivation) to ground that interaction. Dissipative systems, time, complexity itself, are only possible on the basis of equilibrated and near-to-equilibrium phenomena. This again is a description of a 'nested' ontology built on relative plasticity; a theory of eco-auto-organisation replacing the reciprocals of infinite plasticity and universal randomness.

In this context, we can briefly re-examine the claims that Foucault can be read as a theorist 'attentive to material conditions'. Olssen (1999) addresses Foucault's 'modified realism' and gives time to 'considering Foucault as a historical materialist'. First there is the contested notion of an epistemological break in his output. Olssen cites Poster (1984), Mahon (1992), Dreyfus and

Rabinow (1983), (Barrett 1988), (Smart 1985), amongst others, to underscore a movement in interest, roughly from 1968, from discourse to practices.

> There remains, however, a continuity between Foucault's earlier and later periods of writing. Although Foucault's later analysis adopts new methods and strategies, and explores new problems, there is no repudiation of the central theoretical insights of *The Archaeology of Knowledge*. There are shifts of emphasis as well in the problems of interest, and he becomes more manifestly materialist in the sense that he elaborates a theory of power, but there is no disqualification of his insights in *The Archaeology*. Moreover, *The Archaeology* can plausibly be read in a fundamentally materialist way. This view also accords with Foucault's own view that too much had been made of a supposed contrast between his earlier and his later writings: 'I have said nothing different from what I was already saying'.
>
> (Olssen 1999: 41)

Or again:

> The unavoidability of discursive mediation is not changed in Foucault's post-1968 period, yet in his works of the 1970s – *Discipline and Punish* and *The History of Sexuality*, Volume 1 – practice becomes increasingly emphasized as that which exists independent of inter- pretation and as separate from discourse. This increasing recognition of material practice correlates with Foucault's shift in method from archaeology to genealogy. In focusing on archaeology, Foucault emphasizes the structure of the discursive, whereas in focusing on genealogy he gives greater weight to practices and institutions.
>
> (ibid. p. 43)

Whereas Smart says:

> 'a change in Foucault's value relationship to his subject matter' from the 'relative detachment' of archaeology to a 'commitment to critique' characteristic of genealogy.
>
> (Smart 1985: 48)

These comments are fair enough and it is clear that the 'genealogical turn' carries with it a greater commitment to critical engagement. However, is this materialism enough? Compared with the materialism of neo-Marxism, it is somewhat restrained, allowing an autonomy, even a poetic autonomy, to the discursive that neo-Maxism would not, despite the dialectical inclusion of the relations of formulation alongside the relations of production. The problem is the character of this discursive autonomy itself. It may 'reflect' or 'associate'

160

with the materiality of power and institutions, and this is materialism of a sort. But it is not that established in the concepts of auto-eco-organisation and auto-exo-reference. Foucault's discursive and material are loosely bound, they do not form a hyper-networked ontology but differently constituted realms, somehow, and usually mysteriously coming into causative relation. It is this dislocation, again structurally similar to the basic idioms of humanism, that allows the madness of such as Gilles de Rais to be 'interesting' when it is clearly pathological, unacceptable, marginal and largely irrelevant.

Consequently, Foucault's the 'dissident' is also marginalised, not quite in the Heiddegerian sense of passive sanction of the monstrosity of Nazism, but rather in the sense of being confined to a kind of intellectualism, an ironic form of critique, much like Socrates, a preoccupation with the more exotic reaches of sexuality but above all in the intellectual's withdrawal from the dirty business of front-line politics. Of course, critical academics, neo-Foucauldians included, are apt to confuse political postures within academic writing with the real thing. We are not claiming anything more 'active' – only the awareness that the reappropriation of complexity theory to *realpolitik* would require massive work of structural and institutional transformation. The same is even more true of the latent materialism of Foucault.

It is now possible to complete this section with a postscript rather more analytic in tone. It will in turn set the scene for the next part of our study. Recall Law's position outlined at the opening of this chapter:

> [D]ivisions and distinctions are understood as *effects or outcomes*. They are not given in the order of things . . . [A]ctor-network theory may be understood as a semiotics of materiality. It takes the semiotic insight, that of the relationality of entities, the notion that they are produced in relations, and this applies ruthlessly to all materials and not simply to those that are linguistic. This suggests: first, that it shares something important with Michel Foucault's work; second that it may usefully distinguished from those versions of post-structuralism that attend to language and to language alone.
>
> (Law 1999: 3–4)

We repeat: is the semiotics of materiality a reductive expression or the declaration of an intention to confront qualitatively different phenomena? The matter remains equivocal and in transition. Instead of a semiotics of materiality we prefer the notion of an ecology that includes the possibility of the semiotic, however much we as humans might put that first 'in practice'. It is now possible to focus our objections more specifically. Law's position (following, for example, Dillon 1993 op.cit.) reflects a radical form of relationality: '. . . distinctions are understood as *effects or outcomes*. They are not given in the order of things.' This 'semiotic insight' – the assertion that qualitative distinctiveness is 'only' the outcome of relation may now be contrasted with what we might call the auto-eco-organisational insight. It appears to us that there is an implicit confusion in the semiotic insight. First, it draws on the well-rehearsed and entirely correct notion of the arbitrary character of the signifier. Despite, then, the close similarity in spelling and pronunciation between 'battle' and 'cattle', this resemblance is arbitrary and the 'substance' of each term is given by the relations of usage. In passing, it should be noted that visual representations, pictorial signifiers cannot operate in terms of this arbitrary relation: there must be some form of appropriate resemblance. However, Law wants to extend this insight 'ruthlessly to all *materials*'. What are we to understand by this? Is the implicit suggestion that the signified too is arbitrary, or that the signified only exists 'in relation to'? Surely this is what ecology also says.

The answer, however, is negative. It is precisely because the elements of ecological relationships are not arbitrary that they can authentically form the elements of ecological relationships. Both the elements and the system of relationships are necessary. Prigogine notes that the elements of a population 'count' or become energised and are active in the formation of complex dynamics. Whilst different ecologies are possible, unlike language items, their elements cannot be translated precisely because the dimension of arbitrary signification is absent. There is, then, an 'outside text' which is conceptually no more difficult than the mundane absence of a conceptualising human. The immense practical difficulty of effective conceptual, visual or sensory adaptation is then not to be understood through the 'semiotic insight' but through the quite different requirement of auto-exo-reference in the maintenance of complex open systems. Conversely, the arbitrariness of the linguistic signifier only presents itself through and in an ecological space that both allows that character and demonstrates its functional economy over other systems, such as laborious pictorial resemblances. To a reader who cannot grasp, agree with or finds trivial this qualitative distinction, we can only say: then *draw* 'battle' and 'cattle'. From what does the difficulty arise: the graphic trace or the robust complexity of its referents?

This principle, that the irreducibility of a system to the sum of its parts does not make the parts trivial, has a counterpart. Just as the interaction of elements, and chance and environment, constitutes the extra dimensions of systematicity – an interaction based on the further irreducibilty or qualitative specifics of the elements – so the concept of autonomy applied to human or social action is marked by this complex duality. Unlike the sovereign individual, or what Rorty calls Foucault's 'knight of autonomy'; utterly unlike the analytic upshot of 'to refuse what we are' (op. cit.); or Wolfe's translation 'what can be the ethic of an intellectual if not that: to render oneself permanently capable of getting free of oneself?' (Wolfe 1999 op. cit.). The individual who is simultaneously member is both subject and object. Hence the distinction between Bataille whose autonomy derives from his writing literature and those like Hitler whose autonomy impinges upon others directly, again derived and 'permitted' through political structure. The distinction – author/autocrat – is then dependent on the 'robust complexity' of an ecology of systems whose qualitative character(s) make possible and impossible specific, differentiated outcomes, not all of them intended. That is, of course, to say nothing of equally robust and essential substrates of biological and genetic forms.

The reciprocity of systems and their elements must be strongly qualified by the temporal priority of both components and, in the case of systems far from equilibrium, available environmental energy. Such relations are causal and the interrelation that makes the relationships non-linear is still bound by the direction of time. This is precisely Prigogine's requirement. By contrast, the semiotic insight does not see time in respect of signified–signifier (always written the other way round), element and system, or individual and member. Neither are the substantive elements of causality, linear or not, analysed: they remain merely and formally power. Whereas energy is always manifest in qualitative (re)organisations of non-trivial elements.

8

COGNITION AND THE RENEWAL
OF SYSTEMS THEORY
Redundant idioms and disputed positions

Our purpose is not an account of general systems theory or to comment on renewal in the historical sense. Our orientation is qualitative in that we are especially interested in social systems and the status of information, communication and culture. The analytic project is therefore both the means and the object of its own inquiry, but it is not the sole object. From the number of 'systems' thinkers that could have been chosen, we continue to prioritise Prigogine, and to extend our critique of Maturana and Varela, by drawing on the work of Plotkin and Dennett. Eventually this shall extend to a reappraisal of Luhmann's transformative use of their concepts. This is, then, a focused rather than a general study, though it will primarily explore the most basic characteristic of systems theory: the distinction between systems and environment. That distinction and its implications remain badly theorised and philosophically inadequate. These selected thinkers are concerned with theorising the systems and environment relation in terms of the transfer of energy, operational closure along with structural coupling and communication. Priority will be given to Prigogine's (homeo)dynamics rather than the autopoietic closures currently espoused by the others, but the implications and outcomes are not that simple. We seek to re-unite these opposed positions but the work of re-examination falls on the 'autopoietic' side, which is where the 'redundant idioms and disputed positions' are most strongly clustered.

Prigogine's position is important because of an ontology based on the transformations of energy. This is not the place to explore the identity or relation of matter and energy. It is, however, of central importance to provide a coherent and common ontology of external cause, together with the limitations imposed by chance, otherwise we are left with an account of autopoietic processes *ex nihilo*.

Prigogine, then, provides the crucial insight that the organisational complexity exhibited in systems far from equilibrium, including living systems, is a 'solution', possibly a necessary, optimal, or better solution to the transfer of energy from environment to system. If the transfer is seen as a local increase in disorder, turbulence or pressure, then the organisational complexity is an 'order from noise' solution. That is, these systems exhibit active mediation, not passively reproducing equilibria. It is easy enough to remark that such systems are by definition open and only loosely analogous to the regulated openness or closure of a simple cell – to say nothing of more complex organisms, social or communication systems. But the question remains: open in what sense? Certainly not that sense in which the barrier or the autopoietic process itself generates a dualism reminiscent of the persistent bane of European philosophy. This is the possible fate of radical constructivism which, like Kant, prioritises the synthesis or self-organisation of organism and cognitive processes. Rather, energy is seen to be the common origin of the difference grasped here, as the system, as 'in receipt' and therefore as the very reproduction of its qualitative character. And grasped there, as an environment of systems, as qualitatively defining both itself and the type of energy in the event of transfer. Given the importance Prigogine attaches to time and irreversibility, it is necessary to understand this mutual determination chronologically. The transfer has an 'arrow', a history of 'initial' conditions. This does not preclude but rather organises the character of mutuality or 'feedback'. In exactly the same sense, the transfer organises the character of the mutual spaces inherent in the distinctions between system and an environment of systems. At some threshold this 'organised character of mutuality' must involve an increasing informational component. This follows because of the degree of freedom, chance, and non-linearity in the relations between components. Indeed, recursion in such circumstances demands information. If life is seen as driving against entropy, information is life's means of reproduction and navigation.

The intellectual customs of European philosophy have persistently failed to find any viable formulation of the difference between systems and environment in its various forms; especially that implied in the difference between knowledge and environment.

Much the same can be said of sociology. The result is a continual, tragic repetition of estrangement, caught perfectly by Derrida's sense of knowing as ruin built on ruin. We thus require a diversion into cognitive theory as it is presented in biology and, associated with that, a discussion of adaptation or 'structural coupling' with environment which draws on contentious issues in evolutionary theory. The point of this diversion is the transfer of some theoretic tools into theoretical sociology, especially the sociology of knowledge. The focus is again *complexity*, here energised in terms of the difference between organism and environment.

Every organism reconstructs, represents or constitutes its environment. The case made for complexity theory was that this was analytically coupled with the idea that the environment constitutes the possibility of both the organism and its representations. These two themes are ineradicable from the disciplines of Western critical thought. However, we are not content with either their formulation or opposition in the traditional divide between idealism-constructivism-innatism and empiricism. Before we consider the complexities of 'viable' radical constructivism, it is necessary to dispose of the forms of that orientation that are completely unreasonable. In other words, we are speaking of an ill-founded theoretic habit. Ironically, since his *Steps Toward an Ecology of Mind* appears close to the position argued here, we propose to examine one of Gregory Bateson's lectures as an exemplar of non-viable constructivism. We propose to treat this with humour. Bateson is not above calling his audience 'insane', thus we shall treat like with like.

> First, I would like you to join me in a little experiment. Let me ask you for a show of hands. How many of you will agree that *you see me*? I see a number of hands – so I guess insanity loves company. Of course *you* don't 'really' see *me*. What you really 'see' is a bunch of pieces of information about me, which you synthesise into a picture of me. You make that image, it's that simple.
>
> (Bateson 1972, 2000: 486)

The explosion of italics and scare quotes ought to give sufficient warning that this is an old conjuring trick. However, up go the dutiful hands, as they have for centuries. Bateson makes his joke: Aren't you all *silly*? Not one hand throws an egg, or a tomato in response. Perhaps Bateson was right, perhaps we, his audience, are insane.

Though tedious we have to concede that Bateson's ploy is generally effective. Did you go along with it? It works as follows. You ask: *Can you see me?* By 'me' you intend unspecified but sufficient visual information to convince a viewer you are there. Naturally the hands go up. Now you tacitly change the meaning of 'me'. You say: *Oh no you can't*. Strangely, the audience does not reply: *Oh yes we can*. Still unspecified, you rely on their intelligence to fill in something like: Oh, he must mean the 'real' me, all of it, not just the bits I can see at the moment. Then you reply with the devastating punchline: *What you really 'see' is pieces of information about me which you synthesise*. The audience politely giggles when it should say: *That's what we meant in the first place!*

You probably wouldn't get away with this kind of thing anywhere else than a 'critical' theory-oriented gathering. *Oh yes we can* would be much more likely. Then there is the classic scenario in a rough pub: *Who are you looking at?* You wouldn't have enough time to split hairs about the meaning of me or you before you got a split lip. Perhaps 'critical' theory should just be a little less polite. In fact, there is a deeper linguistic custom underlying the 'critical' response. 'Me' has both a precise, even correspondential, meaning: the person speaking. But it also indicates the space of a possible series of predications, not necessarily congruent: me as I am, as I was, as I will be, me if, me without, me *as*. You can see the first me, if I'm here, *to a degree*. You cannot, in principle, see the predicative space indicated by 'me as' without further specification. It is absolutely essential to see that the custom of treating these *together* is logically incorrect. Put more sharply, there is an historic error in 'critical' custom. The error is produced by generalisation, or formalisation, as follows.

Quite rightly, the critical stance does not *only* want to refer to the 'me' visible to a degree. That would amount to relying on anecdotal or partial evidence. Critically speaking, one *wants* to consider the whole. That is where the error seeds itself: 'me' is taken as a set of possibilities *including* the 'me' visible to a degree *and* the 'me as' predicative space. What could be more natural? In fact, it's wrong. Both versions of 'me' are qualitatively different, but their sharpness is blunted by visibility *to a degree*. Similarly, 'me' is neither a set nor category. It is so open that an affirmative answer to the question *Can you see me?* is both true and untrue to a degree. Like experience, like the thing in itself, like me 'in myself' – all of these are accessible to a degree. Not, as Kant says, 'a pure *beyond* of thought'. This will turn out to have profound implications for the distinction between system and environment.

Let's rework the argument from the concluding position we took in Chapter 2. There we argued that the 'thing in itself' (the me in myself) had a 'fuzzy' meaning. If you like, it was conceivable as a fuzzy set of all the predicates that could be asserted about this thing/me. Notice that we have an odd infinity here. On the one hand, the thing/me is bounded by tacit specification. On the other hand, we agree that the specification can be breached. To stretch the point, a piece of 'me' might become a soil particle in due course. Alongside the space of predication, then, lies a space of contradiction, not primarily linguistic but 'in the world'. The thing or me is open to infinite extension but also to precise limitation. I may be 'seen', killed, consumed by wolves, recycled as organic matter. Then the space of predication is routinely invaded, sometimes with fatal results, by the space of contradiction. But the spaces of predication and contradiction are in principle unrelated or are only related empirically. I happen to be seen, or whatever. Then it is clear that the thing or me 'in itself' is a concept void of chance, insulated from impact, a hermetically sealed 'black box' of infinite extent, since there is literally nothing to limit it. Such boxes can have no conceivable place within the ecology of system and environment. The in-itself, Bateson's 'me-myself' can and must be excluded from systems theory. It is then of the utmost importance to distinguish the notion of autopoiesis from the 'black box' it sometimes resembles or is conflated with in Luhmann.[1] Actually this distinction is not up for description because it has not been analysed. It is questionable whether it can be analysed. In any event, it will affect the fate of autopoiesis, related notions of operational closure and structural coupling.

Recall the example in the previous chapter where apples and oranges only belonged to the set 'fruit' to a degree, to the extent that specific characteristics are ignored. Logic and illogic stood together. We can now see that a concept as narrow as 'me' is beset by the same contradiction, simply by its extent, whether understood temporally, partially, conceptually, as an energised process generating an informational and material structure, or as an organism distinguished from but dependent on an environment. Like the Cretan who announces 'All Cretans are liars', this problem – and it is a problem, not a paradox – underlies every conceptual formulation.

We now turn to a more extensive analysis of the model of cognition advanced by Maturana and Varela, especially in Varela's later work.

Recall this passage we cited earlier:

> The living system is autonomous, however. The environment only triggers the changes; it does not specify them . . . By specifying which peturbations from the environment trigger its changes the system 'brings forth a world' . . . Cognition, then, is not a representation of an independently existing world but a continual *bringing forth* . . . to live is to know . . . cognition is embodied action.'
>
> (IOC 30; Capra 1996: 261)

And the rather uneasy truce outlined in our response:

> But the philosophy of complexity would never, ever have formulated such an absurdity as 'the organism bringing forth worlds' without insisting that this is analytically identical to 'the world bringing forth organisms'. If the former is absurd on grounds of auto-*eco*-organisation, the latter appears self-cancelling. Then we appear to have said nothing yet a compelling sense persists. Perhaps the fault lies with the saying rather than the sense.
>
> (p. 39 above)

Varela, Thompson and Rosch (1993 and 2000) develop the concept of living systems' autonomy in relation to 'post-' rather than 'neo-' Darwinist evolutionary theory. First they define *cognitivism* in order to distinguish themselves from it in due course.

> The central tool and guiding metaphor of cognitivism is the digital computer . . . A computation is an operation carried out on symbols, that is, on elements that *represent* what they stand for.
>
> (p. 7, original emphasis)

The first criticism of cognitivism is surprisingly pragmatic. Representations, symbols and their processing are 'local': serial, sequential and chainlike. Any malfunction is likely to be globally devastating. Whereas:

> *Connectionist* models generally trade localised, symbolic processing for distributed operations (ones that extend over an entire network of components) and so result in the emergence of global properties resilient to malfunction. For connectionists a representation consists

in the correspondence between such an emergent global state and properties of the world; it is not a function of particular symbols.

(p. 8)

The terms 'representation' and 'correspondence' are questionable here, at least inconsistent with the way the argument is subsequently developed. The sense would be better expressed as a relation between a complex network and a complex environment, both of which can exhibit quasi-specific or fuzzy 'states'. Obviously, the term 'representation' becomes radically unstable:

> We propose as a name the term *enactive* to emphasize the growing conviction that cognition is not the representation of a pregiven world by a pregiven mind but is rather the enactment of a world and a mind on the basis of the variety of actions that a being in the world performs.
>
> (p. 9)

This, then, is a type of 'radical constructivism' though rather better grounded than others of the same orientation. It presents a particular problem to which the response is necessarily complex: in speaking of the 'actions of a being', are we speaking of a self-constituting autonomy something like a subject? If so, why should it persistently reconstruct its characteristic 'self'? For example, as a human, a member of a species or a society with an identifiable culture. Or is the sphere of enaction, and hence cognition, grounded in both an evolutionary and social history that operates as a powerful attractor? This would generate an adaptationist model very like that argued by Tooby and Cosmides (op. cit.) of more limited plasticity, that is, with content-specific mechanisms. The answer turns out to both subtle and contestable. First let us examine their relation to phenomenology.

> [There is] . . . a reason for the failure of the Husserlian project that we wish to emphasize here: Husserl's turn toward experience and the 'the things in themselves' was entirely *theoretical*, or, to make the point the other way round, it completely lacked any *pragmatic* dimension.
>
> (p. 19, original emphases)

It looks as though a middle course is on offer: a radical constructivism that at the same time is 'nonobjectivist and nonsubjectivist' (see p. 9). Consequently, they cite an intellectual foundation common to both 'their' scientific tradition and to the disciplines of critical sociology and philosophy: Merleau-Ponty, whom they cite at length:

> The properties of the object and the intentions of the subject . . . are not only intermingled; they also constitute a new whole. When the eye

and the ear follow an animal in flight, it is impossible to say 'which started first' in the exchange of stimuli and response. Since all the movements of the organism are always conditioned by external influence, one can, if one wishes, readily treat behaviour as an effect of the milieu. But in the same way, since all the stimulations which the organism receives have in turn only been possible by its preceding movements which have culminated in exposing the receptor organ to external influences, *one could also say that behaviour is the first cause of all the stimulations* . . .

[I]t is the organism itself—according to the proper nature of its receptors, the thresholds of its nerve centres and the movements of the organism—*which chooses the stimuli in the physical world to which it will be sensitive.* The environment emerges from the world through the actualisation of the being of the organism – [granted that] an organism can exist only if it succeeds in finding in the world an adequate environment.

(Cited on p. 174, but shortened by us. The italics are added in the citation.)

Providing we can substitute 'enaction' for the oddly chosen term 'movement', this position is virtually identical to the position in *Autopoiesis and Cognition* where the organism is said to 'specify what counts as environment' and so 'brings forth worlds'. We can see where Varela's *et al.* italicisation wants to lead the reader: rather less toward mutual constitution and rather more towards behaviour as first cause. Merleau-Ponty, with the added voices of Maturana, Verala *et al.* and like-minded radical constructivists, are offering another version of Bateson's unintended conjuring. We follow the animal in flight with our eyes and ears. No doubt about the chronology there. Stimulus and response are conventionally in place. Yet Merleau-Ponty asserts 'it is impossible to say which started first'. Complete nonsense. Here is the variation on the trick.

We know perfectly well that the animal went first and we reacted. The counter-trick says that behaviour is the first cause of all the stimulations because the organism itself 'chooses' or evolves the stimuli in the physical world to which it will be sensitive. Just as Bateson tacitly changed the meaning of 'me' when he asked, Can you see *me*?, so the meaning of behaviour is tacitly changed here. Following the animal, it is clearly reactive and subsequent. But in the case of evolution or choice of sensitivity, which can be taken rather more seriously for human culture, we are clearly speaking of an antecedent. Indeed, its ancestry may stretch back (in the case of sight) well before humans were a dim possibility. So, we have succeeded in making a futile paradox of having capabilities and then using them. Shall we fall down stupefied by the enigma of having a TV and then watching it? The correct answer to Merleau-Ponty is that it is only on the basis of a behaviour of mine already being possible that I can subsequently react to the stimulus provided by the behaviour of the animal.

The fact that I have eyes does not cause the animal, that also has eyes, to 'cause' my eyes to react any more than his eyes 'cause' me to see him. 'Cause' is used so loosely that might equally well mean 'cause me to see' or the quite different 'cause the animal to fly'. Merleau-Ponty's trick works with exactly that equivocation. So when he says 'we could equally well say *my* behaviour is the first cause', in true pantomime style we should say: *Oh no it's not*. Because the cause of my behaviour (seeing) and the cause of the animal moving are not the same thing. They are not even in the same place, or the same time.

This specific strategy of confusion brought about by excessive formalism has managed to attain quite a high status in the speech-customs of critical reason, especially sociology, in the sense of unintended consequences. However, once the issue is spelled out, innocence is a less easy posture. This is not to say that the question is solved as the custom is too widespread. But the issue has been at least partly specified, crucially as an active issue in the reflexive establishment of a set of sociology of knowledge practices. That includes the concession we sociologists insist on for everyone else, namely that knowledge is a material and temporal practice, or trans-formation, or representation. Note here that Prigogine's insistence on the fundamentality of time and space or irreversibility is not a marginal criticism of reason's normal practices. On the contrary, this example shows that reason habitually ignores time.

Yet language, or usage, has an ally in its propensity to mislead us. The argument is subtle, and, moreover, not decidable in principle. It is a matter of inspection. This is the argument put forward by 'post-' Darwinist evolutionary theorists. Just as Maturana and Varela propose structural coupling in the organism and enviroment relation and then radicalise operational closure, so post-Darwinism replaces adaptive constraint and change with autonomous drift. Staying with the former, for the moment, it is ironic that they criticise Husserl's lack of pragmatism when their radicalisation of operational closure means that the organism is so obsessed with reproductive autopoiesis that its environment threatens to become its product. Perhaps the model contains a theme that makes important sense. Organisms do, in a sense, 'bring forth worlds', but on the other hand, they are entirely insensitive to the contradictions in Merleau-Ponty. They cited him, remember, and with added emphases.

The argument for evolutionary drift is put forward by especially Gould and Lewontin and discussed at length by Varela *et al.* (1993/2000).

> Evolution as natural drift is the biological counterpart of embodied action, and therefore also provides a more embracing theoretical context for the study of cognition as a biological phenomenon.
>
> (p. 188)

Where neo-Darwinism presents a view of organisms 'hard-coupled' to their environment by the pressures of adaptation, 'post'-Darwinists operate on the basis of 'uncaused', in the sense of 'chance', variation in the genome. Where the former argues for optimum adaptation and therefore sees environment as final cause, the latter argues only for a principle of *sufficiency*. Now the organism is somewhat freer to organise itself through internal variation. Only those aspects of the organism's recursive self-structuring that cannot be tolerated, given general environmental conditions, will be eliminated. In this case, structural coupling is gathered around the 'attractor' of self-organising reconstruction and replication. For 'harder' neo-Darwinists, such as Dennett or Dawkins, the attractor is specific environmental conditions and the role of chance is diminished by selection processes. One might see these two positions as the two ends of a spectrum and not radically incompatible. After all, we see both adaptation and intense variation. This is sometimes argued from the neo-Darwinist position. But Gould, Lewontin, and especially Varela, insist on a radical difference, which is not circumstantial. They insist that their position is not compatible with neo-Darwinism at certain times, or under specific conditions. They are arguing, then, for a difference in principle that is open to logical inspection. This is the argument.

> The cooperative neuronal operations underlying our perception of colour have resulted from the long biological evolution of the primate group. As we have seen, these operations partly determine the basic colour categories that are common to all humans. The prevalence of these categories might lead us to suppose that they are optimal in some evolutionary sense, *even though they do not reflect some pre-given world*.
>
> (added emphasis)

> This conclusion, however, would be considerably unwarranted. We can safely conclude that since our biological lineage has continued, our colour categories are *viable* or *effective*. Other species, however, have evolved *different* perceived worlds of colour on the basis of different cooperative neuronal processes . . . .Most vertebrates . . . have quite different and intricate colour mechanisms . . . Our colour vision is trichromatic..[S]ome animals are *dichromatic*, others are *tetrachromats*, some may even be *pentachromats*.
>
> (Varela *et al*. p. 181, original emphases)

And the conclusion:

> [T]he vastly different histories of structural coupling of birds, fishes, insects and primates have enacted or brought forth different perceived worlds of colour. Therefore, our perceived world of colour should not be considered to be the optimal 'solution' to some evolutionarily posed 'problem.' Our perceived world of colour is, rather, a result of one possible and viable phylogenic pathway amongst many others.
>
> (ibid. p. 183)

No neo-Darwinist would deny this.[2] We therefore suspect that a caricature of what Varela calls the 'received view' of evolution underlies his 'difference'. He could not have 'received' this view from Dennett or the more extreme Dawkins. They might, however, point to the different ecological positions associated with 'viable and non-viable phylogenic pathways'. What then is being said?

> The first step is to switch from a prescriptive logic to a proscriptive one, that is, from the idea that what is not allowed is forbidden to the idea that what is not forbidden is allowed . . . .This proscriptive orientation shifts our attention to the tremendous diversity of biological structures at all levels.
>
> (ibid. p. 195)

The first salient level of difference then begins to appear. The implication is that neo-Darwinist notions of optimisation falsely imply issues of rank; they are redolent of humans as the highest animals, 'in the image of God'. Such hierarchies are indeed objectionable and humanistic in the most archaic and discredited sense, and, moreover, untenable in analytic terms. They are, so to speak, 'imperialistic' or homocentric. One can see the analytic and political attractions of contesting this position. They are analogous with the politics of pluralism and responsible environmentalism. As opposed to neo-Darwinism, post-'modern'-Darwinism seems an apt name.

> The second step is to analyse the evolutionary process as satisficing (taking a suboptimal position that is satisfactory) rather then optimising: here selection operates as a broad survival filter that admits any structure that has sufficient integrity to persist.
>
> (ibid. p. 196)

The logic here is both 'fuzzier' and more accurate; a higher level of complexity is permitted which, moreover, is clearly required by the subject matter; the homocentrism of relative moral worth is completely absent. 'Sufficient integrity to persist' looks, however, like the kind of opening that might allow tight-coupled adaptationism to reinstate itself, albeit at a higher level of complexity and variation. The 'integrity to persist' requires the consumption of environmental energy, in Prigogine's sense, therefore predation, in the biological sense, to say nothing of the current political power expended on securing reserves of oil, water, and other material necessities. Perhaps Varela's terms are a little understated?

Recall the objection to our colour-perception reflecting a pre-given world. Recall also the idea that responses distributed through a complex neural network radically undermine older notions of representation and the processing of symbols.

The crucial point is that we do not retain the notion of an independent, pregiven environment but let it fade into the background in favour of so-called intrinsic factors.

(ibid. p. 198)

Are we to understand then that the environment simply varies or that organisms and environments influence or specify each other? These ideas are hardly new, hardly worth the theoretic effort, hardly worth the term post-Darwinism. Perhaps this is a further attempt to play the Merleau-Ponty gambit: in favour of so-called intrinsic factors? Are both insistence and denial at work here? On the one hand:

[L]iving beings and their environments stand in relation to each other through mutual specification or codetermination.

(ibid. p. 198)

On the other:

[E]xtraorganismal environment is made internal by psychological or biochemical assimilation, as internal state is externalised through products and behaviour that select and organise the *surrounding* world.

(ibid. p. 199, our emphasis)

Are these positions contradictory? Mutual specification is perfectly acceptable, it is the core of auto-eco-organisation, it is the basis on which any sort of evolution is conceivable, including human evolution, including social evolution. But it is not new. There is no pre-given world 'out there'. This is an archaic, constantly repeated assertion. What about products and behaviours that select and organise the surrounding world? We appear to be back in Merleau-Ponty country, where human sight, the response, is causally equivalent or near equivalent to the animal's flight (the stimulus), a world in which time has got lost. Prigogine would have none of that. It is that old trick again confounding the conjuror. Perception simply does not organise the surrounding world but only its own internal synthesis. Varela seems mired in total confusion of both. Sometimes 'world' is a series of viable, constructive-responsive syntheses by which the organism operates. But equally 'world' or 'environment' oscillates between 'independent externality' and 'independent internality'. It cannot be both wholly independent and synthetically 'coupled'. Structural coupling is open in the sense of process and so cannot be described in terms of a given or closed state of non-dependence. A frog is this state would not respond to anything, including the fly. A member or a society in this state would be incapable of adaptive response. In this sense, it is not neo-Darwinism nor the organism nor common sense that confuses the synthetic and the independent environment, but theorists of Varela's persuasion. The confusion exists in space, time and language.

Theorising the cognitive process is essential to a proper sociology of knowledge; indeed, it is the complex-systems approach to what has hitherto been only approached with excessive, over-formalised or misplaced simplicity. The result has been confusion, repetition and stagnation. Evolutionary adaptation as opposed to drift is an enormously important but circumstantial matter. Both are inherently possible, essentially dependent on the scale of energy transfer and the integrity of structures, material, organic or social. If extrinsic adaptation and intrinsic variation are both true to a degree, they should not exclude each other in a purely formal or logical argument. Of course, there will be concrete occasions of exclusion or predominance. Now we see the disadvantage of sufficing:

> [E]ach species will ignore whatever it can afford to ignore in its environment, a risky policy that may blindside it in the future, when a heretofore bland variable . . . suddenly takes on fatal relevance.
> (Dennett 2003: 163)

Dennett is an ultra-orthodox neo-Darwinist. The rationality is also orthodox risk management, that is, a kind of insurance. One only needs a minor but critical change to find that the 'world brought forth' cannot be brought forth any more. Another word for 'insurance' is intelligence.

We begin with the distinction between systems and environment. However, we intend to take that in Prigogine's sense, which emphasises their mutual qualitative specification. There are, then, these essentials: energy, difference, space, time, chance and causation, including the dimensions of feedback or reciprocity.

With respect to cognitive processes, the crucial dimension of energy is that which can enter into a stimulus-response relation in a neural network. In the case of humans, this is undoubtedly extremely complex, yet auto-organisation requires the mechanisms to be simple enough to evolve complexity. The 'connectionist' model owes its origin to something like the simplicity of the signal processing model it proposes to supersede. That is, the perception of light 'means' best escape route; the perception of heat 'means' retract; an acid or alkaline gradient 'means' move this way. In other words, a perturbation triggers a response of a qualitatively different kind. This is not to reinstate a representation model but to specify the need for qualitatively specific association. What we emphasise here is representation in a different sense, rather more akin to processes like eating, that is, a representation in the sense of transformation is taking place. Environmental energy, stored or presented in some form, is transformed by the organism into the specifics of its own organisation. This is the very stuff of life, or more prosaically, the excretion of entropy.

Varela et al. stress visual perception whilst insisting there is no pre-given world 'out there'. Fair enough, if what is meant by 'world' belongs to the synthetic domain of embodied or enactive cognition. However, there must be a transfer of energy, in this case light, which must be first of all 'out there' to elicit a response, which belongs to and only occurs in the organism's self-organisation. We have, then, clear, if complex, dimensions of time, space, energy, transformation and the rudimentary mechanics of causation. It is singularly hard to see why so rudimentary a relationship is constantly mystified. That is not to say that the developed processes are not complex. But then, so too are the processes of eating and digestion. Perhaps if that analogous transformation were to be kept in mind, less theoretic chaos would result when the process in question is, instead, cognition. Consequently, when Varela *et al.* argue that because our colour vision is trichromatic, yet other animals are dichromatic, tetrachromatic, or pentachromatic, and so there is no pre-given world 'out there' – one must reply that there is light, including that beyond the visible-to-us spectrum. And so there is a pre-given world quite apart from a derived world of qualitatively differentiated types of cognition. This does not preclude causal reciprocity. Quite the contrary, the viability of the organism's cognitive processes is apt to make it materially effective, as the human example now so disastrously shows. Perhaps we should underscore this with our eating analogy. The fact that the bacon one ate last week is no longer bacon but 'human' does not mean that there was no pre-given bacon 'out there' to begin with. It just means digestion works. Could it be argued that his scenario trivialises the problem of cognition? Well, not unless a single cell trivialises the complexity of embodiment.

Let us now turn to the role of chance and to the Kantian axiom that experience is contingent upon the domain in which it does or can take place. Let us take our examples above: Bateson's *Can you see me?*, Merleau-Ponty's '*eye following the flight of an animal*', and let us add, say, a tree that we can agree is 'visible'. It is surprising just how fragmentary the correct response to Bateson actually is. Assuming he was dressed in the conventional manner, we would actually see very little of him, the head and hands perhaps. Then, of course, there is the question of the angle of view. Add to this factors due to distance, movement, obstructions to vision, interruptions, the quality of eyesight and the percentage of Bateson we actually see is really quite small.

What we 'see' is not an incident ray that happens to strike the retina but a constant synthesis of vast numbers of such incidents. Here, we tacitly changed the meaning of 'see' to a small number of contingencies (low-percentage Bateson) then changed it back again to mean 'see' as *synthesis*. Synthesis of what? *High*-percentage Bateson? That might be a shorthand way of saying it. Even Bateson says that:

'What you really 'see' is a bunch of pieces of information about me, which you synthesise into a picture of me. You make that image, it's that simple.'

(op. cit.)

176

For us, *much* more is involved, preferably without unnecessary confusion about the meaning of 'me' or 'see'. The total situation, including Bateson, is the truer and fuzzier object of our gaze. Here you can see that we cannot possibly be arguing for a return to simple or immediate cognitivism, there is no single representation but a network of highly mediated interconnections. Incidents are not simply 'collected' where the aim is to get a better percentage or to fill in the blanks. We prefer the term 'enrichment' but at the same time emphasise its qualitative procedures. These must rest on adaptations in the sense of content-specific mechanisms in several senses. The character of memory, for example, is important; we did not presume that he had lost his legs when all we could 'see' was a pair of trousers. Then there is the whole cultural structure of presumptions and prohibitions. *Can you see me?* didn't prompt the audience to undress him to get a better look. The innate ability to learn a language is clearly implicit here as is the ability of a complex mind to reconfigure, reassociate or manipulate the Bateson we see for the task in hand. A clear economy is also at work. There are questions of concentration, multiple association and the directedness of consciousness. For example, in realising, despite the trousers, that Bateson still has legs, we need no conscious or detailed memory of the structure of the knee. Indeed, the image is hardly there at all. Consider the extent to which you needed to imagine a knee when it was mentioned. How far did the intervention of the word 'knee', that is, the inter-connection to language, mediate the requirement of a visual image? Is that sort of substitution dependent on the architectural inter-relation of the neural systems of vision, hearing, memory and speech, unique to humans? Is culturally acquired knowledge dependent on these interconnected neural systems? Has 'culture', the ecological requirement of being a social animal, driven their evolutionary development? How far is culture limited by mental capacity? We are not invoking 'what came first, chicken or egg?'-type scenarios here. Clearly there is a chronology at work, evolutionary theory demands that. But it is a process in which effects produce positive feedback that interact, influence or change their 'original' causes. This is what is meant by auto-eco-organisation.

How are we to think of this complex world 'brought forth' by environmental energy and an array of receptors and also by constant syntheses of enrichments, interconnections and species-specific mediations? Which is the more real: the tiny percentage of Bateson we discern through the discrete action of incident light rays or the complex of images and words we imply by the concept 'Bateson'? Perhaps that way of framing is simply redundant? This runs to the heart of any attempt to treat knowledge as a complex system, it destabilises the distinction between the systems of cognition and their environment. It certainly corrodes that central postulate of the critical attitude, which is that the 'real' is stable whilst perception is unstable or 'virtual'. Given the localised and essentially random character of the transformation of energy that is implied in sensory perception, is not the 'virtual' better understood as

177

the more stable? This is the kind of radical constructivism implied by auto-exo-reference. However, this sense is inexpressible in the speech idioms of ordinary philosophy. That is, where 'me' and 'me as' are treated as the same thing instead of the complex of difference and oppositions they signify. Where the inhibiting concept of the thing *in itself* – the most radical expression of the confusion between an ordinary thing, with a simple name (me) – and the thing *as* (me *as*) *guarantees* that philosophy is bound to fail. Conversely the thing in itself is an open complex, open to conceptual re-presentation.

We want to argue that this actually runs counter to Kant's conception of experience, as 'could have been otherwise', but is congruent with his concept of imagination. The whole drift of the synthesis of experience, exactly like Varela's organismic self-synthesis, is quite the opposite of a random principle. On the contrary, it marks the reproduction of a complex unity. Kant defines imagination as the faculty to re-member 'that which is not itself present' (Kant 1973: 165), then defines three such syntheses: the past, the present and the future. These syntheses, somewhat simple no doubt to modern cognitive science and, of course, innocent of the literal re-membering functions of DNA, allow and constitute the unity of the subject in Kant and, analogously, the organism's self-organisation (see Varela). This is the information requirement outlined by Prigogine. Given any measure of chance, here provided by the spatio-temporal extent of environment in relation to the cognitive system, in order that organic systems can re-produce themselves or their previous state, sufficient information must be stored about the relationships between system components. Space, in the distinction between the organism and the more extensive environment, and time, in the form of continual re-production or differentiation *vis-à-vis* an environment, require what is variously called the imagined, the virtual, information. It is essential to see that this existential difference between the world as environment and as information-saturated synthesis comes necessarily out of the difference, out of the relation itself. Prioritisation of either (mind first, world first, world as 'in here' *versus* 'out there') loses the sense of that requirement. Correspondingly, the system, organisation or organism must have a non-contingent or non-random structure. This also excludes a logically formal structure such as Kant's subject. Its experience certainly could have been otherwise but only because it lacks any structural identity. Consequently it can have no environment either.

Once the subject is specified, however loosely, that structural identity commences its cycle of complex reconstitution, with the dimensions of chance or disorder increasingly excluded. These dimensions are conceptually identical with entropy, or the collapse of the system- environment distinction. Thus the subject unspecified can have no place in systems-theory. Neither can Luhmann's black boxes or Varela's prioritisation of 'intrinsic factors', because to re-cognise, re-member, re-produce, re-present the organisation of the systems is to distinguish between intrinsic and extrinsic phenomena. To re-present, to re-cognise, to re-member must be heard in this transformational sense. Varela's critique of representation as symbol-processing is fair enough but to base one's critique on so weak a model of representation, digital computing, is to miss its deeper significance and to have one's own work marked by that omission.

Content-specific structures in Tooby and Cosmides' sense can be deduced from the same set of considerations. Consider again the idea that open systems, far from equilibrium, in Prigogine's sense, evolve complex structures in response to the inward transfer of environmental energy. They can then be said to excrete, or avoid, entropic decay or the tendency to randomness in the very transformation of environmental energy into the properties of components of the system's own homeodynamics. Contrast this with Varela's notion of autopoiesis, which allows 'the notion of an independent, pregiven environment . . . to fade into the background in favour of so-called intrinsic factors' (p. 198 op. cit.) In the view expressed by Prigogine, Tooby and Cosmides, content-specific structures of response are absolutely necessary because organic systems require information not only about themselves but about their environment. This is entirely because any organic system's integrity, to use Varela's term, depends on identifying those elements in the environment that it is about to transform into itself. Remember the 'bacon' analogy. Information is a structural component of an organic system every bit as much as its material parts; in humans, arguable more so.

The more inwardly oriented version of autopoiesis, compared to eco-auto-organisation and its reciprocal exo-auto-reference, seems possible where issues are not 'critical', where the sufficiency principle will 'do'. It is contradicted, however, by Varela's own chosen example: vision. Vision exemplifies a critical relation to an environmental given, namely light, which is why, as Mayr points out, the eye has evolved separately so many times. The eye is both 'attracted' and is an attractor.[3]

Varela's model implies a high degree of unity or homeostasis. The persistent image is that of a relatively closed, if not insular structure that 'drifts' in its internal composition. Consequently the implied environment does not impinge greatly. Despite the fact that his principle of 'sufficing' is supposed to allow diversity, this situation also implies stasis or uniformity. We are not especially concerned with the diversity in the sense of diverse separated structures, such as distinct species, but diversity in the sense of structures participating in the cognitive process. Clearly, the eye is connected to, or co-implied in advanced cognitive processing. It therefore has both integrated but specific systems within the brain. Even this relation is not a principle focus here. Look instead at those structures that belong to the generality of consciousness itself, that which we call 'content.' Does Varela imply 'drift' here too? If so this is again an unconvincing model of relative uniformity. Note instead, especially in humans, the emergence of qualitatively distinct conceptual structures. Drift is not an option when such content-laden structures arrange themselves in hierarchies, oppositions and confirmations, replacements and realignments. Conceptual drift resembles the naïve and sentimental version of post-modernist pluralism that never produces intolerable difference. Our version instead exhibits continuity with material structural requirements. Conceptual chaos is congruent with material randomness; the integrity of the system, organic or conceptual, must minimise this. A measure of random-ness is acceptable, and necessary (the order from noise principle), but conceptual content must exhibit emergent qualitative structures, just like organisms do, and for the same reason: to possess an identity, however plastic. Just as the abstract subject can have no boundary and so no environment, so the most radical connectionism must exhibit qualitative structure in order to connect. That is the unseen requirement in formal connectionism. It exactly parallels the disintegration of humanism's formal subject.

9

THE EVOLUTION OF
INTELLIGENCE, CONSCIOUSNESS
AND LANGUAGE
Implications for social theory

The previous chapter showed that adaptive and autopoietic or constructivist approaches to cognition were not at variance. If it is true to a degree that organisms 'bring forth worlds' and also true to a degree that they are adapted, both autopoietic and environmental attractors are at work. They are not mutually exclusive at a formal level, though concrete conflicts are conceivable, even likely. It was also argued that the virtual, or synthetic, or 'imaginary' aspects of cognition are driven by the contingencies of environmental input, such as sense perception, *vis-à-vis* the relative autopoietic constancy of the organism. The term employed was 'enrichment'. What we sought to exclude was the analytic inadequacy of mutual exclusion, the old dichotomy of synthesis *versus* correspondence. Further exposed was the widespread logical fallacy embedded in critical formalism of confusing the thing as it immediately presents itself with the thing as all the ways in which it might present itself, the thing 'in itself', as it is sometimes put. This expression is wrong as the thing is nothing for itself in quite the opposite sense from Kant's intention. It has no conceivable essence, merely a series of 'appearances' *as* or *for*. This does not simply mean appearances 'for an observer', far less a human observer. Rather, its reality is entirely relative to an environment. A tree may be a source of oxygen for the aerobic biosphere, a carbon sink in the Earth's temperature maintenance systems, wood for a builder, a source of food or shelter for a bird, a component of the soil or unit of fossil fuel for a later time. It did not become fuel but merely a set of volatile molecules until we developed an appropriate technology. Its realities are radically local and temporal. The thing 'in itself' is merely the semantic residue of the paradigm of external creation, bluntly, God. But the ontology presented here is one of self-organisation. This is to preclude the 'in itself'. Steven Hawking will not know the mind of God unless His authorship is strictly limited. It is time to choose one's faith.

This requirement reminds us of the view that people do not generally believe in God because there is 'something out there', but because there is not. This dilemma is as active in contemporary reason as complexity theory as it was for Durkheim's analysis of religion. He could not at the same time maintain the function of religion and its analysis. Despite every protestation he showed it to be false and to function because it was false; it covered or enhanced or 'spun' the truth. This contradiction is inevitable in the evolution of intelligence, not simply as the overcoming of superstition, discipline or tradition but as the emergent usurper-counterpart to Kant's previous distinction between phenomenon and the thing in itself. It is the enriched imagination, not contingent, impoverished or localised experience that reflects upon but can never realise its own limits; the recourse to the 'in itself' is denied. Yet the denial is itself contingent; it depends on circumstance and intercourse.

The identity of the organism, or more especially the culture, presupposes the emergence of a principle of non-contradiction, not primarily out of logical but out of existential necessity. This wrought identity lives, so to speak, in constant fear of its dissolution at the hands of an environmental other, which it both knows well enough and yet knows insufficiently. It would not be intelligent if it did not grasp the threat of that equivocation. Now the existential principle of non-contradiction, faced by contradiction, declares itself; it is analytically inseparable from the fear of death. This requires qualification; organisms, minds, cultures do not live in abject terror, or if they do it is by sublimation. The issue here is network proximity; analagous to Durkheim's moral density, it says that non-contradiction is a requirement but not an absolute requirement, just as Kant's famous criterion could never operate absolutely. The issue is connectivity where close coupling to external phenomena is assumed; the looser the coupling the lower the degree of critical interaction. Prigogine's thermodynamics exemplify the former, evolutionary reorganisation is necessary. Maturana's and Varela's more optimistic versions of autopoiesis assume the latter. In taking the discussion of cognition in its rudiments to the evolution of intelligence, language and culture we shall argue that both strong and loose coupling are important determinants and therefore that a type of parallel, as opposed to serial, modelling becomes necessary at the levels of both individual consciousness and collective manifestations such as language, group and culture. The model we are seeking to establish consists of highly differentiated but networked subsystems exhibiting widely varying levels of connectivity. This is not unlike the picture of content-specific mental adaptation discussed in Tooby and Cosmides and is also analogous to Luhmann's concept of subsystems of society. However, the comparison is illustrative.

Are we not perhaps reinstating Kant's criterion – experience teaches us that a thing is so and so but cannot be otherwise? That it is true to a degree but that degree is determined circumstantially. It is not so much necessary in the logical sense but vital in the operational sense; it has to be part of intelligence's tool kit, not its global specification. Its 'truth' necessity or vitality is not a property of the statement, as humanism would have it, but of the critical degree of connectivity, as self-organisation would have it. It both emerges and absents itself by virtue of the networks of interconnection. Intelligence as the ground of that statement is itself an emergent property of the network to which it relates. The best, most accessible account of this process, certainly the one most congruent with Prigogine, and therefore with intelligence emerging from less complex systems, can be found in the work of Henry Plotkin (1994, re-issued 2003).

One of the charges levelled against the idiomatic practices of philosophy was excessive formalism, the idea that the thing as (or me as) connoted a series of predications in which the possibility of contradiction was not to be taken seriously. Much the same can be said of post-modernity's sentimental pluralism; it ignores contradiction in the analytic sense and therefore also conflict in the concrete and political sense. It is reasonably easy to demonstrate that the thing in itself is redolent of authorial rather than self-organisation. It is less easy to see or to show that an unproblematic or non-contradictory extended space of predication is dependent on the same kind of limit or origin. However, if our ontology is one of self-organisation and there is any degree of interconnection or response, how can one possibly expect that contradiction will not arise? That expectation seems farcical, especially where we confront that domain we routinely grant to be auto-eco-organisational, namely, the biosphere. Here we meet diversity and competition, or contradiction, as a consequence. Why should we think otherwise about human construction, perhaps because we still consider it to be privileged?

Much the same argument can be placed against autopoiesis. The idioms associated with autopoiesis speak of 'organism' or 'social system', rarely of fox or rabbit, or democracy or theocracy or global capitalism. The content of Prigogine's position suffers the same problem not because of lack of specifics but because of analogy; his specific materials are not social phenomena. The crucial move in Plotkin is to see that the move from cognition in general to intelligence in particular is a qualitative one and it depends on qualitative relationships with an environment. Cognition is commonplace in the biosphere, intelligence is rare. Is this more plausibly understood as drift, or adaptation, or both? Is there a qualitative distribution?

Plotkin (2003:51) begins with a re-iteration of Prigogine's emphasis that the entropic principle makes complexity, especially living complexity improbable and that its possibility therefore depends on acquiring environmental energy to sustain itself. The tacit reply to the 'drift' argument, then, is that a drift 'downhill' (to equilibrium uniformity) is inherently more likely. We might say that life is not so much drifting as driven; though both positions can be, in principle, maintained, so long as drift 'suffices' its energy requirements. Plants, then, provide a foundation layer of photosynthesisers. This method of obtaining energy is qualitatively distinct. Compared with sunlight as a more or less evenly diffused source, indirect sources of energy are scattered and localised. Locomotion, equipment for extraction and the relatively complex neural apparatus that goes along with that requirement is qualitatively necessary. Such requirements are unquestionably adaptations, unless 'drift' is accompanied by an anthropic principle offering a series of cast-iron guarantees. Drift, especially post-adaptation, is not ruled out but appears much more path-dependent and easily threatened than Varela's more formal presentation. Suffice to say that drift and fitness are potentially antagonistic processes, or that at each critical event, the latter determines the fate of the former. Here again, we meet the deformalisation of chance; variation is not a formal or genuinely random property but a qualitative movement gathered around both internal and external series of attractors.

Plotkin points out:

> Three points should be noted here. The first is that individual development is a complex cascade of, as yet, little understood processes and mechanisms. Its importance, however is undeniable. Second, because of the dependence of genes on an appropriate environment and developmental sequences for the information coded in them to become embodied in neural structures and their behavioural outcomes, genes are only ever part-causes of adaptations of this or any other kind. This should not be taken as downplaying the important role of genes as crucial repositories of information that can be transmitted across generations. Indeed, in the overwhelming majority of animals this is the *only* way information is transmitted . . . Genes are, however, wholly dependent on individual development for their expression.
>
> It has become fashionable to decry the terms *innate* and *instinct*, especially amongst social scientists and especially when applied to our own species. This is nonsense.
>
> (Plotkin 2003: 52–3)

Plotkin adds, '[A]daptive behaviours – instincts – wholly caused by a combination of genes and development do not in their enactment result in long term changes of central-nervous-system states' (ibid.). The question is not that old, sterile debate of nature *versus* nurture but the indication of an essential threshold, that of parallel processing.[1] The point can be taken two ways; instinctual processes are necessary and therefore not transformative. The opposite is true of learned and modifiable behaviours. Equally, it would be an invitation to rapid extinction if either were to be infiltrated by the essential characteristics of the other. How would it be if our involuntary nervous systems were infused with choices, or if our learned behaviours became totally reflex? There must be a series of interconnections, but also of boundary maintenance. This is Tooby and Cosmides' requirement of seeing the brain as a complex of organs and content-specific structures.

This takes us back to the earlier objections to the *serial* bottleneck of the *cogito*. But this is not only a Cartesian failing. How often is the contemporary sense of reflexivity extolled as including the active contribution of the observer? On this reading it is trite simply to include the observer as an active factor in descriptions. Why not the eater, the sexually-attracted, the depressed, the competitive, the neurotic? Is it being suggested that by 'including the observer' the dimensions or outcomes of reflexivity are adequately addressed? The conditions of 'parallel' processing are infinitely more complex and demanding.

The dimensions of this problem are both complex and subtle. Plotkin cites Lorenz, the father of *ethology*, as the first to show as a consequence of evolution 'that not only is learning constrained, but constrained in ways that make learning mesh with other biological characteristics of the learner' (ibid. p. 56). This is a radical constructivism indeed, but one grounded where Lorenz and Darwin's self-organising, interactive dynamics are cited, not the insular will of Nietzsche or Berkeley.[2] This constraint may be taken to indicate the power of intrinsic attractors. There are also extrinsic attractors. Plotkin puts forward the position of longer-lived animals. The position is equally applicable to those open to a diverse environment. For such organisms genetically-coded information is too liable to be rigid or out of date. The considerable extra biological costs of intelligence are therefore offset. Yet the rarity of developed intelligence should give us pause for thought. Despite our prejudices, intelligence may not always pay for itself and instinct may offer radically more effective and certainly quicker solutions. The flight mechanism is one such instinctive imperative. Compared with instinct (and think of predator and prey interactions), intelligence is slow, cumulative but flexible. It takes over where evolution cannot pre-programme. Without invoking a structural anthropology in which culture mirrors the human mind, it is unlikely that culture does not exhibit structural complexities related to this nested hierarchy.

There are three central issues here: cost, constraint and adaptation. For those who associate pluralism with the absence of structural limitations, this list of limitations will signal a political threat. In a sense they are right, but the threat is levelled at the doctrine of non-limitation, not at the aspiration to pluralism. Pluralism, after the complexity turn, is both a mental and a material practice.

Plotkin expresses the multiple dimensions of cost as follows:

[I]nstincts are adaptations honed over long periods of evolutionary time. They are effective because they work instantly. An animal that had to learn to freeze when confronted with mortal danger would probably not survive the learning experience. Many instinctive behaviours have to be fully formed the first time they occur, and the intervention of intelligence of any sort would be distinctly disadvantageous. Instincts also win out over behaviour driven by intelligence because they are energetically less costly. The evolutionist G. C. Williams' principle of the economy of information asserts that living things evolve in such a way as to maintain information in the cheapest form possible. The nervous systems which is an aggregate of nerve cells each of which is constantly using energy to maintain a particular balance of ions across its membranes because that is the basis of neural activity, is energetically a very expensive form of tissue. It is cheaper to code information in DNA then in neural form.

(Plotkin 2003: 68)

Here we see something akin to Prigogine's insights of thermodynamic input translated into the specifics of cognitive processes. Interestingly, we see both an energy-expensive and an energy-inexpensive solution. In terms of behavioural economy, instincts are inexpensive solutions to adaptation requirements. At the same time, though rare, there is sufficient energy surplus to evolve and store information in neural networks. This too is adaptive. As Plotkin constantly reiterates, intelligence provides the information that evolution cannot handle. It deals with shorter term fluctuations or complexity, the predictably unpredictable to which DNA is blind. How, then, are we to understand the notion of constraint in relation to learning?

The connotation, from the human point of view, and certainly from the pluralist traditions of critical sociology, is that constraint forbids. That is, a domain perfectly possible, perceptible or even desirable is ruled out of bounds usually by some interest group in favour of exclusive possession. In the animal kingdom, Plotkin cites birds learning only the song of their own species; the situation is reversed. In this context constraint is rather a path forged into a region that is otherwise featureless or only governed by instinctive response. If intelligence takes over where DNA is 'blind' then it 'brings forth worlds' previously unseen, unknowable and certainly therefore previously unintended and undesired. There is no sense of prohibition here and the world brought forth along this path is surrounded by 'chaos' in the sense of not-knowing and not-conscious, not 'presenting itself' at all. Something approximating to but still far short of the sense may be grasped by hearing another language as simply a cascade of sounds. Imagine placing oneself in the role of a very different other; 'losing' would be more apt then placing. What is connoted by constraint in this sense is path-dependence. In one sense, the path itself is an attractor, especially in human cultures. In another sense, it is the advantage the path confers that attracts its development or maintenance. It is not customary in sociology, an incorrigibly optimistic discipline, to dwell on the interplay of advantage with disadvantage. Qualitative path-dependence is apt to define in the sense of demarcating the more from the less possible and finally the actual from the impossible, however temporal its extent. The question for critical sociology is: what connotation of constraint should be attached to human intelligence and culture? Present but forbidden lands, or path-dependence where ostensible alternatives cannot literally be realised?

The answer must be both. We must be open to the insistence of contradictions; this is no easy compromise. Yet again we must make recourse to the expression, 'to a degree.' Here it is especially apt in relation to the path itself. It has no hard edges; indeed, it cannot have hard edges, in principle, for that would require the outside to be known. Path-dependence is quintessentially fuzzy both because it is in or of the world and yet excludes it. Paths, or possibilities and impossibilities, *not* worlds, are 'brought forth' and Plotkin's 'definition' of intelligence is tantamount to increasing reflection on this limiting condition. This is what we have in mind in speaking of intelligence as adaptation. It is like, but also importantly unlike, the schema of appearances set against things in themselves. The in itself in our sense is not completion but chaos, the chaos from which intelligence is protected by its evolution, though not fully – that is its own task.

This section of the book began by describing this sense of horizonality not as the global definition of intelligence but as part of its toolkit. What emerges from that argument is the suggestion that sociology as we now conceive it should dispense with that defining name *homo sapiens*. *Sapiens* is now a part of the evolved complex *homo*. Correspondingly, intelligence is part of that which we commonly call culture, yet we deny culture's complexity by habitually formulating intelligence, or its symbolic manifestations, as its predominant cause. Human intelligence may be a necessary but not a sufficient condition for the emergence of culture. That would be to dismiss or at least diminish all of those crucial functions of human life such as nutrition, shelter, reproduction, whose roots lie in other areas of our biology or our physical environment.

Before moving onto the topic of 'grounded' language and culture, it is instructive to consider Cilliers' (1998) analysis of the relationships between post-modernism and complexity from the somewhat different connectionist perspective. Where Maturana, Varela and Plotkin contribute to the philosophy of cognition via biology, Cilliers enters by way of computer modelling and Artificial Intelligence. He, like Varela *et al.*, also promotes connectionism as a more viable proposition contrasted with what he calls 'rule-based systems'. Here is a much-abbreviated slice from his argument:

- Every symbol in a rule-based system has a precise pre-defined meaning – this constitutes a local representation. In a connectionist network individual neurons have no pre-defined meaning. Changing patterns of activity over several nodes perform meaningful functions. This is often referred to as distributed representation.
- Formal systems have well-defined terminating conditions and results are produced only when those conditions are reached. Connectionist systems tend to dynamically converge on a solution, usually in an asymptotic fashion. The process does not have to terminate; as a matter of fact it will not arrive at a single, final conclusion.
- The internal structure of a connectionist network develops through a process of self-organisation where rule based systems have to search through pre-programmed options that define the structure largely in an a priori fashion. In this sense learning is an implicit characteristic of neural networks. In rule based systems, learning can only take place through explicitly formulated procedures.

(Cilliers 1998: 19)

As such his argument is startlingly persuasive. Patterns or 'weights' of neuronal activity distinguish meaningful differences that lead to both self-organisation and learning within the connectionist network. 'Rule-based' systems, on the other hand, are helpless without their controller, blind unless instructed otherwise and prone to crash in the face of contradiction. Which form models human intelligence better, unless your persuasion is Creationist?

The point is set to be sharpened through Cilliers comments on Derrida's critique of Saussure.

> Derrida's critique of Saussure's description of the sign is related to his critique of a tendency in the whole tradition of Western philosophy, which he calls the 'metaphysics of presence.' In the case of Saussure the metaphysics of presence is affirmed by his insistence that the sign has two components, the signifier and the signified, one of which, the signified, is mental or psychological. This would imply that the meaning of the sign is present to the speaker, when he uses it, in defiance of the fact that meaning is constituted by a systems of differences. That is also why Saussure insists on the primacy of speaking. As soon as language is written down, a distance between the subject and his words is created, causing meaning to become unanchored.

> Derrida argues, however, that Saussure has no reason to be anxious about this state of affairs. He insists that the distance between the subject and his words exists in any case; that the sign is always unanchored, even when we speak. Thus the signified . . . never has any immediate self-present meaning. It is itself only a sign that derives its meaning from other signs . . . Stripped of its signified component. Since the signified is also constituted through a system of relationships, it functions just like a [another] signifier that has to take its position in the endless chain of signifiers . . .

> The deconstruction of the sign . . . is closely linked to the deconstruction of the subject and of consciousness . . . The subject is no longer in control of meaning that can be made present, but is itself *constituted* by the play of signifiers.

> Put in the language of systems theory, Saussure still understands language as a closed system whereas Derrida wants to argue for language as an open system.
>
> (Cilliers 1998: 42–3)

The argument is by now a familiar, indeed repetitive and persuasive one, so far as critical sociology is concerned. Derrida catches the excess, deferment and complexity of the relation between the subject and language. However, this conclusion is false in the sense of over-simplistic not over-complex. To make that criticism of Derrida is indeed a shock. Unfortunately this is what the complexity turn and its interdisciplinary implications require. Our counter-argument can placed in two parts corresponding to Cilliers' and Derrida's positions.

Cilliers offers a persuasive argument about the superiority or credibility of connectionist networks over rule-based ones, in respect of their ability to organise themselves. It should be noted, however, that all of his descriptions of connectionist networks are auto-exo-referential. However, that describes networks that need to learn. This is indeed a common presumption about humans and according to Tooby and Cosmides learning is something of a catch-all for describing processes we do not understand. Here the converse is the case. Following Plotkin's argument on the difference between intelligence and evolved behaviours or instinct, it is essential that some neural networks do not learn. Otherwise they would be converted from the energetically-conservative, rapid response systems of involuntary control to the slower, energetically-demanding, but more flexible systems of learning. The parallel construction of Plotkin's model insists on at least a degree, possibly a high degree of insulation. This is absent from Cilliers' model; it is only networked. The distinction between information stored in DNA and neural networks, however, is important. It is because of the limits of DNA that intelligence represents a further adaptation, and because intelligence is dependent upon that link, it is not free to create itself. Instead it is tied to this foundation. In this sense the creationist argument contains a half-truth. The plasticity of intelligence is the 'path-making' child of the relative fixity of DNA. This may be derived from Prigogine's position; if the universal origins of complex self-organisation are thermodynamic then the autopoiesis of intelligence is a direct result of the limitations of DNA in handling the information that is necessary for recursive organisation. That is of course speculative, though it is clearly implicit in the 'forced' theory of complex self-organisation. The alternative is the notion of drift and the principle of sufficiency. Perhaps both are necessary. Indeed 'drift' may itself be a response to energy inputs. It is clear from the biosphere that, drift or driven, the resulting organisms are just as energy-hungry for their reproduction. It seems paradoxical that any organised system that simply drifts into existence should be so voracious once specified.

Derrida's argument can be countered in the same manner; the chain of signifiers is not endless. It may be extremely long, for example, 'the situation in Iraq', or really quite short, for example, 'look at that tree.' Endlessness is an over-simplification. Ironically, it is an idiomatic simplification. True to the tradition of philosophers, Derrida is allowing himself the licence to speak at the maximum level of formality, that is, 'all' signifiers 'in general', and thus blinds himself to the difference between specifics. So Derrida, far from showing the endlessness of signification, shows in fact that his own idioms are altogether rather limited. What we can see here is the decay of auto-exo-reference

189

into repetitive auto-reference. This is possible as the tradition of radical constructivism in critical theory so often demonstrates. It is ironic that Derrida should speak of the metaphysics of presence when the metaphysics of absence is so much more apt, certainly in respect of Kant, of Nietzsche and his strongest influence, Heidegger. Heidegger is explicit in this respect: Being is 'absented' through the predomination of things. So is Nietzsche: God is dead. Kant's thing-in-itself is more elliptical but we have demonstrated often enough that it connotes a complete character independent of self-organisation. What unites these major figures of Western humanism, Derrida included, is the dialectics of presence or absence of external causality or a Creator in variously thin disguises. It is essential to see that the corresponding idiom of maximum formality rests on collectability based on this common external cause and the corresponding guarantee, formulated by Kant, that what is collected is merely appearance. Given eco-auto-organisation and exo-auto-reference the doctrine of maximised formality and the idiom of unproblematic categorisation become groundless, or simply academic habit.

It is sometimes given this expression in complexity theory: *complexity cannot by 'compressed'*. This expression, derived from the non-linearity of complex phenomena and therefore the constant production of qualitative difference, says that one simple representation, sign or programme cannot adequately 'stand for' the complex manifold. This may be the greatest difficulty faced by post-humanist complexity theory. In particular, it cuts across that most cherished sociological prejudice that all opinions or cultures are of equal standing. It may even cut across the discipline in the sense of destabilising the categories 'human,' 'culture,' or 'society'. Something of this sense is currently emerging from complexity theory in relation to globalisation. Given that caution, we now turn to the relationships between intelligence, language and 'culture' and the domain of their organisation.

The chains are not endless, the wells may be full or run dry, paradigms with sufficient attention, disclose something of their own extent and limitations. That is both their strength and weakness.

At this point it will be instructive to consider one of the great strengths of Saussurian signs, incorporated but lost, in contemporary post-structuralism, namely the arbitrariness of the sign. Are they fundamentally or accidentally arbitrary? The common answer seems to be that they are functionally arbitrary but the reasons given seem too dispersed or unsatisfactory. Instead let us reason backwards from the invention of the phonetic alphabet and the 'discovery' that it was so apt for the codification of language. Why should this be? The circular answer is that language is phonetic, but what is excluded by that tautology is interesting. Of particular importance is the exclusion of visual representation. Despite the sophistication of human art, vision and visual culture, it entails production difficulties that speech does not. These are of two kinds, the transformation into viewable media and the requirement of resemblance. Neither of these is immediately available and their actual sophistication requires considerable skill and resources. An arbitrary name, however, will 'do' and on the basis of relatively simple agreement. Simple, that is, to the human brain. Layers of adjunctive meaning can then be added. Let us not speculate on origins here, except to indicate that as a system of communicated representation its emergence is made infinitely more possible by both its 'portability' and its arbitrariness. What we intend to picture here is language's groundedness as opposed to the groundlessness assumed by post-structuralism. Furthermore, it attains its complexity by arbitrariness. As Wittgenstein says in a remark that unites his early and late writing: 'the number of names cannot be specified'.[3] That could not be the case if they were not arbitrary.

There is nothing wrong, then, in demonstrating the learned conventionality of culture or the complex self-reference of linguistic signifiers, just as there is nothing wrong with neural networks that organise themselves. The question is, what do they interact with? If there are no structural attractors either within the human brain or the material environment, then their productions are analytically random. If there are inter-actors, we have production centred around attractors and consequently degrees of possibility or impossibility. There is a world of difference between complex variation simply built on itself and that gathered around certain structural attractors. The former is not complex but chaotic. Whereas the discipline of sociology after the complexity turn is gathered around the interface of emergence between chaos and self-organisation.

Speaking of global networks, Urry notes:

> They do not derive directly and uniquely from human intentions and actions. Humans are intricately networked *with* machines, texts, objects and other technologies. There are no purified *social* networks, only material worlds that involve peculiar and complex socialities *with* objects.
> (Urry 2003: 18, original emphases; also citing Latour 1993 and Knorr-Cetina 1997)

This emphasis will be elaborated in the closing chapters; here let us continue to consider the reverse implication, that the network of linguistic signifiers is never purified nor exclusively social but is also intricately networked with both the physical body of the individual human and the materiality of environmental conditions. Compounding the picture are two further interactive domains: that part of the cognitive apparatus most embedded in or related to the physical body, and that part most receptive to the environment. Connoted with the former are the necessary substrates that connect physical and emotional necessities: the experience of pain, hunger, sexual desire, the fear of death. Connoted with the latter are not simply the senses, however crucial, both the whole panoply of consciousness – might we say self-consciousness? For in that term is embedded that curious, possibly uniquely human feature, that to be human is to theorise the mind of other humans. Given the bounded infinity exemplified in that phrase, 'other humans,' all conceivable other humans, we see the staggering parallel complexity involved. Perhaps we are beginning to grasp that it can only work on the basis of fuzzy but compelling approximations, open to trial and reconsideration. We can also see that the humanist model is hopelessly serial. Decartes' bottleneck of the *Cogito*, Kant's 'black box' of the transcendental subject, Derrida's infinite endlessness of signification, Foucault's abyss, even finally 'order from *pure* noise' amount to serial simplification in the sense of guarantee or the theoretic comfort of assured randomness. The world, including the social world, is enormously stranger than that.

Plotkin constantly remains us that intelligence and language are adaptations. Cilliers, Derrideans and radical connectionists dwell on the emergence of meaningful patterns of difference from distributed representation. Despite the total discreditation of truth as correspondence, Plotkin's 'adaptive' position implies a degree of 'matching', which he concedes, and connectionism requires 'weights' to be given to sensory inputs. Both models then appear to ally themselves with common sense in that they, so to speak, reserve the right to do some pointing 'outside'. Derrida, with greater consistency and arguably less practical intelligence, allows no limits, presumably even those that 'mistake' the crocodile's smile or the everyday insistence that you've taken something the wrong way. The issue becomes explosive at the level of culture where the *sui generic* and adaptationist approaches are polarised as the grounds for pluralism and of authoritarian rationality respectively. This argument carries some weight, for example in the constructivist rather than psychological empiricism's approach to special needs in education.[4] But the one position collapses into the other, finite correspondence is a recipe for perspective, not truth, and radical constructivism, connectionist or not, needs a stimulus-response relation to activate itself. Even at the most *sui generic* or Geertzian notion of culture, the familiar polarity is re-asserted in the difference between individual and society, and re-denied in the notion that individuality is only expressible in membership. There is a better way to formulate this apparently irredeemable condition.

Varela is apt to refer to naïve realism. Indeed, the everyday world runs on the basis of naïve realism, until it becomes infected with Cartesian anxiety (Varela *et al.* 2000: chapter 7). Before we take this too seriously, let's imagine a predator (a lion) and a gazelle on the horizon. Does the lion conclude that the gazelle, being distant, looks so small it would make no more than a mouthful? That would be indeed naïve – and unthinkable. Yet we are to believe that humans are more gullible?

Laplace's demon lies concealed in this conundrum. The total correspondential synthesis of a world is hopelessly uneconomic and much the same applies to a truly exhaustive description of any part. But cognitive representation bears no relation this. It is more plausible, realistic and economic to think of interconnected neural pathways able to respond to a stimulus. The inter-connections do not consist of representations, certainly not conscious ones, but rather of means of associating or managing differences and relationships in time and space. This would accord with both connectionist and adaptationist positions. Yet, following Kant's notion of imagination as re-presenting some-thing that is not itself present, something like a strong notion of re-presentation is presupposed in both the notion of memory and the compatibility of further stimulus reception. Representation is here understood in the sense of trans-formation, as opposed to correspondence. Much the same presupposition underlies the social functions of visual, verbal and embodied culture or com-munication. Similar to the argument about Gregory Bateson, the primary mechanism must be 'simple', or easily managed, or 'available'. Otherwise both its rudimentary evolution and the accumulation of internal complexity would be ungroundable. This means that stimulus-response correspondence is both necessary and rudimentary.

The example of the predatory lion, indeed any analysis of visual perception, shows an auto-critical process below the level of consciousness. Vision creates something akin to a reliable or believable world by sampling, weighing, judging. This is anything but naïve, except in the sense that vision takes care of a self partly or substantially unaware of vision's executive role. This does not undermine but rather enhances vision's 'picture of the world'. Perhaps this is what Varela convolutedly means. On the other hand, it is possible to conceive of a manifestly false picture that is still an evolutionarily stable strategy. Language attains that status in extreme formalism; it is false through misplaced compression. We are emotionally incapable of treating vision as critically as we treat language, it lacks conventionality.[5] This is reasonable or natural, barring pathology. At the same time, it is clearly not correct in Laplace's sense. Such correctness is impossible. Is it the fault of vision that it is adapted? Vision is, or appears, reasonable, that is, reasonably adapted. But the formal linguistic conventions of humanism are beginning to fall apart.

Vision is saved from naivety by its innate (i.e. eco-auto-organised) reflexivity, which is to say that it is interconnected with memory; this is to indicate parallel adaptation processes. Memory is coupled with everything else, or rather every-thing it has been, by adaptation, instructed to interconnect with. In that sense, to 'see', utterly unlike the camera and the associated notion of one to one correspondence, is a part-conscious process of sampling, comparing, analysing, re-examining, acting in accord, re-acting in altered accord. All of this based on sedimented layers of the evolution of ecologically effective ways of exploiting visual stimuli. Think of the entirely unconscious, self-organising visual contest between the predator and the camouflaged prey. Is this bringing forth worlds? Perhaps this is what Varela, convolutedly, means. We might rather say, 'There *is* a world out there.' It is adequately simulated by cognition. Laplace remains unhappy, so might Baudrillard. Varela's convolutions rest on this. What if we should say that rudimentary correspondence is the preferred choice and that

Laplace's demon or total one to one correspondence, like the naïve realist, are amongst the least satisfactory simulations human imagination has invented.

Dennett (1991, 2003) constructs a complexly parallel model of consciousness on similar grounds. His first argument, strongly reminiscent of Cilliers' pragmatism, is to dismiss what he calls 'The Cartesian Theatre' on the grounds that it would crash. This 'theatre' is the illusion or metaphor of a central processing location, usually equipped with a screen, in which the self 'sorts out' all the conflicting mass of data coming in, not to mention imperatives from within and so arrives at a picture of its own state *vis-à-vis* the world. In humans this is compounded by the importance of the social world, no doubt populated with selves having similar illusory theatres. Dennett's alternative to Cilliers' 'distributed representation' in connectionist networks is 'the multiple drafts model'. The essential point is that there is no final draft. Rather, data, information, representations are stored, possibly for a fleetingly short time, possibly for longer according to their perceived importance throughout the neural network. Whilst certain areas are specialised for particular kinds of input–output, the network as a whole relies on hyper-connectivity to summon up relationships as necessary. This *ad hoc* arrangement is crucial; only stimuli that matter at the time are granted full conscious consideration. Others are given less attention. This is a situation familiar in so-called expert routines. One is not entirely conscious of the route or traffic whilst driving. Yet the concentration is successfully divided, the driving gets done reasonably expertly and should an emergency stimulus arise, your concentration will instantly shift. This is not a model of relative negligence; the more expert the driver, the more viable is this division of concentration. By contrast, we all remember the almost irresistible desire to look at our feet when learning to drive. How much more concentration is needed for a route you do not know than for one that is familiar. Much the same sensation can be experienced with playing a musical instrument, the concentration can be one hand, both hands, the sound, the visual picture of the movement, the flow of the phrase, or any such combination. The key is parallel options, multiple drafts, relative levels of consciousness. In visual processes, the almost total non-consciousness of processes of sampling, adjusting for position, adjusting for what a camera would experience as 'shake', prediction, re-prediction, the co-ordination of hand and feet in response.

Commenting on Libet's experiments that seemed to indicate minute delays that suggested explicit consciousness inexplicably lagged behind, for example, motor commands, Dennett comments:

> When we remove the Cartesian bottleneck, and with it the commitment to the ideal of a mythic time *t*, the instant when the conscious decision happens, Libet's discovery of a 100 millisecond veto window evaporates. Then we can see that our free will, like all our other mental powers has to be smeared out over time, not measured in instants. Once you distribute the work done by the [imaginary] homunculus

> . . . in both space and time in the brain, you have to distribute [con-
> scious] moral agency around as well. You are not out of the loop; you
> *are* the loop. You are that large. You are not an extensionless point.
>
> (Dennett 2003: 242)[6]

The picture of human cognitive activity that emerges from these considerations
radically reshapes both the more static or insulated forms of autopoiesis and
hermetic closure of consciousness within mind or language that is characteristic of Western humanist epistemology. In particular, the conscious mind is
no more of a unity within itself than in its relations to its environment. Like the
multiple drafts metaphor, this is a constantly wrested, provisional or fuzzy unity
constantly approaching other states. In other words, part of the perceived
problem of getting outside is the insistence that the mind is container-like, a
black box. Whereas the notion of mind in Dennett has smeared boundaries in
time and in space. Where or when for example does the faculty of sight begin
or end, in the non-habituated explorations of the infant, at the 'outside' of the
lens or the surface of the retina and so on? Would it not be more reasonable to
put these either/or questions aside and admit to a demystified temporal and
spatial domain in which the process of re-presentation takes place, simply
because the organism/environment distinction is an existential necessity?

Another prejudice of humanist epistemology is that, unlike the occluded outside, the self, or consciousness, is somehow more available for introspection on
account of its ostensible unity:

> Philosophers and psychologists are used to speaking about an organ
> of unification called the 'self' that can variously 'be' autonomous,
> divided, individuated, fragile, well-bounded, and so on, but this organ
> does not have to exist as such.
>
> (Ainslie 2001; Dennett 2003: 245)

In a grimly amusing example, Ainslie[7] describes the thoughts of a recovering
alcoholic being variously tempted by and refusing a drink, imagining or
'discounting' the various outcomes and further consequences:

> . . . what immediately determines her choice is the interplay of
> elements that, even if well-known in themselves, make the outcome
> unpredictable when they interact recursively.
>
> Hyperbolic discounting makes decision making a crowd phenomenon,
> with the crowd made up of the successive dispositions to choose that
> the individual has over time.
>
> (ibid. p. 131; Dennett, p. 212)

A key idea in this crowd phenomenon, clearly a version of multiple drafts, is
what Dennett (following Wegner 2002; Dennett 2003: 246) nicely calls our

'underprivileged access to consciousness'. In this case, it arises out of the inability to decide which draft is 'final', that consciousness is the loop, or in this case the crowd, and any privileged self-interpretation is impossible and another bit of the loop or crowd. It has, however, another route.

> This ghost army of unconscious actions provides a serious challenge to the notion of an ideal human agent. The greatest contradictions to our ideal of conscious agency occur when we find ourselves behaving with no conscious thought of what we are doing.
>
> (Wegner 2002: 157)

Dennett (2003: 246) cites this with reservations. His main aim, after all, is to ground the strongest possible notion of moral agency. However, in this instance he is speaking of such things as inadvertently signalled betrayal of sexual desire, so-called 'ideomotor automaticity'. The clear conclusion is this:

> For Descartes, the mind was perfectly transparent to itself, with nothing happening out of view and it has taken more than a century of psychological theorising and experimentation to erode this ideal of perfect introspectability, which we can now see gets the situation almost backward. Consciousness of the springs of action is the exception, not the rule, and it requires some rather remarkable circumstances to have evolved at all . . .
>
> In most of the species that have ever lived, 'mental' causation has no need for, and hence does not evolve, any elaborate capacity for self-monitoring.
>
> (Dennett 2003: 246–7)

This is very close to Plotkin's notion of the rarity of intelligence, and the conclusion is structurally identical. Humanist sociology has responded with the counter-argument that it is precisely the rarity of human consciousness and its cultural concomitants that makes us and sociology unique. Here, to borrow Dennett's phrase, the situation is 'almost backward'. In Plotkin, Dennett, Deacon, Visgotski and to a very slightly lesser extent, in Pinker and Chomsky, a developed social lifestyle, consciousness, symbolism and language are co-evolved phenomena.

> It is only once a creature begins to develop the activity of communication, and in particular the communications of its actions and plans that it has to have some capacity for monitoring not just the results of its actions, but of its prior evaluations and formation of intentions.
>
> (ibid. p. 248)

How is this so different from humanist epistemology? Well, because its origin is social or exo-auto-referential. The whole phenomenon resides in the spaces of the relationships, not in the sealed space between the ears. In a world of perfect Cartesian introspection, the socialisation of thought represents a kind of degradation. So too in Derrida, but this time on account of language's total self-reference. In the society represented by Dennett *et al.*, socialisation is the origin, the sustenance and the enrichment of symbolic consciousness. Which is the more sociologically appropriate model?

> People become what they think they are, or what they find others
> think they are, in a process of negotiation that snowballs constantly.
> (Wegner 2002: 314; Dennett p. 250)

In a telling phrase that underscores the ecology at work, Dennett says, 'We are transformers' (p. 250). All of this emphasises the importance of what has variously been called the ability to have a theory of mind, or more precisely, of others' minds – the faculty that is so disastrously lacking in autism. This implies that language, as one of the crucial domains in which minds are 'enacted', for this is a supremely practical account of reason, is not simply self-referential but geared toward influencing outcomes, including the negotiated identity of the self. It is at this point that one of the tenets of humanism has the possibility of entering the picture.

Does not 'snowballing negotiation' reinstate some or all of the problems of conventionality and contingency? Well, it could, and that is why it must be checked. Wegner's words are: 'snowballs constantly'. This implies duration, constantly, in time. If we were truly speaking of contingency in the sense of 'could have been otherwise', what is it that grounds duration? This brings us back to the constantly overlooked dimension in Prigogine's notion of system. Recall how systems close to equilibrium, all reactions more or less finished, were composed of undifferentiated particles, indifferent to each other. When the system was 'energised', the tendency to entropy reversed, metaphors such as particles 'begin to see' or 'are sensitive to intitial conditions' or 'take on an active identity' were used. Less figuratively, there were degrees of freedom, resonances, in other words increasing self-organisation as a system-preference for one set of possibilities over another. One solution was better than another, however temporary that situation might be. The same sense is conveyed by saying that self-organisation demands 'strong' particles and is moreover apt to strengthen their specific identity, perhaps until a catastrophic bifurcation becomes necessary. A similar strong and strengthening identity of human beings is the outcome, and in many senses the 'project' of culture. Of course, it too may be subject to catastrophic change. This will be the subject of our next chapter.

10

COMPLEXITY, LANGUAGE AND CULTURE

Social systems in qualitative, i.e. not formal, terms

Humanism rarely expresses its epistemology in systems terms. If it did, it would tend to present a closed, organised, unified faculty capable of responding to chaotic impulses that it 'synthesises' into some more orderly conception, presumably by detecting relative constants. That, in a sense, is the empiricists' version: constants are accumulated, become more certain, form bases for methodologies and routes of explanation. The phenomenological version, initially derived from Kant, differs only insofar as the order of conceptualisation is not so much derived as imposed. We shall not draw distinctions between these variations on a theme, but on the theme itself, the organised unity and relative closure of consciousness *vis-à-vis* an external manifold. In its modern form, especially in Heidegger, Derrida and Foucault, it is the self-reference of language that provides the image of closure and the mechanics of convention; enframing, representational thinking ground the persistent imagery of loss, ruin, abyss, or horizonality. What is outside language, tragically or ecstatically, according to your preference, stays out.

Explicitly in Dennett or Ainsley's notions of consciousness and language, less so in Cilliers' connectionism, there is no such boundary; the inside is no more accessible or unified, no less of a manifold or 'crowd' than the outside. Much like our discussion of path-dependency, hard edges require knowledge of both sides of the imagined boundary. Multiple drafts, according to Dennett, 'smear' the boundaries of the self: 'you are the loop.' Tooby and Cosmides' picture of adaptation-enaction and to a lesser extent the innatist notion of language derived from Chomsky describe 'hard-coupled' or content-specific neural mechanisms that describe specifiable domains, unified and distinguished by function. It is essential to see that this is not a contradiction, or a reinstatement of a kind of phenomenalism, but a highly likely outcome of complexity theory and evolved self-organisation.

Of course, it is possible to point to the physical container of the self, to name it, to influence it, to show it as the boundary of gradual morphological change, to cure it, kill it or watch it die. But what of factors such as approval, status, sanction, punishment? In these respects, what is the extent of the self? Is it commensurate with the dimensions of the body? Which notion of dimension is more appropriate to sociology or philosophy? There is, then, a strong argument that says, to begin with the physical container and the notions of restraint given by this version of inside-outside is to begin in exactly the wrong place. The epistemology of humanism takes exactly that mistaken strategy. For complexity theory, the body might be taken as the locus of the self's extension. But this would clearly not be enough, and in two related senses. First, the human self is social and therefore we should speak of loci of extension, both as an analytic requirement and as part of the social-material conditions of such extensions. Second, the human self is an evolutionary outcome, or more pointedly, one of the possibilities in the history of terrestrial self-organisation. Qualitative complexity theory begins as we move beyond this formal specification; in place of inside or outside there are two fundamental attractors whose interaction causes specification. In the first (social-material conditions), culture is one, increasingly important, subsystem. In the second (the sphere of cognitive possibility), intelligent self-consciousness is an ecologically defining subsystem.

We must not return this important insight back into the bottleneck of Cartesian serialism. Here we are speaking of innately parallel processes, some closely networked, others necessarily insulated. Equally important is the notion of 'strong' components in eco-auto-organisation as most forcefully demonstrated by Prigogine, without qualitative distinctions between more and less possible, or loss of symmetrical randomness; orders cannot appear at the interface with chaos. Without this qualitative seed, self-organisation in its entirety is impossible.

It is possible to concede certain aspects of our analysis of the co-evolution of intelligence, self-consciousness, language and the origins of culture and yet argue that developed culture is so far from these beginnings that evolutionary attractors have entirely lost their value as structure-builders and explanatory models. Thus, whilst Durkheim can admit to something like our inter-personal attractor in the notion that social facts are capable of exerting a constraint on individual action, they remain *sui generic*. This stance is routinely stated to be the foundation of sociology and its related disciplines:

> The founders of American anthroplogy, from Kroeber and Boas to Murdock and Lowie, were equally united on this point. For Lowie, 'the principles of psychology are as incapable of accounting for the phenomena of culture as is gravitation to account for architectural styles' and 'culture is a thing *sui generis* that can be only explained in terms of itself.
>
> (Tooby and Cosmides 1992: 22)

The choice of gravity and architecture here is at least ironic and, at most, blind. Of course, gravity is a major attractor in architectural structure and style. So are a host of other non-cultural factors, from climate to available materials, to say nothing of the universal and therefore non-cultural human need for shelter. A prime example is the invention of the so-called style of Georgian architecture as a series of functional regulations drawn up in response to the disaster of London's Great Fire. In our more complacent moments, we might credit humans with the invention of fire. More realistically, we can claim its partial management, its 'enculturation'. But the Great Fire broke that human bond only too easily and so forged another attractor to which 'style' was then subject: fire regulations. What Lowie demonstrates, then, is not an analytic position but an idiomatic prejudice. In other spheres we might call this bigotry.

Similarly:

> Our ideas, our values, our acts, even our emotions, are, like our nervous system itself, cultural products – products manufactured, indeed, out of tendencies, capacities and dispositions with which we were born, but manufactured nonetheless.
> (Geertz 1973: 50; Tooby and Cosmides 1992: 28)

Plotkin (2003: 248) interprets such statements as not denying the reality of 'dispositions', but as asserting 'their causal force and explanatory power is trivial'. With Plotkin we argue this position is not tenable. The assertion that non-cultural attractors, including physical, ecological and genetic ones, are trivial, with the underlying assumption of culture as *sui generic*, simply says that culture is never open to environmental influence; as a system it is absolutely closed. This is absurd. We may as well say that everything but human culture is subject to the laws of physics and then, like Geertz, allow that mistake to appear in our wordings – our nervous system itself is a cultural product. This is not disconnected from the generality of science, nor is it reason. It is simply creation *ex nihilo* either in the Christian sense or in the not very different beliefs of Nietzsche and naïve Post-modernism. The cause of all this hysteria, according to Plotkin, Tooby and Cosmides, Cohen and Stewart and practically everyone writing from a biologically informed notion of complexity, is the ghost of determinism. In other words, the *sui-generists* feel forced to explain the complexity or variety of culture by a correspondingly complex source, that is, unbounded self-creation. But as Cohen and Stewart point out, this 'conservation of complexity' is completely unnecessary once we admit to non-linear outcomes from relatively simple or similar beginnings. This version of sensitivity to original conditions completely removes the need to explain complexity by complexity; or in this case the complexity of culture by the prior complexity of culture as unbounded. Ironically, it is the *sui generists* that espouse determinism in the implicit linear requirement that complex results must stem from equally complex beginnings. Conversely, once we accept that culture is a eco-auto-organisational phenomenon, it is the relative simplicity of dispositions that becomes trivial as an obstacle to complexity and foundational in 'kick-starting' the manifold needs, respected, satisfied or invented by the emergent phenomena of culture.

This argument provides some discursive space for the reconsideration of human culture as an active component of the systems of terrestrial ecology, by removing the illusory threat of an implicit biological determinism. We shall directly address some sociologies of culture in more detail below, but it must be understood that attention cannot be directed to the many versions of culture as *sui generic* without becoming over-extended and diluted. Let us look briefly at one equally general sociological assumption, this time from Berger and Luckmann's classic, *The Social Construction of Reality* (1966). We propose to analyse this succinct but essential motto:

> . . . man is capable of forgetting his own authorship of the human world.
>
> (cited by Plotkin 2003: 265)

This remark – the routine indicator of a commitment to pluralism – displays an utterly chaotic notion of 'authorship' or 'social construction' or the degree to which the social world is *sui generic*. This confusion lies at the political heart of humanism in its sociological manifestations and however well-intentioned its sentiments, it is analytically false. Strong moral sentiments, however attractive, cannot stand on such weak ground.

'Humankind', we argue, is not a unity. The idiomatic assumption that it makes sense to fail to distinguish between past or present or future humanity, between the powerful and the powerless, between the young, the old and the dead, between genders, between those bound by quite different political regimes, between the killer and the killed, is absurd. It is also a pervasive characteristic of humanist discourse, especially in its academic forms. Neither we nor you, nor anyone else 'authored' the human world and therefore it is impossible to forget an authorship that did not ever happen. For the most part, we tinkered at the edges. Perhaps a few kings, scholars, religious leaders, technologically oriented scientists, 'great' artists or 'great' criminals had marginally more impact. But sociology never tires of reminding us that such 'individual' greatness is actually a travesty of communal action.

Even if we take out this routinely glossed epistemic fallacy, the situation is hardly improved. Suppose we say instead: 'In the last analysis humanity has authored its own world.' We should remember that the structural fallacy remains in the implicit assumption that the world is defined as human product. Even if we distinguish between the world and the human world there is still a classically Cartesian split: *Res* and *res cogitans* with no reciprocal ecology. Each represent a separated unity out of what was an interaction. The expression 'Man' is a similar trope. It is essential to see that once interaction is admitted, the unity of these categories collapses. Each becomes a qualitative and dependent outcome of the specific sites and processes of interaction. This is just another way of stating that central axiom of complexity theory: extreme sensitivity to initial conditions. Berger and Luckmann and their followers can and regularly do say, 'So what?' This is the Geertzian premise that non-cultural phenomena are trivial in the explanation of culture. So we reach the position of saying that one cannot maintain that the social construction of reality is an interactional outcome, with or without material conditions, and at the same time an act of authorship. Indeed, the emergent phenomena of complex interaction are not reducible to simple agents. Berger and Luckmann's position describes such an emergence but that is then throttled by their humanist concept of agency, or by their speech idioms.

This is not another case of the conservation of complexity, the idea that complex outcomes depend entirely on complex origins. The idea is quite different. Nor does it say that interaction, however simple, is the key phenomenon and that without interaction no party has any identity. This is entirely why the humanist version of agency looks limitless. To assert that identity, or order, emerges from interaction, between populations or ensembles of non-trivial component particles or through some sort of system-environment distinction, is not to predefine or fix the process of emergence. Nor should we force process onto relatively stable identities. Both are possible to a degree, according to circumstances. There is no way to compress these multiple dimensions into a single formal principle. Complexity theory must forego, identify and avoid that epistemic closure. Formalism is unavailable after the complexity turn in any sense that resembles humanists' usage.

How then is an account of the emergence of 'culture' possible when formalism presents so many epistemic dangers? The formal principle is dissipative structure in Prigogine's sense, that is, the transfer of environmental energy to a system to stave off entropy and to fuel its reorganisation. Such a system is necessarily eco-auto-organisational. Beyond a certain level, the role of chance demands that such recursive structuring must be informed about its own structure and the environmental properties it proposes to make use of. Hence the requirement of exo-auto-reference. Energy and information, then, are both the material bases of recursive structures. They are also primary characteristics of the living. It should be remembered, moreover, that despite the variety and scales of classification in which we view living things, they also represent systems 'far from equilibrium' as at least part of their structure. 'Birds' are, for example, viewed in stable families and species. They are also viewable as chains of electro-chemical reactions; hence their mortality. The co-existence of stability and instability, networked relation and insulation, are not contradictions but outcomes of complex self-organisations, underlining their parallel character. We should not allow the possibility of useful classification to reintroduce Cartesian dualism or its serial consequences. Instead, what classification, that is, the identification of relative constants, means is that energy and information exist in characteristic forms, or eco-logically.[1] Energy is materially available and transformable into the structure of the living.

Information is materially available as the adaptive coupling of organism and environment. We are not speaking, then, of hardware and software but of re-production. This is the sense in which radical constructivism is correct. Information is species-specific. Horse-sense differs from insect-sense, which differs from human-sense. It is less convincing in failing to stress viability, that is, the significance of the relationship itself and prone to space-time errors, not to mention conceptual irrationality, as we saw in the discussion of Bateson and Merleau-Ponty.

It has proved difficult to describe the origins of consciousness, language and culture. The influence of Chomsky's 'language acquisition device' – a fully fledged faculty – is testament to that. It is not a description at all, far less a theory. Yet the co-postulation of consciousness, language and culture is now common ground, emphasised by both theoretical and empirical demonstrations of the necessarily social character of language acquisition. Yet it is perfectly possible to model the analytic requirements placed on their prototypes given the requirements of eco–auto–organisation and exo–auto–reference.

The hermetic seal of one individual's consciousness, the black box, set against both a general environment and a specific environment of other individuals, appears far more as the product of verbal idiom than a statement of fact. An early criticism of humanism was the hardening of images into the status of facts. Eco–auto–organisation suggests that an opening appeared in a somewhat general sense in which a population of individuals might prosper as a social group given the 'amplification' of co-operative tendencies into something akin to what we could call developed 'communication' by means of symbols. To use Cohen and Stewart's apt phrase, this development seems necessarily 'downhill to' a less developed phase; some ecological advantage must have been gained. The consequences of this model are important. First, this is Prigogine's constant requirement, the matter of population is important; whether we speak of particles in a system or individuals in a social system, the properties of the systems cannot be reduced to the components. Interaction is what gives the system its complexity, that is, the possibility of self-organisation. Second, however, the individual, the particle or the human, is not a random, symmetrical, or merely quantitative specification. Such individuals must have a qualitative character in order to enter into interactive organisation. Chance is not then a general or formal variable that describes components, nor their relationships. Prigogine's position says instead that chance too takes on qualitative dimensions.[2] This is the upshot of his metaphor that particles become 'active' or 'begin to see' or become less 'indifferent to each other' in conditions far from equilibrium. Once-random possibilities become more defined as complex order increases: some configurations are more possible or 'better' than others. What does this imply for the most problematic relation of all, namely that between a human individual and a group or culture?

Given the consensus on the co-implication of the human brain, consciousness, language and culture, and especially Deacon's (1997) radicalisation of their co-evolution,[3] we can see that the relationship might equally well be inverted. The human individual, the member of our species, might just as well be regarded as the outcome of co-evolutionary processes. Much the same might be said of the member of a specific culture. The one-way-ness of this process, that is, Kant's subject constituting the phenomenal world or conversely 'socialisation' theory, is another habitual idiom. Given the analyses of cause, the idea of positive feedback in complex systems, and the notion of interactivity, we must insist, cause flows all ways. Not in Merleau-Ponty's sense; time is still irreversible. The problem is not how to get the black box, the blank slate, to have some content. Rather, the processes of eco-auto-organisation and exo-auto reference are constantly influencing the multiple, qualitative dimensions and possible content of the brain, consciousness, language and culture. Each emerges through ecologically viable relations. This is not to say that every such outcome is equally valid but that on balance ecology has 'favoured' their general development. It is an open question whether the ecosystem is capable of sustaining that development.

Before we move to the direct comparison of this model with those more usually described in social systems theory, we should note several features that must not fall out of epistemic attention. The first of these is Dennett's notion of multiple drafts with no final draft, or what we might generalise as 'provisionality'. Dennett's concept is explicitly tied to the parallel-provisional organisation of self-consciousness. Take a similar mixture of provisional-alterable decisions, or states, as complexity theory's response to Derrida *et al.* and the 'undecidability' of meaning. The second refers to the non-uniform character of systematicity. This indicates both the propensity to operate in parallel and the idea that the network of relations between the system may be intensely connected or relatively insulated. It may be crucial that some systems stay constant or do not learn, whilst some must have flexible-response characteristics, including learning and innovation. These are not meant entirely exclusively; the involuntary nervous system must stay that way, yet the taken-for-granted movements of the hands and feet may be focused on with uncustomary, acute consciousness in dance, music, visual art.

Luhmann provides a series of important insights into how this autopoietic complexity may be modelled for sociology. The notion of autopoietic closure recommended here is somewhat different. Let us begin with the issue of closure.

> Our thesis, namely, that there are systems, can now be narrowed down to: there are self-referential systems. This means first of all, in an entirely general sense: there are systems that have the ability to establish relations with themselves and to differentiate these relations from relations with their environments. This thesis encompasses the fact of systems, the conditions of their description and analysis by other (similarly self-referential) systems.
>
> (Luhmann 1995: 13–14)

The logic of this position is impeccable. One of the more interesting consequences is the idea that the relative simplicity of the system or organism *vis-à-vis* its more complex environment rules out any question of one to one correspondence. Hence the telling remark in Knodt's *Foreword*, 'Systems theory, in other words *simulates* complexity . . .' (ibid. xix). It is instructive to re-inscribe this situation in human terms. The 'member' 'simulates' the complexity of its physical and social environment. Such a position would be commensurate with Maturana, Varela and radical constructivism, and also with Derridean conceptions of meaning and interpretation, or the general thrust of phenomenology as a component theory of society. However, it potentially or actually shares the same formalism, or rather the same misplaced formalism. For the implication is a distinction in which the system, organism, or member is self-referential with respect to itself but only capable of simulations of complex altereity. But as Luhmann insists, self-reference is an emergent reality confronted like any other. Then the logic and methodological requirements collapse. As Dennett's notion of multiple drafts and 'impeded access' to the self suggest, no privilege can be attached to self-reference; it too is self-simulation. Both 'exo' and 'auto' reference are something quite different.

This rather abstract formulation appears counter-intuitive but relatively easy to illustrate. 'My' self, as the *cogito* demonstrates, is traditionally understood to be more certain or stable for me than its contents, which are taken as radically more contingent. Hence Kant's axiom. This is normally taken as the distinction between two spheres, consciousness and consciousness *of*. It is better taken as a simple distinction within forms of speaking. The 'conscious self' (contentless) is an altogether more formal idea that the self that is conscious *of* something. That is the sole source of the former's apparent stability. Even with Dennett's provisional draft model the formal self is not particularly constituted circumstantially. I, formally understood, remain 'me' despite circumstance. But the concrete me, what I can say or do, depends acutely on circumstance, despite the influence of memory or my self-history. The self is path dependent and path dependence has a route, but is always intensely sensitive to actual position. The formal self, however, has no historical precedent in this path, except as idiom. If we accept the fundamentalism of self-organisation, the formal self has no status, no prehistory, no environment. It is a reality that has to be excluded from the ontology of eco-auto-organisation. And that statement is itself an emergent reality in and of a 'system', which Luhmann would call the subsystems of science, amply demonstrating that 'self-reference' is not privileged access. The path-dependency of self-reference obscures as much as it illuminates. The role of contingency appears to have been amplified; indeed this was always the upshot of our critique of Kant, in that contingency can no longer be reserved or excluded in the realm of content or experience or alterity. It is then appropriate to turn to Luhmann's conception of 'double-contingency'.

The basic situation of double contingency is then simple: two black boxes, by whatever accident, come to have dealings with one another. Each determines its own behaviour by complex self-referential operations within its own boundaries. What can be seen of each other is therefore necessarily a reduction. Each assumes the same about the other. Therefore, however many efforts they exert and however much time they spend . . . the black boxes remain opaque to each other. Even if they operate in a strictly mechanical way, they must still presuppose indeterminacy and determinability *in relation to one another.* Even if they themselves operate 'blindly' they proceed in *relation to one another* more effectively if they assume determinability in their system environment relationship and observe themselves through this. Any attempt to calculate the other will inevitably fail. One could be more successful and could gain experience by trying to influence the other from his environment. Incalculability is absorbed – one might say 'sublimated' – by concessions of freedom. The black boxes, so to speak create whiteness when they come upon each other, or at least sufficient transparency for dealing with each other . . . they can try to influence what they observe by their own action and learn further from the feedback. In this way an emergent order can arise that is conditioned by the complexity of the systems that make it *possible but that does not depend on the complexity's being calculated or controlled.* We call this order a social system.

(Luhmann 1995: 109–10, original emphases)

We have quoted this in full with minimal abbreviation. What is being expressed here? Well, two black boxes come to have dealings with one another but remain, by definition, 'closed' to each other. Nevertheless an emergent order is possible. It does not depend on 'definitions' of systems but on 'actions' or 'ploys' in an intersecting environmental space. Luhmann does not quite say so here (but does elsewhere throughout the text) that these strategies, moves, errors, vexations, feedbacks and so on are necessary to the autopoiesis of the system. That continuous process is the key point.

This, remember, is intended to model human interaction. How helpful then is the conceptualisation 'black box'? Whether we imagine an infant struggling to enter the social world or one adult struggling to interpret another, we confront a determinate and influential history. In the case of the infant, it could be conceptualised as a mixture of instinctive disposition and active experimentation. The infant's 'recipient-adult' is in approximately a similar position with rather more accomplishment. In the case of adult co-interpretation, cultural histories are presupposed, possibly similar enough to lend itself to the emergence of comprehension, possibly different enough to frustrate it, but in every case influential.

Whatever heuristic function 'black boxes' serve *vis-à-vis* double contingency or the construction of meaning, the emergence of order from noise, they also carry with them the weight of their specific imagery. Is it then accidental or in some obscure sense factual, or idiomatic, or all of these, that the imagery of the black box subtly but completely erases the counter-image of path dependency that is so central to systems-theory, not least in the key dimensions of biological and social evolution? In such imagery the black box mutates into shades of grey interspersed with white. Noise is certainly possible but within roughly determined spaces. This is approximately the same as saying that chance is not a general or formal but a specific ecological dimension. Then 'double contingency' becomes a space of qualitative possibility and impossibility; the infant's cry will not be read as aggression. Certain kinds of sociological modelling, at certain levels of abstraction, are prone to throw away such qualitative insights. They are the stuff that complexity theories must be made of. Parallel to arguments made above, 'black boxes' and qualitative path-dependence are mutually exclusive. The latter is central to any theory of eco-auto-organisation. Now contrast 'black boxes' and their counterpart, order from noise, with *eco-auto-organisation* and its counterpart, order from order and noise. The latter expresses qualitative path dependency in the precise sense of sensitivity to original conditions, in this case, the preconditions of the biosphere and antecedent social structures. These may be taken as variations on themes or more precisely as gathered around multi-dimensional attractors. The black box, for all its heuristic value, is simply too compromised with the residual sense of starting from scratch, more precisely as order *ex nihilo*. One could dispense with these nuances by insisting that 'noise' has a character of sorts. Then one must also concede that randomness is similarly 'asymmetric': probability always occurs within frames of ecological influence.

Luhmann's concept of interpenetration is much stronger. The whole concept of 'black boxes', parallel to the formal subject, defies autopoiesis so long as it remains 'black'; once this situation changes, the image becomes at best redundant and at worst obstructive. Conversely, the whole concept of interpenetration insists that an active relationship of 'negotiated alignment' is the entire basis of autopoiesis. The difference is emergent. Otherwise we are again speaking of equilibrated identities, the 'close of business' situation, the triumph of entropy. This image haunts every notion of consciousness as closure. One of the interesting nuances Luhmann proposes in the context of interpenetration is the distinction or relation between psychic systems and the social system of communication. This places the latter, broadly all of those phenomena that can be described as linguistic or capable of carrying meaning, in social space. Such a premise is congruent with Durkheim's location of social facts, yet it is also congruent with the notion of *memes*.[4] These, first proposed by Dawkins, developed by Dennett and Blackmore, are units of cultural iteration that are only possible on account of the human mind, but, on the other hand they parasitise or preoccupy its social operations. If we introduce Dennett's multiple drafts, without finalisation, or even allow Derrida's altogether less analytically neutral 'endlessness', we can see clearly the implication, a homeodynamic capable of interrelation, response and mutual constitution. The 'provisionals', the psychic system, language, culture, all describe 'states' of that dynamic: spatio-temporal 'mappings' or structures.

Look again at the notion of parallel differentiation or we might repeat the failures of post-modernism. To say that structures are radically spatio-temporal, or autopoietic, is not to say that a common duration, character or distribution is to be expected. With characteristic abstraction, Luhmann refers to all such considerations as difference between systems, subsystems and so on. Plotkin uses rather more concrete images in understanding the difference between intelligent systems that 'learn' and systems whose requirement is not learnt innovation but constant repetition: the involuntary or instinctive dimensions of mind and brain. Somewhere between these extremes lies Tooby's and Cosmides' images of content-specific mechanisms and 'adaptation enaction'. Nothing is to be gained by treating these as analytically similar. They are clearly qualitatively distinct. Likewise, nothing is to be gained by treating their expression in, or relation to culture, as though the distinctions are erased in that 'medium'. On the contrary, the implications are related, qualitative differences within the cultural milieu. The characteristic of path dependency remains decisive; the identity of a system, subsystem, culture, member or 'meme' lies at the intersection of many such paths. They are inescapably structural, having very little to do with the post-modern notion of conventionality or contingency or the sudden explosion of innovation at the whim of members.

We are now in a position to make plain our thesis. Where Luhmann says 'there are systems' we say there are, in the most general sense, attractors. Given our interest in attractors shaping social possibility, these fall into five relevant categories:

1. Those attractors that predate but persist in the human species, such as dependency on oxygen, food, shelter, sexual reproduction.
2. Those that are exclusively human, such as developed intelligence, the use of language and symbolism.
3. Those that emerge from the material interaction of human societies and the world: tools, technology, the means of material transformation.
4. Those that appear to gain their stability only 'memetically': custom, habit and convention which sociology may credibly claim to be merely repetitive or whose apparent necessity has long been lost to rational analysis.
5. Meanwhile, the fourth category has manifestly divided itself, so that the fifth is the requirement of self-reflexivity. Some disciplines may not recognise that requirement; they may, for example, begin in faith, belief or the conviction that something is morally unacceptable. Our risk and strength lies entirely in taking on the requirement of reflexivity.

The fifth condition may be taken a little differently, again following from Luhmann's thesis. The distinction between systems and environment is specifically a reduction of complexity, hence the 'simulation' argument discussed above. Therefore the absence of one-to-one correspondence is simultaneously the production of risk, named in the difference itself. This is trivialised as 'the precession of simulacra'; it is the existential outcome of the unity of identity and difference. As such it may be taken as a sixth requirement, or a unifying requirement that grounds the emergence of the previous five. It is, in effect, another occasion of the emergence of eco-auto-organisation and exo-auto-reference from the logic of the text. Like Luhmann, our position is decisively and inescapably 'circular'.

> The theory of evolution is itself a product of evolution, action theory could not develop without action, and so on.
>
> Traditional epistemologies consider circles of this sort as grounds for suspicion that statements are false, if not gratuitous. The opposite is true. They force themselves upon us. One cannot avoid them. One can sharpen them as a paradox and leave it at that. But one can also build them into the theory of science, for they provide precise instructions for self-control. Theories must, as a minimal requirement, they must always be formulated so that their object is subject to comparison. If they themselves appear among their objects they subject themselves to comparison. As their own objects they must continue to function under the pressure of comparison.
>
> (Luhmann 1995: 482)

Luhmann would insist that such a position places us within 'the subsystem of science' and is so bound, in his terms, by the 'binary' code true/not true. This is an uncomfortable place for a reflexive theoretical sociology to find itself returned. But not returned in the narrower sense of 'pure' self-reflexion, for what is described is constantly open to comparison. This clearly implies the dual sense of eco-auto-organisation and exo-auto-reference; indeed the one dimension constitutes the other; they are mutually autopoietic. Perhaps we should admit, then, that 'our' science is, like Dennett's self, somewhat smeared-out, less a distinct subsystem and more an interdependent feature of explanations that might make recourse to more mixed criteria: belief and dis-belief, sacred and profane, exhaustion and renewal, even self-disgust at humans' domination of the planet, or our obsessions with words, words, words.

The first category of attractors, those that predate but persist in the human species, such as dependency on oxygen, food, shelter, sexual reproduction, might now look ripe for reconsideration. We are speaking of domains associ-ated with the senses that, to repeat, predate but persist in humanity in a form that is species-specific *to a degree*. This exposes our susceptibility that the old prejudice, 'information is mainly human', is merely homocentric. Information, as we have constantly reiterated, lies at the very centre of recursive self-organisation. We shall return to the counter-implication shortly, that language is not the 'highest' and certainly not the most neutral or reliable information-managing resource. It is simply our most species-specific resource and the one we have spent most time 'analysing', by linguistic means of course. Narcissus does not so much look at, as speak to, himself.

Let us begin with embodiment.[5] This is what autopoiesis means in its fundamental key. Stripped of its grace-notes the melody is simple. You are the consequence of sexual reproduction and dependent on nutrition for your continued identity. Are we, in the West, so complacent that we think we have long ago 'solved' these basic requirements and, having forgotten the poverty of the human majority, concluded that sociology need no longer begin at the beginning? Is the truth yet more ridiculous, we are so idiomatically absorbed in our special wordings that we have forgotten that there is a beginning? For all sociology's arrogance that is not an amnesiac trait shared by other sciences. We are alone here, even when we whistle into this oblivion by calling others reduc-tionists. Whilst we insist, *Il n'ya pas dehors texte!* – the 'reductionist' majority might register our embodied dependence on, aside from nutrition, say, climate, and global warming, or disease and preventative healthcare, or kin-preference and the reproduction support systems of family institutions; on the availability of building materials and the mobilisation of labour and so on. Or, unlike Geertz, might recognise that such materials actually do obey the laws of gravity and 'discovered' it long before we arrived on the scene, and take steps to mitigate its effects (such as water transport, railways and roads). We might even make the shocking discovery that cities owe far more to such physical depend-ences than to 'text'. We might even concede that the majority of texts, however mistaken, are dedicated to the management of such problems of dependency, or that language originates in this mundaneity and constantly responds to this environment as the basis of its autopoiesis.

Part III

THE FIELDS OF
COMPLEX ANALYSIS
Contemporary complexity theory

11

THE ETHICS OF PRAGMATISM

Politics and post-structuralism in transition after the complexity turn

Post-structuralism currently holds the ethical and political high ground. Its practitioners write with a tone of confidence and expectation that their position is justified and anyone who wants to suggest otherwise better have a very good argument and know what they are taking on; or better, what we all stand to lose if post-structuralism's authority is overturned. A challenge to what appears to be the best-founded critical paradigm is a serious business with serious consequences. Its dominance is nevertheless in question and, indeed, from within. A sense of transition is obvious in the best writing from that field. Cary Wolfe's *Critical Environments: Post-Modern Theory and the Pragmatics of the 'Outside'* (1998) is the most informative crystallisation of what is at stake.

> ... the critiques of the traditional philosophical paradigms of positivism, empiricism and the like, which stress instead the contingency and social construction of knowledge (pragmatism, post-structuralism, material feminism), would seem politically promising because they hold out hope that a world contingently constructed might also be *differently* (i.e. more justly) constructed. On the other hand the ... constructivist account has left intellectuals ... without foundations ... Having undercut the philosophical footing of those in power, contemporary intellectuals find their own supposedly more progressive claims in danger as well of being 'just another' contingent (and ... self-serving) interpretation.
>
> (p. xii)

This is an extremely frank statement. It is staggeringly Modernist, for a postmodernist: 'more justly ... more progressive'; at the same time, he spends a lot of time decrying consensus-production (Habermas *et al.*). Wolfe is one of the very few that grasps that relativisation of others is equal to self-relativisation. So the spectre of self-serving 'discourse' arises. Indeed, the cited paragraph opens: 'In his characterization of the double crisis of post-modernism Lyotard puts his finger on what is perhaps the *central* challenge ...'

(ibid., our emphasis). To cite a routine positivist response: Wolfe's facts are not lonely. Despite a number of analytical and ontological counter claims the preoccupation is primarily ethical. We must put ontology or 'foundation' first. Rosen, faced with a similar dilemma, memorably declared that second is extremely high but . . .[1] There is, however, a completely disingenuous comment: 'how can a North American published author, citing Lyotard, one of the most influential, still refer to '*those* in power'? Perhaps the regular idioms of post-structuralism and 'material feminism' are responsible for this 'understatement' passing without notice. Are the dynamics of hegemony so badly understood?[2] That offers a more compelling perspective on the contingencies of self-reference. Self-serving interpretation is so much more complex than the implicit but limited presentation cited above. In the same way that the self, who is served, in part rests on the Cartesian mode of address where privileged access to the interior is taken for granted and strategic, so this restricted notion of self-reference is just another massively determining, routine figure of speech. It is a matter of idiom, usage and complicity, not interiority. Note that this is from an author who feels impelled to put the pragmatics of the 'outside' in scare quotes. Might we say at the very least that the inside/outside polarity is becoming problematic?

The issue can be further developed. Is this not exactly Foucault's point when he dismisses the centrality of the Subject and insists on strategies without strategists?

Is not Wolfe's 'self' the very thing that is lost in this self-organising play of power? Is it not exactly this loss that the theorist as dissident and Wolfe in particular throughout this book is trying to reconceptualise; to find, as Deleuze puts it in reading Foucault, 'new co-ordinates of praxis'? Our response is: Yes, to a degree. In that sense, the word 'transition' in this chapter's title does not describe 'someone else' but forces at work in the episteme *we* share. So what difference is emerging that we-as-authors seek to represent? Are we not simply working that old, ironic game from Socrates to Deleuze where the theorist (paid, published and authoritative) engages in the self-description as dissident, civil disobedience, the permanent re-invention of the self. Permanent, that is, in the sense that the game has gone on for centuries. Here the answer is a decisive rejection. If anything we see ourselves as complicit in the episteme. How then can we be critics? The answer is simply to reject the polarity and with it complicity in the sense of crime or guilt. If we reject the polarity and its demonisations, the writer might be seen as the episteme reflecting upon itself. That of course is too monolithic and invites the counter-charge of Hegelian 'megalomania'. We intend instead to grasp the episteme as one of the networked structures of our social (eco-auto) organisation and locate the critical writer at one of the points of pressure where eco-auto-organisation and exo-auto-reference are engaged in re-production. One can take this as homeostatic or homeodynamic, but not in itself, not without development, as an ethical issue. It is first ontological. Our wording below tends also toward the notion of 'adaptation' without losing the autopoietic propensity toward re-production. As observed above, dynamics of the adaptive or de/re-constructive kind pre-suppose a degree of homeostasis

The 'dissident' is located first at that ontological pressure point and not in the absurd posture of disobedience that led Socrates to his entirely consistent but avoidable death (which he chose *not* to avoid on no sustainable logical or ethical ground compared with the alternative)[3] and to the deserved public indifference to philosophy ever since. If Socrates had anything worth saying he should have found it to be his duty to stay alive and say it. On the other hand, if he is to be believed that he could not value social life above death, he is (philosophy is) hardly in a position to offer reasoned social criticism. If philosophy 'alive' is complicit, so be it. The 'transition' consists then in this: in freeing philosophy from the Socratic posture and trying to occupy its new responsibility to reasonable effect. That is where our ethics should begin, not in ancient posturings about others as demonic, power crazy, con-spiratorial or plain stupid. We are weary of academics who see themselves primarily as better people, the priest class. We are working students: pragmatists of a sort.

Wolfe's opening chapter espouses the general notion of pragmatism whilst condemning some of its particular forms in American philosophy for failing to engage their reliance on the technological, economic and political structures of that country. This resembles our dislike of Socrates. Wolfe cites Lentricchia:

> To proceed with the illusion of purity is to situate oneself on the margin of history ... It is to exclude oneself from any chance of making a difference for better or worse.
>
> (Wolfe 1998: 9)

Commentating on James' pragmatism:

> For [Cornell] West as for Lentricchia, Jamesian pragmatism insists on the gap between concept construction on specific discursive sites and concept circulation in a broader set of contexts, and it is in this gap that the possibility of the social and the historical resides.
>
> (ibid. p. 10)

This is an entirely acceptable position that still, however, breeds its discontents. First there is the question of deferral, dispersion or contingency that makes it 'hard to see how we can reflect on ... what what we think does' (sic. ibid.). Second, and interlinked, the results are, so to speak, open to inspection: we are implicitly *involved*. This [Jamesian] position then leaves us with both a correspondential and a constructivist version of truth. Propositions must agree with some reality in order to be counted true whilst human action has 'a revisionist role ... in the construction of that reality' (ibid. p. 11).

We must express some dissatisfaction with this formulation; it courts an unhelpful polarity; it is too formal in that the differential access to both concept formulation and 'inspection', elsewhere ruthlessly exposed, is glossed. The result, whilst Wolfe intends it as criticism, is to invoke the dismal, outworn distinction between theory and practice: 'In Lentricchia's reading of James it is as if theory and practice are engaged in a never ending battle on the terrain of belief' (ibid.). Characteristically 'practice' is merely taken to be differentiated (i.e. treated formally) whilst 'theory' takes its equally characteristic position 'above' the fray – variously described as 'a kind of conceptual imperialist within' or (following Lentricchia) 'the need to generalise' and 'obliterate differences' (ibid.).

This marks the slippage in the transition. On the one hand, theory and practice are distinguished and potentially granted different kinds of agency. On the other is the guarantee of conceptual imperialism, the obliteration of differences. This simply erases the first distinction. In re-granting the hegemony of the theoretical, what is lost is the locality, specificity and strategic ploy of such formulations.

The professional theorist (James, Lentricchia, Wolfe and us) habitually works in this imperialistic way. That is both a matter of specialism and of custom; both rely on epistemic assumptions we have repeatedly criticised, most prominently in Kant. Let us try to resist the traditional confines, which are almost bound to configure the issue in the same terms. Set theory suggested that in order to belong to a more inclusive, or formal category, or set, specifics have to downplayed for the sake of that strategy. Our earlier example was apples and oranges subsumed under the category 'fruit' to which they can belong only to a degree. The subsumption, then, is contradictory. What is it that makes the more general set (fruit) more theoretical than the more limited sets apples and/or oranges? Nothing. From a creationist or creator point of view it makes more sense (though Hegel might take issue with that).[4] From a Nietzschean point of view, when God is dead, it appears that we can play fast and loose. Nonsense too. From a complexity theory point of view, where God never was alive, all that is ever at stake is strategy with effects or costs. The question of rank, especially as theory or practice, is largely beside the point.

We can illustrate this by concrete example. The policy of integrating pupils with special or additional educational needs (ASEN) into mainstream schools is active in British education at the time of writing, not without controversy. We are not especially thinking of those in favour of maintaining separate provision; they are probably the majority but have no political voice. Instead we mean a more radical debate, indicated above, between those who argue that ASEN is 'constructed' and so could be constructed otherwise: classic post-structuralism; and those who say the dimensions of relative disability are real in the sense of unavoidable. This sometimes called the medical model because it focuses on remedy as opposed to social reform. This time, we do not want to argue for or against either position. Both are inherently possible. The question now is this:

suppose as a teacher, or governor, or ASEN manager, or a learning support worker, or a parent, your contractual, civic or common law responsibility is to ensure the best outcome for a child with ASEN in school, which is a legal requirement; are you in a position to consider both sides of this debate (both *possibilities*) or are you obliged to place one above the other? Is the construc- tivist strategy as equally open as the medical model in these circumstances? The answer must be no; not because the issue is unthinkable; it would be a fairly standard part of the debate in any education degree. Rather it isn't worth the cost given the priorities of the classroom. We could reduce this to theory versus practice but that would be to neglect the ecology that makes one strategy more viable than another. If we resist that temptation theory has a different feel; rather than ask about social values it asks instead about the processes of knowledge acquisition, especially when it fails to be viable. When that happens, the practitioner has both the right and the necessity to counter certain theoretical tendencies as not-practical, that is, to overturn the hierarchy. The imperialism of total theory, the obliteration of difference, then rests on an occupational trait. Both professional theorists and professional educators risk the downside of the contradiction of inclusion, not in mainstream schools, but rather in the classificatory ambitions of their own professions. Does 'strategies without strategists' model this situation reasonably or, instead, do we need to invoke the concept of qualitative attractors?

This example shows that a universal theory-practice distinction elevates, but obscures, local, mundane classificatory practices. 'Local epistemologies' might be an apt phrase. We could then point to the contradiction in every classification (that to belong to any set is only true to a degree) alongside a corresponding contradiction here at the level of differential intent. Heard in that sense 'local epistemologies' might seem, indeed is, the statement of an intention to neglect some other, perhaps less local, epistemological possibilities for good reasons. That this neglect is functional for practical purposes cannot absolve it from its effects. The question is one of re-presentational practice which for Wolfe and those he cites, judging by what he cites, remains too close to neutral in its effects, too simply just theory despite its 'imperialism', an innocence which trades off the remnants of truth as correspondence. Re-presentation heard in its fundamental key is more like felling trees for (re)construction timber. No doubt Wolfe as an exemplary post-structuralist will be astonished by this response. Is not his whole thrust the relation of knowledge and power: that knowledge reconstructs? Yes, but this is writing in transition; that is, the aim cannot be realised in the epistemic limits of the work.

Consider then Wolfe's conclusion to this section, again citing Lentricchia:

> Theory cannot be identified with agency and the conscious individual ... theory is the sort of force that tends to control individuals by speaking through them. The epistemological generalisation may be an 'appetite of the mind' ... but the economic and political move to

generalise – the global generalisation of labour known as capitalism – is not an unhistorical appetite; it is a locatable historical phenomenon whose role tends to blurred and repressed by James's liberal ideology of the autonomous self.

(CW12)

Then:

> James's gamble is that he is too much within the dominant discourse of the liberal subject, but his payoff is to unleash that discourse's radically democratic tendencies against the private property side of liberalism that threatens always to recontain them.

Surely this more than answers our criticisms? It would if our epistemic assumptions were the same. But they are not. First there is the familiar demonology: '. . . theory is the sort of force that tends to control individuals by speaking through them.' Whatever the critical intent, we are right back at strategies without strategists which robs individuals (when we should say 'members') of both responsibility and power. This is the Nuremburg defence: I was only following orders. This may be a mitigating defence in crude polarity of forced judgement between legality and illegality. As an analytic model of human agency it is simplistic.

Which orders are being followed? Capitalism's of course. And there are unspecified alternatives that dispose of private property (in unspecified ways) and build a new unspecified democracy that hopefully (but not specifically) promotes equality when every other social system is characterised by inequality. Presumably, unlike every other ecology, contest in the form of predation will be also overcome. In this context there is considerable mention of animal rights premised on the post-humanism of the text. This is laudable. It would be more so if handled more frankly, for example, the rights of animals reared for food. If capitalism (or meat-eating) is so avoidable, why is it so widespread? Is it because evil walks in the world blinding us to the truth or because it is a viable attractor for human conduct? What if, instead of being ethically 'bad', a very easy pronouncement, liberal democracy is the 'least worst' alternative?

The problem with distancing oneself from capitalism and its effects (which is not without irony for North American and West European theorists who derived enormous differential benefit from its operations) is that agency is always located elsewhere. This elsewhere is not specified but is exemplified in expressions like 'those who have power'. We have power, however limited. In the terms used earlier we have to confront the fact that capitalism, judged on the evidence, is an ESS partly dependent on our powers, however limited their exercise, and partly on a host of other factors including scarce resources and the dependence of innovation or development on 'stored up' capital. It cannot be changed by our wish-list because it is not an ethical but an ontological matter.

That is to say that the networks of interaction that constitute 'capitalism' are not simply ethical or simply human. This is why Lentricchia's theory/practice distinction is outworn: it treats 'things' as if universally generalisable, as if they were be-spoken, as though concrete necessities expressed in the relation of speech to material objects were primarily 'formulations' and finally, then, as ethical.

This represents the persistence of a language saturated by a creationist past. But even if that is not an acceptable formulation for many readers the distinction can be expressed differently. Recall earlier that we spoke of the issues of transgression raised by Bataille, de Rais and Hitler. We rejected the idea that what was at stake was moral belief, that de Rais did not simply cut into the corpus of belief but into the bone and sinew of his victims. We then pointed to Hitler, the Krays, the Wests, distinguishing between 'essayed' (in writing) and material transgressions. We formulated the difference in terms of material costs. Perhaps that understates the issue so let us state it even more frankly: Hitler and Co. are not primarily immoral but literally unacceptable; they pursue non-ESS strategies in which the cost of non-response outweighs the cost of response. That is why apparently amoral strategies are pursued by politicians (such as wars, sanctions, hegemonic control of regions) and why social orders invest in a complex apparatus of sanctions. This is not to say that amoral or exclusive strategies are *per se* acceptable or absolved from criticism. It is to say, exactly in the dove and hawk example, that an ethical optimum is not necessarily as ESS – not when there are large differences amongst humans, cultures and between species. The conflation of ethically desirable and optimum stability is therefore dependent on an identity of interest, which is highly unlikely. To pursue an argument from the position of ethical desirability is not to meet but to ignore the complex ontology of difference and differentiation, as Lentricchia rightly puts it but without due reconsideration: 'the need to generalise' and 'obliterate differences' (op. cit.). We have never quite understood why 'everything' is col-lectable, generalisable, or capable of having its differences obliterated; is it just the careless usage of 'every thing' or the careful cultivation of the concept of things as uniformly created? In which case it follows naturally that they can be re-col-lected. Given the notion of eco-auto-organisation that underlies complexity theory, such sweeping speech 'theoretical' practices seem, frankly, unreasonable.

This issue was live in the Platonic-Christian culture of the Italian Renaissance. The drive behind Michelangelo's classicism, for example, is based on the idea that the 'elect', God's elect, is capable of seeing the perfection or ideal behind mundane appearances and it is the elect's duty to give that vision substance. Hence there are very many ideal heads or figures in his work but only two faces considered worthy of portraiture.[5] That seems bizarre, but a similar hierarchy underlies the curious acceptance of total categorisation and the ignorance of incident on the part of 'theorists'. Does the same hierarchy underlie the widespread post-modern assumption that all social organisations are to a large if not total degree conventional? What is it – care*ful* or care*less* formulation that so easily undermines the very heterogeny that post-modernism appears to champion, so long as it *is merely* conventional? Is there an essential or merely curious continuity between Socrates or Michelangelo who see beyond the mundane and, say, Foucault who likewise is 'acutely critically aware' when so many fellow-citizens are not? Is the post-modern essentially different from, often blatantly hypocritical, 'civic' theism of the Florentine Renaissance or just another version served up with a Nietzschean sauce? The requirement of complex eco-auto-organisation is not met by a theory of absence, especially of a Christian God.

Perhaps we are trading off a similar hierarchy? There are scant similarities but rather more differences. This can be seen by considering Wolfe's reading of Rorty.

Discussing *Philosophy and the Mirror of Nature*, he describes Rorty's rejection of what Jay (1993) has since called 'ocularcentrism'. Jay's full title, *Downcast Eyes: The Denigration of Vision in French Twentieth Century Thought*, indicates that this is more than a 'Rortian' idiosyncrasy. Levin's (1988) *Opening of Vision* thoroughly formulates similar misgivings in Heidegger's philosophy. The character of vision will become immensely important in due course.

> Rorty suggests that we abandon the representationalist position and its privileged ocular figures and agree instead that 'our only usable notion of "objectivity" is "agreement" rather than mirroring'.
>
> (Wolfe 1998: 12; Rorty 1979: 191)

The equivocal notion of 'agreement' is clarified immediately before: 'Dewey, Wittgenstein and Heidegger . . . [hold] that words take their meanings from other words rather than by virtue of their representative power and their transparency to the real.' (ibid.) And immediately below: 'Rorty's Deweyan reduction of objectivity to solidarity aims to dispose neatly of all sorts of traditional philosophical problems.' (ibid.) The elision of Heidegger, Wittgenstein, Dewey and Rorty is a little hard to swallow. What we want to emphasise is not simply anti-ocularcentrism but the consequent eventual diminution of ontology *vis-à-vis* ethics, not a Heideggerian position. Second, we want to open an important distinction between the neuro-biological systems associated with sight, not just human sight, and the ideology, contested or not, of ocularcentrism and anti-ocularcentrism. These are not ocular apparatus but philosophical positions, articulated in words.

Rorty seems to be wide open to the charge of self-serving ethnocentrism but the issue is not quite that simple:

> it is not clear why 'relativist' should be thought an appropriate term . . .
> the pragmatist does not have a theory of truth, much less a relativistic
> one. As a partisan of solidarity, his account of the value of cooperative

human enquiry has only an ethical base, not an epistemological or metaphysical one.

(Wolfe 1998: 15; Rorty 1991: 23–4)

Wolfe seems half convinced that this move 'works' but also asks 'how can the outside of belief be accounted for *at all*' (ibid., original emphasis).

The answer is that Rorty 'allows' external causality (we would say he *begins* to admit it): 'the pragmatist "takes off from Darwin rather than from Descartes, from beliefs as adaptations to environments rather than as quasi-pictures"' (Wolfe 1998: 16; Rorty 1991: 10).

We must interject here that this concession to Darwin is analytically inadequate; the last thing neo-Darwinism needs is assimilation into a weak pragmatic defence of American liberalism. Though he is anything but a Darwinist, Wolfe's criticism of Rorty is resonant:

> [Pragmatism] modulate[s] philosophical debate from a methodo-logico-ontological key into an ethico-political key. For now one is debating what purposes are worth bothering to fulfil, which are more worthwhile than others, rather than which purposes the nature of humanity or of reality obliges us to have. For antiessentialists all possible purposes compete with one another on equal terms since none are more essentially human than others.
>
> (Wolfe 1998: 16; see also Rorty 1991: 10)

We shall shortly part company with Wolfe's account of American pragmatism and return to his discussion of Maturana, Varela, Luhmann and Deleuze. Suffice to say he argues that Rorty exemplifies 'a more complacent and uncritical pluralism' (ibid.) because he fails to deal adequately with the divisions that potentially open up within his version of 'our' solidarity. Let us now reconsider Wolfe's – Rorty's breathtaking passage above. It is clear how minor his espousal of Darwin really is. 'For *antiessentialists* all possible purposes compete with one another on equal terms since none are more *essentially* human than others.' It is hard to imagine a more contradictory sentence. *Nothing* competes on *equal* terms unless you begin with that perverse definition. Hard-headed *experience* (no doubt a dirty word) obviously shows that some outcomes are more desirable than others. Even Rorty admits to debating 'which are more worthwhile than others'. But the constraint comes precisely from the interaction of the nature of humanity and reality. All purposes do not and cannot compete because the field is neither equal nor abstract and certainly not firstly ethical. Infanticide, especially of other people's children, is not possible because those others will be compelled to stop it. The same applies to Nazism. The ecological contingencies of the Holocaust cannot be understood otherwise; we must face the fact that the Holocaust *was* possible and became *impossible* solely by the exercise of real power. Rorty's (and many others') position is a dangerous illusion, especially when those judging are insulated by social advantage. Aside from Rorty's negligent definition, purposes are not in any sense equal; they may not even resemble each other. Something of the dilemma is illustrated by North America's relation to Islamic fundamentalism. One could say, glibly, that Rortians could not get away with the equality of all purposes after 9/11. It is amazing that such a statements were half-credible in a century that experienced two world wars.

Consequently Rorty is forced to detach his philosophy of 'equality' from his politics of preference and therefore exclusion or inequality.

> The pragmatists' justification of tolerance, free inquiry and the quest for undistorted communication can only take the form of a comparison between societies which exemplify these habits and those that do not, leading up to the suggestion that nobody who has experienced both would prefer the latter . . . not by reference to a criterion but . . . to various detailed practical advantages.
>
> (Wolfe 1998: 17; Rorty 1991: 29)

There can be several levels of criticism: those that question 'undistorted communication' and those that point to the inequality of distribution (of power, wealth, information etc.) in 'free' liberal democracies. But we want to go further. 'Various detailed practical advantages' is a gloss for an intricate network of costs and benefits which constitute a series of criteria that we do not have to 'experience', but only consider or imagine to evaluate. This does not mean that outcomes will tend towards a norm; heterogeneity and the perception of advantage and strategic forward planning ('betting') ensure this process is to a degree non-linear. Even self-sacrifice can be perceived as beneficial but that is not an ESS for a majority. The more important point is that the philosophy of equality is immediately suspended when *any* notion of preference is put into play. Conventionally this is formulated as a distinction between theory and practice (Rorty included). Rather, it completely erases what once passed for theory (the idioms of the philosophy of equality) by resituating theory, not in the play of formal categories but in the various assessments of cost, benefit and risk. Theory and practice are thus united in the formulation of viable strategies. The poverty of the philosophy of equality is exposed: it may be a routine, idiomatic feature of a certain discipline, but as a model of social action is it literally inapplicable, and as a conceptual strategy in the sense intended here it is worthless. Indeed one can argue that since such idioms 'cost' but yield no advantage they constitute a diseconomy; in ecological terms they are tending toward extinction. Why should this happen now when in the long history of Western philosophy they are commonplace. Well, the semantic environment has changed such that their vitality, in every sense, is rapidly diminishing. The change can be marked in successive stages: God creates creatures; God is dead; God never was alive. In other words auto-eco-organisation refutes a separate domain called 'theory' or 'philosophy' and offers instead the embeddedness of informational imperatives in self-organisation – exo-auto-reference.

Let us formulate this informational 'practice' as transformation. It does not mean that 'theory', in the sense that we clearly *are* theorising, becomes impossible. Yet its ontology is markedly different. In place of the system-environment distinction we speak of specific transformations. A continuity of sorts is premised. This is not to revive an approximate to the certainties of 'correspondence' but on the contrary to emphasise the risk of the process of transformation or translation.[6] But that risk is also multi-dimensional; only fractions of any environment can be transformed, re-presented, translated and only through substrate-specific processes, for example, visual systems. Only what is available to be transformed is transformed. Only that which the substrate can transform is transformed. Such processes, therefore, are at grave risk from that which cannot be transformed either through unavailability or incapability. Such a sense of transformative 'theorising' bears more relation to processes such as nourishment than it does to the Platonic Idea, to the Platonic-Christian tradition of enquiry, to its secular modernisation in Kant, Nietzsche or Marx or to their contemporary philosophical descendants.

Let us conclude this section by noting how Rorty denounces and yet becomes analytically congruent with Foucault, amongst other post-structuralists, and how they in turn are tangled in the same web of unviable strategies. Again Wolfe's treatment rewards attention.

For Rorty, Foucault poses as a 'knight of autonomy – but only in the private realm.' Similarly, we can 'dream up as many contexts as possible' but 'it is only when a Romantic intellectual begins to want his private self to serve as a model for other humans that his politics tends to become illiberal' (Wolfe 1998: 19) Wolfe's response, citing Nancy Fraser, draws attention to the tangled relation of personal and political expressed in the feminist slogan 'the personal is the political'. The point is insufficiently developed. There is a deep similarity between the philosophy of equality and 'private' autonomy: 'all possible purposes compete with one another on equal terms since none are more essentially human than others' turned through very few degrees becomes 'all things are humanly possible'- the posture of the knight of autonomy. Both offer no description of actual human privacy but only the semantic space of excessive formalism; they are the sounds of an idiom. In short, 'privacy' is here exactly the same kind of 'fantasy rather than conversation' that Rorty accuses Foucault of peddling. The private/personal/imaginary is grasped as exempt from the double requirement of eco-auto-organisation and exo-auto-reference. The fantasy consists in precisely this exemption which in turn guarantees that philosophy or 'theory' abruptly ceases when it meets 'practice', that is any environment. What kind of 'theory' is possible in, or better, defined by the absence of any environment? This is the Platonic-Christian tradition in its unconcealed state. It illustrates perfectly the difference between what it is to be influenced by Nietzsche, the voice at the funeral, and the secular characteristics of complexity theory.

This drama of entrenchment and concealment is relentlessly exposed in the decidedly French roots of post-structuralism and the decidedly North American roots of modern liberal democracy. This is not to claim that some of Europe is exempt. Wolfe provides an extensive analysis of Cavell's responses to Emerson which we must reduce to the central proposition of North American political philosophy: 'the claim or the good of freedom'. But that is destined to produce the self-possessed or authentic individual 'exercising' freedom as the 'freedom to be alone adrift in the vacuum of autonomy' (Wolfe 1998: 37) ending in the extraordinary re-invocation of man *as* God, *in* God, *trammelled by* God: 'God delights to isolate us every day' (Emerson, *Experience*, p. 280, in Wolfe 1998: 37). It is worth quoting Wolfe at some length to expose the confused identification of and the paralysis induced by the consequent *de-politicisation* of liberal-democratic aspirations to freedom.

> How you feel about that isolation . . . will depend in large part on what you think philosophy is – or rather . . . *what you think it can afford to be.* (our emphases) . . . [I]f philosophy can fulfil its social function only by 'turning' away from society and in that silence exercise its own exemplary freedom – my response is 'so much the worse for philosophy.' That does not mean that what Cavell regards as the function of philosophy is not a very important *part* of philosophy; its imperative that we never cease to think the fact of contingency, difference and openness, that philosophy never allow politics to forget this . . .
>
> [P]hilosophy can have, as Cavell wishes, its autonomy and necessary insulation from polemics and public discourses . . . Or it can its privileged socially representative function. But it cannot have both. [By taking the first option] then philosophy declares as *not its problem* a whole host of material and discursive and institutional challenges that bear directly on the creation of the material conditions whereby philosophy's ideal of freedom, which it rightly takes up, might become a reality . . . But if philosophy so declares itself, then it also ceases to be socially representative, because it then becomes only one of many specialised discourses and practices (including of course polemics) . . . that likewise declare other things (like philosophy) not *their* problem.
>
> (ibid. 37)

The first paragraph, especially the telling phrase 'what you think it [philosophy] can afford to be,' is partly congruent with our position. Can we agree then that 'turning away from society' is part of the function of philosophy? This seeks to promote the deconstructive role of philosophy, the constant reminder of contingency and difference. Everything turns on what is meant by contingency. If we mean to apply something like the notion of individual freedom to political process, then the result is equally spurious. Contingency and self-organisation construct a topology of mutual limitation. Contingency is not a formal backdrop to political constructions that permits us to declare 'they could have been otherwise' but rather occurs in a site of spatial limitation, for example, the Earth, the North American continent, or a city; and temporal limitation, for example, an age, a century, or a year; permeated by a whole range of qualitative dimensions from climate, to economy to technology, to natural resources, to population density. Contingency in this sense means 'contingent upon' and therefore describes not the formal concept of chaos but the ecological notion of relative plasticity, opportunity, inter-dependence. Philosophy in this sense does not allow itself to be free, isolated or to deconstruct 'in principle', but rather to spot an opportunity, another niche, a reorganisation, an unintended consequence, a new synthesis. Of course, then it will become 'one of the specialisms' and certainly, at long last, lose its 'privileges', leave the Church and engage in the dirty business of competition for viability. At this stage it might become worthwhile, at the cost of being reconceptualised, not as the old distinct discipline but embedded in the characteristic, reflexive strategies of ordinary thinking.

Wolfe's second paragraph appears to offer two options, yet only one seems visible. This is not petty textual analysis; one rather then two is importantly parallel to our previous analysis. If philosophy 'distances itself' (option one) it inevitably also exercises option two and becomes a specialism, not a 'representative', that is, its insulation was always only idiomatic. In terms of our notion of informational transformations, all representations *of* are substrate and context-specific. This is not to re-introduce simplistic notions of conventionality and contingency. The collecting power of formal language is both limited, focused and substrate-specific. Anything else, such as Laplace's demon, defies the energy-economy relations of system (substrate) and environment. A total description is impossibly costly since the system is necessarily simpler and smaller than its environment. Even from the perspective inside the system, there are structural needs other than information. Given the existential field thus dominated by scarce resources all representations will be specialist, so creating areas of focus and active ignorance. This will shape the protocols of the system, from Maturana's frog to the sampling processes of the National Statistics Office.

What once formed a distinct discipline 'philosophy' enters a diaspora of embeddedness. What then are *we* writing? We want to argue that *at times* (such as this) it is strategically viable to topicalise philosophy, and as a relatively distinct set of concerns. This is risky, no doubt, a partial exercise of traditional hubris, being 'above' the fray. And so in that topicalisation there are protocols of attention and active, risked, ignorance. Perhaps in speaking critically of

225

'philosophy' we are identifying those modes of address we want to jettison, leaving the formal panoply and sanctuary of the old discipline for the sake of the diaspora of embeddedness. The pragmatic truth probably lies between the two, for we should not entertain romantic illusions; embeddedness does not 'solve' our relations with everyday world. We are still claiming a kind of authority as the only basis for our communal work of reading and writing. In this sense, the discipline is probably destined, for good or ill, to re-constitute the basis and range of its identity. That is what complexity theory may become but the journey will be worthless unless *qualitative* complexity informs what is meant by complexity *theory*.

Wolfe's criticisms of American pragmatist political philosophy turn on its ineffectiveness and lack of comprehension of its embeddedness in the relationships of political power. The implication is that pragmatism could function better if it were more critically detached whilst at the same time conceding that this is 'problematic'. This, however, is impossible; embeddedness is inevitable. The *complexity* theory of politics, especially where we topicalise qualitative complexity, is a form both of embeddedness and of differentiation. Whilst its political ecology is liberal democracy, qualitative complexity is not itself a democratic ethic but a differentiation in that ecology. Whilst it pays heed to ethical demands, it is not itself an ethical programme; the prior concern is a homeodynamic ontology. 'Politics' heard in its fundamental key connotes *policies,* so that qualitative complexity is related to, observes, partly approves but *differs as a policy* from both democracy and its political philosophy. It is not passive but active 'observation'. For the moment, our concerns lie at the foundational and so epistemological stage; we are disputing the rights to particular grounds of and for analysis. In its later, possibly more mature stages, the 'active' phase of applied analyses, our concern is likely to lie less in the field of ethics but that of dynamics: self-organisation, its environment and its unintended consequences. Let us return to epistemological considerations and Wolfe's pragmatics of the 'outside'.

Having found scant solace in pragmatism, Wolfe turns first to Maturana and Varela (how pervasive is their influence!), then to Luhmann, eventually to Deleuze and Guatarri. His considerations are prefaced by and suffused with the problematics of representation which also opened Wolfe's consideration of pragmatism. Referring to Haraway, he writes:

> What is interesting about this desire for 'objectivity' is that it issues from a line of critique that has reminded us again and again that putatively 'objective' scientific accounts are just as socially constructed as any other, and moreover, that what we might call the ideology of objectivity has typically operated much to the detriment of women and other marginalized people. In a passage justly famous for its candid statement of the contradictory theoretical desires that characterise much feminist philosophy of science, Haraway writes:

226

'I think my problem and "our" problem is how to have *simultaneously* an account of radical historical contingency for all knowledge claims and knowing subjects, a critical practice for recognising our own "semiotic technologies" for making meanings and a no-nonsense commitment to faithful accounts of a "real" world . . .'

(Wolfe 1998: 45–6. See also note 12, ibid. p. 162)

Now the question of representation:

[W]hat is important for my purposes is the linkage between the ethical and political values . . . and the 'faithful' accounts of the 'real world' that should underwrite or otherwise serve as a foundation for the practice of those values. This strategy in Haraway, Evelyn Fox Keller, Sandra Harding, and other, I now want to argue, is counterproductive because it thrusts the discussion back into a representationalist frame that is both epistemologically inadequate to the task at hand and potentially troubling both politically and ethically.

(ibid.)

These passages bear and reward close textual analysis.

Proposition 1

'[P]utatively "objective" scientific accounts are just as socially constructed as any other.'

This assertion, not directly Wolfe's but the wording suggests his agreement, is also routinely made in the sociology of science. We are tempted to say that it is simply not true. But we cannot say so because the situation is so much more complex than that. That is why the proposition is misleading. It is true only to a highly qualified degree. The Newtonian theory of gravity, notwithstanding revisions from relativity theory, is not in any sense 'just' as socially constructed as its alternatives such as: flat earth, ether–glue, magnetic attraction, invisible strings, or whatever. This objection cannot easily be dismissed as 'sophistry' as Latour argues elsewhere.[7] It is rather hugely inconvenient to the constructivist case; Kuhn would call it 'incommensurable' and see it as signalling the approach of paradigm change. On the other hand, some scientific statements we may find, with the enormous benefit of hindsight, to be false or at least questionable, and so socially constructed. The term *just as* socially constructed is then not 'just' (in the other sense); indeed, it has no basis whatever for the assertion of equality. Why then has is been made? Why is it routinely repeated? Because that is the idiomatic practice in critical social science.

227

Proposition 2

'[W]hat we might call the ideology of objectivity has typically operated much to the detriment of women and other marginalised people.'

This assertion is equally groundless and for the same reasons: it is marginally improved by the word 'typically'. 'Sometimes' would be more honest but less academically likely, possibly because that sort of equivocation tends to under-mine the authority of the pronouncement. That would not be politically pro-gressive. To cite a specific example, the disciplines of obstetrics are not 'typically detrimental' to women.

Stripped of these idiomatic conceits the two together say:

> Some putatively 'objective' scientific accounts might turn out to be socially constructed but we can't find out without recourse to some-thing like 'objective' testing. Neither can we say very much about the status of socially constructed accounts without similar recourse. Some-times what we might, perjoratively, call the ideology of objectivity has operated to the detriment of women and other marginalized people. (We do not see the need to supply evidence.)

This is both unimpressive and still shot through with half-concealed evasions and untruths. However, this is not an accusation; or rather it is not an accusation directed at someone else. This, we must understand, is our custom. In saying that, we risk exactly the same evasion, falsehood and condemnation.

Extract 3 (Haraway)

> '[O]ur' problem is how to have *simultaneously* an account of radical historical contingency for all knowledge claims and a no-nonsense commitment to faithful accounts of a 'real' world.

We cannot accept radical contingency for all knowledge claims and a no-nonsense commitment to faithful accounts of a real world. 'No-nonsense', what an absurd expression! Try out this revision:

> '[O]ur' problem is how to have simultaneously a *no-nonsense* account of historical contingency for all knowledge claims and a *radical* commitment to faithful accounts of a 'real' world

The sense, perversely, remains the same. 'Radical' and 'no-nonsense' applied to the contingencies of social construction simply says: social construction is unproblematically contingent. It is a matter of fact, not of intellectual strategy; or more precisely a strategy treatable as fact because it carries no risk or cost. This is simplistic.

'Radical' and 'no-nonsense' applied to 'commitment to faithful accounts of the real world operates in the same manner. For 'no-nonsense' read 'no cost';

for 'radical' read 'no obstacle', no counter-claim. The proposition of 'a critical practice for recognising our own "semiotic technologies" for making meanings' is rather more promising but infertile buried in such weak earth. Our semiotic technology ought to include the reflexive attention to the cost, benefit and risk of our shared idioms. Haraway (or Wofle or 'we') have the key in the notion of simultaneity but it remains unused and indeed needs to be reversed. For what is shown here is the operation of contradiction, that radical contingency can only describe knowledge claims, knowledge practices by ignoring their specificity, especially of those that are less, or not, radically contingent. Reciprocally, that no-nonsense commitments to faithful accounts of real worlds is only a fair description for those aspects of the real world that can be described 'without nonsense'. Radically contingent and faithful accounts are one and the same thing put into a complex environment which itself decides their actual qualitative fate. It is not 'our problem' in the humanist sense but an ontological process that sets out the quality of our various subjugations. In this sense, Haraway's phrasing, her semiotic technology, conceals what is open to inspection and dispute if we were prepared to use less formal, and more complex, categorical grouping.

Extract 4

> [W]hat is important for my purposes is the linkage between the ethical and political values . . . and the 'faithful' accounts of the 'real world' that should underwrite or otherwise serve as a foundation for the practice of those values. This strategy . . . is counterproductive because it thrusts the discussion back into a representationalist frame that is both epistemologically inadequate to the task at hand and potentially troubling both politically and ethically.
>
> (ibid.)

Wolfe spends some time arguing that 'faithful accounts' of 'real worlds' cannot be agreed on or pursued because no 'neutral' space for negotiating what this might mean is conceivable. Yet he does not take his own advice and so pursues yet another fictive neutral space, this time the avoidance of representationalism. Ironically he partially states and then ignores the issue we are about to explore.

> [We] cannot very well critique the use of 'objectivity' and at the same time offer . . . a transdisciplinary paradigm that claims universal validity. But the rejoinder, as we shall see, is that if we agree that all critiques or theories are reductive of difference (because they are all contingent, which means that we could have described things otherwise), then the issue becomes how to build a confrontation with that fact into the epistemology one is using, rather than continuing to

pretend that this contingency does not exist by strategically repressing it.

(ibid. p. 52)

This proposal, having raised the problem of 'reduction' whilst at the same time claiming universality is going to go hard for the contingency-constructivist alternative whilst insisting that the other alternative, that is, real worlds, faithfully accounted, the representationalist frame, has not been discarded because it was never an alternative in the first place – it was an illusion. This is not an attempt to undercut this writer but to analyse the character of post-structuralism in transition. This writer, in fact, offers the best crystallisation of this difficult process. We chose him because of the quality of his engagement with the process in which we are all embroiled.

The proposal (extract 4) that a return to 'representationalist frame . . . is both epistemologically inadequate . . . and potentially troubling both politically and ethically' takes an unexpected turn. Given the requirement to confront the contingencies of one's epistemological position, clearly a pluralist move, then Maturana's and Varela's proposals that organisms 'bring forth worlds' or 'specify what counts as environment' is called into play. This 'bringing forth', the whole panoply of autopoiesis, is a thinly concealed form of genetic determinism, as opposed to environmental determinism. Consequently, the abandonment of the representationalist frame is at the cost of autopoietic, or less fancifully, automatic self-determination. This is hardly a progressive or pluralist move. And yet this is precisely the painful convolution that post-structuralism must perform in order to abandon representationalism. Indeed, all that is on offer in the wake of that rejection is a position situated precariously between Berkeleyan subjectivism and genetic determinism. If there is an answer, and it will be quite different from the traditional aspiration, it will consist in not making a choice. Neither, however, will we be caught by Haraway's 'simultaneity' because the 'two' alternatives will be redefined. Maturana and Varela cannot 'deliver' the promised alternative to a representationalist frame.

Maturana's and Varela's wordings are inadequate and misleading from a 'complexity' point of view. That organisms 'bring forth worlds' can be easily confounded by 'worlds bring forth organisms'; both must stand, both are *true to a degree*. Neither is conceivable without the other. We are aware that Maturana and Varela insist that they do not prioritise one side of this relationship. Yet there remains an emphasis, more extensively presented in our earlier analyses. Their position tends to emphasise the autonomy of the organism. They diminish the status of presence with respect to representation. This accords with Derrida's position in several important respects. It also marks a turn in the linguistic presentation that we want to attribute to the wisdom of language over and above the idioms of philosophical specialisms. Presence must precede re-presentation. This 'complex' presentation has nothing to do with the kind of juxtapositions Derrida and others articulate in their 'denials of originary presence'. The originary is largely beside the point. What we refer to instead is the matter of cause and chronology that Maturana and Varela, and their co-formulators in Francophone philosophy, allow to become confused. Indeed, they cited Merleau-Ponty in this respect. Let us take the example of vision, recalling our assertions that vision becomes crucial, that the distinction between environment and organism ought to be represented in terms of transformation.

In terms of the laboratory frog, whatever one chooses to specify as origin, there is an issue of response - rapid movement elicits neural activity; other movements do not. This is badly formulated as 'bringing forth worlds'; however well it describes the embodiment or situation of 'this' frog, it remains a caricature. In the language of the previous analysis, where Maturana and Varela want to avoid 'the recourse to adaptationism' in favour of auto-genetic drift, the former must be presumed in order to account for the latter. The structure of separation precedes all of these considerations. For Maturana and Varela and their descendents, (especially Luhmann) this is 'autopoiesis'. If this is understood as the routine distinction between system or organism and environment, the point is lost. If the structure of separation instead rests on the viability of transformations that presume an exchange and a vital transformation of energy then the situation is completely different. This is the situation described by Prigogine's thermodynamics and in the double concepts of eco-auto-organisation and exo-auto-reference. Exploring this difference pinpoints exactly what is at stake in the transition – *yet to be accomplished* – between post-structuralism and the theory of complex structure.

The organism must respond. It is a moot point whether its recursive structure is primarily adaptationist or the product of autonomous morphology. Prigogine must insist that the exchange of energy is the driving force. In order for the organism, or society, to carry out its recursive processes its perceived relationships to an environment must be viable. There is nothing stated about accuracy or truth here; the point is infinitely more pragmatic than anything Rorty dreams up because the organism, society, political persuasion etc., are bent on their own survival. The hierarchy here is not that of being above ordinary politics but the difference between positive and negative, advantage gained toward improving the prospects of survival or not, life or death. We are all 'representationalists' to a degree.

In truth, the opposition to representationalism does not and cannot come from Maturana and Varela but from 'connectionism'. Connectionism holds, along with Maturana and Varela, Wolfe and just about everyone else, that there is no pre-given information out there. Conversely, what counts as information, indeed the whole process of learning, results from the patterning of neural response to perturbations. Whilst it is perfectly true to cite everyman's phrase (though some claim it is Luhmann's own) 'the systems can only see what the system can see', it is also true that this is an inescapably routine stimulus-response model, whatever is bolted on later. Luhmann is caught in the difference between connectionist and autopoietic modelling. What is unsatisfactory is the poor or absent topicalisation of dependence on both models, but most particularly the willingness to discourse at that level of formality, for example, the black box instead of the human infant.

Let us provide a more developed response to Haraway (extract 3). Her espousal of both the radical contingency of knowledge and the despairing desire for faithful no-nonsense *'empiricism'* is no more then a particularly incoherent version of Kant's criterion: Experience (being radically contingent) tells us that a thing is so and so (no-nonsense, faithful description) but not that it cannot be otherwise (back to square one). We repeat, this understanding is unviable. True, we cannot altogether escape from it, but we think we can be more resourceful in our attention.

The first development is to see that 'contingency' of knowledge claims actually rests on a model of accretion; that is, it becomes 'constructivist', because neither experience nor knowledge claims can be discrete. The second is to see that such constructions are not simply or formally contingent but depend, as Haraway ironically points out, on 'semiotic technologies'. Third, then, they are as such rooted in an ecology that includes physical, inter-species, inter-culture and resource requirements. The fourth question is this: how are we to model this situation, with the recursive closure expressed in the more extreme formulations of autopoiesis or in the dynamic interplay of eco-auto-organisation? Closed, recursive 'identity' tends to present 'knowledge practices' as both contingent and self-constructed. This is an image of inability to learn, of stereotype and predisposition and this is precisely why *autopoiesis* cannot be marshalled into forces of liberal democracy. They are opposite. Similarly, the world of politics is closed to the pre-programmed frog.

The fifth consideration is now this: does the limit of autopoiesis belong to simpler species (think of the frog)? If so, to the extent that he is a sociologist and not just a formal modeller of interaction, Luhmann's admiration for Maturana is misplaced. What is lacking here is precisely Plotkin's distinction between systems that cannot and must not learn (usually embedded in DNA) and systems that can and must learn. These are neurologically based and, you recall, plastic, expensive, probably unreliable but necessary to respond to short-run variation when DNA-based systems monitor relative constants. This is the parallel model of relative independent operation as opposed to what we called the serial bottleneck of the *cogito* which clearly still throttles Western thought (especially contemporary philosophy in its insistence on the primacy of language).

The sixth and final proposition then comes into view. Are we contemplating a structure that is recursive in perpetuity (institutionally bigoted?) or a constantly provisional dynamic that assumes a 'smeared' shape in relation to an environment, a relationship of mutual stabilisation, difference and interpenetration? Can we 'solve' the schizophrenic figure of radical contingency and faithful description (both thoroughly Cartesian) with a new emphasis on provisional topologies much more like the dynamics described by Prigogine? Topology here is not a metaphor for consciousness, but rather models the ecological spaces and processes in which consciousness is one player, or a category of players in many customary guises. It is important that we do not assimilate this topology into post-Cartesian logocentrism.

The dimension, or better, the qualitative difference implied by the visual is again axiomatic here. We are all representationalists to a degree, we all users of 'empiricist' strategies from time to time, we presume chronologies and technologies of stimulus and response. These are ecologically-rooted strategies, not schools of thought, prompted by suspect theorist bent on panoptical regimes of supervision. Empricism-representationalism is not a doctrine practiced by bad people with political hidden motives, it is *our* problem. We are all traditional-methodical empiricists to a degree: to the degree that we rely on experience with *some*, if not a full, understanding of its limitations. We all make recourse to evidence to the 'there-to-be-seen', to its ability as spectacle to impinge upon us. That vision impinges, that other senses impress, that a direction of energy is conceded to which we respond, however much that stimulus is transformed but has its necessary origin in the priority of energised stimulation and a 'technology of sensitivity', is not primarily doctrinal, even if it is a description, but necessary. This is another dimension of the topology demanded by complexity theory: the provisionality of the distinction between organism, the system, and the environment finds its parallel at the social level in the provisionality of the disinction between 'them' and 'us', at the personal level in the provisionality of the 'I' and 'me'. At the level of analytic protocol it consists in the refusal to speak in the quasi-demonology, both ancient and modern, that presumes that the incorrect, misguided or plain evil is 'out there' in some relation of decidable opposition, as though we wore uniforms and badges like so many armies. But this refusal to understand the strategic differentiation of the 'we' to resemble nation states, oppositions or types of pathology does not diminish but rather intensifies and sharpens critical engagement, because it is ourselves that we critique, not some caricature that once pronounced 'simulacrum' can be safely abandoned as though dead.

Luhmann is apt to argue (e.g. 1989: 11–13) that a system's priority is autopoiesis and therefore closure, as opposed to adaptation, even to the extent of 'ecological self-endangerment' (ibid. p. 13). We do not propose our more smeared or interpenetrative notion of system-environment relationships to model or imitate so called 'high-rationality outcomes' or optimised risk procedures. Luhmann says that the system can see (do) only what the system *can* see (do). But this does not undo the relation of presence and re-presentation; indeed the maxim overtly refers to its foundational quality. We are not arguing for the kind of infinite flexibility that radical adaptationism might envisage. Indeed this is more characteristic of radical constructivist tendencies in post-structuralism. Note here the profundity of the contradiction implicit in this association. It is normally glossed under the rubrics of 'mutually-assured' conventionality, the proposition that any construction, for example, knowledge practice, 'could have been otherwise'.

Luhmann (1995: 106) writes: ' Something is contingent insofar as it is neither necessary nor impossible . . . though it could also be otherwise.' But the undifferentiated space between these two extremes is implicitly 'defined' (that is, defined by the absence of definition, or better, by not recognising the need for any further comment) as chaotic.

In keeping, and following Granville and Varela, Wolfe also insists:

> [T]he distinction between the inside and the outside, system and environment, mind and nature, always contains a paradox that makes the distinction turn back on itself to form a 'strange' loop . . . a paradoxicality, that, second-order cybernetics forces us to say [we] *must always accompany the assertion of the contingency of the observer [with] the fact that that an observation could always be otherwise.*
>
> (Wolfe 1998: 58 original emphases)

There is an important contradiction here: we cannot maintain at the same time that a system sees only what the system can see whilst at the same time asserting that every observation is contingent in the sense of 'could have been otherwise'. The former states that the system can only see what it can see and therefore connotes contingency upon a technology of vision that imposes, in relative terms, extremely strict limits. 'Could have been otherwise' is out of the question. The problem is not a logical contradiction of the form X = non X but a confusion of registers that betrays an unconscious confusion of epistemological strategy. It is true in a general sense that every observation is contingent and could have been otherwise but that cannot be squared with the particular system that 'only sees what it can see' and is therefore contingent because it cannot be otherwise. The confusion of epistemological strategy consists not in the inability to distinguish formal registers, that is, systems as opposed to this system, but the idiomatic habit of mixing the strategies or genres, as though it did not matter. It is likely, perhaps idiomatically inevitable, that we have habitually defined contingency in these over-formal or confused formal terms. But that is enough to severely limit the definition. Whereas in speaking of what is likely we connote complexity, rather than assumption of chaos that infects the notion of contingency as 'could have been otherwise'.

Similarly, where in Luhmann's usage 'autopoiesis' underlines operational closure, in ours, 'autopoiesis' as 'eco-auto-organisation', emphasises that operational 'closure' rests on viability or feasibility. It is a situation that system and environment can agree upon, a 'bargain.' That word is also formally apt, it suggests an autopoietic 'economy'. No system or environment difference can remain stable if the costs to any component are insupportable, in Luhmann's terms 'ecological self-endangerment'. This should be understood plurally as the environment is an environment of systems. 'Costs' might instead be understood as coercive or negative energies. They will tend to undermine operational closure and possible force extinctions. Extinction is only possible on the basis of relative operational closure. Contingency as 'could have been otherwise' cuts through this dimension entirely. Its resident-resonant image of an undifferentiated universality may resemble God or nothingness, according to your disposition, but it clearly announces a 'being', an entity, a concept void of content or determination and also void of the prospect of extinction. What is announced here is simply chaos, not complexity, voiced in the heart of a formally fractured epistemology. It persists like Kant because it cannot have any character other than the avoidance of character, it neither lives nor dies but 'simulates' in the backdrop of all determinate existence. This is the 'thing in itself' understood as the chaotic, formal suspension of provisional determination, masquerading as engaged criticism. This thing in itself signals the active idiom of ignore-ance. It is a mark of how far secularisation has so far failed to articulate itself. It is the dialogue of the Neitzschean once-present-now-absent, not of the abiding presence of the living and its ancient roots. God-nothingness-radical contingency, dead or not, is the enemy of the freedom and the finitude of all that is replete and living, the guarantor of dissolution in the absurd acid of philosophical idiomatics.

We have to distinguish this false infinity, void of the prospect of extinction, or as Hegel has it, merely the not-finite,[8] from provisionality or parallel probability within 'attracted' limits. We do not want to counter indeterminate chaos with either entrenched essences or discrete serial manifestation. We must embed the notion of provisionality more viably within eco-auto-organisation and exo-auto-reference, to the extent that it is reasonable.

Luhmann's, that is, the normal, concept of contingency is directly at variance with his concept of autopoietic organisation. We can translate the latter as specific difference 'erupting' on the ground of undifferentiated chaos. We must understand that once this symmetry is broken the idiomatic register of 'general contingency' or the condition 'could have been otherwise' has also been surpassed; it has ceased to model the ontological conditions that are now and henceforth denoted by the notion of appearance or self-organisation. Chaos now lives 'only' in the spaces between islands of self-organisation. Therefore the concept of contingency must be modified. If we now 'run time forward' and envisage an ecology of mutually-influencing and feedback-rich differentiated orders, it is clear that time has set limits to the rationality of the postulate 'could have been otherwise'; it is no longer a valid description. Contingency lies rather in the 'spaces' or more precisely in the ecology of interactions. This can be seen in perfectly concrete and understandable examples, such as where law or order is suspended or broken, contingency has an ecological opportunity to manifest itself. In Prigogine's terms this would primarily result from a critical shift in the influence of environmentally-available energy. There are many places in the political world where that process is observable. It is also clear that the chaos we speak of in such situations is actually compromised by a range of orders, ambitions, pretexts, power struggles and so forth, such that 'compromised chaos' or 'provisional contingency' is actually the better description. Precisely the same condition invades the concept of order or autopoiesis.

Time, or recursive self-organisation, requires that the identity of any autopoietic system is to some extent provisional. That would be a minor comment if time did not present the systems concerned with a degree of chance or random variation. Clearly we are back with Prigogine's model. If the system is equilibrated, for most practical purposes, given a moderately stable environment, the causal effects of chance and time can be ignored. The strength, for example, of a crystal lattice is provisionally sufficient to exclude the influence of such factors unless the amount of environmental energy available to the system is significantly increased. The central consideration for complex systems, far from equilibrium, however, is quite different. They depend on continuing inputs of environmental energy to stave off entropy, yet the characteristic of non-linearity requires that every autopoietic process cancels 'alternative solutions' through informed systems of self-monitoring. Alternative solutions' might be understood in the form of cancers, political cessations, invasions, extinctions, bifurcations, revolutions. The constant watch for such reproductive systems may be caught in the simple maxim: am I me? Thus the inertia noted by Luhmann in the tendency for autopoiesis to reproduce at the risk of endangerment or indeed the citation of evolutionary 'drift' can be grasped as grounded in provisionality and reproduction. There is no in principle solution to the degree of provisionality any more than there is a definition of complexity, they both describe the same problem. The process outlined above remarkably resembles the functions of sexual reproduction in ensuring that the copy does not degenerate. What we can rule out, however, along with symmetrical contingency, is the black box – which equally precedes both time and the operations of chance and self-organisation.

What we describe as the failure to distinguish between formal registers – that is, to practically or idiomatically ignore the distinction between *undifferentiated* 'systems' [+chaos] <u>and</u> specific eco-auto-organisational *local* systems [+ complexity] – seems at first only an error of a strategic kind, too much col-lection or excessive formalism. The error, however, is one of fundamental ontology. Given eco-auto-organisation it represents the idiomatic failure to distinguish between 'time 1' *and chaos* and 'time 2' *and complexity*. Note the close association with Prigogine's insistence that time cannot be factored out of our considerations, nor treated, along with chance, as just the backdrop to evolved complexity. On the contrary, both time and chance in the eco-auto-organisational sense has an intense local form, saturated with information. Information should be seen here in a double sense as that which *in-forms*[9] in the 'active' or prior sense and that which is sometimes called passive but ought to be called *re*-active. An example of the former is DNA and an example of the latter would be sense perception or post-natal 'plastic' neural response and formulation. The relative interplay and insulation of each should be seen as parallel phenomena as argued above.

In this sense, the illustrative expression, 'am I me?', does not primarily describe a communication system and certainly not a conscious one. It rather refers to an information system , understood in both senses, whose foundations as an ontological requirement predate and ground the possibility of both consciousness and communication in the more ordinary sense. Luhmann's foundational strategy, treating society as a communication[10] and all its associated metaphors turns out to be ontologically unviable, not just strategically weak, because it literally absents the relations of time, form and information. If classically Cartesian in its reductions to conscious communications, the black box as the *Cogito,* it is equally an equally classic *sui generis* error. Despite communication Luhmann's autopoiesis is the kind of creation *ex nihilo* that does not need, depend on or finally recognise the requirement of reference or context. Those who find Luhmann's modelling persuasive or even somewhat compelling (Wolfe is obviously one) will respond to this with exasperation. What *are* we saying? Precisely this: that information understood in the complex sense of that which informs, makes or commands forms necessarily exists in the world prior to communication in the simpler sense. This is the correct response to Wolfe's, Luhmann's and Maturana's *et al.* simplistic arguments against so-called representationalism. It is the informational context that rules out both the 'unecology' of the black box and the thing in itself. It is the materially-encoded substrate of what used to be called determinate, now responsively complex, structure. Far from existing, as the term post-structuralism suggests, apart from structures other than those of interpretation, what Hararway calls semiotic technology, such a notion of information is actually embedded within structures. It is never substrate neutral, nor does the notion of its being 'substrate specific' improve matters much, because the notion of substrate is too linear, too redolent of base-superstructure modelling. Complex, parallel inter-penetration is the actual requirement, such that the distinction between structures, substrates, material and information, if not erased, connotes instead a topology of interacting energies and outputs. Such a topology is utterly unlike the simple linear rigidities of Cartesian insides and outsides or the infinitely variable properties of the imaginary *sui generic,* or the uninformed black box.

We spoke earlier of a shared epistemology in transition; whereas our analysis inevitably produces Wolfe as contestant. His dissatisfactions are not entirely congruent with ours but related reasoning is demonstrated in his ambivalent consideration of Deleuze's *Fold (le plis).* This citation we consider to be strongly resonant with our criticism of Cartesian modelling:

> the body surpasses the knowledge we have of it, *and that thought likewise surpasses the consciousness that we have of it* . . . the model of the body according to Spinoza, does not imply any devaluation of thought in relation to extension, but, much more important, a devaluation of consciousness in relation to thought: 'a discovery of the unconscious' – a

non–Oedipal unconsciousness, of course, – 'of an *unconsciousness of thought* just as profound as the *unknown of the body'*

(Wolfe 1998: 121)

Wolfe's own interpretation is extremely instructive:

[W]hat is being described in the 'twisting,' 'folding,' and 'doubling' of Deleuze is a kind of 'overcoding' . . . or, better still, a 'transcoding.' In the example from Spinoza, the effect of the effect of the impingement is a transcoding of the stimulus from the outside (the body's 'idea' of the impingement) which is then transcoded again by consciousness (the 'idea' of the 'idea'). The theoretical payoff for Deleuze here is obvious: he is thereby able to say that the thing, the stimulus, the event, is therefore *the same and not the same.* And this enables, in turn, an epistemological break with phenomenology; thought may no longer be seen as intention oriented toward an object , because thought is now re-theorised as a non-linear transformation, at each level of which the input is transcoded by a self-referential system that is selective according to its own rules . . .

From this vantage, the picture we get of the process of folding is thus one of fractal recursivity of this sort described by Francisco Varela.

(ibid. p. 122)

That appearance turns out, however, to be deceptive according to Wolfe. Deleuze, despite the cuts and folds is seen to preserve a kind of 'informational continuity' (ibid. p. 123), whereas Varela insists that it is the self-referential 'system's structural state that specifies what perturbations are possible' (ibid.). Deleuze thus trades of an implicit representationalism or the idea that information exists in the world. Wolfe continues, suggesting this 'paradox' of internality-externality remains irresolvable, producing the well-known 'blind spots' of Luhmann's systems theory. Deleuze is then seen to 'perform the complexity of the [interior/exterior] distinction' or 'traffic between the two sides of the strange loop' (ibid. p. 127). Our response is that the formulation is philosophically weak and linguistically dysfunctional, the metaphors of connection do not work well enough.

There is no informational continuity in Deleuze's model. As ever in the humanist model, once God as agency has been made absent, agency becomes unspeakable, energy has been entirely ignored in this formulation. True, it allowed the name 'peturbation' or stimulus or impingement but then the work is over. It is not seen that the energy that perturbs, impinges or stimulates can only do so on the basis of neural receptors dedicated to that energy. They are first responsive; and second, energy specific. So far no information exists. That dispenses with Varela's charge of representationalism. If the energy concerned impinged upon, say, a stone, information would not be generated. There might be some physical effect. If the impingement acted upon a system far from

238

equilibrium, its dynamics may be altered. There is still no information. Only the connection of a neural receptor to a neural system capable of 'processing' it as information produces an informed phenomenon. Contrary to Varela, 'processing' here constitutes or creates information. The linguistic fallacy that haunts the discussion throughout Varela or Wolfe is therefore simply the failure to distinguish between energy and information.

The form of energy in question here is light and we should remember that light energy exceeds the visible spectrum. Organic responsiveness to light ranges from processes such as photosynthesis, the synthesis of vitamin D through the impact of sunlight on human skin, to the production of complex visual images. How odd Varela's wording now seems, 'the input is transcoded by a self-referential system that is selective according to its *own* rules.' (op cit). Are the rules set by the organism, or by light, or both, or by their relation? 'Its *own* rules' only asserts an impossible insulation. Is photosynthesis best understood as a function of the autopoiesis of green plants or as a possible outcome of the relationship between the Earth and sunlight? Both are absolutely necessary. It is strategically possible to treat photosynthesis as a function of the autopoiesis of green plants but it is unforgivable to then fall over the debris of one's strategic decisions, as it were, 'in surprise' and cry 'paradox'. Much the same can be said of 'blind spots', they are facts, not paradoxes.

The differences Varela *et al.* refer to, such as tetrachromatic visual systems[11] are actually stretched rather further; photosynthesis is not a visual system at all. These differences rest upon or are attracted by the characteristics of energy in the form of light. Such an emphasis connotes an ecology, not the idea of the system's 'own', insular, determinations. It also reinstates a rational chronology of precedents and subsequent possibility; the organism now 'belongs' to the originating conditions of the biosphere; the wave and particle and its energy to the conditions of the universe. What follows is the proposition that receptors, previous to any question of passive information are actively pre-informed by the characteristics of detectable energies, such as heat, sound, light and pressure, and their more subtle combinations, such as low-energy gravity or acute molecular detection by the sense of smell. These considerations both generate and limit the requirement of parallel processing argued for by Plotkin in the sense that any organism restricted to response patterns to a limited range of energetic inputs is likely to be at risk, through its own limitation. A situation of this kind is not ecologically impossible but would require compensatory strategies, such as large numbers of offspring. The analytic issue remains, however, that an organism capable of pre-informed multiple responses is likely to be better informed afterward about the environment it faces. None of these considerations presuppose the straw-man absurdity of information 'out there', 'only' the capability for eco-auto-organisation. They have the opposite requirement, namely the interior evolution of systems (not Cartesian theatres) capable of allowing the cacophony of different inputs to permit the constant, 'smeared' re-postulation of the relation between I, me and other(s), consisting of relative constants and variables. Given these considerations, we should be in a better position to formulate our response to 'blind spots' and their ilk.

Here is Wolfe's presentation of Luhmann:

> . . . the observing system must remain 'blind' if it is to engage in that observation at all.

Hence:

> The source of a distinction's guaranteeing of reality lies in its own operative unity. It is, however, precisely as this unity that the distinction cannot be observed – except by means of another distinction which then assumes the function of a guarantor of reality. Another way of expressing this is to say the operation engages simultaneously with the world which as a result remains cognitively unapproachable to the operation.
>
> The conclusion to be drawn from this is that the reality of the external world is established by the blind spot of the cognitive operation. Reality is what one does not perceive when one perceives it.
>
> (Wolfe 1998: 118)

The statement: the observing system must remain 'blind' if it is to engage in that observation at all – is false. The system will marginally add to its stock of visual information by observing. It will 'know', in a limited sense, that its stock of such information is limited. But unless we are to repeat the costly fallacy of colossal demons capable of knowing 'most things' such conclusions are largely irrelevant. The question is simply are the limited images ecologically sufficient? And, if not, can we improve matters? Wolfe and Luhmann seem, then to rule out the pragmatics (which is where Wolfe begins) of making an observation, then reinforcing it by reinspection, for example, by simply moving the view-point. The wordings are therefore perverse. The topology needs to be redrawn to allow multiple, self-monitoring inputs, whereas Luhmann's perversity simply describes a non-viable system. But we know that living systems are viable. What then does Luhmann describe or is his modelling is itself simply unviable? It is notable in this respect that he allows both communication and observation but few other developed sensitivities or content specific processing systems and that those allowed are modelled so badly as to inhibit rational development.

To complete the circle then, the role of rational criticism lies neither in the asocial posture of Socrates, nor the marginally more engaged position of Rorty. Foucault's and Deleuze's civil disobedience. The 'knights of autonomy' often obsessed by trangressive sexual practices are equally marginal in our view. Our stance is rather that of the ecologically, politically and culturally complicit critic. More precisely, at this point, we need to reorganise the 'pragmatics of the outside' *without scare quotes* and in terms of the topology of complexity.

12

THE TOPOLOGY OF COMPLEXITY

The foregoing has emphasised the complex, doubled relations of eco–auto–organisation and exo–auto–reference, set against the more radically constructivist, closed and self-referential models advanced by Maturana, Varela and Luhmann, amongst others. It is instructive to reconsider how our position arises from the dynamics of systems theory. Before we begin to expand what we mean by 'topology' it is instructive to look to the lucidity displayed in Von Bertalanffy's early formulations of systems as opposed to the received notion of systems in sociology.

> The systems problem is essentially the problem of the limitation of analytical procedures in science . . . 'Analytical procedure' means that an entity investigated be resolved into and hence can be constituted, or reconstituted from, the parts . . . This is the basic principle of 'classical' science which can be circumscribed in different ways: resolution into isolable causal chains, seeking for 'atomic' units . . . etc. [T]hese principles . . . are highly successful in [analysing] a wide range of phenomena.
>
> Application of the analytic procedure depends on two conditions. The first is that interactions between 'parts' be non-existent or weak enough to be neglected for certain research purposes . . . The second is that the relations describing the parts be linear; only then is the condition of summativity given, i.e. an equation describing the behaviour of the total is of the same form as the equations describing the behaviour of the parts; partial processes can be superimposed to obtain the total etc.
>
> These conditions are not fulfilled in the entities called systems, i.e., consisting of parts 'in interaction.' The prototype of their description is a set of differential simultaneous equations which are non-linear . . . A systems or 'organised complexity' may be circumscribed by the existence of 'strong interactions' . . . or interactions which are 'non-trivial' . . . i.e. non-linear.
>
> (Von Bertalanffy 1969: 19)

241

Our emphasis is on the new or self-organisation that emerges from the interaction of what formerly were simply elements. They are no longer elements, or not in the original sense; which is to say that the temptation to 'analytic procedures', that is, the reductionism of the kind indicated by essences or even categorical collection on the basis of resemblance, risks missing that new organisation. This problem is redoubled when systems interact with other systems. The resulting 'ecology' is similarly not reducible to component (sub)-systems. What is underscored here is the temporal succession of organised complexities. The distinction between open and closed systems now becomes fundamental.

Closed systems, through the application of the second law of thermodynam-ics, the principle of entropy, or the tendency of heat to flow from high to lower concentration, have a clearly defined finality. The total amount of energy in the system will tend toward equilibrium. Despite this simple outcome, it is clear that one of the characteristics of complex systems, sensitivity to original conditions, also applies here. If the system is theoretically or, for all practical purposes, closed, the final state of energy in the system will simply follow from the eventual homogenisation of the energy originally present. This shared characteristic of simple and complex is one of the many ambiguities that this chapter seeks to examine; not in the spirit of 'resolution' since they generally cannot be resolved but in the sense of exposing and taking into account as one of the causes of, or contributors to, complexity.

Here, we want to emphasise that the closure of any system may be the result of a theoretic model, an effective practical boundary, a temporary balance of system structure and environmental energy, a contingent insulating factor, or all of these. Other descriptions of closure are no doubt possible but we must stress that discrete closure is simply an actual or temporary state of affairs, contingent on the practical availability of environmental energy and its access to the closed system. To illustrate, a chemical reaction in a closed flask may be completed, the heat-content of closed container of water may be equilibrated. The simple fact of opening, an energetic act in itself, will potentially expose the equilibrated state to further disturbance from the energy-environment. In principle, then, only the totality (which may be taken as the Universe or the 'relevant universe') is closed, because any local closure is re-openable by the application of sufficient energy. Apparent or practical stasis, closure, equi-librium may therefore be, or is even likely to be, a sort of pseudo-stasis. The final stasis is the postulated heat-death of the Universe.

One characteristic of such 'closed' systems is fundamental to what follows; they are incapable of performing work. That is tautological, a closed system is energetically closed. Suppose that system to be a tank of water. Subject it to opening such as removing a plug or providing a heat input, the resulting output is able to work, that is, its energy can be transferred to enabling the operations of another system. In this case we have described, respectively water and steam-driven engines.

Stated in terms of the title of this chapter we can see in this case that the topology of system and environment is both a consequence of energy and a way of structuring its influence or operations. To the extent that we as humans can make use of this topology, it is as a conduit or facilitator of energy-influence through practical or theoretical knowledge of appropriate procedures. This is the sense of 'constructivism' that informs our and other 'materialist' stances. It is in the first instance exo-auto-referential as the basis of its eco-auto-organisation. So, the simplest living structure is informed by the need to obtain nutrition, that is, self-constructive energy from outside itself. Dynamic, non-living complex systems are also informed by the energy that drives them. Consequently, when constructivists of the Maturans-Varela-Luhmann or post-stucturalist schools insist that 'there is no information out there' might this not be taken as far too logocentric? We should be aware that the complexes of DNA-RNA and the nano-technology of operating cellular components are clearly information bearing, and whilst essential to life are not living themselves. It would be absurd to say that they are not therefore either 'informed' or 'informing'.

Bohm insists that the electron is informed by its wave-packet.[1] At the opposite scale, Lovelock's *Gaia* hypothesis insists that the Earth should be conceptualised as a living and self-regulating system, if not quite in the same sense of the life that exists on it or 'in' its systems, then with a great deal more continuity than is routinely granted. This harks back to the old debate between evolution and intelligent design. Evolution is at least not as preposterous as the designer who designed the designer who designed the design. For 'information' to suddenly appear if not with humans in its fully developed sense, then with higher animals in a more rudimentary sense seems to require a distinction of the kind intended by acts of will or design springing *ex nihilo*: who designed the designer? Energy makes information possible in the sense that 'informs' the non-living, the simple cell, the rudimentary thinker, the cerebral development that characterises humans and the information-saturated structures of technological society. In this sense only can information share a common ontology that we grant to material structures, including the human and social body. This intimate and evolving relationship between energy and information distinguishes our position from those preferring to stress informational closure, self-reference and its attendant paradoxes, especially in Luhmann's work. This does not imply any return to a correspondence theory of truth or any simplistic schema of stimulus-response. It rather implies transformation in the sense of adapted, content-specific gathering and stabilising protocols, mechanisms, functionally-differentiated 'subsystems' in the sense advanced by Tooby and Cosmides and subject not to the criteria associated with truth or necessity or of the arguments for and against relativism but simply with the requirement of ecological viability, that is, vitality. This is, of course an extremely simple but universal requirement, which echoes that self-organising complexity must evolve from simple beginnings. The contrary requirement is the fallacy of the conservation of complexity, what is complex must have begun complex. Whatever sense then belongs to the problems of self-reference is threatened by the continued insistence of its paradoxical autopoiesis, as opposed to trans-formational protocols. Paradoxical self-reference is the design designing the designer (or *vice versa*) precisely the fallacious conservation of complexity. Our position does not solve the problem so much as redirect the manner of our attention to how self-reference contributes to complexity.

We are now in a position to consider functionally open systems.

> [W]e find systems which by their very nature and definition are not closed systems. Every living organism is essentially an open system. It maintains itself in a continuous inflow and outflow, a building up and breaking down of components, never being, so long as it is alive, in a state of chemical and thermodynamic equilibrium but maintained in a so-called steady state . . .
>
> (Bertalanffy 1969: 39)

Or again:

> [W]e see the close relation between one fundamental characteristic of the organism, i.e. the fact that it is not a closed system in thermo-dynamic equilibrium but an open system in a (quasi-) stationary state with another one, equifinality.
>
> (ibid. p. 133)

And perhaps the best encapsulation:

> [C]hemical equilibrium is incapable of performing work. For main-taining the process going on no work is required nor can work be won from it . . . In order to perform work it is necessary that the system be not in a state of equilibrium but tend to attain it; only then can energy be won. In order that this is achieved continually, the hydrodynamic as well as the chemical system must be arranged as stationary – i.e., a steady flow of water or chemical substances must be maintained whose energy content is transformed into work . . . The apparent 'equi-librium' found in an organism is not a true equilibrium incapable of performing work; rather it is a dynamic pseudo-equilibrium, kept constant at a certain distance from true equilibrium; so being capable of performing work but, on the other hand, requiring continuous import of energy for maintaining the distance from true equilibrium.
>
> (ibid. p. 125)

These passages underscore some of the points made immediately above. They also echo the positions outlined earlier in our discussion of Prigogine's insistence that systems 'far-from-equilibrium' are capable of running against the entropic tide, thus increasing their internal organisation and complexity. However there is one new emphasis – 'equifinality'. Let us first distance Bertalanffy and ourselves from 'vitalism',[2] which he roundly condemns, or 'design' or 'intentional stances'. We can then say that organisms are taken as 'equifinal' in the sensethat despite the constant alteration of conditions, presented by openness to the environment, the organism (or more generally any dynamically complex system) extracts energy to perform work directed at re-enacting its final or 'steady' state (within certain parameters) which is nevertheless presented as 'dynamic pseudo-equilibrium'. This then is the counterpart to autopoietic closure and recursive self-reproduction. In part the positions are interlinked and indeed co-posited, no organism 'wants' exposure to its environment, that would be fatal. Hence the notion of operational closure in the form of skins, boundaries, ecological robust identities etc. Yet the organism needs energy to work the re-production of its components and overall systematic identity. So also the need to construct the environment 'informationally'. This is another avoidance strategy, yet the construction must be such that vitality is maintained, the construction must, literally, work.

This energy-exchange and transformation must be possible. Robust homeodynamic systems, living or not, are a consequence of what is possible within a specific system-environment relationship, even if entropic equilibrium is the more generally-distributed outcome. This again underscores how despite its improbability, or possible uniqueness, the relationship of Sun, Earth and Moon is foundational to counter-entropic complex dynamics. The Earth is open to the Sun to a degree but in such a thermal and gravitational range as to permit a possible atmosphere in which water exists in all three states. The moon has been pivotal to tidal erosions and the formation of soils, being less distant in its earlier history, its gravitational and therefore tidal effects were once many times greater than now.

Similarly, continental drift and the prehistory of simple life is one condition of the biosphere's current diversity. We want to place information, especially in its human socio-cultural manifestation firmly in, rather than distinct from this context, even though distinctness, boundaries and so constructions are existentially necessary. The complex topology we describe, then, is energy driven, results in qualitatively-differentiated dynamics both open and closed to a degree and therefore presenting degrees of both determination and freedom. We may now turn to the analogy or, the homology of complex living systems, non-living systems and those like social systems that are strongly associated with such dynamics.

In the above and our earlier discussions of Prigogine's thermodynamics, the capacity of systems to evolve complex new orders, given the inflow of environmental energy, is stressed. We also noted the operation of chance: for any system to return to a previously-ordered state the interactions of disorder[3] must be minimised. Energy-driven evolution toward a new level of complexity cannot support the assumption that if the energetic drive is removed or diminished, the 'backward' path will match or even resemble the forward one. Only by minimising chance and presuming linear relationships will the forward and backward momentum be symmetrical. This should not be confused with entropy, nor does it in any sense contradict it. Entropic equilibrium is merely the most probable state; it says nothing about the qualitative character of intervening states of the system. The simple example of an inexorably cooling cup of coffee is sufficient to illustrate this point: the process of cooling in no way resembles the process of its original preparation; the only constant is ambient temperature.

The generation and storage of information about previous states must occur in living phenomena where a constant process of reproducing a steady state is required at the same time as risking disorder through the acquisition of environmental energy in order to make reproduction possible. Such systems must risk chaos to generate order. Only the regulation by information makes this 'pseudo-equilibrium' feasible. Organic systems are thus informed or structured by information-bearing substrates. It makes no sense to insist that information is not 'out there' because it is an integral part of the organization of a large and significant class of systems. No information out there thus violates the very foundation of systems theory since it suggests, tacitly though finally unmistakably, that the system's organisation or interrelation can be ignored. Also tacit is the assumption that re-production, without information embedded within it, will somehow take care of itself or happen 'naturally', by which must be meant linear relationships. This clearly violates Bertalanffy's founding conditions of systems *per se*. The point should be taken further, however, because the commonly-made distinction between material reality, out there, and information, in here, is fallacious on the basis that both are self-organising and indeed interactive. The distinction then is 'pre-systematic' or possible only before a systems-ontology of eco-auto-organisation. In other words it strongly resembles classical, reductive or atomistic analysis applied inappropriately. Finally it makes no sense to insist that information is unique 'because it only exists in minds' because it does not only exist in minds, and further, its requirement of existing only in or by virtue of a substrate is not unique. That would be something like saying that because electricity requires a conducting medium it does not really exist. It is surprising that this level of confusion exists.

Unlike closed systems, open systems are driven by available energy. Living systems thus create their own order at the expense of disorder because they are driven by the requirement of energy, available or not. They excrete entropy by transforming whatever differently-ordered energy they can capture into their own organisation. Such disordering and re-ordering inevitably produces waste, excretion in the normal sense. The ecology of the biosphere 'manages' this phenomenon through manifold systems of recycling. Social systems, on the other hand, share the same requirement of energy-need and hence also create disorder around them, the counterpart to their drive to self-organisation is pollution. If the insistence that information does not exist out there has not yet been defeated by our arguments so far, perhaps we can now concede that the production, distribution and consumption of information in human societies is itself a major pollutant. This energy input and waste output is hard to square with a phenomenon that does not quite exist. The ontology of eco-auto-organisation is not marked by entities with hard, material boundaries but by emergent orders. Information is not a special case.

We are now in a position to present a rudimentary classification of the topologies that interest us here. The first class is that of closed or equilibrated systems which are closed only provisionally subject to the balance of forces between their own structure and that of available environmental energy. DeLanda, commenting on the translation of Deleuze and Guattari's 'metaphors' puts this well.

> [I]t is still possible (and enlightening) to say that sedimentary rocks, species, and social hierarchies are all instances of strata, while igneous rocks, ecosystems, and precapitalist markets are meshworks. And if this typology (with all its underlying immanent, topological mechanisms) is correct, then many interesting philosophical consequences follow from it. At the very least, Deleuze and Guattari have shown us how to make nonmetaphoric comparisons like these, that is, how to go about identifying the roots of these deep isomorphisms. Beyond that, their conception of specific abstract machines that govern a variety of struc-ture generating processes blurs not only the distinction between the natural and the artificial but also that between the living and the inert. It points us toward a new kind of materialist philosophy, a neomaterial-ism in which raw matter-energy, through a variety of self-organizing processes and an intense, immanent power of morphogenesis, generates all the structures that surround us. Furthermore, such a neomaterialist account renders matter-energy flows, rather than the structures thereby generated, the primary reality. Let's elaborate this crucial point in more detail. There is a sense in which the thin, rocky crust that we live upon and call home is not a fundamental part of reality but simply a side effect of deeper morphogenetic processes. Indeed, if we waited long enough, if we could observe planetary dynamics at geologic time scales, we would witness the rocks and mountains that define the most stable and durable traits of our reality dissolving into the great under-ground lava flows which drive plate tectonics. In a sense, these geologic structures represent a local *slowing-down* in this flowing reality, a temporary *hardening* in those lava flows.
>
> Similarly, we can say that our individual bodies and minds are mere coagulations or decelerations in the flows of biomass, genes, memes (behavioral patterns established and maintained through imitation), and norms (patterns originating in and reinforced by social obligation).

247

Here too we, as biologic and social entities, would be defined *both* by the materials we are temporarily binding or chaining into our organic bodies and cultural minds *and* by the time scale of that binding operation. With longer scales, what matters is the flow of biomass through food webs, as well as the flow of genes through generations, not the individual bodies and species that emerge from these flows. Given a long enough time scale, our languages would also become momentary slowdowns or thickenings in a flow of phonologic, semantic, and syntactic norms; standard languages would thus result from institutional interventions to slow down the flow, to rigidify a set of norms, while pidgins and creoles would emerge from accelerations in the flow, with such languages as Jamaican English and Haitian French being produced in a few generations. The worldview that this 'geological philosophy' generates can be encapsulated by means of some technical terminology.

(DeLanda 1999: 130–1)

Notice the proper attention and respect given to time and temporal flow in this passage. Contrast it with the carelessness of Varela's and Merleau-Ponty's 'mind-first' inversion of stimulus and response. Think also of the hubris of Law's 'semantic insight, ruthlessly applied to all materials'. Does the Earth that emerges in DeLanda's writing only exist through that relation? Would it be more respectful to say that the Earth is the condition, mother and midwife to which DeLanda offers proper deference? This is not, of course, to argue for correspondence, a kind of Earth-clone in language; that would be Lapalcean and, frankly, demonic. It is also a matter of acute moral responsibility to realise that our productions and reproductions of material and informational kind bear directly, causally and often disastrously on the planet and its biosphere, including ourselves. The first class, then, which we dryly call 'equilibrated' or closed systems, some of which are our chemical composition and our fuel, may be topologically and literally described as our temporal foundations. It is reasonable to stress, like Deleuze, Guattari and DeLanda, that such foundations are also temporary but the epistemology and ethics that follow from that are at times questionable. We must return to that in our discussion of Gray (2002) and what we shall call the spectatorial ethic. For the moment let us recall that it tacitly invites the philosopher to raise again the Platonic-Christian, indeed Hegelian standard: the demonstrable inauthenticity of the mundane as temporary. Our position is that the temporary is authentic.

The second group within our rudimentary classification must truly, then, be second. We are speaking, given our topological foundations of those living things that Prigogine's thermodynamics and Bertalanffy's teach us are 'open', counter-entropic, steady-state or in pseudo-equilibria. Yet according to Luhmann, Matrurana and Varela and a host of exceedingly interesting work, we can collect under the heading 'embodied cognition' these systems that are

248

'operationally closed' but structurally coupled. Add to this the debate between Darwinian adaptationists (Dennett, Plotkin, Barkow *et al.*) and those like Gould and Varela who specifically opt for the principle of sufficiency (4) there is something of a topological equivocation here. Given also that sociology has placed great store on principles of functional differentiation, from class to gender, to law, to economics etc., and insists, as we do, on their extreme significance, then this 'topological equivocation' enters inevitably into our third category. These are phenomena that arise from the ethology and ecology of living things; what Dawkins would call the 'extended phenotype': from ant's nests to human societies.

If we remain with the contested topology of the living and its informational requirements, whilst recognising that this second distinction, like the first, is an abstraction, a strategic formulation. We do not intend to repeat the previous detailed arguments. What is essential here is the chronology, we are speaking of the living and its informational requirements as the second classification and as the foundation of the third. Path dependency is more apt and indeed essential to this topology. The path concretises a history and the space of a present. Only from the point of view of linear determination based on minimal or trivial interactions is a future determined. The most we can say in formal terms is that the past and current concretisation is influential or an 'attractor' in the foundational sense.

The theme that resonates throughout all the writers we have examined and many beside, is the necessity of recursive reproduction, whether this is understood in operationally closed sense of autopoiesis, the adaptive-constructivist sense advanced by Tooby and Cosmides or neo-Darwinism generally, or the patterned dynamics of Prigogine. The minimum requirement, the fundamental level, then, in the discussion of any human phenomenon is the reproduction or simply the continued existence of the species. Whatever their elaborations, then, the roots of all cultural formations must be requirements of this kind: sexual reproduction, child-rearing, social co-operation (and competition) nutrition and its organisation, shelter, defence, the functions of the senses and their social organisation, languages and their social organisation, the social organisation of memory and knowledge, the construction of forms of symbolism and representation, methods for generating and discharging instinctive emotions, means for subjecting them to rational inspection or control, acknowledgement of successes and failures, measures to discern or estimate relative advantage and disadvantage, the management of death. The topology invoked here is not that of contingency or conventionality where one form arbitrarily replaces another, nor the linear causality of simple determinism and 'inevitability'. Instead we see find rooted, tree-like or delta-estuarine networks marked by successes, failures, trials and provisionality, different levels of freedom and determination, certainties, uncertainties, truths and outright fictions. None of this is necessary in the sense Kant and philosophy generally tries to secure. It is rather 'vital', or not, in the sense that applies to the rootedness of any species, plant or animal, and dependent on an ecology that allows its possibility. In this sense Varela's emphasis on sufficiency, as opposed to close-coupled adaptation, appears appropriate, but sufficiency cuts both ways – *for* organism, *from* environment. Where those collide, adaptation must be finely honed at all levels: the organism, the culture, technology and information. This interlinked topology, then, rules out anything resembling the Foucauldian-Derridean abyss, their absences and ruins are replaced by the niche and the soil.

Like DeLanda, we do not find the 'tree' and the 'delta' simply illustrative metaphors but structures that reveal deeper isomorphisms. The tree, for example, is inescapably qualitative. The ash remains an ash and 'excludes' being an oak. Nevertheless, neither are defined by the seed but rather by the developing interaction between limits set by the seed and further limits set by the environment, some of which the seed's resources may be in a position to surpass. The resulting tree, or structure, is therefore not a space of infinite possibility but a space of constrained probability whose number of configurations are large, possibly immense. Similarly, culture has roots and dispositions, some of which are considered above. Sexuality may find many expressions, child-rearing and diet may take many forms; technological innovation may free up further options. Variation may be immense but the roots remain. The sociologist operating on the basis of radical notions of social phenomena as *sui generic* can then be compared to a biologist who is prepared to consider the variety of the canopy of leaves but refuses to consider the influence of seed, root, trunk, branch or bud. With this qualitative emphasis, the terms 'conventional' and 'contingent' become redundant and worthless.

The branched structure of the tree and crucial relationships of photosynthesis transform light energy into living structure demonstrate an interpenetration of organism and environment. In the same way, the structure of the river, delta and estuary demonstrates an inseparability of water and terrain. Water is both subject to and the producer of terrain; the reverse must also be true. The ecology of culture and terrain demonstrates similar interdependence or inseparability whether consider from the point of view of the origins and development of cities or the 'unintended' consequences of pollution. Two recent examples of highly differentiated or 'essayed insulation' are horribly instructive. The operational closure of The World Trade Centre and the specific functions of passenger airliners needed only the energy stored in two fuel tanks, minute by global comparison, to undo the closure. Similarly, the functional differentiation represented by the school at Beslan needed only the confluence of our emotional investment in our children, the typical organisational systems of a school and a minute amount of very specifically-directed energy to produce disproportionate effects.

This disproportionality of outcome is a well-documented characteristic of complex systems – the butterfly effect. However, we also must consider the response. Post-structuralism, given this phenomenon, would tend to emphasise the transgressive or contingent. We emphasise instead the openness of operationally closed systems to attack and defence, to wounds and to healing processes, and to the re-adjustment of operational closure with better defences or weapons of response. This is the adaptive-enactive model of Tooby and Cosmides in action. Like the evolved complex differentiation of the brain, the economy that the Trade Centre represents sought to repair and to protect itself: successful or not, it precipitated a previously isolationist administration into an extreme interventionism. Similarly, schooling will continue, but the security systems that were rare twenty years ago are now commonplace in Britain and will no doubt become mandatory wherever they are possible. Again the terms 'contingent' and 'conventional' are at best redundant and at worse systematically misleading. Post-structuralism represents, for us, the institutionalisation of this tendency to ignore, to the point of intentional blindness. It represents only a slight advance, a minor politicisation, of traditional idealisms. Some writers, like Deleuze and Bourdieu, escape or partially escape this characterisation; some concepts of some work - Foucault's archaeology perhaps. Yet the option is usually kept open to play the Socratic dissident, to 'refuse what we are', to find massively exaggerated political importance in minority lifestyle choices; to allow oneself the illusion of philosophical detachment. This is simply an idiom.

As idiom, however, it rests on that old topology of inside-outside with privileged access to interiority: *cogito ergo sum*; to which an appropriate response might be: but that tells us nothing about thinking. Operational closure, especially in its formal expression takes us little further. The topology is still that of an ascertained and ordered 'inside' pitched against a chaotic externality with little concept of how precarious either the insulation or the self-ordering, conscious or not, might be in awkward circumstances. The imagery here is spherical, amoebic, cellular, a space enclosed by a boundary. Set that against the historically interactive branching and differentiation of the tree, the delta, the city, the language, the art form, the building tradition, the economy, the emergent intellectual discipline. We now confront the central issue: Is the concept of autopoiesis consistent with the functional differentiation we find in organic, cognitive, technological, cultural, political and economic, *emergent*, complex orders?

> [A]pplying Luhmann's autopoietic formulation to the global or 'world society' would result in a global functionalism . . . This position is unconvincing. But so too is an alternative view that treats the global as the clear and determinant outcome of a partially self-conscious transnational capitalist class.

> Thus the notion of global self-making seems plausible but *the* global system as a whole should not be viewed as autopoietic. How to combine these positions here?

> It is necessary here to return to Prigogine. He shows how new pockets

of order arise that are often far from equilibrium. These islands involve dissipative structures, islands of new order within a general sea of disorder.

(Urry 2003: 101)

We agree: it is necessary to return to Prigogine; but our agreement is qualified by a difference of emphasis. Despite arguing 'Luhmann's argument is couched at too high a level of abstraction to grasp the very specific character of the global networks and fluids I outlined ...' (ibid. 100) Urry's image of Prigogine's dynamics is here expressed so formally that it threatens to re-instate the 'cellular', or island, topology with order inside and disorder outside. This is most unhelpful since it reinforces the polarity of inside-outside with the corresponding polarity or order-disorder. If the issue is qualitative structuring, then let us look at some examples. Taking atmospheric phenomena as given, the energetic constant that rules the appearance of an ordered delta from the interplay of water and sediment is gravity. Its intrusive presence at every molecular level not only invades the insularity of the components, water, sediment, living organisms, thus creating disorder – a mixture of previously distinct entities – but forces a new dynamically-ordered resolution of difference. There was no sea of disorder first or 'generally'. Indeed the idea seems strangely Biblical.

The tree is a classic topological response to a system far from equilibrium. The ostensible disordering agent here is the differential availability of light. Of course we should say it is the energetic capability inherent in the ordered structure of light that is re-ordered by photosynthesis. The specific material form of the tree is then determined out of the interplay of genetic and environmental influence. Neither are 'dis'orders; nor is fire, predation, grazing, parasitisation, leaf fall and decomposition, to say nothing of beavers' dams, shipbuilding or furniture making. The key notion in Prigogine is the circulation and conversion of energy, the sedimentation of layers of interactive orders but above all the de-formalisation of both order and disorder. Both are ecological 'outputs'. The counter-entropic orders in systems far from equilibrium will 'excrete' or make 'disordered' waste products whose energy is in turn reconsumed, including that 'absorbed' in the system or organism as it collapses or dies. Only in this sense is a system, or order, at, near, or far from, equilibrium is conceivable. Otherwise we only have discrete, mechanical and extremely limited action. It should be kept in mind that there are two senses of disorder in Prigogine. One is driven by energy causing interactions which lead to patterned dynamics and eventually life. The other is entropic homogenisation, again driven by tendency of heat to equilibrate. Disorder is not the best way to describe process that lead on the one hand to the dual complex of eco-auto-organisation and auto-exo-reference and on the other to the inexorable heat death of equilibrated structures and eventually the Universe.

This confusion is most pressingly exposed in the entirely humanistic metaphors: islands of order; seas of disorder. Devils, enemies, predation, natural disasters are only instances of disorder as the disordering of the human. We do not formulate our own food or energy requirements as disorder despite their polluting effects. This is the more rational viewpoint. Pollution-causing or not disorder is not the backdrop to but an inherent process constantly at work in the interaction of participants in an ecology and, in particular, the effect of counter-entropic strategies. Prigogine's image of emergent order in systems far from equilibrium is emphatically not a story about order arising from disorder. Instead, an equilibrium is, so to speak, 're-opened' by the action of environmental energy. Neither of these are 'disorders' but processes and interactions. Any new or emergent order is made possible solely by their interaction: both the energy and that which it acts upon are structured and determinate; they cannot be formal or contingent. So also, then, is the emergent order as an outcome made possible by their interplay. The element of 'disorder' or non-linearity is given solely by the degrees of freedom, or role of chance, given by the character and interaction of the elements. Though it seems counter-intuitive, we hold that the degree of disorder or chance is itself auto-eco-organisational. Interactions are not disorders but counter-orders, what we have in chance is not the absolute but the entirely more realistic, 'pseudo' or ecologically limited form; we are not speaking of chaos but determinate complexity. This lesson, it seems, is constantly learned and lost again. Perhaps the most productive corrective is, again, the non-linear topology of the tree-like.

Now let it be demonstrated how organised the seed is. Penrose has said the same thing about the first milliseconds of the universe (Radio 4 Thursday 17th March). The 'nothing' that haunts origins in Biblical and philosophical usage is completely superseded. There is no absence in this model, only the determinate spaces of the seed and its environment.

The seed is organised. It erupts into a qualitative 'opening' an apparently viable space. Now the quality of this space which may be regarded as linearly-structured reacts with the quality of the seed, which if not strictly linear is predetermined, and we have non-linear interactions. No such process could originate if either or both of the actants-reactants were blessed or cursed with random-chaotic-conventional, could-have-been-otherwise-ness. Non-linearity needs linearity in exactly the sense we discussed above: non-linear interaction between elements is trivial unless the elements are themselves non-trivial.

The set pieces of complexity theory demonstrate this perfectly: for want of a nail a kingdom was lost. The King's horse loses a shoe in battle and . . . defeat follows. It would *not* have followed except for the 'critical state' previously represented by the King and kingdom. Similarly, the grain of sand that 'disproportionately' causes an avalanche in the sand pile, when the previous n grains only added to the cone. Here the critical state is given by the interplay of forces in the pile. The grain has no more or less significance than those that preceded it. Its importance is given, like the King, by the prehistory of forces accumulated in the pile. These are aggregate not occult effects. If the sand had not been sand, the King not been King, none of this would follow. These are qualitative interactions, not occult disproportionality. Let us emphasise the complex and chaotic grow out of the fixity of components; not despite, but because of, their interactions. Water would not produce the same structural disturbance as sand, frozen water would generate different dynamics on different time scales. Kingship and liberal democracy are not subject to nails, or whatever, in quite the same way. Would the King's mistress or propensity to confiscate wealth be as bad as that nail? Would a democratically-elected leader's sexual promiscuity or financial corruptibility ever be balanced against his ability to drive a tank or fire a gun?

The consequences for sociology are immense and ubiquitous. First, the *sui generis* thesis, hitherto the basis of sociology, collapses. Impelled into the spaces are socio-biology, social psychology, socio-economics, human geography, human evolutionary psychology and culture, social ecology and their ilk. All of these point to the interaction or expression of one qualitative field in at least one qualitatively distinct other. They are avowedly empirical, replete with all the difficulties implied by the empiricism of the complex. The current critique and understanding in contemporary 'sociology of science' is completely inadequate to the task, not least because it begins with the separation of sociology and science; that is with the pretence that sociology is formally neutral or analytic and its object, science, is a qualitative, if not ideologically-shaped discipline in every sense of that term. This is a position as old as Plato, the critical stance, the standpoint of irony, the deconstructive impulse. No doubt it will continue to sustain itself, it seems fertile. It will also have to change, because its formalism is now exposed as qualitative and idiomatic. The old stance is no longer enough.

The etymology of the distinction between analysis and synthesis aids us here. The connotations of the latter are well-enough known, structure, making, replacing, the exercise of will, the critique and control of nature, civilisation, convention and culture. But analysis, under its paradoxically transparent cloak means 'to spread smooth or level', to deconstruct. This is clearly not neutral, as Socrates' accusers were well aware, but instead depends on the existence of a 'synthesised' object to work upon and a work of particular character. If we can avoid the pejorative resonances, the relation is more obviously parasitic. This may be beneficial, especially to humans since we are, arguably, omnivorous parasites. The parasitic function is fundamental to the cyclic systems of planetary ecology. Yet the more ordinary sense of utterly self-serving remains persuasive and for good academic reasons: 'professional sociologist' is a distinct ecological niche. All of these must figure in our considerations.

Perhaps the argument can be defused through another metaphor. Consider the term 'culture' in its active sense and its deep, necessary relation to agriculture. Now place the meaning 'to spread smooth or level' in this qualitative context. The analyst is to the syntheses of culture as the land-clearer is to agriculture. 'Cut and burn', so to speak is part of the violence of the clearing-analytic process. But there is no point in that violence unless it is directed towards new or at least altered structures of provision or protection. The ethical problem of the analyst in this figure is not then the avoidance of parasitism but the altogether more culpable destructive and unnecessary intervention in an ecology which did not need nor invite us in the first place. Socrates was elected to 'gatecrash' by the Oracle; Jesus by Messianic warrant. Both were able to ground the formalism of their analyses, or deconstructions, on the wholesale negativity of the finite. Hegel claims similar grounds. Unless you wish to invoke anamnesis or religious fundamentalism, that is now ridiculous. The analyst has become a secular figure or should have by now. Analysis, then, becomes inevitably political in the proper sense.

The actual problem that confronts us, then, is this. Analyst as citizen cannot aspire to detachment in the sense that Rorty essayed, nor operate under the terms of the functional differentiation that 'objectivity' in the old sense implied. Given the proliferation of hybrid analytic forms discussed above, socio-biology, social ecology etc., the problem is exacerbated. Thus the central problem for complexity theory applied to our field is exactly the same as it must be for every application of a theory of emergent, dynamic order: In what sense can we speak of functional differentiation? Then it is clear that autopoiesis versus adaptation can never be far from our considerations.

Despite Varela's explicit objection to the application of autopoiesis to social systems, it is clear that such systems can be formulated as operationally closed, but structurally coupled to its environment. This is the basis of Luhmann's repeated insistence that social systems can place themselves at ecological risk, presumably by reproducing their characteristic closure in or despite environmentally unfavourable circumstances. The fact that such risks cause social systems to make adjustments or suffer systemic failures, or catastrophic extinctions also shows that adaptation, for good or ill, successful or not, can in one way or another be forced upon the system by the environment. The situation that the analyst as a functionally differentiated role rests upon a development of this question. What Luhmann wants to stress is the development of subsystems of specific and specialised autopoietic characteristics (for example the legal system, the economic system) that can efficiently perform their operational closure or 'reduce' their structural coupling to a matter of binary coding such as legal/illegal.

> [E]very binary code resolves tautologies and paradoxes for the sytems that operates with this code. The *unity* that would be unbearable in the form of a tautology (for example legal is legal) or in the form of a paradox (one cannot legally maintain that one is legal) is replaced by a *difference* (in this example the difference of legal and illegal). Then the system can use this difference to steer its operations. It can oscillate within it, and develop programmes that regulate the coordination of

the operations to the positions and counter-positions of the code *without ever raising the question of the unity of the code itself.*

(Luhmann 1989: 37, original emphases)

We do not find the temporal immediacy of 'overcoming paradox' in any sense convincing, though it may be abstractly viable. The temporal 'smear' is for us more satisfactory; it was possible to assert the legal is/as legal in the former rights of Kings. More recently, the unity of law and leader in authoritarian dictatorships has been repeatedly essayed. Our emphasis is on subsequent operations of the legal system, given the body of written law. Luhmann's position, in our view, conceals through abstraction such issues as the interpretation of law; the coding is not so simply binary. Then the execution of the subsystem's duty is not simply binary, and autopoietic, but interpretative, and therefore adaptive. This adaptation may be driven to, or attracted by the functional differentiation 'ideally' expressed in binary coding but is highly equivocal at the margins. Granting the temporal extent of accrued law (think of the claim the ancient religions still cogently make here) the image is less that of a closed system and subsystem and more that of path-dependency and branching, mutually influenced part-definitions, part openings and closures of varying robustness.

Has 'our' functionally-differentiated subsystem, the discipline of the sociologist, been made untenable on the grounds that the complexity turn has shown the insufficiency of the *sui generis* paradigm? If so, how do we re-write our job-description? Actually, there is nothing standing in our way but custom, once we renounce the monolithic, formal differentiation ostensibly granted us by the *sui generic* and accept the necessary diasporas of new qualitative studies and functions. These may consolidate into 'specialisms' like those found in the sciences, but surely only on the basis of a common ontology that links auto-eco-organisation, auto-exo-reference, the interplay of organisation, reorganisation and generated 'dis'order; in other words, on the ontological and ethical requirements of radical secularisation. Science has long accepted this necessity; whether it has enacted the mandate is questionable. Whatever else might be said, the notion of post-humanist qualitative complexity presents us with the most favourable opportunity to beak with the misplaced formalisms of an onto-theo-logical past. Whilst the *sui generis* thesis is just too conceptually, ethically and aspirationally close to creation *ex nihilo*. The humanism announced by Nietzsche when 'God is dead!' only makes a claim to an inheritance.

13

RE-INTERPRETING GLOBAL COMPLEXITY AS AN ONTOLOGY

Human ecology

A central conclusion to this book is the proposal for a redirection of the sociology of global complexity and its interest in such things as networks or complex human interactions towards a foundational ontology of complexity. The difference lies in the reliance of the former on the *sui-generis* thesis, despite the readiness of globalisation theory, unlike post-structuralism, to admit that humans are 'also' networked with non-human phemomena (Urry 2003; Castells 1997; Latour 1993; etc.), including technological relations to 'materials'. From the standpoint of a foundational ontology of complex emergence, a specific chronology and history must be emphasised. The sociology of complexity constantly recognises this; indeed it must do to the extent that Prigogine's influence is felt or so far as complex systems theory is assimilated into its corpus of knowledge.

> [Global] complexity derives from what I have described as the dialectic of moorings *and* mobilities. If to express this far too simply, the social world were to be entirely moored or entirely mobile, then systems would not be dynamic or complex. But social life seems to be constituted through material worlds that involve new and distinct moorings that enable, produce and presuppose extensive new mobilities. So many more systems are complex, strangely ordered, with new shapes moving in and through space-time.
>
> (Urry 2003: 138)

The dialectic of moorings and mobilities is hugely preferable to the simpler autonomies of post-structuralism, indeed Urry's 'material worlds' are intensely technologically structured. Our emphasis, then, particularly following the 'topology' of the previous chapter, will lie on the landscapes of possibility and impossibility that now ground our possibilities and impossibilities, including what may and may not be 'cognised', constructed, represented or assimilated into cultural praxis. Our post-humanism is decidedly not of the kind that sees the cyborg as the emancipation of the human, but rather as the opening of a specific relationship between the technological and the human. This is not to prioritise 'mooring' over 'mobility' but to argue that the great variety of 'mobilities' are saturated in the ecology of human being and its world.

The car, telephone, mobile phone, computers and the internet do not so much 'free' us as demand qualitatively new structural changes in the relationships of human ecology. If the sociological-humanist position emphasises the freedom of humankind to deconstruct or reconstruct, we emphasise with Tooby and Cosmides the more complex but more finite notion of relative post-natal plasticity, its ecological rootedness and its capacity to respond to further ecological pressures. If human freedom follows, for post-Nietzschean genealogies, from the death of God, relative post-natal plasticity is granted by the evolution of the biosphere. Its God, so to speak, is a Goddess, not unlike Lovelock's *Gaia* and manifestly *not* dead. The crucial implication is this; where Heidegger can argue that after Kant ontology 'becomes epistemology' (for example, Heidegger 1973: 88) – the essential characteristic of modern humanist philosophy – our emphasis requires that ontology cannot be assimilated under epistemology. This must stand as a principle despite the intrinsic difficulty of getting outside human understanding. This 'phenomenological horizon' still exists but not through the reflexive turn that amounts to repetition (the notion of autopoiesis as reproduction) but as the endless proliferation of provisional drafts that interact and supersede each other as cognitions with material relations and effects. The inside-outside relation is, using Dennett's term, 'smeared' rather than defined. Indeed, it is smeared along a complex, branched and richly figured topology of understandings and praxes, not the familiar Cartesian 'container'. This is not a soft version of the humanist skull.

We want to stress the rationality of *Gaia* over the *sui-generis* thesis. *Gaia* may be locally extraordinary, we do not yet know of other such configurations, but it does not locally violate the laws of the universe to anything like the extent that the *sui-generis* thesis implies and sometimes proposes. For example, unlike the proposal of radical relationality, a contestable view of language applied with scant attention to 'materials' (Urry 2003; Law 1999), the ecologies manifest in the biosphere recognise that, like language, the 'fixing' of certain qualities, habitats, populations, meaning, customs in turn acts upon the possible determination of further and subsequent such phenomena. Some 'relations' are ruled in or out. If the linguistic relationship of signified and signifier is formally, and correctly, described as arbitrary. That is the essential fact of language's absolute economic advantage over pictorial representations' equally necessary but cumbersome requirement of resemblance; subsequent relations are conventional in the opposite sense of 'could be otherwise', that is, they are strongly rule-guided and historically path-dependent. The 'extra-ordinary' position of *Gaia* does not rest on arbitrary relations in the same sense; 'translation' is not available. Foundation is more appropriate.

Gaia, to employ the same term, is one of the immense foundational systems 'far from equilibrium'. Whilst Mars or the Moon, for example, are currently at equilibrium: without major disruption of the solar system, all that can happen has happened; reaction is over. At the same time, as the evolutionary result of massive historical turbulence, *Gaia* has an intensely organised character. It is important to see that this is 'downhill' to its previous states. The laws of possibility have been confirmed, not usurped. The only engine of this counter-entropic development is the specific but dynamic relation of the Sun as energy-giver and the Earth as active receiver. This is the sense in which Lovelock claims that the Earth is an actual or quasi-living system; hence *Gaia*. Before we return to more philosophico-sociological considerations, it is instructive to look at some of the senses in which *Gaia* is both an immense system far from equilibrium and the ground of every similarly emergent 'inhabitant' sub-system.

It is not practically possible to give anything but an impression of Lovelock's position. However, we can begin with the common, scientific ground, the issues of entropy, and negative entropy and emphasise again that *Gaia*, whilst metaphoric or arguably poetic, is not irrational or even 'ecstatic' in the sense that Heidegger 'listens to' Being. The more general point is the ability of *Gaia* to maintain or regulate a viable temperature range. 'Viable' is indeed a loaded term and connotes the charge of teleology. Lovelock has his own answer (Lovelock 1998: chapters 2 and 3), that is, 'viable' in the sense of creating negative entropy. In contrast with the atmosphere of Earth, then, 'The atmospheres of Mars and Venus are like . . . exhaust gases, all energy spent.' (ibid. p. 28). A related but more precise calculation is also offered:

> [Contrasted with Mars and Venus] How have we kept our oceans? It seems likely that the presence of life has done it . . . There are several ways of retaining hydrogen on a planet. One is to add oxygen to the atmosphere or environment so that it captures hydrogen to produce water. Life in the act of photosynthesis splits carbon dioxide into carbon and oxygen. If some of the carbon is buried in the crustal rocks [or, say, in the structure of plants] there remains a net increase in oxygen. Each atom of carbon buried, therefore, is in effect four atoms of hydrogen or two molecules of water saved.
>
> (ibid. p. 82)

The implication is the co-evolution of life and the planet and, in particular, the active force of life in shaping the planet, not simply living on a dead surface. The contribution of life to atmospheric oxygen is well known; so also is the contribution of calcified animal remains to rocks such as limestone. As in most instances of complex emergence, the distinctions become smeared or dynamic; this time not the relations of inside to outside but those of 'in' or 'on' Earth. The temporal dynamic is also startling.

> The Earth, just before it became the habitat of life, then, must have been a dead planet whose atmosphere was near to equilibrium. At this

THE FIELDS OF COMPLEX ANALYSIS

time just before life, before Gaia, the atmosphere would have been in what scientists call the 'abiological steady state' . . . [O]n its surface [were] the chemical components from which life is assembled . . . these . . . are also the products of the abiological steady state. The mere presence of such compounds on an oxygen-free planet is not by itself evidence for life. It is evidence of the possibility of its formation . . . The existence of life and pre-life chemicals [also] requires a temperature range between 0 and 50 degrees C. The Earth could not have been frozen, nor . . . hot enough for the seas to boil.

(ibid. pp. 68–9)

The picture here is one of an exhausted planet whose transformation into the series of systems far from equilibrium that Lovelock calls *Gaia* may be surprising but it is eminently, locally possible. To use Cohen and Stewart's apt term, such complexity is 'downhill to' the previous equilibrium, given those local conditions, whilst the absence of life nearby is analogous to the landscape of impossibility that surrounds actual social relations, actual human ecology. Surrounding absences, impossibilities, impinge massively on the ecology of the Earth, including human ecology. One has only to think of the massive historical and contemporary influence of the Sahara on Africa's development to illustrate this. But the principle can be developed.

The notion of 'downhillness' illustrates that the metaphors of topology we have employed, such as 'trees' of possibility or path-dependency, not only have qualitative characters capable of qualitative interactions but they are also, thereby, energised in certain directions. Reversals, diversions, inversions are dependent on counter-energy of sufficient magnitude, position and opportunity. This in no way violates the unexpected outcomes of complexity theory, though it does caution us about the use of so-called 'disproportionate' effects. The grain of sand that causes the well-known avalanche in the sandpile is no different from the one that maintains the growing cone. It is instead the build-up of critical forces or a 'critical state' in the cone that allows the fortuitously placed grain to seed an avalanche. The avalanche is entirely proportional to the interplay or disposition of forces in the critical state and the strategically placed 'excess' provided by the new grain(s). Disproportionality invites mysticism, proportionality connotes determinism. The issue is easily resolvable: effects are deterministic, proportional and predictable for simple relationships or for relations between objects that can be treated as simple. But complex objects, like the sandpile, and complex systems produce complex (not chaotic or disproportionate) outcomes whilst still obeying rational laws of probability. This can now be generalised into a rule of procedure that can guide an ontology that must refute and supersede the modern assimilation into epistemology.

We now have in 'downhillness' a binary coding of the more or less possible and a requirement that sufficient energy must be applied to influence or disrupt the ensuing qualitative direction. This not only applies to the meta-systems connoted by *Gaia* but also to its subsystems, whether at the individual or aggregate level. The formal particle has a formal direction and a formal probability of redirection. Only when this ratio is exactly half can the outcome be genuinely said to be contingent. Otherwise, 'could have been otherwise' has a specific probability. The formal notion of convention in social science is similarly modified, it will actually turn on the 'disputes' of qualitative probabilities. Conventionality, whether applied to social or natural phenomena, especially emergent structures, is only rational to the extent that one is speaking entirely formally (or when the probability is exactly 50/50). Otherwise it is irrational. Is it therefore possible to discourse formally about qualitative emergence? The answer has to be negative. Formalism – and this is formalism – rationally limits itself. What part of it, if any, remains secure or epistemologically viable?

This consideration is close to Lovelock's critical evaluation of *Gaia* as possibly teleological. Lovelock's response was experimental, ours is theoretical. So far as we concede 'emergence' as auto-eco-organisation, we must also concede the binary of more or less possible. Implicit in that are the thermodynamic laws of entropy and negative entropy, though sociology, even after the 'complexity turn', often merely acknowledges that.

Energised emergence and binary processes therefore appear both reasonable and inevitable. From that it follows that a modified version of the concept 'evolutionarily stable strategy' (ESS) must also be conceded, in the form of an ecologically stable structure. Let us call this an ecologically 'robust' structure (ERS). One could identify a number of such phenomena, ranging from ice caps to kinship systems, to money. The intention here is strictly formal; such structures are simply possible as opposed to impossible. No further description of dynamics, robustness, decay, interaction can be appropriate at this level. What we can say, however, is that energy has been 'invested' in every ERS. The term 'invested' implies one observable polarity, which is that humans invest in robust structures from houses to legal systems. However, we might simply say that energy has 'flowed' into the ERS. This cannot, however, be contingent; it must be likely. Now the neutrality of 'flowing' and the self-interest expressed in 'investment' become somewhat more parallel: the achievement of another different ERS requires a relation of opposition. What can be called a 'conflict of interest', which is in fact simply an energised conflict between structural dynamics, enters our considerations even at the most formal stage. This resembles the complex development of interdependencies whether we think of food chains, price mechanisms, stock market fluctuations, forest fires, earthquakes, hydrodynamics.

Lovelock's emphases also expose another formal level that is 'universally' present: what we shall call 'punctuated' re-circulation. It is essential to *Gaia* that, for example, animal remains become part of the limestone cycle, that plants become part of the carbon cycle, and so on. Re-circulation is necessary or energy is lost to the total system: which would tend to limit its regeneration, it is also ecologically opportune to 'store' materials in more robust structural containers. The importance of rain forests to rainfall is one example. Forests as 'carbon sinks' are currently under scrutiny. Fossil fuels are another example, specific to human purposes, though the ecological opportunity seems destined to limitation. What is shown in all these examples is that even at the formal level, the transport, confiscation, or conversion of the energy co-opted to one ERS from another is constantly present and is concretely expressed in phenomena such as predation, scavenging and competition. The Sun's energy would not do this. It would lead to equilibrium instead: the abiological steady state that preceded *Gaia*. Pollution is a special case in this respect, a waste product that cannot be recycled effectively or which destroys the self-organisational possibilities of the   environment on which it depends. It threatens a way back to the abiological steady state, precisely by freezing or insulating the energy store that allows re-organisation, far from equilibrium. Thus pollution threatens to disorder in the exact sense of simplifying complexity by increasing the tendency toward equilibrium.

The importance of this ontology, organised chronologically and energetically, cannot be over-emphasised. We confront a downhill process towards inexorable equilibrium and a downhill process towards complex eco–auto-organisation. The only factor on offer in this analysis is energy, as opposed to intentionality or design. It is still formally possible to identify distinct stages of demarcation. The first of these is acquiescence at equilibrium. A mundane example is a closed vessel, such as a kettle of water, that is 'allowed' (when we should say 'destined') to approximate ambient temperature. The second is a heated or energetically altered system, such as a heated kettle of water, that will exhibit the characteristic reactions of water molecules when subjected to heat transfer. Note that the roles of intentionality and chance are minor in this situation, the key factor is an energy differential; the key respondent is the qualitative form of the water molecule. This seems to have violated our rule, our 'desire', for maximum formality, in this instance. Let us say that 'our' formality has limited itself, again. The situation is broadly deterministic, so long as input A causes output B. But if there is any probability in this sequence – that A could 'cause' B1, B2, B3 or C – then the outcome is to a degree both deterministic and non-linear. Now the question of chance, or degree of freedom, is intrinsic to the qualities of the interaction. Formalism has again limited itself, despite allowing what has hitherto been called 'chance' or contingency to enter the relation. This is simply because random elements are mis-named as 'disproportionate outcomes'. Both are ecologically appropriate relations, of qualitatively specific magnitudes; they do not inhabit, nor impinge from, any 'other' domain. This ontology, crucially, is self-contained and sufficient.

Water does not 'care', but a new dimension has been transcended, formally. The new dimension is a question of degree, but also a qualitative question. What is the crucial break between water that persistently exhibits its molecular structure and life that insists on its reproduction? Does God breathe life or does *Gaia* offer, or represent, an opportunity for a series of tiny gradations in which the molecule that has to be itself, allows the just living system to re-interpret being itself to reproducing itself? Those inclined to see a less-unified ontology might stress the reproductive information-bearing advent of DNA. Yet the water molecule is 'informed' (in Bohm's sense) if only by the no less mysterious imperative of being itself. Organisation again; not chaos! Let us say that the closed imperative of being oneself in the case of the molecule, reproducing oneself, no less imperatively in the case of the living, and 'maintaining relative stability' in the case of cultures, might be said to lie along a continuum. In Dennett's terms, the evitable may be said to evolve from the inevitable. The intentional represented by the living and the encultured need not stand and is better understood as not standing in opposition to the unintended. Now God (the agent of intention and design) may absent Himself from the scene without chaos, Nietzschean genealogy or post-structuralism (post-Hegelianism), claiming our Being.

In the last chapter we argued that the notion of post-humanist *qualitative* complexity presents an opportunity to break with the misplaced formalisms of an onto-theo-logical past; whilst the *sui-generis* thesis was taken as too conceptually, ethically and aspirationally close to creation *ex nihilo*. The appropriation of *Gaia* exposes the humanism of traditional onto-theology by emphasising a 'goddess' that is distinctly non-human and amoral. In this sense, *Gaia* transforms itself into a distinctly secular figure with no 'interest' in the human latecomer, at the same time providing a simple binary dialectic that allows the gradual emergence of intentionality. First we have the gradient of possibility, downhill more possible than uphill, then minimal emergence of 'preference' in the autopoiesis of the living, finally the complexes of human cultural intentionality. Clearly demonstrated here is the accumulation of complexity from simple origins that in turn 'feeds back' upon its rudiments. However, where humanism (or the *sui-generis* thesis, or the more radical protestations of autopoiesis) think 'feedback' amounts to a kind of sovereignty, we describe that as an error, or less credible than the figures of path-dependence and limited retro-action, whether applied cognitively, in the form of relative post-natal plasticity, or in terms of praxis in the material conditions and outcomes of technology and culture. Both, but especially the latter, can be seen to bear a far closer relation to what Dawkins calls the extended 'phenotype'. The resemblance turns entirely on the history of the interplay between energy and the emergent structures it makes possible. One class, though an extremely varied one, is the types of structure that can store and enact information. Despite human reliance and some knowledge of DNA or cognitive processing, our understandings remain incoherent or speculative, especially about the replicative precursors to DNA.

This picture of a causal cascade in which emergent elements are themselves incorporated in the conditions of emergence presents us with a kind of necessity and a sort of reductionism. Hence, the emphasis on roots of all kinds, including human evolutionary psychology. However, this sense of necessity or reductive explanation must be carefully distinguished from those it marginally resembles and the words suggest. We are speaking of a cascade of emergence that obeys the binary logic of more, not less, likely but whose interactions are so complex that 'linear' determinism can only operate in local conditions of suppressed or insulated interactions. Nevertheless, this process, itself an energetic interruption of the more universally likely tendency toward equilibrium, is *complex*, not chaotic. Therefore our ostensible 'general inability' to predict future outcomes rests on the complexity of interaction, the diseconomy of an information system immense enough to chart the complexity of interactions and the even greater complexity of the probabilities of outcomes (and not irrationality or occult sovereignty). The upshot of these reservations is that analysis and prediction is not impossible, nor is it complete; both are locally viable, to a degree. Similarly, the oft-repeated idea that emergent complexity does not 'forget' its history is manifestly a genuine half-truth.

We are still speaking formally in this context. If the image of the Earth, before *Gaia*, as an exhausted planet, is credible (and this is extremely close to saying if the second law of dynamics is true, then the persistence of counter-entropy, or emergent complex organisation requires a principle of re-circulation). Contrasted with Bataille, or the more general religious symbolism of the Sun as inexhaustible life-giver, *Gaia* is an altogether fiercer Being. In turn, the 'benign' Sun is recast as the engine of inexorable heat-death, staved off by the life- and death-giving *Gaia*. If the Sun is set to boil us, *Gaia* commands an energy-economy of maximised efficiency; otherwise it too would suffer the entropic inevitability, or more simply, run down. This means, makes possible or requires competitive predation. Lovelock's title, *The Ages of Gaia*, illustrates that the evolution of photosynthesis makes possible the energy-strategy of the herbivore, which in turn makes possible the strategy of the carnivore. And all are key 'players' in the construction of ecologically robust population dynamics. This can be presented as a kind of complementarity (see Margulis), but only so far as the co-operators thereby derive benefit.

The radicalisation of this interrelation can be grasped in the postulate that complex, emergent order is this process of energy-transfer, punctuated, slowed, interrupted in qualitatively differentiated 'temporary' forms (see DeLanda 1999). Just so, light is interrupted as the body of the tree is reconverted to energy in the forest fire or the human furnace; just as light, by analogous processes, becomes the body of the antelope or bird, or carnivore. It now remains for us to re-deploy this formal specification of energy-interruption in the context of an omnivorous animal that furthers its actual ecological opportunities in social organisations, employing higher degrees of post-natal plasticity than other animals and with an almost exclusive development of language, information and technology.

[M]ost significant phenomena that the social sciences now deal with are in fact hybrids of physical *and* social relations, with no purified sets of the physical or the social. Such hybrids include health, technologies, the environment, the Internet, road traffic, extreme weather and so on. These hybrids, most of which are central to any analysis of global relations, are best examined through developing complexity analyses of the interdependent material-social or 'inhuman' worlds. Through examining their dynamic interdependencies via complexity, their emergent properties can be effectively understood. The very distinction between the 'physical' and the 'social' is itself a socio-historical product and one that appears to be dissolving. The complexity sciences seem to provide the best means of transcending such outdated divisions between nature and society, between the physical sciences and the social sciences.

(Urry 2003: 18)

We agree, but not without some misgiving. Elsewhere, Urry stresses radical relationality- 'there are only relationships' (ibid. p. 20) – which seems to limit chronology. It may be formally correct, to a degree, but objects and systems can precede, ignore or destroy each other. It seems to us, then, a non-*qualitative* statement, belonging to its actual beginnings in formal semiology, rather than human ecological complexity. Thus, a trace of hesitation seems evident in the curious 'distinction between the "physical" and the "social" is itself a socio-historical product'. Of course, this is true, but if so, the distinction is false: a socio-historical error. The authentic vocabulary of complexity is still squeezing between the spaces of an older 'outdated' discourse rather than being in full voice. For example: where does that leave his newer position, just another contingency or a more necessary, that is vital, articulation? How does the 'science' Urry invokes stand in relation to the 'social product that appears to be dissolving'? Perhaps they cannot be finally disentangled, but everything turns on confronting **that** contested space not on letting it pass by, unrecognised.

Let us consider **those** aspects of complexity in socio-physical dynamics that are generally emphasised, that we no longer live in, nor is science primarily concerned with, i.e. *stable* objects. We are instead faced by the patterns of action and reaction that constitute systems and, in particular, with the positive feedbacks that drive the dynamics of complex emergence. In the terms that opened this chapter, let us first consider the mobilities rather than the moorings. Our intention is to emphasise the dependence, designated or limited plasticity of these dynamics; that their variety is neither contrary to nor frustrated by, their ecological foundations or antecedents. On the contrary, that is the ground of their qualitative variation and also, crucially, the ground of multiple forms of resistance. We should not extrapolate our inability to predict into a theory of near-chaos. Hidden variables are the more likely ecological contributor to unexpected and unintended outcomes. The paradigm example here is our 'theorisation' of disease which, until the discovery of 'hidden variables', namely micro-organisms, was also thought occult, arbitrary, hyper-complex and inexplicable without invoking such things as evil, spontaneous emergence, causelessness, divine retribution.

The first (hyper)mobility we want to consider is the growth of network society. As ever, we are collectively guilty of poor usage. We tend to mean the networked growth of communications, markets and the like and these are clearly new, generating a new social topography that blurs, undermines or replaces older borders, such as the nation state. But networks are not new. They are everywhere in the biosphere and non-living structures. 'Network' does not mean 'like the internet'. It would be more accurate and more respectful to say that our society and its technology has availed itself of one of the most enduring topographies of Nature and has thereby reinvented itself. Perhaps it would be more reasonable to say that society has modified itself through one of the topographical opportunities that Nature had already provided. Reinvention starts to resemble fate, at least it recognises the imperative of 'downhillness'. We must be careful to distinguish this position from Platonic notions of form. The latter precede and are given best mundane expression in human definitions. The former emerge; there is no distinction between the mundane and the exalted; indeed, there is no place for the exalted. Human definitions are irrelevant except for the furtherance of human ecological opportunity; here they may, or may not, be advantageous strategies.

Networks are intrinsically powerful, whether in crystalline structures, nervous systems or social systems. This is not a socio-historical construct. Networks are morphological forms made use of in socio-historical contexts that are in turn transformed. We emphasise both the qualities of the constant (the network) and those of the dynamic context of application and reaction. Without both, echoing Urry, '[social] systems would not be dynamic or complex' (op. cit.). Further, over-formal analyses will yield sufficient insight. To cite 'networks' as opposed to structures is to acquiesce in the demand that complexity theory is conducted at a qualitative level, but acquiescence must become an explicitly different onto-methodology.

Castells (1997, 1998) argues that the morphology of network society de-stabilises or replaces those of bordered region and more stable structure. We need to recall the force of temporal 'layering' here, that the newer morphology works upon the old, not upon a formal or nondescript social landscape. Here is one of the possible centres of resistance that Castells lucidly identifies. There is a question of power and advantage at work; namely network society may and must be a social construct, but that it is able to impinge so forcefully is not. Nor is the threat it poses to certain kinds of identity simply a matter of perception, it is at least as much a matter of fact. This is the awkward, fuller voice of complexity theory when it engages the actual consequences of their being no pure social or physical phenomena, only hybrids. There are no 'pure' socio-historical constructs either, in the sense that is normally used. If one were to

266

object that 'construct' instead refers to emergent orders, then the difference between constructs, facts, constraints, conditions, operations upon (including informational operations) would have to be massively reworked, to say the least. The humanist constructivisms of post-Saussurean semiology and post-structuralism would be marginalised in that re-alignment.

In Castells' presentation, network-information society is, through its morphology, able to connect and disconnect, diffuse, spread, subvert and reconfigure. Where older boundaries are relatively fixed and literally legislated, information networks are open, dynamic, evolving; both chaotic (i.e. indestructible) and characterised by emergent orders, opportunities and reconfigurations. Thus, networks supply advantages to global businesses and political powers but also to their counter-movements: organised crime, global terrorism and unintended consequences. This is the picture:

> Castells's network analysis is of major importance because it breaks with the idea that the global is a finished and completed totality.
>
> (Urry 2003: 10)

This version of Castells could be assimilated to the kind of post-humanism that sees us as emancipated cyborgs or with the idea of unlimitable technology and its vast capacity to transform. The position and language of *The Power of Identity* (volume 2 of Castells' trilogy) must then come as a surprise.

Commenting on the rise of Christian fundamentalism in the USA:

> The American patriarchal family is indeed in crisis . . . There is an obvious reaction by men to defend their privileges . . . But there is something else, shared by men, women and children. A deep-seated fear of the unknown, particularly frightening when the unknown concerns the basis of everyday, personal life. Unable to live under secular patriarchalism but terrified of solitude and uncertainty in a wildly competitive, individualistic society where family, as a myth and as a reality, represented the only safe haven, many men, women and children pray God to return them to the state of innocence where they could be content with benevolent patriarchalism under God's rules. And by praying together they become able to live together again.
>
> (Castells 1997, 2004: 29)

This is an astounding and chastening extract. It is particularly resonant for these writers, whose secular ambitions are extreme and evident, it also mocks implicitly Durkheim's vain protest that his *Elementary Forms* was not a rationalising attack on but an 'explanation' of religious sensibility. It represents one of the few places where the sociology of the emotions is allowed the discursive space to voice itself as an ontological equal with secular rationalism. Secularism is, and was, never particularly good at community, from Kant's transcendental but insular subject to Foucauldian dystopias. The shock is that Castells feels able to use such terms as 'terror' or 'fear of the unknown' and the 'return to innocence'. In the context of this extract, there is a collision between two old forces, rationalism and emotional need. In the context of Castells' trilogy, it is this desire for emotional and physical identity that is threatened by newly emergent, globally integrated networks. True, there are new techno-logical elements, but the shock is not only 'the shock of the new'. Rather, it describes the collision of two morphologies, both pre-existent, both with inherent, qualitative advantages and momenta. Set against the kind of social constructionism that liked to dismiss structures in favour of the multiplicities of deconstructed and reconstructed contingencies, we witness instead the con-frontation of two morphologies which we can call necessary in the sense of vital. Neither the patriarchal family nor the network would 'count' or stand in salient opposition unless they represented in quite different ways the kind of fundamentals we have dryly called ESSs.

Our analysis is implicitly involved in this oppositional relationship. We must now make that explicit and at the same time reject the traditional stance of pragmatic or idiomatic detachment that has so emaciated philosophy ever since Socrates' standpoint of irony. In taking the rationalising position, we put at risk, discount or even alienate the sensibilities Castells calls 'fundamental', half by accident, half through grim realism. Then our analysis becomes a 'specialism' in the sense outlined in Chapter 10. Just as Wolfe *et al.* point out, from the post-structuralist standpoint, this makes 'our' specialism (or philosophy) contingent in the routine sense of conventional and 'could have been otherwise'. Even from the standpoint of autopoiesis, this would be just a type of discourse re-membering itself; from the standpoint of Bourdieu, it would exemplify the most repetitive sense of *habitus*. Our position must be that our 'rationalism' is strategic. This takes us no further, of course, unless we ground that strategy as necessary to human ecology, part of our vital, adapted relations with our environment. Such a position inevitably makes a truth-claim, even if it cautions that its insights are only true to a degree. That limitation should be seen as a commitment to greater accuracy. In this sense, something more of our strategy is revealed, we are placing a stress on understanding, or rather, on trying to understand inter-relations. In saying that networks and human needs precede the phenomena of globally integrated network societies, we are not claiming to predict, certainly not to *have* predicted. But this does not mean that the globally integrated networks were an entire sur-prise; they were, in part, designed. Neither the impetus behind the design nor that which motivates this analysis would have gone forward unless they were perceived to be both possible and positively beneficial. Set against the amazing growth of globally integrated networks, we want also to place stress on this less amazing, actually rather mundane process of furthering one's ecological advantage by small steps, which *may* aggregate in non-linear fashion (De Ventos, in Castells 1997: 34)

Furthering one's ecological advantage, as nature and history shows us, is often at the expense of another. In the domain of understanding this is equivalent to the denial of another's truth. This is ironically, unconsciously and savagely underscored:

> Through a community of history and destiny, memories may be kept alive and actions retain their glory. [O]nly in the chain of generations . . . can individuals hope to achieve a sense of immortality. [T]he formation of nations and the rise of ethnic nationalisms appears more like the institutionalisation of a 'surrogate religion' than a political ideology, and therefore more durable than we care to admit.
> (Smith 1986: 125, also Castells 1997: 34 in slightly different form)

What a tangled text! How ambiguous is the 'we' that does not care to admit that it actually doesn't and can't understand others' 'surrogate religions' operating as tacit political ideologies; nor that its own commitments are viewed in much the same derogatory light by those exact others. Imagine the disgust of, say, the Taliban at the charge of surrogacy; and ours (or Rorty's) at the suggestion that liberal democracy is irrational or nationalistic, the emblem that legitimates our hegemony. Of course, such accusations are made all the time and with frank disbelief in the accuser's 'sanity' both ways. Neither standpoint is therefore contingent, both are 'vital' in the sense of self-sustaining. On the one hand, they are no more or less contingent than any other ecological opposition (the zebra, the lion). On the other, there is no meta-ecology that would allow the absurd proposition that both, or all, are equally valid. That, only time will tell; for now there is only the perception of interest, strategy, intelligence and reflexivity. Just as the zebra and the lion, these dimensions are never worked out formally, but only through a qualitative history of development, an entrenched set of ecological relationships of varying importance or intensity and the limited opening of opportunity. So we are speaking of structures, not arbitrary contingencies, complex, dynamic but qualitative possibilities not misnamed 'chaotic' pseudo-dynamics. Or again, we have to insist on the complexity thesis whilst conceding that the other, in this exchange, cannot and must not agree. From a conventionalist position, both entrenchments would be absurd, but that position is itself a self-cancelling entrenchment.

It is essential to see that our problem is not globalisation and the provocation of nationalisms and the like, but rather that processes of influence have structural-qualitative characteristics and so too have phenomena of resistance or, indeed, accommodation. Processes of influence will tend to expose these characters, even where the ultimate effect is erosion. Nor is this pattern of action and reaction, typically 'systematic', confined to human dynamics. Much the same can be seen, for example, when the laminar flow of water is interrupted, the resulting turbulence reveals both the character of the substrate over which the water flows and the molecular structure of the water itself.

Castells cites:

> Rubert de Ventos, in an updated and refined version of Deutsche's
> classical perspective [on the causes of nationalism] has suggested a more
> complex theory that sees the emergence of national identity through
> the historical interaction of four series of factors: *primary factors*, such as
> ethnicity, territory, language, religion and the like; *generative factors*, such
> as the development of communications and technology, the formation
> of cities, the emergence of modern armies and centralised monarchies;
> *induced factors*, such as the codification of language in official grammars,
> the growth of bureaucracies and the establishment of a national
> education system; and *reactive factors*, that is, the defence of identities
> oppresses and interests subdued by a dominant social group or insti-
> tutional apparatus, triggering the search for alternative identities in the
> collective memory of a people. Which factors play which role . . .
> depends on historical contexts.
>
> (Castells 1997: 31–32)

This is an impressive and complex formulation with which we can agree, with
one proviso – that the dimension of human *need* coheres each of these factors,
which, without it, would amount to no more, literally, than a set of conventional tendencies. This need has yet deeper roots: in physical survival.
Each refers through this need to the basic strategy of its assurance, the social
bond. Then it becomes clear that we are no longer speaking of the confined
phenomenon of nationalism but to a multiple, complex isomorphism that,
with suitable modifications, can relate to most phenomena of solidarity and
differentiation; from culture, to class, to gender, to age or occupation group;
from political allegiance to sexual orientation, to dietary practice; from visual
art, to dance, to cuisine, to medical priority and research expenditures; from
criteria for students' assignment marking to penal codes, to the marking of
birth or death. Each of these rests (as Luhmann demands in somewhat different
though related context) on a simple binary coding, that is, the perceived
difference between advantage and disadvantage. Of course, this is 'only' a
sociological-philosophical description whose *imperative* – the true author of
this work – cannot be treated by its sub-authors as conventional. From this
observation our title, *Qualitative Complexity*, is demanded.

In Castells' and his commentators' readings, the spread of network society
generates or exacerbates 'resistance attractors'. Thus, as is well documented
(Castells 1997; Gray 2003), the rise of Islamic fundamentalism is seen as
modern and reactive. We doubt that fundamentalists themselves can see it
that way. Perhaps the enemy is new; perhaps there are calls for renewal or
restoration; but *modern* and *reactive*, never! That would be preposterously close
to having God discovered by increased American hegemony. Rediscovered
perhaps, but only through recognising modern error. There is more than

convention or dogma at work here, indeed we have argued throughout that convention and dogma are misconceptions in this and like 'disputes'. Where Castells is seen as important because he shows the global is not 'a completed totality' (Urry 2003: 10) and like the sciences of complexity is concerned with dynamic emergence, perhaps the insistence in fundamentalisms on *constants* is not so much doctrinal as the exemplification of a set of needs that we cannot analytically dismiss. This is not a kind of pluralist diplomacy, but rather a concern that the influence of post-structuralism has over-emphasised incompleteness or 'incomplete-ability' at the expense of constants. In other words, the question is that of more adequate modelling on our behalf. Structurally, it has much in common with the insistence in systems theory and Prigogine's thermodynamics that the components (particles, structures, members, species, *constants*) 'count' more than ever and express their qualities in energetic far-from-equilibrium interaction.

Consequently, the simple notion that networks both connect and isolate or differentiate as they develop, interact and change, and that successful groupings exhibit growth and unsuccessful ones exhibit decay, can be taken further. That earlier topology, the idea of *regions*, that networks so readily destabilise now enters the dynamic not as the surpassed form, nor even as that revealed by the new form of agency, but necessarily as both. That the region's 'interruption' can be compared with the obstacle around which fluids flow indicates, further, that it is not exclusively, or even primarily, a geographic limit but one that in principle can be attached to a number of phenomena, so – gender is 'regioned', the tolerance of crime is regioned, likewise the disposal of waste, the size of state expenditure. These represent 'resistance attractors', certainly moderately entrenched factors of the environmental ecology which energetic dynamics, networked or not, will have to negotiate. This is no more than the insistence that qualitative components matter to the sytem's evolution, and also that like DeLanda, Deleuze and Prigogine, the essence of qualitative dynamic patterning represents an 'interruption' in either entropic or counter-entropic processes. These may be described as 'slowing' but also as other kinds of resistances, ranging from rebuttal to diversion to absorption. Where we eschew the model of deconstruction, which for the most part is sentimentally and modernistically taken to be 'progressive' (that is, the dismantling of convention) and instead model dynamics ecologically, no implicit nor explicit moral claim is made. On the contrary, where that which has been ecologically stable is destabilised, one can expect, analogously *wounds*, not the overturning of convention, *hurt*, not liberation, *debris*, not a virgin field, *resentment*, not celebration. It may be, and certainly the West would claim, that the destabilisation will become a change for the better, but the predatory aspect of the transformation is as important as its reconstructive ambitions.

It is time to disabuse ourselves of that old lie, modernist and usually imperialist, that change is progressive, cost-minimal and in everyone's rational interest. Conversely, region, structure, resistance, identity are first qualitative

271

and structural, ecological imperatives, not contingencies. Not even, or perhaps especially, when threatened by overwhelming new forces.

This may be seen through another topological figure that interests theorists of global complexity, namely fluids. Consider the kind of information exchanges the Net facilitates, and those it resists. It aids and itself thrives on those things like prices, discrete specifications, news items but is unsuited to those not so transmissible. It may serve the military aims of fundamentalist groups but is not a natural ground of the transmission of theology or precise matters of observance. In the field of the arts, it is a powerful market organiser, advertiser, price-setter, scheduling instrument, but not sympathetic to the nuances of performance-teaching or visual discipline. The metaphor of fluids, on the other hand, stresses first directionality, that is, fluids flow where they can, they are not direction-sovereign. They also require continuity, a fluid contained is only active in distributions within itself. Fluidity lends itself to the teaching and exchange of complex value precisely because it lacks the speeding, branch-interconnection of integrated networks but instead operates by proximity acting on proximity, the repeated nuancing of influence and value-'correction'. It exemplifies the to-and-fro of the one-to-one teacher–pupil 'contacted' relationship. It describes precisely those aspects of community that are constructed not despite, but because of, boundaries and regions. Where 'network' institutes or exposes resistance and difference outside or against its 'self' which, like the weaker notions of rationality, assumes the disguise of neutrality, fluids bounded within regions create difference, or rather, identity within themselves. This process of fluid distribution and dispersal within a bounded region is intensely resonant with the key processes of speciation; a construction not disguised in neutrality but unequivocally qualitative and quality-building. At which point the equivocation of quality in the dual sense of 'specific' and 'good example' necessarily reasserts itself, together with the inevitable perception of environmental influence as advantageous or not. The dialectic of 'mobilities and moorings' then begins to look like a promising expression that admits to a difference, but not yet to the explosive variety of qualitative structures that ought to inform the transformation of sociology – resting on vestiges of the *sui-generis* thesis to ecology, and then, *human* ecology. The crucial difference is given in opposition to *sui generic*, not the arbitrary making of the new, nor the imposition of new forms on old, but the interaction of possible, specific, sometimes new, more likely pre-existing, morphologies, generating related and mutually influencing complexities. In this discipline, the word 'arbitrary', that which is not subject to intense and complex influence, ceases to have much meaning.

Conclusions or 'reminders'

It seems ironic to speak of a position in the early stages of preparation and use the term 'conclusions' – and yet there are several specific results. It is important to see that these results are beginnings. They are not intended to substitute for the detailed arguments of the text. Hence we use the less ambitious term 'reminders'. Here the irony is redoubled – how much have we inadvertently, inevitably, left out or 'forgotten'?

1. Despite our concessions to the emotional needs that underpin fundamentalisms, and the clear admission that for any fundamentalist our position is wrong, we find it necessary to begin from the notion of a universe in which entropic equilibrium is highly likely. However, far-from-equilibrium systems are possible, driven by environmental energy and are capable of 'evolving' dynamic structures out of the interplay between components and the levels or character of energetic actions. Such structures, whilst describable or predictable formally, will have specific, qualitatively distinct, though dynamic forms, which are highly likely to exhibit patters of path-dependency and can be described as emergent or self-organising.

2. Unless the universe, region or environment in which self-organisation takes place is uniform (and Earth is not), local characteristics will become manifest. To the extent that they co-exist, mutual influence is possible and likely. At the formal level, orders can be described as emergent or auto-organisational. At the level of qualitative interaction, either between one system and 'an environment' or many systems constituting each other's environment, they are necessarily auto-eco-organisational.

3. Since energy will be present in a specific form – level of intensity, temperature range, gravitational influence, etc. – it has no general form. Similarly, the object or system upon which it acts is specified, however loose the actual parameters. Without both sets of relative specifications no system-dynamic is possible. We should not, therefore, confuse the ability to speak about systems formally with the existential requirement of relative specificity. Formal systems are postulates, discursive strategies, that must not be mistaken for factual descriptions. Much the same could be said of 'people', 'citizens', 'right-wingers', 'footballers' wives', fantastic animals, ghosts and perpetual mobiles.

4. The parameters of our study are, principally, the distinction between objects (that used to be called natural phenomena) and dynamic systems (that used to be called *sui generic*). Without going into the nuances of how such classifications might be undone, the contrast under the new rubrics is the distinction between systems, or objects, at equilibrium and those far from equilibrium.

5. Correspondingly, the former contrast between the natural or fixed 'object' and the contingent, arbitrary or conventional – the 'construct' – is now simply the question of the relation of the equilibrated to the far from equilibrium. All of the terms that connote 'chance' or chaos are merely metaphors that underscore our lack of knowledge of the *complexity* of

far-from-equilibrium dynamics. Like formal postulates, the designation 'arbitrary' or 'contingent' should not be taken as matters of fact, which they routinely are, but as admissions of either inadequate knowledge or the impossibility of adequate knowledge. Much the same could be said of the pet cat who cannot understand your motives or less the engineering of a bridge or the processes of politics. They are not made contingent by the cat's or the human's intellectual limits.

6. Points 3 and 5 can now be connected *via* the familiar 'dichotomy' of agency and structure which its advocates (e.g. Urry 2003) claim complexity theory has resolved. Our position must be that what is represented here is a necessary difference, not a dichotomy, which cannot, and theoretically *must* not, be 'resolved'. *Qualitatively* speaking, agents can only operate in and through structures, and complex structures are evolved through the action of agents. Both require, therefore, organised or relatively determinate precedents. Any notion of radical relationality at once subverts agent-identity and therefore also reduces apparent structure to an illusion on the point of collapse. Post-structuralism sees this quite correctly, indeed this formulation describes that paradigm. What it does not see is that this reduction of agency to relativism and structure to chaos is a contradiction that subverts both. It cannot possibly, then, be the ground of the progressive politics it ostensibly espouses. Post-structuralism is simply a contemporary manifestation of excessive formalism. Even in its use of arbitrariness in the Saussurean sense, it is contradictory; or rather, there are an infinity of nuances for arbitrariness in that sense. The first signifier may be arbitrary; the second is limited by the first, the third by the first and second, and very quickly the language becomes extremely determinate. This, of course, leaves out all of the neurological processes that give language shape, a priori. The key point is that even if we begin with arbitrariness, more acutely if it arises during structuring, chaos is rapidly surpassed. This dynamic is badly understood even amongst those (like physicists) who deal in fundamental probabilities. Whether we are speaking of particles or populations is constantly elided and therefore the 'uncertainty principle' has many conflicting interpretations. Prigogine is firm on this point, the issue is energised, interacting populations and uncertainty are represented by 'degrees of freedom'. His readership, especially in sociology, is confused.

7. This directly impacts on the distinction between linear and non-linear causality. They are different but not opposites and certainly not in the sense of order *versus* chaos. Moreover, that which *appears* non-linear or arbitrary, our example was disease, may simply reflect ignorance of a moderately simple, determinate relationship. Linear causal processes may have an array of non-linear effects, an infected person may in turn infect no one, many, or spark a pandemic. Similarly, the 'harmless' match of minute energy may do virtually nothing or begin a forest fire whose energy is massively disproportionate to its 'seed'; the acorn may fail or will seed an oak, nothing

else, but will only loosely determine shape, age, and hardly at all whether ivy clings or a woodpecker nests. Prigogine is firm that non-linearity arises from the complexity of interactions. We must all be equally firm in rejecting fantasies.

8. We proposed that information entered the scene as, or with, the advent of living or life-like or life-related phenomena, such as societies, because of non-linear causality. To maintain what von Bertalanffy calls their 'pseudo-steady-state' in the face of multiple possibilities of causal outcome, such phenomena must have 'control mechanisms'. These must be auto-exo-referential. The most fundamental is DNA, the most economical in terms of organism/environment relations is 'coded' response or behaviours to long-term environmental chracteristics. 'Intelligence' is expensive and necessitated by short-term variation and the advantages conferred by consequent plasticity of response. Following Plotkin, we described these processes as necessarily parallel. We do not propose to reopen or detail the distinction between Cartesian or phenomenological notions of consciousness and that argued by Plotkin, Dennett et al., described above, but simply to underline the crucial distinction between serial and parallel models.

9. Tooby and Cosmides are instructive in this respect. They insist that 'learning' is too diffuse a metaphor for human adaptation to environment and society. Instead they propose the brain as a complex of adapted, content specific mechanisms, subverting the impossibility of ' learning how to learn' by predisposed acquisition, language being the prime example in humans. We argued above for the dimension of human need to energise difference, hostile or not, as opposed to convention. Similarly, Barkow, Cosmides and Tooby's project is to 'reconstruct' human culture on the back of the demands of evolutionary psychology. Why then have we not championed a full-blown socio-biology as argued by E.O.Wilson (1975) and more recently, for example, by Maasen et al. (1997) with a limited inclusion of complexity theory? The difficulty is in the 'directionality'; more precisely, the opposite direction from post-structuralism. We need to begin somewhere nearer the middle. We cannot agree that the social can be accounted for by the social, sui generis, nor by construction premised on the priority of human 'species' requirements. The great strength of Durhkeim's reconceptualisation of morality along the lines of the normal and the pathological indicates most clearly what is at stake. The 'normality' of slavery in this paradigm shows that an ESS is possible in contradiction to a 'homogenised' conception of humanity and human need. The differentiation of the 'human' is a routine part of social practice because it is an ESS. Of course, a modification of human purpose, along the lines of promoting self-interest can then be reincorporated into the species-led model. Simply, then, our argument is: begin from the ESS.

10. In this context we must consider the difficult position in which complexity theory of all kinds finds itself. Claiming increased scientific accuracy (fuzz

up, accuracy up; facing up to actual uncertainty), complexity theory must also concede a distinct inability to predict and so control: the prize of normal science. There are truly serious political and research implications here. Gray (2002, 2003) comes close to the politics of the spectator, not unlike Heidegger, whilst fate takes its course. This is not viable politics except for any extremely well-insulated elite. However, we must be modest, whilst well-informed prediction seems extremely difficult, it is eminently possible for us to turn our research attention precisely to relationships between the unexpected outcome, the prior expectations, the relationships or constants, if any, and the driving energies. Suitable fields of inquiry within political, economic, educational and cultural phenomena are numerous and obvious. Again, the message is: *begin* from the ESS, even if its dynamics seem temporary.

11. Considering the morphologies inherent in ESS or near ESS, we also need to question whether the phenomena are new in the *sui-generic* sense or the re-energising of existing morphologies and therefore producing characteristic co-responses. Such phenomena may not be predictable in any simple mechanical sense, but may be subject to period oscillations, limit cycles, attractors and regions. The very least we can topicalise in the cultural-political-economic sphere is the system-characteristic of action and reaction.

12. We are at the beginning, we propose – and *only* the beginning – of a multi-dimensional reunification. The insights we have proposed from science seem to us to enrich philosophical and sociological considerations without compromising anything but the dysfunctional idioms. The objects of such enquiry remain, indeed are intensified. The hierarchy that traditionally places physics at the 'top' has become radically re-networked and re-organised by self-styled go-betweens like Prigogine and by the strange but massively influential 'hybrids' between the living and the non-living, like *Gaia*, like quasi-objects and quasi-subjects. The trite position is to say that we, the lesser, have much to learn from science, especially physics, the greater. In fact we are met with a truly exciting criticism of reductionism from the study of ESS, which challenges a whole series of weaknesses of formulation and paradigm construction with, for example, physics. The notion of chance, probability and its relation to fuzzy logic in this respect is clearly inadequate in its present form and open for re-inspection. In turn, we must lose the distinction of our discipline based on *sui-generic* social phenomena and embrace the topologies of path-dependency. What is at stake here is not simply the relative boundaries of disciplines but the entire question of what it is, how one can, to what degree it is possible, to enter into formal considerations. Heard in its fundamental key, this asks: What does it mean to *conceptualise*?

NOTES

1 COMPLEXITY THEORY: A POSITIONING PAPER

1 See Law (1999: 3–4). It is essential, we shall argue – and Law agrees along with Latour (1993, 2004) – that sociology must undo its traditional distinction between the human-social and the non-human, non-social. The application of *semiotics*, however, and Latour's *Politics of Nature*, threaten the absorption of 'materiality' into an intensified humanism.

2 See Douglas Kiel, L. and Elliott, E. (eds) (1997 and 2000) *Chaos Theory in the Social Sciences: Foundations and Applications.* Michigan: Michigan University Press; Waldrop, M. (1994) *Complexity.* London: Penguin; Cohen, J. and Stewart, I. (1995 and 2000) *The Collapse of Chaos.* London: Penguin; Ball, P. (2004) *Critical Mass.* London: Heinemann; Eve, R., Horsfall, S. and Lee, M. (eds) (1997) *Chaos, Complexity and Sociology: Myths, Models and Theories.* London: Sage; Hayles, N. K. (ed.) (1991) *Chaos and Order: Complex Dynamics in Literature and Science.* Chicago: University of Chicago Press.

3 See Buchanan, D. (2000).

4 See Prigogine, I. and Stengers, I. (1984: 146–60).

5 Maturana, U. and Varela, F. (1980 and 1998), Varela *et al.* (1993).

6 See Hayles, N. K. (1999).

7 These expressions are abbreviations of Maturana and Varela. Full details, sources and discussion begin in Chapter 3.

8 The etymology is significant: co-*lect*. For a fuller discussion, see Rosen, S. (1969).

9 That is underscored in the notes with a ringing endorsement of Lovelock, J. (1988) – an endorsement we share.

2 FROM DESCARTES' CONJECTURE TO KANT'S SUBJECT AND THE *COMPUTO*

1 The essential work is 'The Question Concerning Technology' in Heidegger, *Basic Writings*, ed. by Farrell Krell (1978).

2 The list itself is endless. From the last half of the twentieth century, one could include figures as diverse as Popper, Feyerabend, Heidegger, Latour, Lyotard, Foucault, Derrida. They have in common the philosophical starting point of Kant's criterion, discussed and rejected below. Except for Prigogine, Bertalanffy and those they influence, their work remain formalistic and does not address the qualitative viability of different interpretations.

3 Lyotard is key. The question is: have we lost faith absolutely or 'to a degree'? The difference is of the utmost importance.

277

NOTES

4 We have Derrida in mind. The limits (the horizons) of language are taken as matters of fact. They are also viable adaptations. This gets lost in the Derridean metaphors of ruin. We counterpose: the 'virtual' is an *authentic* condition of consciousness *of*.

5 The persuasive view that Descartes is *wrong* is put forward by Dennett (1991, 2003), Damasio (1995) and less explicitly by many others involved in the interface between theoretical neuroscience and philosophy. The implication of more 'tolerant' thinkers is that Descartes' model can work 'alongside' more recent work. We think there is an intolerable difference.

6 Expert routines, for example, operate below the level of fully directed consciousness. Also a condition of consciousness *per se* is the duration or repetition of a stimulus. Part or subconscious 'cognitive' processes are then only contradictory to a rather strange model that both requires uniformity and discounts the continuum of multiple stimuli, or the enduring 'performance-and-revision' of conscious thought.

7 Popper's 'falsification' thesis rests on this idea, as does the widespread, but in our view inadequate, notion of the innate conventionality or contingency of knowledge 'practices'.

8 Whilst it both precedes and endures beyond, Maturana and Varela's (1980) formulations are arguably the most influential. Variants and critiques occur throughout the text.

9 Jay documents this beautifully, with more detachment than Levin's (1988) ruthless, Heidegger-influenced attack on 'the predominantly egocentric character of vision in everyday life'. This passage (from the rear jacket) culminates in praise for Levin's interpretation of the 'visionary life'. When we mistake the complexity of the living for the stiff preferences of philosophers' ideology, such 'mistakes' tend to emerge out of the wisdom of language. However, the book is intensely strong, serious and challenging, not least because it exposes the chasm in our understandings at the highest level.

3 AUTOPOIESIS IN COGNITIVE BIOLOGY

1 Above all, their influence on 'second wave' cybernetics.

2 For a brief introduction, see Chapter 1. More precise definitions and fuller discussions are in Chapter 5.

3 See Hayles, N. K. (1999: 222–46).

4 See von Glaserfeld, E. (2002: 91): 'Like Bishop Berkeley (1710), I do not know what to *exist* might mean, unless it simply refers to the things one perceives . . . Constructionism does not deny reality. It merely says one cannot know *independent* reality. [I]nstead knowledge only has to be viable, to suit our purposes. It has to function, that is, to fit into the world as we see it, not into the world as it might be' (original emphases). Kant revisited! The notion of sufficient function is promising but subject-centredness is evident in the metaphor 'fit in the world as we *see* it'. Adaptation to other senses, other systems of sensitivity (immune systems, allergies) are left out. The inside/outside distinction is commonplace and simplistic. Consequently, the function is simply assumed. This problem will be extensively developed. Keep the concept of auto-exo-reference as the counterpart to 'radical' (i.e. simplistic) constructivism.

4 EMERGENTISM, EVOLUTIONARY PSYCHOLOGY AND CULTURE

1 For fuller discussions, see Skyrms, B. op. cit., Peyton Young, H. (2001) and sources cited therein.

278

2 See Dennett (1985 and 1993). For a different and longer presentation readers may refer to Smith and Jenks (2001), the opening and closing chapters.
3 See Dennett (1995: 81) and Dawkins (1989: 331).
4 '[I]n a "certain Chinese encyclopaedia" . . . animals are divided into: (a) belonging to the Emperor (b) embalmed, (c) tame, (d) sucking pigs, (e) sirens, (f) fabulous, (g) stray dogs, (h) included in the present classification, (i) frenzied, (j) innumerable, (k) drawn with a very fine camelhair brush (l) *et cetera* (m) having just broken the water pitcher, (n) that from a long way off look like flies.' See Preface to Foucault (1974: xv).
5 This theme was outlined in Chapter 1.

5 PRIGOGINE'S THERMODYNAMICS, ONTOLOGY AND SOCIOLOGY

1 On the one hand, Gleik (1988) ignores him whilst Prigogine himself suggests a cosmology that by no means fits with the general 'big bang' consensus. On the other, he belongs to the tendency that 'observes' self-organisation, whilst Gleik belongs to the group (including the important mathematicians Mandlebrot and Feigenbaum) interested in 'constants' that underlie apparent chaos, such as fractals, attractors and phenomena that obey laws of similarity across scales.
2 The concept is Bataille's. It could be translated here as 'waste'; his usage approximated more to 'sacrifice'. Our analysis is in Chapter 7.
3 See Prigogine and Stengers (1984), especially chapter 7.
4 See Dawkins (1976), Dennett (1991) and Blackmore (1999).
5 Cohen and Stewart (1995: 92–4).

6 MODERNISM AND DETERMINISM: LINEAR EXPECTATIONS AND QUALITATIVE COMPLEXITY ANALYSES

1 Prigogine and Stengers (1984), chapters 1 and 2.
2 This will be discussed at length throughout the text. Our position is that this routine and widespread usage becomes completely unviable after the complexity turn.
3 See Lovelock (1988 and 1995). We return to Lovelock and *Gaia* in our final chapter. In this context it is important to see that Earth is not an equilibrated, or 'exhausted', planet but a complex dynamic system, far-from-equilibrium (in Prigogine's sense) not only permitting the evolution of new forms (such as life) but also maintaining a series of moderately stable states; water, for example, is both turbulent and cyclic; life is itself partly responsible for the existence of a life-viable temperature range.
4 This exchange is adapted from a fuller version in Smith and Jenks (2000: 152).
5 Once called the 'New Art History' and associated with such writers as Woolf, J. and Pollock, G. The best exponent, in our view, is Tim Clark, whom we discuss below.
6 These contemporaneous extracts are cited by Clark (1985: 88, 94, 96) and discussed by us in Smith and Jenks (2000: 118).
7 Manet's *Dejeuner sur l'herbe* had enraged the public and critics by depicting a lunch in which a naked woman sits amongst a group of clothed men. According to Zola, the only motive was 'to obtain vivid contrasts' or 'the opportunity to paint a bit of flesh' (Hamilton 1954: 97). This *formal* distinction between the reality to which the subject matter refers and the reality of the painting (or the book, or story, etc.) is a most important matter, not only for Modernism (which we discuss here) but also in the Renaissance. It depends on the Platonic distinction between essence, appearance

and image. Many theorists of many periods implicitly follow the Augustinian axiom that a painting *cannot* be true (to its subject matter). Kant's thing in itself is a related concept. It rarely seems to occur (except among the artists) that the limited discipline of painting (writing, etc.) may limit but also inaugurates inquiry.

8 The relation is anything but simple. Whilst the promotion of 'American-type painting' with New York as its critical and commercial centre is overt, the declared politics of modernism tended toward the 'progressive' and anti-capitalist. In any case, the doctrine presents itself as true and therefore superior, whatever the reflexive consequences on American culture. Whether this should be seen as a commitment to political equality or a claim to hierarchy, or the perverse and pervasive synthesis of both, is open to question. For a fuller discussion, see Frascina (1985).

9 Waugh puts these words in the mouth of Collins, 'an embryo don', in the opening chapter of *Brideshead Revisited*. 'Significant form' is Clive Bell's identification of the 'one quality common to all works of art' (see Harrison and Wood 1992: 113) – another attempt, like Greenberg's, at permanent classification.

10 The Copenhagen Interpretation stresses *actual* randomness of *individual* events at the quantum level. A minority of physicists (Bohm is the most prominent) insist that the quantum mechanics must operate at the level of *ensembles* of particles. Here, interaction would allow complex processes to emerge that may *look* random or chaotic, due to 'hidden' (unknown/unpredicted) variables. This is the more likely position at the level of social processes and coincides precisely with Prigogine's thermodynamics of *ensembles*. At the risk of repetition, none of Prigogine's dynamics are applicable at the level of 'individual' particles. Following conversations with physicists, they tend to elide individual and ensemble but concede this may be unacceptable 'post-complexity'.

11 Pierre-Simon Laplace (1749–1827). The 'demon' is the customary shorthand for the position described above, taken in the Introduction to his *Essay on Probability*.

12 Heterodoxy of position, or more broadly the idea that information-bearing substrates are not neutral, is altogether different from the 'embodied philosophy' or 'naturalised phenomenology' position where 'information' (e.g. number) is not 'out there'. The former has more in common with connectionist and adaptationist forms of constructivism. The latter is analytically indistinguishable from the kind of idealism that has the subject construct the world (and, therefore, in principle, all other subjects). Whatever may be said of its relation to onto-theology, or human(ism's) hubris, it is certainly incommensurable with the notion of a human ecology. This theme will be analysed thoroughly in the following chapters.

7 COMPLEXITY THEORY AS A CRITIQUE OF POST-MODERNISM

1 This is where Latour (2004) leaves us. He grants the notion of communities that consist of the human and the non-human. Even if that negative is not prejudicial but existential, the boundary remains intact yet unexamined.

2 Certain commentators who claim post-structuralism as a key influence are apt to inexplicably forget its saturation in, and obsession with, language. Nevertheless (in contradiction), they claim post-structuralism has moved on from its naïve phase. This is self-evidently inadequate. We agree: it has moved on – but the shift is minor and inconsequential. For us, post-structuralism is, and has always been, just another take on old idealisms: if not Kantian, then Nietzschean.

3 For the evolution of sexuality and its functions, see Maynard Smith (1978).

4 For an etymology of 'analysis', see Rosen (1969: 51).

5 This extract is a modified version of an argument first presented in Smith, J.A. concerning the *difference* between visual and verbal representations. It traces

relationships between Derrida's 'frame' and Heidegger's 'enframing ', emphasising that Derrida's 'parasitisation' thesis must be understood reciprocally. As such, it may operate as a precursor to complexity theory and not a recycling of Heidegger's politically compromised philosophy.

8 COGNITION AND THE RENEWAL OF SYSTEMS THEORY: REDUNDANT IDIOMS AND DISPUTED POSITIONS

1 Black boxes model (doubly) contingent order-from-noise processor; autopoisis is recursive.
2 At the same time, the arguments are extremely heated in their nuances. Sterelny (2001) provides an excellent, highly readable account and also puts the problem cogently: 'the facts that make stasis easy to explain make speciation hard to explain' (p. 78). Issues of separation and isolation have to be brought into play. Clearly, Varela *et al.* propose a very specific version of 'isolation'. We shall in turn propose that structural topography is a vital factor in social 'identity'. See Chapters 12 and 13.
3 Tooby and Cosmides discuss the evolution of the eye in a section titled *What Adaptations Look Like*, and Mayr's remark is on pp. 56–7. Mayr is amongst the most significant figures in this debate. His interventions stress the speciation-separation issue, but *this* one also underscores that environments and not just organisms 'bring forth worlds': 'worlds', that is, in the sense of embodied-informed cognition. Obviously, the availability of light energy is not a sufficient condition for the evolution of the eye (or photosynthesis), but it is a necessary condition. The organism stands in the parallel but inverse relation. Both are necessary but insufficient conditions *by themselves* for the interaction we call 'vision'. The attempt to make this 'one-sided' (so to speak) seems to us totally unreasonable. This is not to deny the *variety* of worlds, no more than to deny the variety of species, but like real species that variety must be properly and viably rooted.

9 THE EVOLUTION OF INTELLIGENCE, CONSCIOUSNESS AND LANGUAGE: IMPLICATIONS FOR SOCIAL THEORY

1 See Ridley (2003). Taking something as relatively simple as a seed, the genetic material is expressed in a form limited by environmental opportunity. The opportunity is often not available at all. In the case of human genetic expression, the apparently massive plasticity of self-transformation (for example, from bipeds to rapid transport-users) describes not an environmental restriction but an environmental opportunity. Of course, it bears costs. But the idea that genetic material can be expressed without environment 'constraint' is delusional. The parallel but partly independent development of distinct but related domains of auto-eco-organisation is fundamental here.
2 We can no longer neglect to remark that these positions are fundamentally opposed.
3 The number of names cannot be specified. That could not be the case if they were *not* arbitrary. This does not mean that the number of names is infinite, though it may be immense: 'Elementary propositions consist of names. Since, however, we are unable to give the number of names with different meanings, we are also unable to give the composition of elementary propositions' (*Tractatus* 5.55).
4 The constructionist argument says that differences in ability are not innate but socially constructed. We take this to mean that some abilities confer greater social status or value than others. The argument has run for a very long time: see

Tomlinson (1982) or Thomas and Loxley (2001) for a more recent version. The attraction for educational theorists is that socially constructed status and value are open to reinterpretation. This may be true and is clearly kinder than some older attitudes. Philosophically, however, it is indefensible since difference in ability is presupposed even for the most liberal *subsequent* policies. Pressed by such considerations, the suggestion arises that educational disabilities are actually somehow manufactured by anonymous systems. At worst, this resembles conspiracy theory, usually class-based. The better postulate, that a social ecology is at work, distributing value, also sharply reduces the assumed effectiveness of educators' interventions.

5 This is not to deny *illusion*. Clearly, perspective is both a fact, or true, and *in* fact, an illusion. Every image is also necessarily partial. This is not conventionality in the cultural sense, nor is it arbitrary in reality. Rather, what is described is the operating relationship between vision and its object. According to Bateson (1979 and 2002), this means 'There is no objective experience' and 'The *processes* of image formation are unconscious' (pp. 28–9, our emphasis). He goes on to cite Ames (pp. 29–33), who dealt with and experimented on *defects* of vision and deliberate manipulation of otherwise normal vision. This cannot be squared with: 'There is no objective experience' – and the processes, however unconscious, are therefore objectively functional.

6 Libet suggested that there was a paradoxical delay between the initiation of a voluntary act, such as moving a hand, and consciousness of it. See Dennett (2003: 228–42).

7 See Dennett (2003: 207–17).

10 COMPLEXITY, LANGUAGE AND CULTURE: SOCIAL SYSTEMS IN QUALITATIVE, I.E. NOT FORMAL, TERMS

1 The ordinary humanist position stresses the contingency of information, data or experience. Hence Kant's criterion, the limitation of experience, can be said to apply to a number of fields: sensate intuition, statistical 'sampling', Popperian critiques of scientific method, etc. But this is to begin in the middle of the story. The prior question is: what makes sampling, data, sensory perception *possible*? This is not a chaotic relationship but an adapted one, between an ordered kind of energy and an energy-specific receptor. The best example is the eye. Rather than exclusively stressing the contingency of what is seen, we must also take into account the *structured order* of 'seeing-light'. Then, for example, perspective becomes a stable property of seeing systems and not a distortion of reality. As such, its 'error term' can be managed. We also note that all of this precedes what we ordinarily know as conscious understanding.

2 Where the participants in an encounter have qualitative characteristics, the interaction itself becomes qualitative, i.e. not formally random but *limited*. Two quite different interactions can illustrate this: again, the eye and light; sexual relationships. A third, completely different phenomenon displaying determinate chaos, or complexity, is traffic flow. 'Chance' too takes on qualitative dimensions and as such becomes not the formal background but the degrees of freedom present in the interaction. Differently put, in statistical terms chance is the area bounded by and under the normal curve.

3 See Deacon (1997). For a simpler, more schematic view, see Maynard Smith and Szathmary (1999).

4 In this context, we want to stress the propensity (elsewhere called paratisation or preoccupation) of humans to seek patterned iterations. Like the order from noise principle in Luhmann's communications theory, the drive is to interpret pattern to

supercede contingency. The concept 'meme' expresses the social drive to qualitative structure.

5 This is, of course, Maturana and Varela's imperative. A rich literature has developed from it. It is bedevilled, however, by 'their' problem: is knowledge (or information) out there or in here? Interestingly, maths and physics have the same problem (see Penrose 2004) and are driven to Platonic worlds or degenerated forms of phenomenology. The topology of the loop will be discussed below as an alternative to this dilemma.

11 THE ETHICS OF PRAGMATISM: POLITICS AND POST-STRUCTURALISM IN TRANSITION AFTER THE COMPLEXITY TURN

1 In Rosen's case, 'the problem of nihilism is only secondarily one of morality. Second is indeed very high: I do not mean to trivialise morality but to suggest that what counts as moral is a derivative of our concept of reason' (Rosen 1969: 23). It rapidly becomes clear that reason and ontology are inextricable.

2 We got it used from New York after repeated British orders were delayed for months.

3 See the *Apology* and Kierkegaard's account in *The Concept of Irony*.

4 Hegel sees differentiation or self-alienation, or 'making a division within himself', as the nature of God, as opposed to the distinction between the sacred and the profane, or the primacy of essence/design over appearance/product. See, for example, Hegel (1971: 17, endnote).

5 See Summers, D. (1981), Smith and Jenks (2000), chapter 2.

6 This notion is central to Luhmann. See also the sociology of translation in Brown and Capdevila (1999).

7 See Latour (2004: 12).

8 Hegel's objection is again correct. The false infinity is the not-finite, the bit left over or determined by the finite. The truer infinite must be inclusive. But Hegel does not go far enough: his post-historical is *merely* negative; for us, that is an inconceivable 'amputation' of Being.

9 See Bohm and Hiley (1993), especially chapter 3.

10 See Knodt's foreword to *Social Systems*. This is the basis for the validity of an autopoietic interpretation.

11 See Varela *et al.* (1991), chapter 8.

12 THE TOPOLOGY OF COMPLEXITY

1 Bohm insists that the electron is informed by its wave-packet. This is *active* information. Bohm's analogy is that of a ship, which has its own energy, guided by a radio signal of much lower energy that propagates across a vast area but whose 'potential' is only actualised by the ship's reception systems, connected to its own propulsion mechanisms. See Bohm and Hiley (1993), especially chapter 3.

2 We have used the terms 'vital' and 'vitality' but in the specific senses of self-organising systems 'being possible' or 'able to endure'. We do *not* mean 'living' or anything like a spark of life. The appearance of the living is no spark, but a gradual transformation. Equally, a non-living complex system can display the characteristics of vitality in every sense: for example, the market economy; the ecology of the oceans. The reference to *Gaia* puts assumed distinctions between the living and the non-living back into question.

3 *Dis*order is understood in the strictly relative sense of another order detrimental to

the continuity of the system. The general or formal notion of disorder ceases to have much meaning.

4 Throughout his work, Luhmann stresses the relationship of autopoiesis and risk. In Luhmannesque terms, the system does what the system does – or can do. This is the condition of its difference from an environment, even if that endangers the very existence of the system. Operational closure and the principle of self-sufficiency then serve to *specialise* both the competence and 'incompetence', or risk, that the system must face. This is the basis, in Luhmann, for the specialised distinction and 'binary coding' of such systems as economy and law. They are 'blind' to the considerations that lie outside their specified field. This may be taken two ways, which in our view are mutually confirming: the increase in operational closure or differentiation is also an increase in ecological inter-dependency. The law, for example, could not operate *as such* unless the functions it is incapable of are undertaken by some other system.

13 RE-INTERPRETING GLOBAL COMPLEXITY AS AN ONTOLOGY: HUMAN ECOLOGY

1 In Kant, the transcendental subject; in Maturana and Varela, the organism, 'brings forth worlds'. The centrality of the subject-system, given by its operational closure, guarantees this. But as Luhmann is apt to ask: which one of us is the transcendental subject? Of course, in our terms, he has the same problem, which we can put cryptically as: which one of us is the black box? To the extent that an organism has a specific, if plastic, character its 'operational closure' is subsequent to adaptive processes. This is the Tooby-Cosmides model. Epistemology therefore *follows* the ontology of structural adaptation. Indeed, it also follows non-conscious, information-bearing substrates. It cannot then be *simply* grounded in any one subject or organism.

2 Autopoiesis simply as reproduction is redundant. Bertalanffy's notion of the pseudo-steady state indicates instead that an open system has to reclaim its identity in the face of change due to the transfer of environmental energy. Reproduction is also then suppression. Hence our insistence on auto-exo-reference. Multiplicity of drafts, even if we restrict this to so-called higher animals with significant levels of post-natal plasticity, reinforces the active nature of autopoiesis because it implies that some 'drafts' are prioritised over others: some kind of *selection* is at work. The process is not homeostatic but homeodynamic.

3 See, for example, Rose (1966: 361–7), Capra (1996: 92–4) and Woolfson (2000).

4 See Margulis and Sagan (1986 and 1987).

5 See DeLanda (1999).

6 This issue still bedevils the most interesting contemporary maths. Penrose (2004) is drawn to locate mathematics in a Platonic realm, whilst Lakoff and Nunez (2000) are forced to insist that human babies (and other animals) discern number but it is not 'out there'. Then why should the ability to 'count' arise at all? If it is an adaptation, it has to have an origin for its 'abstracting' responses. One might reply that the ability to swim is not 'in the sea'. Where does that take us? Into the labyrinth of an irritating, ancient word game.

7 Kierkegaard's account remains the best. Socrates sets out to demonstrate human ignorance, especially his own. He refuses to take any finite human knowledge seriously. This is *practised* ignorance. How is it that he can ground this practice when, on the face of it, some humans are less ignorant about x or y than others? According to Plato this is given by the Oracle: 'Human wisdom is worth little or nothing . . . he amongst you is the wisest who, like Socrates, knows that this wisdom

is worth nothing at all' (Kierkegaard 1965: 197). See also Smith and Jenks (2000) chapter 4.

8 The notions of value and quality expose what is at stake. Within the fluid proximities of communities, disciplined practices determine quality and value. By such practices we mean, for example, religion, moral codes, cuisine, art, music, fashion, etiquette. Nor should these be taken in the 'high' sense; all are manifest and developed in popular culture. Where a cohesive, critical-appreciative community is diluted, price-quantity relations or commodification will predominate. Whether this universalisation of value in terms of price per unit will in time dissolve all, or most other systems of value is an open question.

BIBLIOGRAPHY

Ainslie, G. (2001) *Breakdown of Will*. Cambridge: Cambridge University Press.

Ball, P. (2004) *Critical Mass*. London: Heinemann.

Barkow, J., Cosmides, L. and Tooby, J. (eds) (1992) *The Adapted Mind: Evolutionary Psychology and the Generation of Culture*. Oxford: Oxford University Press.

Barthes, R. (1971) 'From Work to Text', in C. Harrison and P. Wood (eds), *Art in Theory*. London: Blackwell.

Bataille, G. (1991) *The Trial of Giles de Rais*. Los Angeles: Amok Books.

Bataille, G. (2001) *Eroticism*. London: Penguin.

Bateson, G. (1972, 2000) *Steps to an Ecology of Mind*. Chicago: Chicago University Press.

Bateson, G. (1979, 2002) *Mind and Nature*. Cresskill: Hampton Press.

Bennington, G. (1995) 'Introduction to Economics', in C. Gill (ed.) *Bataille: Writing the Sacred*. London: Routledge.

Bertalanffy, L. von (1969) *General Systems Theory: Foundations, Development, Applications*. New York: George Braziller.

Best, S. and Kellner, D. (1991) *Postmodern Theory*. Basingstoke and New York: Palgrave Macmillan.

Blackmore, S. (1999) *The Meme Machine*. Oxford: Oxford University Press.

Bohm, D. and Hiley, B.J. (1993) *The Undivided Universe*. London and New York: Routledge.

Buchanan, D. (2000) *Ubiquity*. London: Weidenfeld & Nicholson.

Buchanan, I. (ed.) (1999) *A Deleuzean Century*. Durham, NC: Duke University Press.

Byrne, D. (1998) *Complexity Theory and the Social Sciences*. London: Routledge.

Capra, F. (1996) *The Web of Life*. London: HarperCollins.

Carroll, D. (1989) *Paraesthetics: Foucault, Lyotard, Derrida*. London: Routledge.

Castells, M. (1997, 2004) *The Power of Identity*. Oxford: Blackwell.

Castells, M. (1998, 2000) *End of Millennium*. Oxford: Blackwell.

Cilliers, P. (1998) *Complexity and Postmodernism*. London: Routledge.

Clark, T.J. (1985) *The Painting of Modern Life*. London: Thames & Hudson.

Clark, T.J. (1999) *Farewell to an Idea*. New Haven and London: Yale University Press.

Cohen, J. and Stewart, I. (1995) *The Collapse of Chaos*. London: Penguin.

Damasio, A. (1995) *Descartes' Error*. New York: Penguin Putnam.

Dawkins, R. (1976, 1989) *The Selfish Gene*. Oxford: Oxford University Press.

Deacon, T. (1997) *The Symbolic Species*. London: Penguin.

DeLanda, M. (1999) 'Immanence and Transcendence in the Genesis of Form', in I. Buchanan (ed.) *A Deleuzian Century*. Durham, NC: Duke University Press.

Deleuze, G. and Guattari, F. (1987) *A Thousand Plateaus: Capitalism and Schizophrenia* (trans. Brian Massumi). Minneapolis: University of Minnesota Press.

Dennett, D. (1991) *Consciousness Explained*. Boston: Little Brown.

Dennett, D. (1995) *Darwin's Dangerous Idea*. New York: Simon and Schuster.

Dennett, D. (2003) *Freedom Evolves*. London: Allen Lane.

Derrida, J. (1981) *Dissemination* (trans. B. Johnson). Chicago and London: Chicago University Press.

Derrida, J. (1982) 'Signature, Event, Context', in A. Bass (trans.), *Margins of Philosophy*. Brighton: Harvester.

Derrida, J. (1987) *The Truth in Painting* (trans. G. Bennington and I. McLeod). Chicago and London: Chicago University Press.

Descartes, R. (1968/75) *Discourse on Method and the Mediations* (trans. F. Sutcliffe). London: Penguin.

Dillon, M. (1993) *The Political Subject of Violence*. Manchester: Manchester University Press.

Dissanayake, E. (1992) *Homo Aestheticus*. New York: Free Press.

Douglas Kiel, L. and Elliott, E. (eds) (1997, 2000) *Chaos Theory in the Social Sciences: Foundations and Applications*. Michigan: Michigan University Press.

Dreyfus, H.L. and Rabinow, P. (1982) *Michel Foucault: Beyond Structuralism and Hermeneutics*. New York and London: Harvester Wheatsheaf.

Eve, A., Horsfall, S. and Lee, M. (eds) (1997) *Chaos, Complexity and Sociology*. London and New York: Sage.

Foerster, H. von (1984) *Observing Systems*. Seaside: Intersystems.

Foucault, M. (1977) *Language, Counter-Memory, Practice*. New York: Cornell University Press.

Foucault, M. (1982) 'The Subject and Power', in H. Dreyfus and P. Rabinow, *Michel Foucault: Beyond Structuralism and Hermeneutics*. New York and London: Harvester Wheatsheaf.

Frascina, F. (ed.) (1985) *Pollock and After*. New York and London: Harper Row.

Glaserfeld, von E. (2002) 'The Construction of Knowledge', in D.F. Schnitman and J. Schnitman (eds), *New Paradigms, Culture and Subjectivity*. New Jersey: Hampton.

Gleik, J. (1987) *Chaos*. London: Abacus.

Gray, J. (2002) *Straw Dogs*. London: Granta.

Gray, J. (2003) *Al Qaeda and What It Means To Be Modern*. London: Faber & Faber.

Greenberg, C. (1961) 'Modernist Painting', in C. Harrison and P. Wood (eds), *Art in Theory 1900–1990: An Anthology of Changing Ideas*. Oxford: Blackwell, 1992.

Grimes, P. (2000) 'Recent Research on World Systems', in D. Hall (ed.), *A World-Systems Reader*. Lanham and Oxford: Rowman & Littlefield.

Hamilton, G. (1954, 1986) *Manet and His Critics*. New Haven and London: Yale University Press.

Harrison, C. and Wood, P. (1992) *Art in Theory*. London: Blackwell.

Hayles, N.K. (ed.) (1991) *Chaos and Order*. London and Chicago: University of Chicago Press.

Hayles, N.K. (1999) *How We Became Posthuman*. London and Chicago: University of Chicago Press.

Heidegger, M. (1973) *The End of Philosophy*. London: Souvenir Press.

Heidegger, M. (1993) *Basic Writings*, ed. by D. Farrell Krell. London: Routledge.

Jaggar, A. (1989) 'Love and Knowledge in Feminist Epistemology', in S. Jaggar and

S. Bordo, *Gender/Body/Knowledge: Feminist Reconstructions of Being and Knowing*. New Brunswick and London: Rutgers University Press.

Jay, M. (1993) *Downcast Eyes: The Denigration of Vision in French Twentieth-Century Thought*. Berkeley, Los Angeles and London: California University Press.

Jenks, C. (2003) *Transgression*. London: Routledge.

Kant, I. (1929–1975) *Critique of Pure Reason*. (trans. N. Kemp Smith). London: Macmillan.

Kierkegaard, S. (1965) *The Concept of Irony*. Bloomington and London: Indiana University Press.

Kosko, B. (1994) *Fuzzy Thinking*. London: Harper Collins.

Lakoff, G. and Nunez, R.E. (2000) *Where Mathematics Comes From*. New York: Basic Books.

Latour, B. (1993) *We Have Never Been Modern*. Hemel Hempstead: Harvester Wheatsheaf.

Latour, B. (2004) *Politics of Nature*. Cambridge, MA and London: Harvard University Press.

Law, J. (1999) 'After ANT: Complexity, Naming and Complexity', in J. Law and J. Hassard (eds), *Actor Network Theory and After*. Oxford: Blackwell.

Levin, D. (1988) *The Opening of Vision: Nihilism and the Postmodern Situation*. New York and London: Routledge.

Lovelock, J. (1988, 1995) *The Ages of Gaia*. Oxford and New York: Oxford University Press.

Luhmann, N. (1989) *Ecological Communication*. Chicago and Cambridge: Chicago University Press and Polity Press.

Luhmann, N. (1995) *Social Systems*. Stanford: Stanford University Press.

Lyotard, J.-F. (1984) *The Postmodern Conditon* (trans. G. Bennington and B. Massumi). Manchester: Manchester University Press.

Lyotard, J.-F. (1988) *Writing the Event* ed. by G. Bennington. Manchester: Manchester University Press.

Maasens, S., Mitchell, D., Richerson, P. and Weingart, P. (1997) *Human by Nature: Between Biology and the Social Sciences*. Mahwah, NJ: Lawrence Erlbaum Associates.

MacCabe, C. (2001) 'Introduction', in G. Bataille, *Eroticism*. London: Penguin.

Malpas, J. and Wickham, G. (1995) 'Governance and Failure: On the Limits of Sociology', *Australian and New Zealand Journal of Sociology*, 31: 37–50.

Margulis, L. and Sagan, D. (1986) *Microcosmos*. New York: Simon & Schuster.

Margulis, L. and Sagan, D. (1987) 'Bacterial Bedfellows', *Natural History*, Vol. 96.

Maturana, U. and Varela, F. (1980) *Autopoiesis and Cognition*. Dordrecht: D. Reidel.

Maturana, U. and Varela, F. (1998) *The Tree of Knowledge*. Boston and London: Shambhala.

Maynard Smith, J. (1978) *The Evolution of Sexuality*. Cambridge: Cambridge University Press.

Maynard Smith, J. (1982) *Evolution Now: A Century after Darwin*. San Fransisco: Freeman.

Maynard Smith, J. (1988) *Games, Sex and Evolution*. London: Harvester.

Maynard Smith, J. and Szathmary, E. (1999) *The Origins of Life: From the Birth of Life to the Origins of Language*. Oxford and New York: Oxford University Press.

Mayr, E. (1982) *The Growth of Biological Thought*. Cambridge, MA: Harvard University Press.

Morin, E. (2002) 'The Notion of the Subject', in D.F. Schnitman and J. Schnitman (eds), *New Paradigms, Culture and Subjectivity*. New Jersey: Hampton.

Olssen, M. (1999) *Michel Foucault: Materialsim and Education*. Westport and London: Bergin & Garvey.

Pefanis, J. (1991) *Hetereology and the Postmodern*. Durham and London: Duke University Press.

Penrose, R. (2004) *The Road to Reality*. London: Cape.

Petito, J., Varela, F., Pachoud, B. and Roy, J.-M. (1999) *Naturalising Phenomenology: Issues in Contemporary Phenomenology and Cognitive Science*. Stanford: Stanford University Press.

Peyton Young, H. (2001) *Individual Strategy and Social Structure*. Princeton and Oxford: Princeton University Press.

Pinker, S. (2002) *The Blank Slate: The Modern Denial of Human Nature*. London: Allen Lane.

Plato (1977) *Euthyphro, Apology of Socrates, Crito*. ed by J. Burnett. Oxford: Clarendon Press.

Plotkin, H. (2003) *The Imagined World Made Real*. London: Penguin.

Porush, D. (1991) 'Fictions as Dissipative Structures: Prigogine's Theory and Post-Modernism's Roadshow' in N. Hayles (ed.), *Chaos and Order*. Chicago: University of Chicago Press.

Prigogine, I. (2002) The End of Science?, in D.F. Schnitman and J. Schnitman (eds), *New Paradigms, Culture and Subjectivity*. New Jersey: Hampton.

Prigogine, I. and Stengers, I. (1984) *Order Out of Chaos*. New York: Bantam.

Prigogine, I., with Stengers, I. (1996) *The End of Certainty: Time, Chaos and the New Laws of Nature*. New York: Free Press.

Reed, M. and Harvey, D. (1992) 'The New Science and the Old: Complexity and Realism in the Social Sciences', *Journal for the Theory of Social Behaviour*, 22: 356–79.

Ridley, M. (2003) *Nature via Nurture*. London: Fourth Estate.

Rorty, R. (1979) *Philosophy and the Mirror of Nature*. Princeton: Princeton University Press.

Rorty, R. (1989) *Contingency, Irony and Solidarity*. Cambridge: Cambridge University Press.

Rorty, R. (1991) *Objectivity, Relativism and Truth*. Cambridge: Cambridge University Press.

Rosen, S. (1969) *Nihilism*. New Haven and London: Yale University Press.

Schnitman, D.F. and Schnitman, J. (eds) (2002) *New Paradigms, Culture and Subjectivity*. New Jersey: Hampton.

Skyrms, B. (1996) *The Evolution of the Social Contract*. Cambridge: Cambridge University Press.

Smart, B. (1985) *Michel Foucault*. London: Routledge.

Smith, J.A. and Jenks, C. (2000) *Images of Community: Durkheim, Social Systems and the Sociology of Art*. Aldershot: Ashgate.

Smith, J.A. and Jenks, C. (2005) 'Complexity, Ecology and Materiality of Information' in Theory, Culture and Society Vol. 22 No. 5.

Sterelny, K. (2001) *Dawkins v. Gould*. Cambridge: Icon.

Suleiman, S. (1990) *Subversive Intent: Gender, Politics and the Avant-Garde*. Cambridge, MA: Harvard University Press.

Summers, D. (1981) *Michelangelo and the Language of Art*. Princeton: Princeton University Press.

Thomas, G. and Loxley, A. (2001) *Deconstructing Special Education and Constructing Inclusion*. Buckingham and Philadelphia: Open University Press.

Tomlinson, S. (1982) *A Sociology of Special Education*. Boston and London: Routledge.

Tooby, J. and Cosmides, L. (1992) 'The Psychological Foundations of Culture', in J. Barkow, L. Cosmides and J. Tooby (eds) *The Adapted Mind*. Oxford: Oxford University Press.

Urry, J. (2003) *Global Complexity*. Cambridge: Polity.

Varela, F., Thompson, E. and Rosch, E. (1993) *The Embodied Mind*. Cambridge, MA and London: MIT Press.

Waldrop, M. (1994) *Complexity*. London: Penguin.

Williams, S. (2001) *Emotion and Social Theory*. London: Sage.

Wittgenstein, L. (1992) *Tractatus Logico-Philosophicus*. London: Routledge.

Wolfe, C. (1998) *Critical Environments: Postmodern Theory and the Pragmatics of the 'Outside'*. Minneapolis: University of Minnesota Press.

Woolfson, A. (2000) *Life Without Genes*. London: Harper Collins.

INDEX

abyss: Foucault (Michel) 143–4, 153, 156, 159, 192, 198, 249; *mise en abyme* 143, 152; representation 141, 198

actor-network theory (ANT) 3, 24, 58, 130, 161

adaptation: bringing forth worlds 100, 126, 181, 231; Darwinism 91, 172, 248; drift compared 174, 183; enaction 105, 198, 208; homeostasis 110; human nature 159; post-adaptation 184

additional educational needs (ASEN) 216, 217

agency: thing-in-itself 45, 46, 56

Ainsley, G. 198

alterity 58, 59, 65, 205

analogy: bacon analogy 176, 179; heterogeny 45; thing-in-itself 43–4

anamnesis 107, 114, 255

appearances: appearances-in-general 31; essence distinguished 44; experience 33, 34, 38, 44; uncertainty 33

architecture: attractors 64; consciousness 52; evolutionary psychology 22; human nature 64; information-processing 55; language 21; mind 20, 22

Aristotelian: identity 41; traditional logic 18, 19, 44

arrow of time 88, 90, 94, 165

attractors: architecture 64; categories 208; determinism 16; evolutionary psychology 63; evolutionary stable strategies (ESS) 12, 66; identity 64; language 12; memes 110; multi-dimensional 73–4; plasticity 72; strange 5, 12; world-systems 20

authorship: self-reflexivity 93; social construction 201, 202; thing-in-itself 183

auto-eco-organisation: autonomy 15; autopoiesis 7, 52, 53–4; biosphere 183; bringing forth worlds 54, 126, 168; causality 151; components 54, 70; *computo* 40; dissipative structures 83; emergence 41, 72, 261; genetic material 281; materialism 161; mutual specification 174; radical secularisation 256; reference 42; self-organisation 53–4, 98, 273; selfish gene 83; thing-in-itself 56; *see also* eco-auto-organisation

auto-exo-reference: complex open systems 162; connectionism 189; Morin (E.) 8, 42, 43; radical constructivism 178, 190

autonomy: Bataille (G.) 162; *cogito* 59; drift 171; humanism 21, 59; knight of autonomy 162, 223; self-organisation 6

autopoiesis: auto-eco-organisation 7, 52, 53–4; cognitive biology 6, 47–60; complexity theory 6–8, 37; cybernetics 6; environment 6, 7; evolution 6; Luhmann (Niklas) 6, 167, 204, 231, 232, 233, 234, 236, 251, 284; representation 51; self-reflexivity 51; structural coupling 6, 55, 57, 167, 255; thing-in-itself 49

Barkow, J. *et al* 21–2, 63, 73, 248, 275

Baron-Cohen 61

Barthes, R. 115, 116, 147, 148, 149

Bataille, G.: autonomy 162; energy 157, 158, 159, 264; excess/transression 137, 152, 153, 154, 155, 156, 219; fundamentum 156; individual sovereignty 131

Bateson, Gregory 166, 167, 170, 176, 177, 193, 203, 282

Printed in the United Kingdom
by Lightning Source UK Ltd.
123501UK00001B/44/A